15778

# INDIRA GANDHI

ZAREER MASANI

# INDIRA GANDHI

*A Biography*

HAMISH HAMILTON
LONDON

First published in Great Britain 1975
by Hamish Hamilton Ltd.
90 Great Russell Street London WC1

Copyright © 1975 by Zareer Masani

SBN 241 89042 X

Printed in Great Britain by
Compton Printing Ltd, Aylesbury

To My Mother,
SHAKUNTALA MASANI

# CONTENTS

# ILLUSTRATIONS

# ACKNOWLEDGEMENTS

My thanks are due to the following:
To Mrs. Indira Gandhi for allowing me access to extensive material with the Prime Minister's Secretariat, including some of her correspondence; to Mr. Sharda Prasad, Director of Information, Prime Minister's Secretariat, and Mr. M.S. Menon, Additional Private Secretary to the Prime Minister, for their good-humoured co-operation and interest and for the time they spent in making the above material available to me; to Mr. B.R. Nanda, Director, Nehru Memorial Museum & Library, for enabling me to consult the Nehru Papers; to the Press Information Bureau and the Photos Division, Government of India, for providing most of the photographs; to Mrs. Sheela Dikshit and Mr. Virendra Prabhakar of the Chitra Kala Sangam, Delhi, for some exclusive and unusual photographs; to all those who were good enough to give me interviews; to the authors of the published works from which I have quoted (see *Select Bibliography* and *Notes*); to Mr. Hamish Hamilton for patiently allowing me to exceed the deadline by four months; to the friends who have assisted, advised or sympathised; and most of all to my mother, Shakuntala Masani, for her constant encouragement and for the financial help without which this venture would not have been possible.

ZAREER MASANI

# CHAPTER I

# HEIR TO THE NEHRUS

THERE IS little to distinguish contemporary Allahabad from other neglected, provincial Indian towns which have been torn roughly from their traditional moorings and cast into the vortex of political and economic change. There are the usual dusty and teeming bazaars and malodorous, fly-infested slums, with an all-pervasive disregard for appearance and sanitation. Only a few neglected Mughal monuments, some gloomy official buildings and a few avenues of derelict villas remind one that Allahabad was till recently one of the leading cultural and administrative centres of northern India.

Known in ancient, pre-Islamic times as holy Prayag, the town was sanctified by its association with the *Ramayana* and by its proximity to the sacred *Triveni*.* For many centuries it was a traditional place of pilgrimage for Hindus, and even today thousands of pilgrims congregate at the annual 'Kumbh Mela' in an attempt to wash away their sins at the sacred confluence. Renamed Allahabad (City of Allah) in the 16th century by the Emperor Akbar, the town became an important seat of Mughal Government, as its surviving Mughal tombs and ruins bear witness. In the 19th century the British chose it as the capital of their North Western Province, and later it became the second city of the United Provinces. In the early 20th century Allahabad, with a busy High Court and a large contingent of British officials, remained an important centre of British administration and justice. Meanwhile, its university, famous throughout the country, was already the scene of nationalist agitation and a fertile breeding-ground for the Western-educated lawyers and intellectuals who would provide the budding national movement with its leadership. It is not so surprising then that Allahabad has provided independent India with all three of her Prime Ministers—Jawaharlal Nehru, Lal Bahadur Shastri and Indira Gandhi.

Indira Nehru Gandhi was born on 19 November 1917 at Anand Bhavan (Abode of Happiness), the palatial residence of Allahabad's premier citizen, Motilal Nehru. Here the Nehru clan had assembled

---

*The confluence of the three rivers sacred to Hindus: The Ganges, the Jumna and the mythical Saraswati.

for the confinement of Motilal's daughter-in-law, Kamala, wife of his only son, Jawaharlal. According to Hindu custom, an expectant mother returns to her parental home for her confinement; but Kamala's anxious father-in-law had insisted that she remain at his own home, where he could see that she received the best medical attention. While Kamala lay in labour surrounded by doctors and nurses, the anxious relatives crowded in the courtyard outside her room. Jawaharlal Nehru in his usual fashion stood apart, trying to appear unruffled. At last the Scottish doctor emerged to announce: 'It's a bonnie lassie, Sir,' 'Oh, but it should have been a boy!' exclaimed Swarup Rani, Motilal's wife. Motilal, delighted at the safe delivery of his first grandchild, is reported to have snapped at her: 'This daughter of Jawahar, for all you know, may prove better than a thousand sons.' She nodded her head pensively.[1]

This exchange augured well for the future of the baby girl whom it concerned. It was normal for the birth of a daughter to be greeted as a misfortune in Indian families. A girl was an economic burden to her father, who had to provide her with a dowry and find her a husband. Indian society had been male-dominated since Vedic times, and the traditional role of a woman was to serve her husband with absolute obedience. Indian history did, of course, provide instances of outstanding women who had played a leading role in politics and other spheres; but these were special cases, favoured by the accidents of royal birth and palace intrigue, for whom exceptions had been made. Total submission had been the general lot of Indian womanhood through the ages, and it was not until the latter half of the 19th century that some westernised Indians, schooled in liberal ideas, took up the cause of female emancipation. It was to this liberal school that Motilal Nehru belonged. Thanks to the emancipated outlook of her grandfather and her parents, Indira Nehru's desires and talents would never be stifled by the oppressive and discriminatory taboos to which most of her sex was subjected.

Motilal decided to name his granddaughter 'Indira' after his own mother, who had been a formidable woman in her time. To this the young parents added 'Priyadarshini' (Dear to the Sight). When she was a few days old, Indira Priyadarshini, swaddled in a Kashmiri shawl, accompanied her grandfather on a solemn visit. Across the garden, in a cottage on the Nehru estate, lived Munshi Mubarak Ali, steward of Motilal's large establishment. Born of an aristocratic Muslim family which had fallen on hard times since the Great Revolt of 1857, Munshiji* had become an institution in the Nehru household, where he was loved and respected as an elder of the family. He had witnessed the birth of Motilal's children, and their earliest memories were of sitting

* '—Ji' is a suffix commonly used as a mark of respect.

on his knee and listening to his tales of the past. Now Munshiji lay dying of cancer. He had said to Motilal: '*Bhai Saheb* (Brother) do not worry. I am not going to die until I have seen and held Jawaharlal's son in my arms and have given him by blessing. I live only for that day.' And now, as he blessed Indira, the dying man is said to have whispered: 'May he be a worthy heir to Jawahar as Jawahar has proved a worthy and wonderful son to you, and may the child illuminate the name of Nehru.'[2] Munshiji died happily unaware that it was a girl he had held in his arms.

\*     \*     \*

The Nehrus were Kashmiri Brahmins,\* with a colourful and distinguished past of which they were proud. Their ancestor, Raj Kaul, renowned as a Sanskrit and Persian scholar, had attracted the attention of the Mughal Emperor Farrukhsiyar, who had invited him to the court of Delhi. The family had migrated to the imperial city in 1716 or thereabouts, receiving a *jagir* or fief from the Emperor. Their house had stood on the banks of a canal, whence the name 'Nehru' (from *nahar* or canal). The empire by this time had entered into an irreversible decline, and the Nehrus had shared in its vicissitudes, their *jagir* dwindling away till it finally vanished. Motilal's grandfather had been the first *vakil* (legal representative) of the East India Company at the shadow court of Delhi; and his father, Ganga Dhar Nehru, had been *Kotwal* (Chief Magistrate) of Delhi at the time of the Revolt of 1857. This had not, however, protected the family from the upheavals of that year. Having lost nearly all their possessions, the Nehrus had fled to Agra to avoid the terrible vengeance of the victorious East India Company, and they had narrowly escaped with their lives.

At Agra the family had struggled to rebuild its fortunes. It was here that Motilal Nehru was born in 1861, a posthumous child who was brought up by his brother, Nandlal. A few years after the family migrated from Delhi, Nandlal had entered the service of the Raja of Khetri, a small princely state in Rajasthan, as his *Diwan* or Prime Minister. Later he started practising law in Agra, and when the High Court moved to Allahabad the Nehrus moved with it. Motilal, whose educational career had been chiefly noted for his wild escapades, had eventually followed his brother into the legal profession. He had found his vocation, and his success at the Bar was spectacular. By the time his son, Jawaharlal, was born, he had become one of the most successful barristers in the United Provinces. 'No one can doubt my supreme contempt for money',

---

*The Brahmins, the Hindu priestly order and the highest of the four main castes in Hindu society, claim direct descent from the original Aryan settlers of India. The Kashmiri Pandits, who belong to the northern-most part of the sub-continent, take special pride in being racially the purest Brahmins in the country.

Motilal once declared to a client;[3] but success inevitably brought riches, and Motilal, who had received a pittance of five rupees* for his first brief, became one of the wealthiest men in his profession. 'Full of the spirit of play and fond of good living in every way' his son later wrote, 'he found no difficulty in spending what he earned. And gradually our ways became more and more Westernised.'[4]

*　　　*　　　*

The Nehrus, at the time of Indira's birth, were one of the most cosmopolitan families in the country. Their outlook and way of life revealed a subtle mixture of three distinct cultural traditions: the scholarly and exclusive Brahminism of the Kashmiri Pandits, the Muslim culture of Mughal India, and the public-school virtues of the British Raj.

Though proud of his Brahmin origins, Motilal was full of the aggressive and restless spirit of Western science and materialism. Impatient of religious and caste prejudice, he had crossed the seas to Europe, violating the customary taboo, and had refused to undergo a purification ceremony on his return, thereby winning a reputation as a social reformer. An ardent Anglophile, he had taken eagerly to Western dress and Western ways at a time when it was unusual for Indians to do so. His own early education had been confined to Persian and Arabic, and he had not learnt English till he was in his teens. But he compensated for this by employing English governesses for his daughters and by educating his son at Harrow, Cambridge and the Inner Temple, whence young Jawaharlal returned 'more an Englishman than an Indian'. Though Jawaharlal later recovered his 'Indianness', Britain was to leave an indelible mark on him. To his years there he owed the liberal values which he was never able to shed, even at the height of his Marxist phase, and a peculiarly Anglo-Saxon sense of discipline and emotional reserve, qualities that he passed on to his daughter.

The Brahmin past died hard, however, and for all their westernised ways, the Nehrus could not escape its influence. For one thing, the older women of the family, especially Motilal's orthodox wife, Swarup Rani, did not share his crusading zeal for westernisation. Notwithstanding the proclaimed agnosticism of their menfolk, they saw to it that all the traditional Hindu festivals were celebrated in the customary manner and that Hindu ritual was scrupulously observed. But ritual apart, Brahminism exerted a more subtle grip. Shorn of its religious trappings it manifested itself in a sense of Aryan superiority and élitism, an aristocratic exclusiveness that the Nehrus have never shed. As Jawaharlal once confessed: 'A Brahmin I was born and a Brahmin I seem to remain

*Ten rupees were then equivalent to one pound sterling.

whatever I might say or do in regard to religious or social custom.'5

'Hinduism clings on to its children, almost despite them,'6 Jawaharlal was to write; yet the Nehrus were peculiarly free from sectarian prejudice and bigotry. For two centuries the family had lived in the plains of Hindustan and had steeped itself in the courtly Muslim culture and manners that characterised upper-class life in Northern India. Urdu—the lingua franca of Mughal India—was the only Indian language in which they felt at home. Both Motilal and Jawaharlal counted Muslims amongst their closest friends, and neither would have dreamt of allowing religious differences to colour their choice of friends or political associates. In later years this secular outlook, translated into political terms, was perhaps the most valuable contribution of the Nehrus to a country divided by Hindu-Muslim rivalry.

The Nehru heritage was a rich and versatile one, combining in a fertile synthesis some of the finest attributes of East and West, of Hinduism and Islam. The family history revealed not only an ambitious and adventurous driving force, but a remarkable resilience and capacity for survival, qualities which are in any society the pre-requisites for successful leadership.

*     *     *

Anand Bhawan, home of the Nehrus, stood on a site hallowed by its associations with Hindu legend. According to some traditions, it was here that Rama, hero of the ancient Hindu epic the *Ramayana*, was met by his faithful brother Bharata on his return from exile. Nearby was Bharadwaj Ashram where the sage Valmiki, author of the *Ramayana*, is reputed to have once stayed.

Soon after the birth of his son, Motilal had moved with his family from the congested old quarter of Allahabad to the spacious European grandeur of the exclusive Civil Lines. A few years later, he had acquired a large estate with a dilapidated, old house, and had set about creating a home appropriate to his social status and his expensive tastes. The result was a whitewashed villa, sprawling round a paved, open courtyard, its terraced roofs and long verandahs enclosed by a series of colonnaded arches. Its rambling interior included over a dozen bedrooms, large reception rooms and a unique indoor swimming-pool. With its marble floors, massive Victorian furniture and silver, Persian and Kashmiri carpets, and scintillating Venetian glass and Dresden china, Anand Bhawan exuded an air of quiet opulence. Its grounds encompassed spacious lawns and gardens, orchards, tennis-courts, a second swimming-pool, outhouses for a battalion of servants, stables, kennels and garages. The estate was enclosed by a high wall, broken by imposing wrought-iron gates. By all accounts, Anand Bhawan was a palatial residence and, as Indira later recalled, it was also 'a delight to children for it had lots of space for play and hiding.'[7]

Here, in feudal splendour, Motilal Nehru held court; and British officials, Indian princes and other notables flocked to his lavish parties and banquets, lured by his magnetic personality and legendary hospitality. Handsome, brilliant and witty, with an imperious manner and strong likes and dislikes, Motilal, like a Renaissance prince, lived life to the fullest. Sir Frederick James, a former member of the Viceroy's Executive Council, has described him as 'a Grand Seigneur—such as those who have appeared in all the great epochs of history... He was the perfect host... His home, which was always open, was the Mecca of all who enjoyed the good things of life and who looked to him as a great lawyer and national leader... Motilal was generous in everything that he did. There were no half-measures'.[8]

It was at Anand Bhawan, amid the ostentatious revelry that marked the hey-day of the British Raj, that Indira Gandhi spent her earliest years. One of Motilal's daughters has described him as a 'shepherd who though apparently unconcerned, kept a vigilant eye on all his flock;'[9] and young Indira was no exception. Many years later, she recalled: 'In days of affluence or in days of hardship, the household was sternly governed by my grandfather—his awe-inspiring temper softened by quick forgiveness and infectious laughter, his strict discipline tempered by his love for his family and his enormous zest for life.'[10] Though famous for his violent temper, to his granddaughter Motilal Nehru was indulgence itself. He wrote to Jawaharlal: 'I am always thinking of Indira. The very thought of a personification of innocence is soothing. By a very easy slip it justifies idol worship and many other things which modern civilisation sets down for senseless superstition.'[11]

Motilal was fond of displaying little Indira to his distinguished guests, and she roamed freely among her grandfather's visitors, solemnly observing them, though she could not yet follow their conversation. Sarojini Naidu, poetess and future nationalist leader, to whom Indira was thus presented, later told her: 'You were the proudest-looking baby I have seen.'[12] Indira Gandhi was later to testify that in these early years Motilal Nehru had a far greater impact on her than her father, whose influence began much later: 'I admired my grandfather as a strong person, and I loved his tremendous zest for life, which my father also developed later on; but I was tremendously impressed with my grandfather's bigness— I don't mean physically—... he seemed to embrace the whole world. I loved the way he laughed.'[13]

Motilal was by no means the only one who indulged Indira. In true Indian fashion, she was spoiled and petted by the whole family and by various friends and relatives who flocked to Anand Bhawan. The strict discipline that had ruled the lives of Motilal's children was waived for Indira, and there were no British governesses to enforce regular hours. When she tired of the dolls and toys with which she was showered, she could rely on the women folk of the family to entertain her: her fond grandmother, who fed her forbidden sweets between meals, thereby winning the title of *Dol Amma*,* and Bibi Amma, Swarup Rani's widowed sister, who was a permanent standby with her exciting tales from the Hindu epics.

The most obvious and the most formative influence on Indira at this time was her mother. It was Kamala Nehru who bathed, dressed and fed her and who initiated her at an early age into the religious mysteries of Hinduism. Tall and slender, with a dazzling smile—inherited by her daughter—Kamala came of old Kashmiri stock. Her family, the Kauls, were prosperous businessmen settled in Delhi and, though orthodox and untouched by Western ways, they could claim as old a lineage as the Nehrus. Kamala's marriage had been an arranged one, in the traditional fashion, and it was not an unqualified success. Years later her husband wrote candidly of their relationship:

'I was twenty-six at the time and she was about seventeen, a slip of a girl, utterly unsophisticated in the ways of the world. The difference in our ages was considerable, but greater still was the difference in our mental outlook, for I was far more grown-up than she was. And yet with all my appearance of worldly wisdom I was very boyish, and I hardly realised that this delicate, sensitive girl's mind was slowly unfolding like a flower and required gentle and careful tending . . . our backgrounds were different and there was a want of adjustment. These mal-adjustments would sometimes lead to friction and there were many petty quarrels over trivialities . . . Both had a quick temper, a sensitive nature, and a childish notion of keeping one's dignity.'[14]

From the very outset, Kamala's ignorance of Western ways had been considered a serious failing in the cosmopolitan Nehru household; and Miss Hooper, governess to Motilal's daughters, had been deputed to rectify the omission. Kamala's gentle and unobtrusive ways soon won her the regard of her father-in-law; but this did not endear her to Motilal's beautiful and accomplished daughter, Vijayalakshmi,** hitherto the darling of Anand Bhawan. Vulnerable in her simplicity, Kamala had to endure the jibes of her sophisticated sister-in-law; and Vijayalakshmi did not hesitate to complain about Kamala to her brother. Jawaharlal, preoccupied with more momentous affairs, took a neutral attitude; but

*A *doli* is a kind of meat-safe for storing sweets and other comestibles; whence 'Dol Amma,' literally 'Meat-safe Mother.'
**Later known to the world as Mrs. Vijayalakshmi Pandit.

this was cold comfort for his wife. He later admitted: 'An unkindness to her would almost have been better than this semi-forgetful, casual attitude.'[17] Vijayalakshmi also carried her complaints to her mother, Swarup Rani, and here Kamala's position as a dutiful Hindu daughter-in-law inevitably placed her at a disadvantage.

'Sensitive and proud, childlike and grown-up, foolish and wise,'[16] as her husband described her, Kamala Nehru retreated into herself, spending long hours closeted in her bedroom, while little Indira sat beside her in silent sympathy. Kamala's pent-up emotions found an outlet in her devotion to her daughter; and Indira for her part, instinctively identified herself with her mother. For Indira, it was an early introduction to conflict and suffering. Her mother's unhappiness must have been a source of emotional insecurity and uncertainty in an otherwise sheltered and untroubled existence. Many years later Indira Gandhi told her mother's biographer: 'We were very close to each other. I loved her deeply, and when I thought that she was being wronged I fought for her and quarrelled with people.'[17]

Meanwhile, forces far greater than a clash of personalities were gathering momentum. In the course of a few eventful years, they would transform Anand Bhawan from 'a stately pleasure-dome' into the headquarters of Indian nationalism. The Nehru household would become a microcosm of the nation that was struggling for independence, a troubled and disturbing environment for a sensitive child.

*       *       *

Towards the end of World War I, Annie Besant, Irish theosophist turned Indian nationalist, declared: 'Autocracy is destroyed in Russia, tottering in Germany; only under England's flag it is rampant.'[18] India at the turn of the century was governed by an irresponsible and ir-removable executive appointed by Whitehall. In the absence of representative institutions, unlimited power was exercised by the Anglo-Indian bureaucracy, an exclusive cadre that was as jealous of its privileges as it was contemptuous of 'natives'. The British Raj existed, not for the benefit of its subjects, but for the greater prosperity and glory of the mother-country; and lest anyone should forget this, Indians were not only denied any share in the government, but were excluded from the services, from clubs, and even from first-class railway carriages and park benches.

Nevertheless, the Raj, despotic as it was, had sown the seeds of its own dissolution. The economic and administrative needs of British imperialism had led to the introduction of Western education and this in turn had opened the way for the growth of a new class of Western-ised Indians, eager for an ever-increasing share in the administration and the economy. At the same time, the gradual growth of Indian industry, shackled and distorted as it was in a colonial situation, had provided this new class with an economic base. The Great Revolt of 1857 had been the last bid of feudal India to oust the foreigner. The battles of the future would be fought by Western-educated, middle-class Indians, who claimed to be as aware as their masters that it was 'impossible to argue a man into slavery in the English language', and whose objective was responsible government.

The Indian National Congress already had a long history when Indira Nehru was born. Founded in 1885, with the blessings of the then Viceroy, as an exclusive debating club rather than a nationalist movement, it had functioned as a loyal opposition, voicing the desire of India's tiny westernised élite for a larger share in the administration. The Nehrus had been long and actively associated with the Congress ever since Motilal Nehru had attended its Allahabad session in 1888. Motilal's legal background had made him a confirmed advocate of constitutional methods, as opposed to the 'extremism' of Tilak and his followers. But his son, Jawaharlal, had returned from England in 1912 with a more radical outlook, convinced that the elder Nehru was 'immoderately moderate'. He had accompanied his father to the various Congress sessions; but it is not surprising that these polite gatherings of verbose gentlemen in top-hats and morning-coats had failed to impress him. Jawaharlal had also dabbled in the activities of the two Home-Rule Leagues founded respectively by Annie Besant and Tilak. Lacking any clear sense of direction, however, he might well have lapsed into a gilded, dilettante existence, had it not been for the coming of Gandhi in 1915.

Fresh from his experiments with non-violent action in South Africa, Gandhi appeared on the Indian political scene at an opportune moment. Indian constitutionalists had been certain that they would be rewarded with a major instalment of constitutional advance in return for India's co-operation in the recent war-effort. Instead they were greeted by the disappointing Montagu-Chelmsford Reforms and the repressive Rowlatt Act. But while there was a good deal of disillusionment with the Raj, there was no clear conception of how to express it in terms of action. Gandhi showed a way out of the impasse with a method of direct action which was as far removed from the impotent Liberal verbiage of Congress resolutions as it was from sporadic and futile terrorism. When he issued a call for *satyagraha** against the Rowlatt Act, he captured the imagination of a large number of young nationalists, among them Jawaharlal Nehru.

*Literally 'the path of truth,' *satyagraha* was Gandhi's name for his brand of non-violent civil disobedience.

Jawaharlal's desire to follow Gandhi brought him into head-on collision with his father. The elder Nehru seems to have viewed *satyagraha* as a form of midsummer madness. The idea that his son should indulge in law-breaking, however non-violent, and court arrest outraged both his aristocratic temperament and his faith in constitutional means. Anand Bhawan rang with heated exchanges as father and son fought in vain to convince each other. According to Motilal's daughter, Krishna: 'The atmosphere was tense all the time and one hardly dared to utter a word for fear of rousing father's anger or irritating Jawaharlal.'[19] These were trying days for the family, and especially for Kamala who was a constant source of strength and encouragement to her husband. Tempers ran high and, at one point, Motilal ordered his son to leave the house, though he soon relented. Although he stormed and raged, Motilal's chief concern was for his son's well-being. It was later discovered that the anxious patriarch would secretly descend from his bed in the dead of night and try sleeping on the floor, in an effort to sample the rigours of prison life which awaited his son.

Thus the conflict might have continued indefinitely had it not been for the massacre of Jallianwallah Bagh, generally rated as the most infamous atrocity in the annals of British rule. On 13 April 1919, at a public meeting organised by the Congress in Amritsar,* an unarmed and peaceful crowd of about 20,000 people—men, women and children— were sealed off in an enclosed space and fired upon at point-blank range by British troops. According to the official estimate, 379 people were killed and 1,200 wounded before the troops ran out of ammunition. The massacre and its justification by the authorities had an electric impact on nationalist sentiment. Many who had believed in the ultimate beneficence of British rule found their illusions shattered overnight. Convinced now that the British would never, of their own will, grant India self-government, they saw that freedom would have to be fought for and turned increasingly to Gandhi's leadership. Motilal Nehru was one of them. Drawn both by paternal affection and by his own disenchantment with the Raj, he moved ever closer to Gandhi. In December 1919, when Motilal was elected President at the Amritsar session of the Congress, the Trinity of Father, Son and Holy Ghost—as the two Nehrus and Gandhi were sometimes called—was already in the making.

When the Congress met at Calcutta in 1920, Motilal finally took the plunge; and it was his active support which tilted the scales in Gandhi's favour and enabled him to capture the organisation. The Congress committed itself to non-violent non-cooperation, announcing a boycott of the legislatures, the law-courts, Government schools and colleges, and

*One of the chief towns of the Punjab.

foreign goods. It was a historic turning point. The Congress was to be rapidly transformed from a 'three-day picnic of the urban gentry' into a mass movement and an instrument of non-violent agitation, with the spinning-wheel as its symbol, *Khadi** as its livery, and a half-naked ascetic as its presiding deity.

\*     \*     \*

Gandhi's impact was no less dramatic in the Nehru household. In accordance with the non-cooperation resolution, Motilal resigned his seat in the provincial legislature, wound up his legal practice and substantially retrenched his large household. He abandoned his Saville Row suits for a simple *dhoti*** and *kurta,*** dismissed many of his servants, and sold most of his horses and carriages. For a man with his zest for good living, these must have been major sacrifices at the age of sixty. Nor could it have been easy for a self-made man, hitherto dedicated to his profession, to abandon his lucrative practice for the uncertain politics of non-cooperation. To many of his English friends Motilal's metamorphosis was something of a shock. Their feelings were said to have 'resembled those of a fond Edwardian father whose delightful daughter became a suffragette and broke his windows'.[20]

Jawaharlal, meanwhile, was changing rapidly from a rather foppish and Anglicised young gentleman of leisure into a charismatic mass leader. Fired by missionary zeal, he was busy discovering the hungry, poverty-stricken peasantry of India, drawing strength and inspiration from their adulation as they did from his new message of hope. 'I almost forgot my family, my wife, my daughter,' he has recorded in his autobiography. 'It was only long afterwards that I realised what a burden and a trial I must have been to them in those days, and what amazing patience and tolerance my wife has shown towards me.'[21] Kamala Nehru, indeed, was far more at home with the asceticism and austerity of Gandhism than with the westernised affluence of the Nehrus, and she had vigorously led the nationalist transformation of the Nehru household. Many years later, her daughter told a women's seminar:

'Many people know the part which was played by my grandfather and my father. But in my opinion, a more important part was played by my mother. When my father wanted to join Gandhiji and to change the whole way of life, to change our luxurious living, to give up his practice, the whole family was against it. It was only my mother's courageous

---

*At Gandhi's instance, the boycott of foreign goods and the promotion of indigenous cottage industries, especially spinning, became a fundamental part of the Congress programme. *Khadi* or homespun was, and still is, the hallmark of an orthodox Gandhian.
**A long, unstitched length of cloth wound around the waist and legs.
***A loose, knee-length tunic.

and persistent support and encouragement which enabled him to take
this big step which made such a difference not only to our family but to
the history of modern India.'[22]

Indira has recorded that her earliest memory was of the day when,
in response to Gandhi's nation-wide appeal, the Nehrus burned their
foreign clothes: 'I can still feel the excitement of the day and see the
large terrace covered with piles of clothes—what rich materials, what
lovely colours! What fun for a toddler to jump on, play hide and seek
in the heaps of velvets and satins, silks and chiffons!'[23] Although it was
well past her bedtime, she was determined not to miss the bonfire and
appealed to her indulgent grandfather. As always, he let her have her
way; but when the flames rose, four-year-old Indira was already asleep.
She was too young to know that the bonfire was symbolic. Among other
things, it marked the end of her brief childhood.

# CHAPTER II

# THE NEW SOUL OF INDIA

IN A letter of congratulations to Jawaharlal Nehru on the birth of his daughter, Sarojini Naidu had humorously dubbed Indira 'the new soul of India'.[1] Her remark was more prophetic than she could possibly have imagined. The story of Indira's childhood and adolescence would be closely interwoven with the history of the new India that was struggling to come of age. That struggle would soon engulf the whole Nehru family and, while she herself was too young to be an active participant, Indira would experience keenly if vicariously the triumphs and the vicissitudes of the nationalist movement.

Her father has left a vivid description of those exhilarating early days of civil disobedience:

> 'Many of us ... lived in a kind of intoxication. We were full of excitement and optimism and a buoyant enthusiasm. We sensed the happiness of a person crusading for a cause. We were not troubled with doubts or hesitation; our path seemed to be clear in front of us, and we marched ahead ... Above all, we had a sense of freedom ... What did we care for the consequences? Prison? We looked forward to it; that would help our cause still further ... We had also an agreeable sense of moral superiority over our opponents in regard to both our goals and our methods.'[2]

But the road to independence would be longer and more arduous than Jawaharlal and other young nationalists had anticipated; and the initial euphoria soon vanished. *Satyagraha*, though non-violent, required a willingness to suffer any consequences—including death—for the cause. And while few had to make the ultimate sacrifice, many faced police firing and *lathi** charges and spent long years in prison, isolated from family and friends. Often broken in health, and sometimes in spirit, they returned as virtual strangers to the world they had left behind. After eight years in a series of prisons, Jawaharlal would write sadly to his sister:

> 'Meeting each other after a long interval shall we recognise each other

*A thick, wooden staff, used by the police to disperse demonstrators.

in the old way? Or will there be a feeling of shyness and strangeness as when we meet those we do not wholly understand? The private world each one of us lives in, worlds of fancy and feeling and imagination, have so long lain apart that they are apt to become strangers to each other, separate circles overlapping less than they used to. Partly that happens as we grow older, but the process is accelerated by the abnormal conditions we have been living in.'[3]

For twenty-five long years chronic civil disobedience and gaol-going were to mean the suspension of normal family life and human relationships. For the closely-knit Nehru family, permanently in the vanguard of movement, these separations must have been especially painful. From the age of four, Indira would be periodically deprived of the companionship of those she loved most and denied a normal childhood. She admitted many years later: 'At that time I did resent the fact, perhaps, that my parents were not with me, as other children had their parents.'[4] On one occasion, some visitors to Anand Bhawan were met on the doorstep by little Indira who gravely informed them that both her parents had gone out to gaol. 'It seemed my parents were always in gaol,'[5] she would later lament. Almost as wearing as the long separations was the constant suspense that clouded the brief reunions. One never knew when the police would arrive to remove one of the Nehrus to their 'second home.'

During the first few years of her life, Indira had been the cynosure of eyes at Anand Bhawan, smothered with attention and admiration by her elders. Now she suddenly found herself deserted by her circle of admirers and supplanted by national concerns which she was too young to understand. In her child's world the change was a drastic one, and it naturally created problems of adjustment. She must have felt neglected and abandoned, and inevitably she built up some bitterness and resentment. Had there been a brother or sister to share her loneliness, she might have adjusted more easily; but she was an only child.

\*        \*        \*

Shortly after the family bonfire, Indira had her first experience of the call of duty and conscience. A relative who had recently returned from Paris called at Anand Bhawan with an exquisitely embroidered dress as a gift for Indira. Her mother, however, politely returned it, explaining that the family no longer wore anything but *khadi*. 'I think you have all gone mad,' the visitor exploded. 'But you are adults and if you want to be ill, I suppose that is your business. But you certainly have no right to make the child suffer and it's for her that I have bought this gift.' Kamala thereupon called out to her daughter, who was playing nearby, and said: 'Auntie has brought you a foreign frock. It is very pretty and you can wear it if you like, but first think of the big fire when we burnt our foreign things.' Indira was tempted, as any little girl would have been. She reached out for the dress, then suddenly stopped short and found herself shouting: 'Take it away—I shan't ever wear it!' 'All right, Miss Saint', the visitor teased her, 'how is it that you have a foreign doll?' 'I was passionately fond of the doll,' Indira Gandhi has recalled. 'I could not think of it, or indeed of anything as lifeless. Everything was given a name and immediately developed its own personality—the doll was my friend, my child.' For days, we are told, she lived in an agony of doubt, torn between her love for the doll and what she considered her duty to her country. Finally the decision was taken. Quivering with tension, she took the doll out onto the terrace and set fire to it. She felt as though she had killed a living person: 'The tears came as if they would never stop and for some days I was ill with temperature. To this day I hate to strike a match!'[6]

The privacy of family life at Anand Bhawan had become a thing of the past. Hordes of serious, khadi-clad politicians and intellectuals thronged the house and held their councils of war on its lawns, where, in former times, bands had played and champagne had flowed. Life in the Nehru household became chaotic, and the women of the family were rushed off their feet by the constant influx. Gandhi, Mrs. Besant, Sir Tej Bahadur Sapru, Pandit Madan Mohan Malaviya, Lala Lajpat Rai and Mohamed Ali Jinnah—these were a few of the political 'giants' who frequented the Nehru home. For Indira it was an early and over-whelming introduction to famous men and women. She wandered freely among them, taking in something of what they said. Asked by an interviewer when her political career had begun, Indira Gandhi would reply: 'I think I attended my first Congress meeting when I was three.'[7] 'Our house was always full of all kinds of people,' she has told the author. 'They were always having political discussions, and even though I didn't understand all of it, I did imbibe something, even though not consciously. It has an effect on one's thinking and development.'[8]

Indira was growing up into a rather tomboyish girl, both in manners and appearance. Kamala Nehru herself had managed as a girl to avoid the constraints of *purdah* by dressing in her brothers' clothes. Now she seems to have enjoyed dressing young Indira in the uniform of a male Congress volunteer. With her close-cropped hair tucked under a Gandhi-cap, Indira could pass quite easily as a boy, and she frequently did, thereby causing considerable confusion among visitors. 'Where is your brother?' they would ask when she appeared in her normal girlish frills. 'I don't have a brother,' she would reply mysteriously. And when they persisted—'but we've seen him with our own eyes!'—Indira, with a child's delight in the discomfiture of her elders, would refuse to divulge the secret which she shared with her mother.[9]

Anand Bhawan was a highly charged environment for a growing child, and it seems to have kept Indira in a state of permanent excitement, sometimes verging on hysteria. Climbing onto a table, she would collect an audience of servants and harangue them passionately with the slogans she had picked up from her elders. 'I haven't the remotest idea what I said to them or whether it made any sense,'[10] she later confessed. Her games were exclusively political. According to the oft-told story, she would mobilise her numerous dolls for battle, dividing them into policemen and *satyagrahis*, with the latter invariably victorious.

Apparently she also had visions of martyrdom. On one occasion her aunt Krishna discovered her in a curious pose. Her eyes burning and her arms dramatically stretched out, Indira stood on the verandah muttering to herself. When asked what she thought she was doing, she solemnly replied: 'I'm practising being Joan of Arc. I have just been reading about her, and some day I am going to lead my people to freedom as Joan of Arc did.'[11] The St. Joan syndrome would remain with her long after she had forgotten and outgrown the fantasy. Transferred to the world of action, it would mean a dynamic sense of mission and an eagerness to respond vigorously to any challenge. But beneath it there may well have lurked a deep-seated fear of inadequacy—of failing to measure up to the achievements of those around her—which would be concealed from prying eyes by an impenetrable wall of reserve.

Indira was not, in the usual sense, a deprived or neglected child. She had affection in abundance from those around her, and her material wants and desires were rarely if ever denied. Even after the Nehrus became involved in the rough and tumble of politics, during the interludes of family life that they were able to snatch, Indira was if anything more petted and indulged than ever. But what she did lack, and what these extremes of indulgence and neglect only served to emphasise, was the even tempo and discipline of a stable and secure home, in which she could be truly a child, free from the anxiety and tension of a world which she was too young to comprehend.

Like so many other children who grow up in a disturbed environment and of whom much is expected, Indira seems to have felt threatened and vulnerable. And like other children, she sought compensation, partly through defence-mechanisms which insulated her from intimacy with people other than the very few she felt she could trust, and partly through fantasies in which she could assert her superiority as a successful and admired figure in the world of action. The result was an obsessive desire to excel and prove her mettle, coupled with a painful shyness and diffidence which, for many years, would cramp her personality and prevent the realisation of its full potential.

\*　　　　\*　　　　\*

In November 1921, when Gandhi proclaimed a nation-wide *hartal* on the occasion of the Prince of Wales's visit, the Government decided to strike at the Congress. The Nehrus, father and son, were among the first to be arrested. For four-year-old Indira it was an early baptism in the consequences of civil disobedience. Though she could not, of course, participate in the movement, she became a regular spectator at the trials of her elders. Sitting in the dock on her grandfather's lap, she witnessed his trial at Allahabad's Naini Prison. According to her aunt: 'Indu* sat very still with her enormous dark eyes fixed intently on the judge, taking in far more of the proceedings than we believed possible.'[12] If, indeed, she was able to follow the proceedings, they cannot have enhanced her respect for British justice. The trial was a farce, with an illiterate witness pretending to identify Motilal's signature on a list of Congress volunteers which he held upside down.

In April 1922, Jawaharlal, only recently released, was re-arrested while engaged in peaceful picketing of foreign cloth-shops and charged with criminal intimidation, extortion and sedition. Indira was present at his trial and did much to enliven the proceedings. *The Independent*, an Allahabad newspaper owned by her grandfather, thus described the scene:

'The stage was set ready for the novel trial to begin. Pandit Jawaharlal and nine others, the pride of the city of Allahabad, were in their proper places on the under-trial prisoners' benches. The judge was in the chair with as solemn an air on his face as he could command. Seats for the audience were arranged neatly in semi-circular rows, and the audience ...sat with attention and gravity writ large on its face.

'The death-like stillness was at last broken by the soft prattle of a child's voice—four-year-old daughter of Pandit Jawaharlal Nehru— as in hopping accents she asked, "Mummie, are they going to have a bioscope show?" The hearts of all listeners were touched by the un- affected simplicity of the child and there was hardly an eye that did not glisten with subdued emotion. It was all over in a minute, however. The faces of the audience brightened up as the next moment they realised the full humour of the situation.'[13]

About this time, Indira had her first encounters with the British police. It was the Congress policy not to pay fines imposed by the courts; and so the police became frequent visitors at Anand Bhawan, carrying away furniture, carpets, silver and other valuables in lieu of the fines. Jawahar- lal later wrote: 'Indira, my four-year-old daughter, was greatly annoyed at this continuous process of despoliation and protested to the police

*'Little Moon,' Indira's pet-name.

and expressed her strong displeasure. I am afraid that those early impressions are likely to colour her future views about the police force generally.'14 Already a strong-willed child, she would fly at the policemen, shaking her fist and shouting, 'You can't take them, they belong to us!'15 Mrs. Gandhi has recorded that on one occasion she almost succeeded in chopping off an officer's thumb with a bread-slicing gadget.

It was now, when he was separated from her, that Jawaharlal first began to take an active interest in his 'Priyadarshini—dear to the sight, but dearer still when sight is denied.'16 Indira was painfully thin and her health was a constant cause of anxiety. 'To dear Indu, love from her Papu,*' Jawaharlal wrote from prison in October 1922. 'You must get well quickly, learn to write letters and come and see me in gaol. I am longing to see you. Have you tried the new spinning-wheel which Dadu** has brought for you? Send me some of your yarn. Do you join your mother at prayers every day?'17 A month later he wrote again, with a string of questions about her visit to Calcutta with her grandfather: 'Love to dear daughter Indira from her Papu. Did you like Calcutta? Is it better than Bombay? Did you see the Calcutta zoo? What animals did you see? Have you seen a huge tree there? You must get strong and plump before I return to Allahabad.'18

It was about this time that Indira first met the man who, for the next twenty-five years, was to have such a pervasive influence on the lives of those around her. In 1922, while their menfolk were in prison, the women of the Nehru family accepted Gandhi's invitation to pay him a visit. Travelling third-class, in the Gandhian fashion, Swarup Rani, Kamala, Krishna and little Indira arrived at Sabarmati, Gandhi's ashram near Ahmedabad in Gujerat. Though accustomed to the comforts of Anand Bhawan they managed to adjust themselves to the rigours of ashram life, which included sleeping on the floor in a dormitory, rising before dawn, and washing their own clothes.

Gandhi forms a part of Indira's earliest memories. Later she 'disagreed with many of his ideas and had long discussions with the usual dogmatism of the very young who think that they have all the answers.' But 'as a very small child,' she recalls, 'I regarded him, not as a great leader but more as an elder of the family to whom I went with difficulties and problems, which he treated with the grave seriousness which was due to the large-eyed and solemn child I was.'19

*          *          *

Surrounded by adults and deprived of the company of other children, Indira was growing up into something of a problem-child, moody,

*Indira's name for her father.
**Indira's name for her grandfather.

self-centred and often refractory. One of her uncles has recalled taking her out in the evenings to buy sweets. 'I used to tickle her, but she never smiled,' he complained. 'She would push my finger away firmly and remain tense and fidgety.'[20] It was an alarming display of propriety from a four-year-old.

Nevertheless, even at that early age, much was expected of her. As early as 1922, Jawaharlal expressed his concern about her education in a letter to his father:

'Kamala writes to say that Indu is becoming more and more intractable and pays no heed to any kind of study. I wish some arrangement could be made for her lessons. I am confident that I could have managed her easily—but I am in barrack number 4—so some other arrangement must be thought of. I do not suppose that she will acquire much knowledge just yet but she must begin to acquire the habit of doing lessons. The longer this is delayed the more difficult it will be for her and for others. As it is she is past the age when she should have begun seriously.'[21]

Indira's education would inevitably suffer from the uncertainty of her home life; and she would also become something of a guinea-pig for her father's experimental ideas. In the days of non-cooperation, Government-aided institutions were being boycotted; and so, after a short stay at a kindergarten school in Delhi, Indira joined the Modern School at Allahabad, a newly-founded nationalist institution. The school was short of resources and staff and included a large variety of age groups. Motilal soon decided that it was unsuitable for his granddaughter, and transferred her to St. Cecilia's, a private school run by three English sisters, the Misses Cameron. The result was a storm in a teacup. The younger Nehru complained to Gandhi that Indira's attendance at a school run by Europeans was a breach of the principles of non-cooperation. At Jawaharlal's request, the Mahatma lodged a mild protest with Motilal. The elder Nehru, in high dudgeon, telegraphed to Gandhi that Jawaharlal had told him 'a tissue of lies from beginning to end', that Indira's school had no connections with the Government, and that Jawaharlal's objections were based, not on the principles of non-cooperation, but on his own peculiar educational views. 'I was solely prompted by desire to give Indira companionship of children of her own age,' he asserted and his son's version was 'absolutely false' and 'too mean for the proudest father in the world'.[22] Motilal might storm and rage, but his son had his way. Indira was withdrawn from school and taught at home by private tutors, removed from the company of other children.

To her loneliness was added anxiety about her mother's chronic ill-health. Ever since Indira's birth, Kamala Nehru had been frail and easily tired. Subsequently, two unsuccessful pregnancies had further weakened her. Neglected and ailing, she suffered in silence. Her remorseful husband later confessed: '...all unconsciously, I almost overlooked her and left her to her own resources, just when she required my full cooperation... She gave me strength, but she must have suffered and felt a little neglected.'[23] It is not surprising then that Kamala Nehru became 'a champion of woman's right against the tyranny of man.'[24] An ardent feminist, she urged women to rebel against man-made laws and the domination of their husbands and impressed upon them the necessity of educating themselves.

*       *       *

As early as 1919, Kamala had been suspected of tuberculosis. When in 1925 the dread disease—then considered fatal—was definitely diagnosed, it was decided that she must go to Switzerland for treatment. In March 1926, Jawaharlal, Kamala and Indira took ship for Venice en route to Geneva. Motilal, anxious lest his granddaughter catch the infection, wrote instructing his son that mother and daughter must be kept at a suitable distance: 'On the journey from Delhi to Bombay I noticed that Indu frequently kissed Kamala. This should be stopped. If possible they should avoid hugging each other in the way they do, as according to the latest theory even perspiration carries the germs.'[25]

The family took a small flat in Geneva, and Indira joined the famous International School. Later she was shifted to L'École Nouvelle at Bex. 'I am sure all the little girls will simply worship her,' Motilal wrote to his son, 'no forced aloofness of the Anglo-Indian girl.'[26] But according to her aunt Krishna, who had joined the family in Geneva, eight-year-old Indira was already too grown-up for her classmates, who were mainly interested in games and certainly not in politics. Indira, as always, kept aloof.

Even so, this was a relatively happy phase in her childhood. She enjoyed the winter sports and soon picked up enough French to roam the streets on her own, thereby winning fulsome praise from her grandfather. In May 1926 he wrote from India to her father: 'Indu is a wonderful little girl to be able to make her way in the streets of a Swiss town in the way you describe. It is not that she is so small—but the fact that she could not possibly have acquired a sufficient knowledge of the language which makes it quite a brave thing to do. But you must not overtax her capacity in this respect.'[27] A few months later he observed approvingly in another letter to Jawaharlal: 'It seems that she can suit herself to any conditions and is well able to look after herself. I am not at all surprised that her mental growth has been remarkable. It has indeed been so from the very beginning. The difference is in the opportunities which were practically nil in Allahabad.'[28]

This proved to be one of the most formative periods of Jawaharlal's intellectual life. Europe in the late twenties was in a state of intellectual ferment and economic crisis. The most important new current of thought was Marxism, which offered a scientific and humane alternative both to the ills of an effete liberalism and to the sinister prospects of Fascism. Jawaharlal was too much of a liberal and a Gandhian to accept the ruthlessness and violence associated with established Communism; but Marxist theory gave him an international perspective and a socio-economic basis for his political thought, both of which were to stand him in good stead when he returned to India. Leaving his wife in the hands of her doctors, he toured the Continent, meeting old friends and making new acquaintances. Indira accompanied him on some of his visits, listening with what her aunt has described as 'the gravity of an old judge'[29] to his conversations with intellectuals like Romain Rolland, Albert Einstein and Ernst Toller. With her father she also toured the museums and historic monuments of Europe. Jawaharlal was an eloquent and indefatigable guide, and it must have been a stimulating if strenuous experience.

In the autumn of 1927, Motilal joined the family in Europe; and his ostentatious ways were a welcome change from the austere regime that Jawaharlal had imposed on them. Kamala had already been pronounced cured, and a couple of months later Indira sailed from Marseilles with her parents, homeward bound. Her stay in Europe had been a pleasant interlude away from the rough and tumble of Indian politics.

\* \* \*

On her return to India in December 1927, Indira joined St. Mary's Convent in Allahabad, her father apparently suspending his objections to European schools. In deference to nationalist sentiment, however, an Indian tutor was appointed to teach her Hindi at home. In the summer of 1928, while Indira was holidaying in Mussoorie, her father decided to write her a series of letters (later published as *Letters from a Father to a Daughter*) designed to awaken her thirst for knowledge. In his opening letter he announced:

'When you and I are together you often ask me questions about many things and I try to answer them. Now that you are at Mussoorie and I an in Allahabad we cannot have these talks. I am therefore going to write to you from time to time short accounts of the state of our earth and the many countries, great and small, in which it is divided.'[30]

The proclaimed purpose of the letters was to show this 'world of ours as a large family of nations'. In a simple account of the early history of the world, illustrated with references to the museums and historic places which father and daughter had recently visited together, they traced the evolution of man and society. Gandhi commented after seeing them:

'They have a value derived not from the truth of your conclusions but from the manner of treatment and from the fact that you have tried to reach Indu's heart and open the eyes of her understanding in the midst of your external activities.'[31]

Two years later, Jawaharlal decided to follow up this first series with a far more ambitious project, a correspondence course in World History from ancient times to the present. Written from Naini Prison on 26 October 1930, Indira's thirteenth birthday by the Hindu calendar, the first letter began:

'On your birthday you have been in the habit of receiving presents and good wishes. Good wishes you still have in full measure, but what present can I send you from Naini Prison? My presents cannot be very material or solid. They can only be of the air and of the mind and spirit, such as a good fairy might have bestowed on you—things that even the high walls of prison cannot stop ... I have liked my talks with you and we have discussed many things ... A letter can hardly take the place of a talk; at best it is a one-sided affair. So if I say anything that sounds like good advice, do not take it as if it were a bad pill to swallow. Imagine that I have made a suggestion to you for you to think over as if we really were having a talk.'[32]

Written in gaol without a reference library, the monumental *Glimpses of World History* (as they were called in published form) could not claim to be an authoritative history of the world. Nor could they escape being coloured by the frustrations of prison life; and their interpretation of events was often superficial and emotional. Jawaharlal himself had no illusions on this score. He cautioned his daughter:

'You must not take what I have written in these letters as the final authority on any subject. A politician wants to have a say on every subject, and he always pretends to know much more than he actually does. He has to be watched carefully... As you will notice, my likes and dislikes are pretty obvious, and so also sometimes are my moods in gaol.'[33]

Nevertheless, with their scientific historical analysis, their emphasis on the then neglected history of the East, their intensity and freshness of approach, and their easy conversational style, the letters justly rank among the best of Nehru's writings. Their charm, however, lies in the sensitive understanding of the mind of a young girl. As Jawaharlal confessed: 'I have decided to write them for my own pleasure. They bring you very near to me, and I feel I have had a talk.'[34] The letters abound in poignant expressions of sympathy for the lonely child who was separated from him when she most needed his love. On New Year's Day 1931, her father wrote: 'Often enough I think of you, but today you have hardly been absent from my mind. Today is New Year's Day ...But you must be rather lonely. Once a fortnight you may see Mummie* and once a fortnight you may see me, and you will carry our messages to each other.'[35]

The series came to an end in August 1933. 'What a mountain of letters I have written,' Jawaharlal concluded. 'Was it worthwhile I wonder? Will all this paper and ink convey any message to you that will interest you? You will say, yes, of course, for you will feel that any other answer might hurt me, and you are too partial to me to take such a risk.'[36] But Indira has recorded how much her father's letter meant to her. They were her only contact with him during those formative years of her life. And although 'they were just letters at that time,' Indira Gandhi would comment many years later: 'Now I realise that they helped to form my mind in a way that no other education did, because they helped me to see things in perspective, and I never saw an Indian problem merely as an Indian problem, but as an international one.'[37]

Spurred on by her father's letters, in themselves a major education, Indira was beginning to settle down to work. 'I study Sanskrit and English regularly now,' she wrote to her father. 'I also go to the convent for French and violin lessons... I have read a lot of books in the library, at least all those that I could understand. Could you suggest some more that I could read? You can tell me when I come at your next interview.'[38]

Indira was becoming a voracious reader, ranging over science, adventure, fairy tales and the biographies of nationalist heroes such as Joan of Arc, William Tell, Garibaldi and Juarez. She enjoyed plays and poetry and was particularly impressed by Oscar Wilde's 'Ballad of Reading Gaol' and Victor Hugo's 'Les Miserables' with its picture of poverty and social injustice. At the same time she enjoyed lighter works, such as those of Lewis Carroll, and dipped into books on natural history like the 'Faber Book of Insects' and Maurice Maeterlinck's books on bees and ants. 'Just the minute I finished one book I wanted another,' she later recalled.[39]

Her father wrote to warn her against excesses: 'It is a good habit to read books, but I rather suspect those who read too many books quickly. I suspect them of not reading them properly at all, of just skimming

*Kamala Nehru had been arrested that very day.

through them, and forgetting them the day after... there are such a vast
number of books which are not worth reading at all.'[40] But he must have
been impressed, because he wrote to his sister Krishna asking her to send
Indira Trevelyan's Life of Garibaldi.

Indira was maturing rapidly, and in one of his letters her father joked:

'...the real reason—shall I whisper it to you?—why I put off writing
was another one. I am beginning to doubt if I know enough to
teach you! You are growing up so fast, and becoming such a wise
little person, that all I learnt at school and college and afterwards
may not be enough for you, and at any rate may be rather stale. After
some time, it may be that you will take up the role of teacher and teach
me many new things!'[41]

*         *         *

By 1930 mass civil disobedience was again in full swing. But this was
after several years of dissension and faction-fighting within the Congress,
during which the organisation had come close to splitting on more than
one occasion. Gandhi's sudden withdrawal of civil disobedience in 1922,
after a minor incident of violence, had shocked and demoralised most
of his supporters, among them the Nehrus, who were alarmed by the
Mahatma's religious obsession with non-violence. In view of the collapse
of civil disobedience, the 'Pro-Changers' led by Motilal Nehru had
questioned the wisdom of continuing Gandhi's policy of total non-
cooperation, and had advocated the opening of a new front in the
legislatures with the aim of exposing these 'sham parliaments' for what
they were. Despite strenuous opposition from the 'No-Changers',
Motilal had formed the Swaraj (Independence) Party within the Congress
to contest the elections under the new Constitution of 1919. A brilliant
parliamentarian, Motilal, as Leader of the Opposition in the Central
Legislative Assembly, had at first been successful in blocking Government legislation and in forcing the Executive to fall back on its wide
discretionary powers. But by 1925 deep cracks had appeared in the
Swarajist ranks, and many of the party's leading figures had abandoned
it in favour of communalism* and constitutionalism. While the Congress
was weakened and divided by its internal feuds, the forces of communalism
had been rapidly gaining ground, and the political atmosphere had been
vitiated by Hindu-Muslim conflict, to the advantage of the ruling power.

Younger and more militant elements in the Congress had, meanwhile,
been growing restive and had turned increasingly to socialism and mass
organisation as an alternative both to the mystical obscurantism of

*Communalism, in the Indian context, denotes politics based upon the rivalry and
competition between different religious or racial groups.

Gandhi and the constitutionalism of the Liberals. Since his return from Europe in 1927, Jawaharlal Nehru had applied himself to the task of radicalising the Congress and making it more representative of the masses. But the younger Nehru's socialism had brought him into head-on collision with Gandhi and his own father. Matters had come to a head at the Calcutta Congress in December 1928, presided over by Motilal Nehru. The Nehru Report, drafted by Motilal as an attempt at a compromise constitution acceptable to all communities and political parties, had caused a sharp cleavage in the Congress with its proposal of Dominion Status. At the Calcutta session, Gandhi, Motilal and the Old Guard had found themselves strongly opposed by Jawaharlal and the radicals, who would be satisfied with nothing less than complete independence. Eventually the sheer force of Gandhi's personality had succeeded in bringinging about a one-year truce. For the Nehrus these had been tense days, with father and son clashing with all the violence of former times while the family looked on anxiously.

By the time the Congress met in Lahore* at the end of 1929, the lack of a positive response from the Government had turned the tide in favour of complete independence. With the active support of Gandhi and his father, Jawaharlal, the hero of the Congress Left, had been elected President, one of the youngest in Congress history. From Lahore the Congress had issued its famous declaration of war, adopting *purna swaraj* (complete independence) as its goal and authorising a renewal of civil disobedience. A few months later, when Gandhi launched mass civil disobedience, beginning with nationwide violation of the iniquitous Salt Law, Motilal and Jawaharlal were among the first to be arrested.

Despite the massive repression to which the Congress was subjected, the movement did not collapse. After the arrest of most of the Congress leaders early in 1930, their womenfolk came forward to man the Congress organisation, filling the breach with a confidence that won the admiration even of officials of the Raj. Equality of the sexes had long been one of the tenets of the Congress creed; but it might well have remained a dead letter had it not been for the role of women in the Civil Disobedience movements of 1930–32 and later in the 'Quit India' movement of 1942–43. With a couple of exceptions, like Mrs. Besant and Mrs. Naidu, women had hitherto taken little part in Congress decision-making; but now they came to the front in large numbers and proved themselves worthy of the status that they had been promised. The active participation of women in post-Independence politics, surprising in an otherwise male-dominated society, owes much to the role of women during the nationalist struggle.

*The capital of the Punjab province.

Kamala Nehru, who had as her husband confessed long been denied 'that comradeship which was her due,'[42] now revealed the potential that lay beneath her gentle and retiring exterior. Despite her ill health, she worked with unflagging energy as President of the Allahabad Congress Committee and later as a substitute member of the Congress Working Committee, the movement's High Command. Unmindful of the summer heat, she kept up a furious pace, organising the women of Allahabad to picket foreign cloth-shops and liquor stores. Her efforts won general admiration and helped to bring thousands of women out of their homes. 'I marvelled at Kamala's energy,' her sister-in-law Krishna later wrote. 'I, who was far more healthy than she, often gave into fatigue or weariness and stayed at home, but not she ... we often grumbled and felt tired and disheartened. Not so Kamala whose faith and spirits never seemed to flag.'[43]

It was in the course of these activities that Kamala is reported to have met Feroze Gandhi, the young Parsi* who was later to marry her daughter. With some other women she was picketing a Government college, while some students perched on the college wall and watched with amusement. It was a blazing summer's day, and the *satyagrahis* were very thirsty. Though it was usual for sympathetic onlookers to offer refreshments, the boys made no such gesture. Suddenly Kamala fainted, and the remorseful students rushed to her assistance and helped to revive her. Feroze Gandhi was one of them. Soon after this Feroze enlisted as a Congress volunteer.

Feroze's nationalist activities soon brought upon him the wrath of his loyalist family, and he began to turn increasingly to the Nehrus for comfort and inspiration. He became a frequent visitor at Anand Bhawan, and Indira and he must have been thrown together a good deal; but it was Kamala Nehru who was Feroze's heroine, and he worshipped her with all the devotion of a teenager to his idol. He became a familiar figure, trotting behind her with her basket of sandwiches and and tea, as she did her political rounds in the villages. Kamala herself later confided to Swami Abhayananda, her spiritual guide, that she looked upon Feroze as her own son.

Kamala Nehru's arrest on 1st January 1931 was her finest hour. She had spent New Year's Eve alone with her daughter, reading Tennyson's 'In Memoriam', when they were interrupted by the ringing of the telephone. Indira answered, and an anonymous voice warned her that her mother was to be arrested the next morning. 'I was stunned,' Mrs. Gandhi has told a woman journalist. 'She asked me to pack and herself spent

---

*The Parsis are a small community of ancient Persian extraction, professing the Zoroastrian faith. They migrated to India in the 8th Century A.D., following the Arab conquest of Persia.

the whole night working ... talking to the local Congress workers, giving them some papers, giving instructions. There was much to be done.'[44]

In a parting message to the nation Kamala Nehru, the Hindu wife in her overcoming for the moment her feminism, declared: 'I am happy beyond measure and proud to follow in the footsteps of my husband. I hope the people will keep the flag flying.'[45] Her husband later wrote: 'She wanted to play her own part in the national struggle and not be merely a hanger-on and a shadow of her husband... She wanted to justify herself to her own self as well as to the world ... but I was far too busy to see beneath the surface and I was blind to what she looked for and so ardently desired.'[46] When understanding came at last, it would be too late to make amends.

'When I was arrested, I was worried about Indu,' Kamala wrote to Jawaharlal from Lucknow Central Gaol. 'I wondered what she would do by herself. But I now feel somewhat reassured about her being able to look after herself. She gave me her word that she would remain cheerful and take care of herself.'[47] To Indira she wrote:

'Let me know your daily routine. Please send your teachers' fort- nightly reports about your studies to your father. I hope you remember what I told you when I left home. Whenever I stroll outside the barrack, I think of you. You must also take a walk every day. When I am released, we shall go out for walks together. That will be six months away, but six months will pass without either of us feeling it.'[48]

Kamala's work had been a shining example to her daughter, no less than to thousands of other women. Indira was twelve at the time, an awkward age. While she was too young to enrol as a regular Congress- woman, she was old enough to be roused by the excitement and enthusiasm of those around her. At the stormy 1928 session of the Congress, she had seen her grandfather as Congress President, driving in state in a carriage drawn by thirty-four white horses ridden by uniformed Congress volun- teers. A year later she had watched her father, 'a knight *sans peur et sans reproche*' as Gandhi described him, riding through the streets of Lahore on a white charger, followed by a detachment of mounted volun- teers and a herd of elephants, while cheering crowds showered him with rose petals. Like the rest of the family, she had watched proudly while Motilal, in the manner of a monarch passing on the crown and sceptre to his heir, had vacated the presidential chair for his son. It had been the first instance in Congress history of a father being succeeded as President by his son. On 26 January 1930, proclaimed by the Congress as Independence Day, Indira had taken the pledge of independence with thousands of others all over the country, reciting after her father the solemn words:

'We believe that it is the inalienable right of the Indian people, as of any other people, to have freedom and to enjoy the fruits of their toil... We believe also that if any Government deprives a people of these rights and oppresses them the people have a further right to alter it or abolish it. The British Government in India has not only deprived the Indian people of their freedom but has based itself on the exploitation of the masses, and has ruined India economically, politically, culturally, and spiritually... We hold it to be a crime against man and God to submit any longer to a rule that has caused this fourfold disaster to our country.'[49]

These were romantic times, and Indira was determined not to let them pass her by. Here was an opportunity to give substance to the fevered fantasies of her early childhood. Even had she wished otherwise, the voice of duty called. If she was a second Maid of Orleans, her father's letters were her 'voices'. They were a constant reminder of what was expected of her. In the opening letter of *Glimpses of World History*, he lectured:

'Do you remember how fascinated you were when you first read the story of Jeanne d'Arc, and how your ambition was to be something like her?... If we are to be India's soldiers we have India's honour in our keeping, and that honour is a sacred trust. Often we may be in doubt as to what to do... One little test I shall ask you to apply when-ever you are in doubt... Never do anything in secret or anything that you would wish to hide. For the desire to hide anything means that you are afraid, and fear is a bad thing and unworthy of you. Be brave, and all the rest follows... And if you do so, my dear, you will grow up a child of the light, unafraid and serene and unruffled, whatever may happen... Goodbye little one, and may you grow up into a brave soldier in India's service'.[50]

Indira had already had an early apprenticeship in social service. As a small child, she would bicycle six miles every Sunday to the home of Sam Higginbotham, an American missionary, to help his wife sort out American donations of clothes, toys and books for children at a Leper Colony. In 1928 she started a children's section of the Gandhi Charkha Sangh (Association of Hand-Spinners) in Allahabad. Now, while her elders were busy with gaol-going, picketing and demonstrations, Indira followed her mother's example and decided to creat a role for herself. Although she was painfully shy and self-conscious, she set about organ-ising an Allahabad branch of the *Vanar Sena* (Monkey Army), a children's

organisation. 'I did that in a fit of temper!' Indira Gandhi proudly recalled many years later. 'I was twelve years old at the time, and I wanted
to be a member of the Congress Party—but they turned me down. They
said I would have to be eighteen or twenty-one, or something like that.
I was exceedingly angry and I said "I'll have an organisation of my own!"
And that's how it began. My father didn't even know about it until I
had completed all the preliminaries.'[51]

Like the legendary monkey army which had helped Rama, hero of
the *Ramayana*, to conquer Ceylon, the *Vanar Sena* functioned as an
auxiliary arm of the Congress, writing notices, addressing envelopes,
making flags and smuggling messages past unsuspecting policemen. It
was also something of an intelligence unit, spying on police-stations for
information about impending raids and arrests. 'I suppose in some ways
we behaved not unlike monkeys,'[52] Mrs. Gandhi has confessed about
her first venture into politics. At the first meeting of the Vanar Sena,
she made her debut as an orator. Unfortunately her voice was drowned
in the large crowd of children that she was to address; and so a chain of
human loudspeakers was improvised to pass her words down the line.
'What is the position in the "monkey army"?' her grandfather wrote to
her from prison. 'I suggest the wearing of a tail by every member of it,
the length of which should be in proportion to the rank of the wearer.'[53]
He seems to have felt that the would-be Joan of Arc was taking herself
too seriously.

Motilal had recently donated his home to the Congress, and the
family had moved into a new house on the same estate. His daughter
later commented: 'Father's plans for the "smaller" house began with the
idea of functional simplicity, but when we moved in, in 1929, it wasn't
simple at all.'[54] Built in tiers like an elaborate wedding cake, with a
whimsical dome perched on the top, the new Anand Bhawan was scarcely
less palatial than its predecessor. The old house, renamed Swaraj Bhawan
(Abode of Freedom), was now the national headquarters of the Congress.
Part of the house had been converted into a hospital, and Indira worked
there with the other women of the family, nursing the victims of police
firing and *lathi* charges. She particularly remembers one boy who was
brought in which a stomach injury that was so serious that the doctors
gave him up; 'but he was my first patient, and I was determined to see
him through. I almost staked my faith in God on his pulling through.'[55]
Apparently her prayers were answered, for she met him twenty years
later during an election campaign.

\*       \*       \*

Indira's part, however modest, in the freedom struggle seems to have
given her a new confidence in herself, and she was beginning to settle

down emotionally. 'Indu is quite happy,' Motilal wrote to her father. 'She has fitted up the old wooden house in which the deer was kept as a sort of a summer house and Betty* and she both spend some time in the middle of the day in it.'[56] But with the rest of the family, she was shortly to suffer a shock which would again unsettle her delicate emotional equilibrium.

Early in 1930, Motilal Nehru had taken over as acting President of the Congress to fill the gap created by his son's arrest, and he had campaigned strenuously till his own arrest two months later. But anxiety and over-work, followed by the unaccustomed privations of prison-life, had broken his health. As his condition grew serious, he was released in September 1930; but by the end of January 1931, he was sinking rapidly. 'Dadu spent a sleepless night yesterday,' Indira wrote to her father, who was still in prison. 'He coughed most of the time and this morning his face is all swollen up.'[57] Although Motilal put up a brave fight, the end was near. On 26 January the Government, in a conciliatory gesture, released the members of the Congress Working Committee, and they flocked to pay their last respects to the dying leader. On 6 February, with his family and Gandhi beside him, the most colourful of the Nehrus breathed his last. He had retained his sense of humour till the very end, announcing that he did not want anyone to pray for him when he was gone: he had made his own way in this world, and intended to do the same in the next.

According to one of Indira's cousins, her earliest memory of Indira is of a lanky girl standing aloof and weeping silently for the grandfather she would never see again. Perhaps she wept, too, for the end of her home life and childhood, such as it had been. Motilal had been an unshakable pillar in the shifting sands of her uncertain environment, a constant source of strength and reassurance. While he lived, his giant presence had filled Anand Bhawan, holding its inmates together by the force of his personality and the depth of his fierce love for them. Now that he was no more, Anand Bhawan, except for brief intervals, would cease to be a home, and the Nehrus would go their different ways. Their sense of loss was best expressed by Jawaharlal in a letter to his daughter:

'Millions have sorrowed for him; but what of us, children of his, flesh of his flesh, and bone of his bone! And what of the new Anand Bhawan, child of his also, even as we are, fashioned by him so lovingly and carefully. It is lonely and deserted and its spirit seems to have gone and we walk along its verandahs with light steps, lest we disturb, thinking ever of him who made it.'[58]

*The family's pet-name for Motilal's younger daughter, Krishna.

# CHAPTER III

# THE UNIVERSITY OF NATURE

MOTILAL NEHRU, for all his many disagreements with his son, had been the younger Nehru's closest friend and adviser and his greatest admirer. Motilal, the practical and hard-headed realist, had been the perfect foil to Jawaharlal's hot-headed and impulsive nature. His death had brought to an end one of the most remarkable political partnerships in the history of the nationalist movement. Before Jawaharlal could recover from the blow, he experienced a major political disappointment. In March 1931, the Gandhi-Irwin Pact brought about a truce between the Congress and the Government. In return for some minor concessions, Gandhi agreed to suspend civil disobedience and to participate in the Second Round Table Conference, which was to be held in London later in the year to discuss India's constitutional future. Gandhi's apparent surrender, following so closely on his father's death, shook Jawaharlal to the core. Suffering from mental and physical exhaustion, he decided to take a vacation in Ceylon with his wife and daughter.

The calm, tropical beauty of Ceylon, away from the turmoil of Indian politics, had a soothing effect on the Nehrus. They spent seven weeks on a leisurely tour of the island's beautiful resorts and ancient monuments. Jawaharlal was already something of a world figure, and wherever they went the family drew large crowds of admirers. Indira—at least to Ceylonese eyes—must have appeared far older than her thirteen years, for one finds Nehru writing to his sister: 'Kamala has often been taken for my daughter. But what do you say to Indu being taken for the mother! This has happened repeatedly.'[1]

When the family returned from their holiday, they found the political future uncertain. Cracks were already beginning to appear in the truce, and there was a possibility of Indira's parents being re-arrested in the near future. It was therefore decided, at Gandhi's suggestion, to send her to a boarding-school in Poona.

The years ahead would be a trying period for her, possibly the most exacting in her life. In addition to the usual strains and tensions of adolescence, she would be consumed by anxiety for the parents from whom she was separated, and most of all for her ailing mother. A lonely exile,

Indira had to struggle as best she could to meet the demands of a formal education.

*          *          *

The Pupil's Own School in Poona* was a nationalist venture, founded in 1928 by a group of intellectuals from Rabindranath Tagore's circle at Shantiniketan.** Originally a kindergarten school, it had been expanded to provide a home for the children of imprisoned politicians, and higher-grade classes had been improvised. Indira was in the first batch of 'political refugees' to be admitted.

The school, which was housed in an old Portuguese Colonial building, had about seventy day-scholars and ten boarders. The system of teaching was a reflection partly of Tagore's experimental ideas and partly of the socialist convictions of Jehangir Vakil, the principal. The atmosphere was informal, and the handful of boarders enjoyed something of the intimacy of family life. Classes were usually held in the open, after the fashion of Shantiniketan. Great emphasis was placed on social service, in the form of Harijan*** welfare work and slum-clearance projects, and on the virtues of self-reliance and manual labour. Nationalist ritual played an important part in the school routine. The day began with a military-type drill, followed by the salutation of the Congress flag and the singing of *Vande Mataram*, the nationalist anthem.

The school was run by an idealistic Parsi couple—Jehangir Vakil, an Oxford graduate, and his wife, Coonverbai. 'Uncle Vakil', an agnostic and a practising socialist who owned no property, believed in free thought and discussion; and he encouraged it at the dinner-table and on walks and excursions. But he was also a stern disciplinarian. He had, we are told, an alarming habit of asking his pupils to name their most treasured possession, and then calling upon them to sacrifice it. Indira was no stranger to the art of renunciation, and her years in Poona must have enlarged her capacity for it.

The Vakils were delighted to have Jawaharlal Nehru's daughter in their charge, and they lavished affection and attention on her. Then and later, Coonverbai Vakil was one of the few people whom Indira felt she could trust completely. A frank and understanding person, she must have been a reassuring influence after the cultivated sophistication of Indira's aunts, who had treated her as something of an ugly duckling. 'Aunty Vakil' encouraged her to do social work, and Indira later observed: 'She had a very great influence on me and it is really through her . . . that

*A town in western India near Bombay; formerly the capital of the Maratha empire.
**Tagore's ashram in Bengal.
***'God's people'; Gandhi's name for the Untouchables—the lowest and most oppressed caste in Hindu society.

I learned to work on the ground-floor.'[2] In later years, she would remain a loyal and devoted friend to her former pupil, always ready to come to the rescue when a crisis threatened.

Nevertheless, these were not happy times for Indira. She was living far away from home in an unfamiliar part of the country, she had recently lost her grandfather, and her mother was ailing again. Kamala Nehru had been moved to Bombay for medical treatment; but as Nehru noted in his autobiography: '...her eager spirit fretted at her inaction and her inability take her full share in the national struggle. Physically unable to do so, she could neither take to work properly nor to treatment, and the fire inside her wore down the body.'[3] Her mother's ill-health must have added to Indira's unhappiness in her new surroundings. One of her school-friends has recalled how often she came upon Indira crying behind a tree or in some other secluded place because she was too proud to share her grief. Loneliness had already become a way of life for her. From an early age, she had been alternately petted and abandoned by those around her. Now she was suspicious of emotional attachments and shy of wearing her heart on her sleeve: far better to be self-contained. Even her parents are reported to have lamented the fact that they could not penetrate her reserve or persuade her to confide in them.

It is not surprising, then, that she found it difficult to make friends at school. As one of her cousins puts it: 'It was as though she was afraid to put out her hand, in case it was slapped.'[4] Perhaps there also lurked a fear—shared in some measure by most celebrities and their close relatives —that people wished to befriend her, not for herself, but because she was a Nehru.

In any case, having lived almost exclusively with adults in a tense and dramatic political atmosphere, Indira naturally found it difficult to share the more juvenile and humdrum interests of her contemporaries. Normal childish levity and frivolity seems to have been somewhat alien to her. The son of some family friends, who was also at school in Poona, remembers being escorted by Indira to the cinema every Friday. On one occasion, they saw a Laurel and Hardy film which sent this six-year-old boy into fits of laughter; but he looked up to find Indira glaring at him with withering disapproval. According to him, she maintained her solemn composure throughout the film and was decidedly not amused. Her young charge was so disconcerted that he refused to be taken by her again, and the weekly outings had to be discontinued.

This somewhat priggish severity did not, however, prevent Indira from being kindness itself to those who needed her help. Early in 1932 her three younger cousins, Mrs. Pandit's daughters, joined her at school. One of them, who was four at the time and missed home terribly, says:

'Indi* was absolutely darling with me. She looked after me like a little mother.'5

*          *          *

Political developments about this time were far from encouraging. The Round Table Conference had ended in a stalemate, and by the beginning of 1932 civil disobedience had been resumed, with Gandhi, Nehru and other Congress leaders back in prison. The Government struck hard at the Congress with a series of ordinances that amounted virtually to martial law. The movement continued, and no less than 80,000 people courted arrest and were imprisoned in the first four months of 1932. But in the absence of leadership and sufficient mass organisation, the enthusiasm of the rank and file proved inadequate to sustain the movement against the Government's violent onslaught.

It was impossible for Indira to remain unaffected by these developments, especially when her family was at the centre of events. She would scan the newspapers anxiously for news of her parents, and her schoolmates recall how often she dwelt proudly but sadly on the sacrifices that her family had made for the freedom struggle. About this time, the Nehrus found themselves in serious financial straits. Most of the family silver and other valuables had to be sold, and Kamala Nehru had to part reluctantly with the jewelry that she had hoped to pass on to her daughter. Mrs. Gandhi has recorded that she often overheard her mother protesting to her father that her jewels were the only security their daughter would have if they were both suddenly removed from the world. This financial insecurity must have told on her, and she acquired a reputation at school for being a hoarder, storing away everything from pencil-stumps to pieces of string. She need not, however, have worried; for Kamala Nehru in her providence made a trust for her daughter, from which Indira was later able to meet her academic and medical expenses and all her other financial needs, without having to depend on her father.

In April 1932, Indira received news that her grandmother had been injured in a *lathi* charge. While leading a peaceful procession in Allahabad, the frail old lady had been knocked down, beaten on the head by police batons, and left unconscious and bleeding on the road. Swarup Rani had spent most of her life as a semi-invalid, spoiled and pampered by her husband and children. But now she wrote to Indira saying how proud she was to have shared with other Congress volunteers the privilege of receiving *lathi* blows.

At home on vacation in May 1932, Indira was herself involved in an unpleasant though non-violent clash with the authorities. Along with

*Indira.

her mother and grandmother, she visited her uncle, Ranjit Pandit, in Allahabad District Gaol. In the course of the interview, Indira showed her uncle a report from the Poona school on the progress of his daughters. With the usual assertiveness of the petty tyrant, the gaoler took strong exception to this. He was extremely offensive, and the visitors found themselves rudely hustled out. But the matter did not end there. The gaoler vindictively complained to his superiors that Indira's grandmother had been 'impertinent' with him and had used 'insulting language'. The result was that when Swarup Rani and Kamala travelled to Dehra Dun to see Jawaharlal in prison, they were penalised by being refused an interview. Jawaharlal, when he was told the reason, was furious at the insult to his mother and refused all interviews for the next seven months to spare his family further humiliation.

*       *       *

Despite political distractions and her own unhappiness, Indira appears to have adjusted herself remarkably well to her new environment. The simple living conditions at the school were a far cry from luxurious Anand Bhawan; but she seems to have had no difficulty in adapting herself to them and asked for no special favours. Her teachers remember her as a conscientious and obedient pupil. In spite of her frail constitution, she enjoyed athletics and was particularly keen on swimming. Climbing hills and mountains, then and later, seems to have fulfilled for her both a psychological and a physical need.* She spent many happy hours hiking in the Western Ghats and rambling amid the ruins of the picturesque Maratha hill-forts around Poona. She also learnt folk-dancing and is said to have had a good sense of rhythm. When the school moved to Bombay in 1934, following an outbreak of plague in Poona, Indira took a leading role in a fund-raising performance of Tagore's dance-drama 'Ritu-Raj' (The Cycle of Spring)—her first and only appearance on the stage.

Her chief talents, however, were her organising ability and her capacity for social work. As the eldest of the pupils, she took the lead in planning the various school entertainments and excursions. Despite her shyness, she served as secretary of the school's literary society, and as 'Prime Minister' of the students' council.

Indira had become a regular visitor at Yervada Gaol near Poona,

---

*Forty years later, Indira Gandhi, addressing the All India Youth Congress appealed to them never to shirk a challenge, and recalled that as a young girl, trekking in the mountains with her family, she had always taken the most difficult and precipitous path, while the rest of the family followed by a more gradual and circuitous route. "My grandfather used to say that I must have been a goat in my previous incarnation", she announced. (National Herald, New Delhi, 15.5.73).

where Gandhi was confined. On 18 September 1932 the Mahatma began a fast unto death against Ramsay MacDonald's Communal Award, which granted separate electorates to the Untouchable community and thereby, in Gandhi's opinion, perpetuated Untouchability. Nehru, tormented by the fear that Gandhi might die, wrote to his daughter from prison:

'I am shaken completely and I know not what to do ... My little world, in which he has occupied such a big place, shakes and totters, and there seems to be darkness and emptiness everywhere. His picture comes before my eyes again and again ... Shall I not see him again? And whom shall I go to when I am in doubt and require wise counsel, or am afflicted and in sorrow and need loving comfort? What shall we all do when our beloved chief who inspired us and led us has gone'.[6]

The fast, however, triggered off a nation-wide campaign against Untouchability. On the fifth day, the Untouchable leaders agreed to give up separate electorates and 'the magician' broke his fast. Indira's school had played its part in the campaign against Untouchability. When Gandhi began his fast, the pupils had observed a twenty-four sympathetic fast and had bathed, clothed and fed Untouchable children in the neighbourhood. Indira herself had worked with missionary zeal and had taken the lead in 'adopting' an Untouchable girl. Taking her cousins with her, she had paid Gandhi a visit in nearby Yervada Prison to report on her activities. 'Indu looked happy and in possession of more flesh', Gandhi had telegraphed her father after seeing her.[7] She seems already to have found great satisfaction in social service.

Her family's visits were the high points in Indira's school life, and they were long and eagerly awaited. Her mother and grandmother came often enough, laden with sweets, chocolates and the other good things of life. In September 1933 she also received a visit from her father. Nehru had just been released from prison and arrived in Poona for talks with Gandhi, bringing with him a trunk-full of books for his daughter, among them a copy of Shaw's *St. Joan*. For a week the school grounds were infested by suspicious policemen, who watched the activities of this dangerous 'sedition-monger' while he visited his daughter. They must have been disappointed to find that he spent his time in such harmless pursuits as playing with the children and airing his political and educational ideas in discussions with the teachers.

In April 1934 Indira took her matriculation examination and passed out of the school. She had spent three years there—her longest stay at any institution during her chequered educational career—and the school seems to have left its imprint on her. It had not drawn her out of her shell: her reserve and aloofness were too deeply engrained for that.

But it had quickened her social conscience, and it had taught her discipline and self-reliance, qualities which she would need in full measure in the difficult years ahead.

*          *          *

Indira had turned sixteen shortly before she left school. 'I had wanted to be a boy', she recalls, 'but at sixteen the delight of being a woman began to unfold itself and, almost overnight, the long-legged tomboy in frocks changed into a sari-clad young lady.'[8] Thin and rather gawky, with enormous, sad eyes and a prominent nose, Indira was not conventionally beautiful, but she had an appealing, gazelle-like grace.

Her father was back in prison by this time, serving a two-year sentence in Alipore Central Gaol, Calcutta. Her mother, too, was in Calcutta for treatment, and Indira joined her there, sharing the precious fortnightly interviews with her father. Kamala's health had been steadily declining, and she seems to have had premonitions of the approaching end. She had always been religious, despite the radicalism of some of her ideas; her daughter has recorded that, during the brief periods when her parents and she were together, the three of them would, at Kamala's instance, regularly read the *Gita* every morning and the *Ramayana* every evening. Now, towards the end of her life, Kamala turned increasingly to mysticism, finding in *Vedanta** a refuge from the sufferings and frustrations of her life, and she had been initiated into the Ramakrishna Mission.** Mother and daughter spent long hours together at the Ramakrishna *Math* at Belur near Calcutta, sitting peacefully on the banks of the Hooghly. 'A new world of thought and experience opened out to me,' Indira later commented.[9]

About this time her grandmother tried to arrange a marriage for her. But her mother came to her rescue, and it was decided instead to send her to the Vishwa Bharati University at Shantiniketan, Tagore's ashram in Bengal. Nehru was now at the height of his Marxist phase, and his political convictions inevitably influenced his plans for his daughter's education. 'I was wholly against her joining the regular official or semi-official universities, for I disliked them,' he has noted in his autobiography. 'The whole atmosphere that envelops them is official, oppressive and authoritarian... Shantiniketan offered an escape from this dead hand, and so we fixed upon it, although in some ways it was not so up to date and well-equipped as the other universities.'[10] In a a letter from Alipore Prison, Nehru told Tagore's secretary:

"I had intended sending her to Europe, probably Switzerland, but

---

*The metaphysical philosophy of the Vedas, the ancient Hindu scriptures.
**A reformist Hindu religious order.

events have a way of taking the initiative out of our hands, and for the last many years we have lived in many ways a hand to mouth existence, finding it difficult to plan out the future. My repeated and frequent visits to prison disturb domestic arrangements...

'The result of all this is that we hop along merrily from day to day not knowing what the morrow will bring. So far as Indira's education is concerned, there is no chance of her going to Europe in the near future. For the present therefore arrangements have to be made for a year or so at least, and perhaps for more... I shall discuss this with her when I see her, for of course decisions must not be imposed on the modern girl!...

'As to her subjects etc... she must choose. My own ideas of education are rather peculiar. I dislike the education which prepares a girl to play a part in the drawing-room and nowhere else. Personally if I had the chance I would like to have my daughter work in a factory for a year, just as any other worker, as a part of her education. But this I think is quite impossible at present in India...'[11]

Indira's views on the subject are not known; but she does not appear to have had any objection to her father's plans, and the necessary arrangements were made for her to join Tagore's university. In a background report accompanying her application to the university, Nehru wrote:

'From her earliest childhood Indira has had to put up with national political troubles and domestic upheavals caused by them. Her education has suffered because of this and there has been no continuity in it. For long periods there has been no peace or quiet in her home atmosphere owing to her parents' and other relatives' preoccupation with public affairs, and often because of their absence in prison. These events naturally left a strong impression on her growing mind.'

He proceeded, nonetheless, to outline his ambitions for his daughter:

'Her parents would like her later to specialize in some subject or subjects which would enable her to do some socially useful work in after-life efficiently, and at the same time enable her to be economically independent, so long as the present structure of society lasts. She is not likely to have an unearned income and it is not considered desirable by her parents that she should depend for her subsistence on a husband or others... We have tried to find out what her own inclinations were, but so far we have not succeeded in bringing out any marked bent... She has a vague desire of doing social or public work, probably because she has a certain admiration for her parents' activities.'[12]

In the India of the thirties, marriage rather than a vocational education was still the accepted end of a young girl's upbringing; but Indira, clearly, was not being groomed for quiet domestic felicity. The goal, a radical one at the time, was the self-sufficiency of an emancipated career-woman. If the fact of being a Nehru had its advantages, it must also have been a strain for a shy and retiring adolescent to live up to the high expectations that it involved. Had she been the child of other parents, she might have found an outlet in the normal revolt of youth. But what was Indira Nehru to rebel against? Her father was the hero of Indian youth, representing all that was liberal, just and progressive in the country. All that Indira could do was strive to emulate her parents' example, and hope that she would succeed.

*     *     *

Founded in 1901, Shantiniketan was the centre of the Revivalist movement in learning and the arts, a somewhat self-conscious attempt at producing an Indian Renaissance by rediscovering India's cultural heritage and revitalising it through contact with the more dynamic influences of the West. Tagore's ashram was modelled on the ideal academic community of ancient India, with teachers and students living and working together in harmony. Students were encouraged to work with their hands, both at domestic chores and skilled handicrafts, and to give free expression to their artistic instincts. Classes were held in the open, and there was a typically Romantic emphasis on communion with nature.

When Indira arrived at Shantiniketan with her mother in July 1934, she felt some trepidation and was overawed by her proximity to Tagore. 'The strangeness of the language and surroundings added to my difficulties,' she has observed. 'I seemed suddenly to have landed in another world.'[13] But the calm and informal atmosphere of the ashram soon dispelled her initial misgivings. 'Although an essentially quiet and introverted person', she has commented, 'I had lived all my life in an atmosphere of noise, emotional and physical strain, and hectic rushing about. The quiet and peace of Shantiniketan was an entirely new experience.'[14]

Ashram life was rigorous and exacting. Indira shared a room with three or four other girls at Sri Bhawan, the women's hostel. There were no servants and the students were expected to do their own cooking and cleaning. The day began at 4.30 in the morning. The students had to perform their ablutions, make their beds, sweep the dormitories, cook their breakfast, and be ready for classes by 6.30 a.m. Living conditions were intentionally primitive. The students had to take cold-water baths, even in winter, and manage without electricity, reading by the light of oil-lamps and enduring the summer heat without electric fans.

After her training at Poona, Indira was no stranger to Spartan living; and she adjusted herself to the ashram routine with an ease that astonished her fellow students. They had expected a spoiled and pampered young debutante; instead they found an unaffected and rather forlorn girl who was always ready to lend a hand.

One of the lecturers remembers her as a conscientious and industrious student; but what impressed him most was 'her utter simplicity of dress and demeanour, her quiet seriousness and a shadow of sadness on her face—due no doubt to her natural anxiety for her parents—with her father in gaol and her mother still bed-ridden.'[15] Less than a month after Indira joined Shantiniketan, Kamala Nehru had fallen dangerously ill with a severe attack of pleurisy. Indira and her father—temporarily released on humanitarian grounds—had rushed to her bedside. But Kamala's condition had improved, and Indira had returned to the ashram to continue her education.

Her anxiety, however, was rarely expressed; on the contrary, she appears to have dealt with it by withdrawing further from emotional contacts, even with her parents. In a letter to his sister Vijayalakshmi, Nehru is reported to have remarked on his daughter's coldness towards him, complaining that she wrote to him only once in three or four months, and then too merely out of a sense of duty. Kamala also seems to have met with the same response; many years later Indira Gandhi confessed that she hardly ever wrote to her mother. 'I could have done much more for her,' she said, looking back with some remorse. 'No doubt I took out my frustrations on her, too, as lots of children do.'[16]

Indira's emotional difficulties, accentuated by the growing pains of adolescence, did not keep her from participating in the lighter side of ashram life. A fellow student remembers an episode which involved an older female resident of the hostel. The lady in question prided herself on her batik work, but the students suspected her of buying her 'creations' from a shop. Among these was a particularly beautiful batik bag which she intended to present to Nandlal Bose, the celebrated painter who headed the university's art school. Some of the students decided that the bag must disappear, and Indira, one of the few people whom its owner trusted, was persuaded to remove it. The self-styled batik artist was greatly distressed and more or less admitted that she had bought the bag. When she threatened to go on a hunger-strike, Indira returned the bag, pretending to have found it under a tree. The woman was furious at having been exposed. 'You look so serious and sweet,' she scolded Indira, 'that I never imagined you would also participate in such devilish pranks.'[17]

Indira, however, seems already to have had a more spirited side to her. Tagore's secretary has described a protest demonstration organised, among others, by her and Ghani Khan.* The provocation arose from the manners of a visiting European scholar who was giving a course of lectures on art history. It was the practice for students and visitors to remove their shoes and sandals before entering the lecture-hall, so that the floor on which they sat remained clean. Despite several polite reminders, the visiting lecturer insisted on keeping his shoes on. The students eventually decided on direct action. On the next occasion, as soon as they heard his loud footsteps, his audience, led by Indira and Ghani Khan, staged a silent walk-out. The incident, despite its trivial nature, is said to have generated much excitement in the ashram, and the news soon travelled to Tagore. Following a brief, and presumably stormy, interview with Gurudev the next morning, the irate academic caught the afternoon train and left Shantiniketan, never to return.

On New Year's Day, 1935, Nehru presented his daughter with *The Science of Life* by H.G. Wells and Julian Huxley, 'in the hope that a study of the science of life will help her to learn the greatest of all arts— the art of living'. 'Do not be frightened by the size or weight of the book', he reassured her in his inscription. 'And do not, at first, try to read it from end to end, or else you will get terribly bored with it. Dip into it and read the chapters that interest you. There is plenty in it that is interesting and that will help you to understand the wonderful panorama and development of life. Later, perhaps, you will read the whole book. It is worth it.'[18]

Owing no doubt to her father's influence, Indira's reading was well in advance of that of her contemporaries, a distinction which won her the title of 'The Red Lady of Shantiniketan' from no less a person than the British Governor of Bengal. Early in 1935, the Governor, Sir John Anderson (later Lord Waverley), was expected to visit the university during a tour of the province. Owing to a recent terrorist attempt on his life, the police insisted on elaborate and humiliating security arrangements. Most of the students—and Indira was one of them—decided, with Tagore's approval, to boycott the visit and spend the day on a picnic away from the ashram. While being shown round the deserted campus, Anderson, who had a sharp eye, discovered in one of the rooms at the women's hostel a desk piled high with books on Socialism. When he asked with a smile who 'The Red Lady' was, he was told that this was Indira Nehru's table. 'Ah!' he exclaimed, beaming with satisfied curiosity. 'That explains everything.'[19]

\*     \*     \*

*Son of Abdul Ghaffar Khan, 'The Frontier Gandhi', and brother of A. Wali Khan, now leader of the National Awami Party of Pakistan.

Indira spent many happy and stimulating hours at Shantiniketan's famous art centre, the home of the Revivalist school of painting.* She had been reared in an exclusively political environment, starved of artistic expression, and this was her first introduction to the fine arts. She became a keen student of Manipuri dance under the guidance of Naba Kumar, the country's leading exponent of Manipuri. The most lyrical and graceful, though the least profound and complex of India's four main schools of classical dance, Manipuri epitomised the spirit of Romantic Revivalism and was Tagore's favourite dance form. Indira took to it enthusiastically and soon developed into a promising dancer.

The most memorable of her experiences at Shantiniketan appears to have been her contact with Tagore, its presiding deity. Though he was seventy-three at the time, Gurudev—as he was known—kept abreast of all the cross-currents in the ashram and maintained a close watch on students and teachers alike. 'His form was frail and bent, his voice rather high-pitched,' Indira has recorded. 'But with his wavy hair falling softly to his shoulders and his flowing beard, his deep-set and penetrating eyes and wide forehead, he was beautiful to look at—a perfect picture of the romantic poet.'[20]

At first she had found Gurudev an awe-inspiring figure and had been painfully shy and tongue-tied in his presence. One day, as she scurried past his house with some friends, she looked up to find him staring at them across the garden. 'Are you afraid of me?' he admonished them. 'Why don't you come to see me sometimes?' Indira and her companions hastened to explain that they had not wished to intrude upon him and waste his time. 'But what is time for?' he queried. 'I like young people.'[21] After this Indira, along with some other students, spent many of her evening sitting at Gurudev's feet, while he painted or recited from his poems. 'These friendly meetings influenced me profoundly and helped in moulding my personality,' she has recorded. 'We had a glimpse of the universality of his spirit, the broadness of his vision and his strong sense of purpose. These were moments of serene joy, memories to be cherished for ever.'[22]

At Shantiniketan, far from the turbulent world of politics, the bitter scars of Indira's unhappy childhood were beginning to heal. But the respite proved short-lived. She had spent less than a year at the ashram when she received an urgent call to her mother's bedside. Kamala was again in the grip of her old disease, which had entered its third and final

---

*Revivalism, which aimed at a synthesis of the forms and techniques of ancient Indian art with the anti-academic and anti-naturalistic trends of Western Expressionism and Art Nouveau, was the dominant influence on two generations of Indian artists. Although it opened the way for future experimentation, it was a somewhat artificial and contrived genre and has left few works of any lasting value.

stage. As a last hope of survival, the doctors had advised sending her to Europe for a lung operation. Nehru was still in prison; and it was therefore decided that Indira should accompany her mother.

The summons arrived on 13 April 1935, the Bengali New Year's Day, while she was rehearsing for her first solo appearance in a Manipuri performance. Tagore called her to his studio to break the news. Her composure must have surprised him. 'My father has trained me to travel alone,' she is reported to have told Gurudev, refusing his offer to send one of the teachers with her to Allahabad.[23] Then, with characteristic stoicism, she took her leave of Tagore and went to pack her belongings. A few days after her departure, Tagore wrote to Nehru:

'It is with a heavy heart we bade farewell to Indira, for she was such an asset in our place. I have watched her very closely and have felt admiration for the way you have brought her up. Her teachers, all in one voice, praise her and I know she is extremely popular with the students. I only hope things will turn for the better and she will soon return here and get back to her studies.'[24]

Indira did not return; but Shantiniketan would remain a treasured milestone on her melancholy journey from childhood to maturity. In December 1936, in a nostalgic and reminiscent mood, she would write from England to her father:

'I am glad of my stay at Shantiniketan—chiefly because of Gurudev. In the very atmosphere there, his spirit seemed to roam and hover over one, and follow one with a loving though deep watchfulness. And his spirit, I feel, has greatly influenced my life and thought.'[25]

\*       \*       \*

On 23 May 1935 mother and daughter sailed from Bombay, en route to Badenweiler in Bavaria, where Kamala was to enter a sanatorium. It must have been a gloomy voyage for Indira. It was seven years since her last visit to Europe. Then her father had been with them; but now he was in prison and she was bearing the tragic burden alone. 'Kamala will live: she has the heart of a lioness,'[26] Gandhi had told a close friend of hers; but according to the same source, Kamala did not expect to return alive. In a somewhat clinical note for his wife's doctors, Nehru wrote from prison:

'The patient has had an emotionally and psychically troubled life for the last sixteen years, chiefly due to political reasons, which have repeatedly caused domestic upsets. She has herself been keenly interested in these political developments and her desire to take part in

them has exceeded her physical ability to do so, and this maladjust-
ment has been a cause of great regret and anxiety to her. She is definitely
neurotic, probably due to some repressions and maladjustments
during the early years. Subsequent happenings, political upsets and
excitements have added to this. When she has herself taken an active
part in public affairs she has been mentally far happier and the neurotic
element has faded into the background. But long continued illness
always bring it to the fore.'[27]

Gandhi, however, later wrote to Nehru:

'As I saw her (Kamala) for two days in Bombay before her departure,
I observed that she never had so much peace of mind as she seemed to
enjoy then. Her faith in the benevolence of God, she said, was never so
bright as then. Her mental disturbance had vanished and she did not
mind what happened to her. She went to Europe because you all
wished it and it seemed to be her obvious duty to do so.'[28]

Badenweiler was a remote spot in the Black Forest, undisturbed by the
tramp of Nazi jack-boots, where even the swastika was not much in
evidence. Indira put up at a *pension* near the Haus Waldeck sanatorium
where her mother was being treated. By September 1935 Kamala's
condition was deteriorating rapidly. Agatha Harrison, veteran of the
India League in London and a close friend of Jawaharlal's, was informed
by an Indian who had visited Badenweiler that he had found Indira
'in a piteous state of mind, having been told that her mother was dying.'[29]
But she seems to have recovered her composure rapidly and wrote to
Miss Harrison on 3 September, briefing her about the situation:

'Dr. Steffen has already cabled to Lord Zetland and the Viceroy of
India. He has also sent a telegram to my father, informing him of
their cables and of my mother's critical condition. Meanwhile my
mother's condition remains the same. She is still getting high temperature, and is unable to take much nourishment, with the result that she
is getting weaker. She has acute pain in her left shoulder and arm and
hardly sleeps during the nights and not at all during daytime.'[30]

Agatha Harrison hurried to Indira's assistance, arriving at Badenweiler
on 8 September. In a letter to Gandhi she described her first meeting with
Nehru's daughter:

'What a pathetic figure—though young in years—old beyond her years
in experience and suffering. I went up to see Mrs. Nehru who looked
to me desperately ill and terribly weak. I only stayed a minute for
she needs to husband every ounce of strength. The rest of that day

I spent with Indira—and we got to know each other and I heard something of her life.'[31]

Released on compassionate grounds by the Government of India, Nehru reached Badenweiler on 9 September. His arrival must have been an enormous relief to his daughter. 'What touched and moved me most.' wrote Agatha Harrison to Gandhi, 'was to watch this father and daughter together. Indira was holding tight to his arm, every now and then rubbing her head against his shoulder, and some of the "years" that I had noticed the day before seemed to have slipped away, and she was a different person.'[32]

On 15 September, Gandhi wrote to Jawaharlal consoling him with his own peculiar logic:

'If she (Kamala) lives, she will live for greater service than she has yet rendered. If she dies, she will do so to come down to earth with a body more fitted for her task than the one she has today. It is well, too, that Indu's literary studies remain suspended for a while, for now she is having a training that is of far greater value than any she would have in a college. She is having her training in the University of Nature... Indu used to write me a few lines when you were not there. Now I suppose she thinks she is absolved from the task!'[33]

Kamala's health showed some improvement after Nehru's arrival, and her husband and daughter were able to snatch a brief visit to London. Her will to live was strong, and she seemed for some time to be holding her own against the disease. Nehru spent long hours by her bedside, reading to her and reminiscing about the past. 'I often wondered if I really knew her or understood her,' he later observed. 'There was something elusive about her, something fay-like, real but insubstantial, difficult to grasp. Sometimes, looking into her eyes, I would find a stranger peeping out at me.'[34]

A frequent visitor at Badenweiler was Feroze Gandhi. Already an experienced *satyagrahi* with four terms of imprisonment to his credit, Feroze had nursed Kamala devotedly in India while her husband was in prison and Indira was at Shantiniketan. Now he had persuaded a wealthy aunt to send him to the London School of Economics, partly because he wished to be near Kamala.

At the end of January 1936, Kamala was moved to Lausanne in Switzerland, while Indira rejoined her old school at Bex. News arrived that Nehru had been elected in absentia to the Congress presidency, and after long consultations with the doctors he decided to return to India for a few months. But before he could leave, Kamala went into a sudden decline, and by 28 February she was dead.

Kamala Nehru was only thirty-six years old when she died. In the course of that brief span of life, she had battled against heavy odds, overshadowed by her husband, humiliated and resented by his possessive sisters, and drained of her vitality by persistent illness. Her own greatest regret, frequently expressed in her letters, had been her lack of a modern education, which had placed her at a disadvantage in the battles, political and domestic, that she had fought. During the long evenings at Baden-weiler, while Indira read to her from Dostoevsky and other novelists, she had never ceased to impress upon her daughter the importance of education. Indira Gandhi has observed that her mother's most pronounced characteristic was her determination; but while Kamala Nehru's determination was moderated by an innate gentleness which embraced even her opponents, Indira would be careful to fight life's battles from a position of strength, sealing up the emotional chinks in her armour. 'I saw her being hurt', Mrs. Gandhi has told her mother's biographer, 'and I was determined not to be hurt.'[35]

After Kamala's cremation at Lausanne, father and daughter spent a few days together at the quiet lake-side resort of Montreux, consoling each other in their mutual sorrow. With the typically ambivalent attitude of Western-educated Indian nationalists, however radical, to British institutions, Nehru had decided that his daughter should continue her education in England. Leaving her in London in the care of Agatha Harrison, he flew back to India. The refrain, 'Kamala is no more, Kamala is no more', tortured his fevered mind throughout the long air journey. At last he knew what his wife had meant to him and how much he had depended on her.

On 30 March, Gandhi wrote to Indira, exhorting her not to give in to her grief:

'Kamala's death has increased your responsibilities somewhat, but I have no fears about you. You have become so sensible that you are well aware of your duty. Kamala had such virtues as are not to be found easily in other women. I have every hope that all these virtues will shine in you in as full a measure as they did in Kamala. May God guide you and give you strength to follow Kamala's example.'[36]

Indira had lived too long in an emotional strait-jacket to give way to despair; but she must have felt utterly bereft and desolate. Much as she loved and hero-worshipped her father, her mother had so far been the greatest attachment in her life. Though life had not been kind to Indira in the past, she had weathered its storms with a quiet and purposeful determination. The removal of her mother's protective presence seems to have shattered the precarious balance that she had so far maintained.

During the next few years, one finds her faltering, unsure of herself and a prey to indecision, torn between conflicting desires.

\*     \*     \*

London in the mid-thirties was a stimulating place for a politically minded young person. These were the days of L.S.E. socialism, hunger marches and Blackshirt parades. The Spanish Civil War was the issue of the day, and the invasion of Abyssinia and the occupation of the Rhineland were only a few months old. While 'dictator-minded' conservatives could scarcely conceal their admiration for the 'achievements' of Fascism and National Socialism, the anti-Fascist Left wavered between pacifism and a Popular Front against Fascism.

Indira's own sympathies lay unequivocally with the anti-Fascist movement. Ideological awareness had come to her at an early age through her father's letters—the *Glimpses of World History*—with their lucid Marxian analysis of political and economic systems. Unlike some of his nationalist colleagues, Nehru had never found any appeal in Fascism, not even as a stick to beat British imperialism. Fascism was as repugnant to his liberal temperament as it was to his Marxism. His ideas had inevitably rubbed off on his daughter, and the seed which he had sown was nurtured by Feroze Gandhi. The London School of Economics was then still busy turning out socialist intellectuals, and Feroze, along with other future leaders of the Indian Left, was one of its firebrands.

Alone in a foreign country for the first time in her life, Indira was fortunate to find in Feroze someone who shared her grief and could sympathise with her. Feroze had been like a son to Kamala. Now that she was no more, he seems to have re-discovered her in her daughter. Drawn together by their common bereavement, Feroze and Indira became constant companions. In course of time, their friendship would develop into love and eventually marriage.

Indira was preparing for her entrance to Oxford and had moved into a tiny attic on Fairfax Road with Shanta Gandhi, an old school-friend of her Poona days. She was still too disturbed emotionally to apply herself to any sustained work. But under Feroze's influence she dabbled in the activities of various Left-wing organisations in London. Though she seems to have been particularly ill at ease with her own age-group, through Feroze she did meet some of the more revolutionary Indian students in England, at least three of whom have continued to be closely associated with her through her long political life.\* While Indira was

*\*Bhupesh Gupta, now a Communist Member of Parliament; Rajni Patel, formerly active in the Communist movement, and now Mrs. Gandhi's nominee as President of the Bombay Congress Committee; and Mohan Kumaramangalam, also a former Communist, who was a leading member of Mrs. Gandhi's Cabinet till his death in an air-crash in May 1973.*

not as politically active as they might have wished her to be, she shared
their concern about the political issues of the day. She sympathised
strongly with the Spanish Republic, and her friend, Shanta Gandhi,
recalls that Indira persuaded her to give some performances of Indian
dance to raise funds for the cause. On one occasion the two girls waited
for hours in the rain to get a glimpse of La Passionaria, the Spanish
revolutionary, when she visited London. Later, during the Sino-Japanese
War, Indira also did some voluntary work for the China Aid Committee.

An important influence on her at this time was V.K. Krishna Menon,
who had recently made the acquaintance of her father and was in time
to become his closest friend. Krishna Menon was then running the
office of the India League. Indira attended some of the League's meetings
and overcame her shyness to the extent of being coaxed onto the platform
by Krishna Menon. She also joined the Left Book Club, became a member
of the Labour Party's youth-wing, and attended Labour rallies. Not
that she identified completely with the party's policies; like other Indian
socialists, she considered the Labour Party too Fabian by far, especially
in its approach to colonialism. But she found it the least objectionable
of Britain's political parties.

Through Agatha Harrison and Krishna Menon, Indira met Harold
Laski, Ernest Bevin, Ellen Wilkinson, Sir Stafford Cripps, Fenner
Brockway and other leaders of the labour movement. Her contacts
with them must have impressed upon her, though not for the first time,
what it meant to be the daughter of a famous man. To most of them she
was simply Nehru's daughter, and they were kind to her for his sake.
More often than not she failed to meet their expectations, and they were
disappointed in her. Reginald Sorensen, Labour M.P. and member
of the India League, observed many years later:

'Indira Gandhi didn't impress me except as the reflection of her
father. I think she was purely her father's daughter, close to Menon
only to the extent that he was her father's friend. But I don't remember
her too clearly. She didn't come very much to the India League.'[37]

A famous historian, who knew her father well, was far more scathing
when he called her 'a silly little girl without an idea in her head'[38]; and
Harold Laski's widow has described her as a 'mousy, shy little girl who
didn't seem to have any political ideas.'[39] Others saw beyond her painfully
shy exterior. Christiane Toller, wife of Ernst Toller, the communist
intellectual, wrote enthusiastically to Nehru:

'Yesterday your daughter Indira came to us for lunch... I only want
to tell you how delighted I was to have met her. Not only that she
is so beautiful, but so pure which makes one feel very happy and very

little against it [sic]. She seemed to me like a little flower which the wind might blow away so easily, but I think she is not afraid of the wind.'[40]

Nehru seems to have thought that too much fuss was being made of his daughter. 'I am afraid all of you are rather spoiling Indira,' he wrote to Agatha Harrison in July 1936. 'She has had a good deal of this kind of thing at home and the treatment continues abroad. It must be very pleasant for her, of course, but I hope that she will not succumb to it.'[41]

\* \* \*

Indira was too shaken up by her mother's death and by her own restlessness to settle down to her studies. She had lost her old moorings and she seems to have been groping for an identity of her own. Throughout her childhood her education had suffered from the fluctuations of the Indian freedom struggle; and even now, when she appeared at last to have eluded its grasp, that struggle reached out to claim her. She had lived too long at the heart of India's nationalist movement to be able to put it out of her mind, and London, with all its activities, was a poor substitute for the reality of Indian politics. Indira felt cut off from the scene of action and she fretted for home. For the next five years she shuttled restlessly back and forth between England, India and Switzerland, and her education was fitful and sporadic.

Early in August, 1936 Nehru received news that his daughter had failed her entrance to Oxford. He wrote to Agatha Harrison:

'I was disappointed of course that Indira had failed in her examinations. I do not attach too much value to examinations. But a sense of failure is depressing and I do not wish Indira to be depressed in that way. And yet if she has any stuff in her, as I hope she has, it will no doubt do her good.'[42]

In the spring of 1937, Indira returned to India for some months. Later she accompanied Nehru on a tour of South-East Asia. Her health was causing some concern. In June 1937 her father wrote to Agatha Harrison:

'Indira's health worries me. She has lost weight since she came here. That of course is not surprising as she has suddenly had to face a hot weather after more than two years of a better climate. Part of her trouble, the doctors tell us is due to her tonsils. So it has been decided to cut them off. I hope this will lead to a permanent improvement in her health.'[43]

It had been decided that she should appear again for the Oxford Entrance, and she took advantage of her stay in India to brush up her Latin, the cause of her initial failure. According to Father C.E. George, the local Catholic priest in Allahabad, the Nehru car brought Indira regularly to his home for a three-week crash course in Latin. He observes with ponderous approval: 'My pupil manifested her acute intelligence in making use of her knowledge of English to pick up vocabulary, and her knowledge of Hindi grammer to explore the intricacies of the Latin syntax.'[44] Thus fortified, she returned to England later in the year.

It had been decided that Indira should join the Badminton School near Bristol to prepare for the Entrance. Badminton was a small town with a peaceful country atmosphere. The school occupied a charming house built with golden and grey Cotswold stone and stood amid terraced grounds that dated back to the 18th century and encompassed rose gardens, old stone balustrades covered with wisteria, and spacious lawns with clipped yew trees. Badminton was a rather exclusive institution, with a more imaginative outlook than was common in other British public schools. 'The questions of the day', its prospectus promised, 'are brought to the notice of the girls, in the hope that they will make the habit of forming independent judgements on matters of national and international importance'.[45] To further this aim, Badminton had an active League of Nations Union. The Headmistress was a member of the Women's International League for Peace and Freedom, which had close connections with Gandhi and of which Mrs. Pandit, Indira's aunt, was also a member.

Little is known of Indira's brief stay at Badminton; and her contemporaries remember her as a frail and withdrawn person who was more at home with the mistresses than with the students. Apart from helping Iris Murdoch, one of her contemporaries, with the production of a play entitled 'A Very Mellow Drama', she seems to have left no mark on the life of the school. 'After all that the British have done to you', the Headmistress is reported to have once asked Indira, 'why do you Indians still come here to be educated?' Indira is said to have answered with a smile: 'Because the better we know you the better we can fight you.'[46] Nevertheless, Iris Murdoch, then a militant radical, has recorded having felt at the time that Indira was not active enough politically, and this seems to have been the general view of her contemporaries.

In the summer of 1938, Nehru arrived in Europe on an extended visit. Indian nationalism was now at a low ebb. The Congress had scored an impressive victory in the 1937 elections, forming ministries in eight of the eleven provinces. But the parliamentary phase had only strengthened conservative constitutionalists in the Congress and had seen an increase in factional strife within the organisation and in tension between the

Congress and the Muslim League. Tired and dispirited, Nehru had decided to get away from it all. He arrived in Europe to find events moving to a crisis, following Hitler's occupation of Austria in March 1938. For Nehru, the world citizen, this was no less disturbing than the vicissitudes of Indian nationalism, and he divided his time abroad between the causes of anti-fascism and Indian independence.

After a visit to Barcelona, during which he met the leaders of the Spanish Republic and spent some time with the International Brigade, Nehru joined his daughter in London. About this time, there was a minor clash between father and daughter about an invitation from the Conservative peer, Lord Lothian, to spend a week-end at Blickling Hall, his Elizabethan country home in Norfolk. In May 1938, before his departure from India, Nehru had informed Agatha Harrison: 'I had written to Indu about Lord Lothian's invitation. Her personal reaction to it was not favourable as she objects strongly to Lothian's pro-Fascist politics.'[47] 'I was violently opposed to the Tories at that time,' Mrs. Gandhi has observed; and at first she refused to accompany her father to Blickling. 'You must control your temper and learn to mix with all kinds of people,' Nehru is reported to have admonished her. And when Lothian wrote asking her to change her mind, she capitulated: 'Much against my grain, I did finally go, but in a very fighting mood.'[48]

These were the days of Chamberlain, Munich and appeasement. Nehru was appalled by the betrayal of Czechoslovakia, and he decided to visit Prague and Sudetenland. Indira was keen to go with him, and she did, in spite of a strong protest lodged by Harold Laski. 'Look, you're just developing your personality,' Laski is reported to have lectured her, 'and if you tag along with your father, you'll just become an appendage.' But it seems to have been water off a duck's back. 'I listened very attentively,' Mrs. Gandhi has observed, 'but of course I went along with my father'.[49] Together they visited France, Czechoslovakia and Hungary.

\*     \*     \*

In February 1938, Indira had gone up to Somerville College, Oxford, to read Modern History. But her first impressions cannot have been encouraging, for by November she had decided to return to India with her father for a long stay. On their way back, father and daughter broke journey in Egypt, where Nehru had talks with Nahas Pasha, leader of the nationalist Wafd Party. One of the results of this meeting was a rumour that Nehru's daughter had become engaged to Nahas Pasha's son. Tongues wagged in India till it was discovered that the Egyptian leader had no son.

Soon after she returned home, Indira, now over twenty-one, was formally enrolled as a member of the Congress; but her health was poor, and she took no part in politics. Most of her five-month stay in India was spent with her aunt Krishna at Almora, a resort in the foot-hills of the Himalayas.

On returning to Cambridge after a visit to India, Nehru had confessed to a feeling of home-coming. It is unlikely that his daughter felt any such elation when she returned to Oxford in April 1939. Both in background and temperament this melancholy 'child of the Indian revolution' was poles apart from the extravagant and debonair young epicurean that her father had been in his student days. Nor was she an intellectual. Academic life held little attraction for her, and she seems on the contrary to have found it rather intimidating. In an article written many years later, she referred to the 'dreadful evening' when, as a 'new and painfully shy under-graduate', she was first invited to dine at High Table:

'I found myself sitting next to the tall, gaunt woman with sinister, dark hollows under her eyes who was our dean. She turned towards me and with an air of putting me at ease, asked: "What are your views on music, art and literature"?'[50]

An essentially practical person who had grown up in the world of action, and direct action at that, Indira was ill at ease in the realm of ideas. Hers was not a reflective and speculative mind, and she must have found Oxford a somewhat irrelevant, though impressive, ivory tower. She was unable to apply herself to her work, and her failure to cope with academic requirements seems to have added to her unhappiness and restlessness.

Nor did she have the self-assurance and boldness necessary for an active role in the student movement. She attended some meetings of the Oxford Union and the Indian Majlis, but was too shy to speak or even to read out a message from her father. She seems, nonetheless, to have had views of her own. At one Majlis meeting attended by her, the proposition that the Indian National Congress should be more revolutionary was debated. Nehru, among others, came in for a good deal of criticism from the more radical element; but when the vote was taken, his daughter was seen raising her hand in favour of the motion.

Indira's one attempt at public speaking ended in something of a fiasco. Krishna Menon had telephoned her from London, asking her to come down for a meeting of the India League to read out a message from her father. When she reached there, she discovered to her horror that she was expected to make a speech. 'I was so terrified', she has recalled, 'I just couldn't get anything out at all.' To make matters worse, a drunkard —'at least I hope he was drunk'—shouted from the audience: 'She doesn't speak, she squeaks.' This sent everyone into fits of laughter and brought Indira's speech to an abrupt close.[51]

In July 1938, Edward Thompson wrote to Nehru: '"What an attractive and promising young woman she seems!"; I will leave you to guess who that is. It is from a letter from Lady Rhondda just received. But you know perfectly well what a darling person Indira has become.' She seems, nevertheless, to have been too reticent to charm her Oxford contemporaries or to participate in the social life of the university.

Most of her time was spent with Feroze Gandhi. Contemporaries who knew them both recall that Feroze had a clearer mind and a better grasp of current affairs. He was also the more adventurous of the two. Soon after his arrival in England, he had tried to join the International Brigade; but his passport had been impounded by the police. Later, however, he spent some time in Spain and also managed a trip to Soviet Russia. In 1938, on a visit to Paris to cover the French general strike for the National Herald, an Indian newspaper, he was arrested and detained for some days by the French police. He later told a friend that he was stripped and photographed from various angles by the police, while he rotated on a revolving stool. He inquired mischievously whether they found him a satisfactory subject for pornographic post-cards, but was told to behave himself.

Feroze courted Indira diligently. He showered her with love-letters and, though he was badly off, frequently bought her flowers and took her out to theatres and restaurants. By this time they were both thinking in terms of marriage; but according to a mutual friend, Feroze had some apprehensions about marrying into the Nehru family and asked: 'Will she become a Gandhi or will I have to become a Nehru?'[53] It was a problem which would plague their relationship in the years ahead.

*          *          *

In the summer of 1939, Indira went to Switzerland for a holiday. 'Indira has come back looking, I think, distinctly better,' Agatha Harrison informed Nehru. 'It was so wet in Switzerland that she lost all interest in being there'. [54] She also appears by then to have lost interest in Oxford and was in two minds about continuing there. Her father left the decision to her. He wrote to Agatha Harrison on 20 September 1939:

'If she has decided to go to Oxford, she should certainly go there... Later she can revise her decision if she feels like it. When she was leaving India in April last, there was some possibility of war then and we discussed this. I suggested that she might remain at Oxford for a while and later, if she felt like it, she might go to America... But I left it to her entirely what she should do... So far as I am concerned I shall agree to any decision in this matter taken by Indu. I do not wish her to feel in the least that I am imposing any decision on her.'[55]

Events intervened and took the decision for her. In October 1939, while walking in the woods in Middlesex, she was caught in a downpour and soaked to the skin. The result was a severe chill which rapidly developed into pleurisy. She was admitted to the Brentford Cottage Hospital, where her condition gradually improved. In December, Edward Thompson informed her father:

> 'I have seen Indu. She looks well, and she is well. She is thin, of course, and there seems no doubt that she is what used to be called "delicate" and will have to go carefully. But she is wiry underneath, and when she is past these difficult days that end adolescence she will pull into real strength... You are not to worry about her.'[56]

He was, however, being over-optimistic. Illness of one kind or another would dog Indira's steps for the next twenty years before her 'wiry' constitution finally asserted itself. Ill and away from home, she must have been a pathetic figure. Her plight attracted the sympathy even of Lord Linlithgow, that most stolid and phlegmatic of Indian Viceroys. In England on home leave, he wrote to Agatha Harrison:

> 'I am truly sorry that Mr. Nehru's daughter is in such poor health. Poor child! It is, or seems, cruel that such a burden should be placed upon youth and innocence, while the father has already suffered too much in that way.'[57]

Indira's illness caused particular alarm in the light of her mother's history of pulmonary tuberculosis. In mid-December, as soon as she was well enough to travel, Agatha Harrison escorted her to Leysin in Switzerland to convalesce. The face of Europe had changed drastically in the course of the last few months. Czechoslovakia was no more, and with the invasion of Poland in August the Second World War had begun. Neutral Switzerland, of course, was undisturbed, and Indira spent the next eleven months there at the Clinique Frenes in Leysin. In January 1940 her father wrote to Edward Thompson:

> 'I have heard from Indira from Leysin. She seems to be happy there and likes the place. The doctor has told her that he proposes to transform her into a Diana in the course of three months. Naturally this has cheered her up immensely.'[58]

Three months later, however, he was writing to Thompson:

> 'Indira is progressing, but I wish the pace was faster. She is terribly keen on returning to India soon and I myself think that she should do so after another three months or so. But the doctors, I suppose, will have the last word.'[59]

Restless and isolated from events, Indira was soon weary of Switzerland, and she fretted at the inaction that had been imposed on her at this critical moment in world affairs. While the German blitzkrieg gathered momentum in Europe, in India, too, matters were coming to a head. Despite its solidarity with the anti-Fascist cause, the Congress had pointed out to the Government that India could not be expected to fight for democracy in Europe so long as she herself was denied freedom. In September 1939, when the Viceroy proclaimed a state of belligerency without consulting Indian leaders, the Congress ministries had resigned. A year later, after abortive negotiations with the Government, Gandhi launched individual civil disobedience. Nehru, though he was the most anti-Fascist of the nationalist leaders, was one of the first to be arrested, receiving the savage sentence of four years rigorous imprisonment.

Anxiety about her father added to Indira's restlessness at Leysin. Her grandmother had recently died, and both her aunts were married with families of their own; she must have known how terribly alone her father was, and her sense of duty must have told her that she should be near him. Nehru, though aware of his daughter's troubled feelings, was determined not to influence her in any way. He appears to have been worried by her indecision and insisted that she must make up her own mind. In May 1940 he wrote to Agatha Harrison:

'She is going through a very difficult period of her life. None of us can be of very much help to her. She will have to find her way out herself. All we can do, and that is very little, is to enable her to find herself. I have been terribly afraid of interfering in any way and thus adding to the difficulties of the situation. When she wrote to me that she was very anxious to come to India, I was put in a difficulty. To discourage her seemed to be wrong, to encourage her was also not very desirable. I was convinced in my mind that she had really no desire to come to India, but her affection for me and a wish to be of some help to me were forcing her to want a return to India. This was not a sufficient reason and it would have led to an intensification of the conflict within her. In a sense this conflict would have taken a shape of what she considered to be her duty overriding her own clear wishes. I do not want her to have that conflict. She should come back to India not because of me but because of herself when she feels that way. I wish she could realise this and put away any sense of obligation from her. That in itself would relieve the tension in her mind.'[60]

By November 1940 Indira could bear her Swiss exile no longer. In spite of the hazards involved in traversing the theatre of war, she decided to make the journey to England. Nehru wrote from prison to his sister Krishna, who had expressed concern for Indira's safety:

'I am glad she has decided to return. There are all manner of risks
and dangers, of course, but it is better to face them than to feel isolated
and miserable. If she wants to return then she must do so or take the
consequences. Life grows harder for all of us and the soft days of the
past already belong to an age that is gone.'[61]

To his daughter he wrote in a more tender vein on 18 November:

'Bear in mind that the good you have derived from your stay in
Switzerland is not jeopardised. I want to see you healthy and strong
and it is better to curb one's impatience for a while if thereby one can
lay the foundations of sound health. All of us, including you of course,
will have to bear heavy burdens in this mad world and the fitter we are
for them the better... Tomorrow is your birthday, my darling one.
At Bex it will pass off rather quietly, but you will be in the minds of
numerous people who care for you, and you will haunt me even more
than you usually do.'[62]

Taking her courage in both hands, Indira embarked on a long and
circuitous air journey, which took her to the South of France, Spain,
Portugal, and eventually London. 'I have no doubt in my mind that she
did well to leave Leysin', her father wrote to Agatha Harrison in January
1941. 'During the last few months she was feeling unhappy and restive
there and the surroundings were uncongenial... As for the future, it is
entirely for her to decide. Everything everywhere is in such a topsy-turvy
condition that it is difficult to advise. She will know best what to do.'[63]

Indira had returned to London to find the blitz at its height. There
were constant air-raids, and strict rationing added to the rigours of a
severe winter. Indira made up for her enforced idleness in the preceding
year by doing relief work. One evening, while helping to put out in-
cendiaries in Piccadilly, she was given an air-raid warden's helmet,
which she has kept ever since as a trophy. Then, having done her bit by the
British war-effort, she decided to return home in February 1941. Any
desire she may have had to complete her education had long since been
drowned in the welter of war and her own illness. Now there was nothing
to detain her abroad, and she knew where her duty lay. Accompanied
by Feroze Gandhi, she sailed for India.

It is unlikely that she felt any pangs of regret as the shores of England
receded into the mist. On the contrary, she had good reason to be happy.
The clouds were beginning to lift and a new life was opening before her.
She was returning to her father and her home. Above all, the man she
loved was by her side and had proposed marriage to her. According to
Bhupesh Gupta, an Indian student who was returning on the same ship,
Indira was in high spirits. Mr. Gupta, now a leading Communist member

of the Indian Parliament, recalls having joined Indira and Feroze in a conspiracy to purge the ship's library. While Feroze and he foraged amid the shelves for pro-Fascist books and threw them overboard, Indira kept watch on the deck.

After pursuing an erratic course as it dodged German submarines, the ship made a one-week stop at the South African port of Durban. The Indian residents of the city had planned a public reception for Nehru's daughter; but Indira, remembering her disastrous experience in London, had stipulated that she would not speak, not even to thank her hosts. Before the reception, Indira and Feroze drove around Durban seeing the sights. They were so appalled by conditions in the Black ghettos that by the time they reached the meeting the Nehru temper had got the better of Indira's diffidence. When the chairman of the meeting announced, after welcoming her, that Miss Nehru would not be speaking, she was on her feet protesting that she would speak. Her speech was a scathing attack on White colonialism and apartheid, which she likened to the Nazi persecution of the Jews. She did not mince her words, and her audience, too, came in for its share of criticism when she condemned the Indian community for being subservient to the Whites and segregating themselves from the Africans. Apparently, they were horrified. 'Though we stayed for some days,' Indira later observed, 'there were no more invitations for us.'[64] The episode confirmed that, for all her shyness, she could when provoked rise to an occasion in the spirited Nehru manner.

In March 1941, Indira landed at Bombay. She had been away for six years, interrupted by two long interludes in India. Her mother's death and her own loneliness and ill-health had made these years something of a trial by ordeal; but she had acquitted herself reasonably well, if not with flying colours. And the experience had not been wasted upon her. She had failed to excel in the academic world; but her years abroad had completed her training in the art of self-reliance and had also given her the cosmopolitan outlook which would be a valuable asset in later life.

# CHAPTER IV

# A WILL OF HER OWN

INDIRA HAD spent her childhood and adolescence at once in the shadow of the Nehru greatness and exposed relentlessly to the public eye. Jawaharlal Nehru's was a name to conjure with, and she, his only child, had endeavoured to conform to the image it evoked. It was not so much the pressure of others as her own conception of her duty that had compelled her to this. Her father, certainly, had never sought to impose his will on her. But the tyranny cannot have been less oppressive for being self-imposed. At the age when youth questions the wisdom of its elders and sets a course of its own, Indira had surrendered her individuality and had clung to the standards and beliefs that she had inherited from her father. Her stay abroad, however, had thrown her into unfamiliar situations and surroundings and seems to have shaken this habit, creating a ferment of sorts. Torn between conflicting emotions and loyalties, she had drifted without any clear sense of direction. But she was soon to show that hers was not a passive or submissive temperament.

'Upto the age of eighteen or nineteen, I was determined that I would never marry', Indira Gandhi has told an interviewer, '. . . because I felt I should devote every minute of my time to the political struggle, and marriage would come in the way. But then, when I decided to get married, I just didn't think out things any more. I just got married.'[1] There had been little enough room in her life for girlish dreams of romance and matrimony. The whole trend of her upbringing had been to emphasise the virtues of self-sufficiency and public life. Nevertheless, she was not destined for spinsterhood. By the time she returned to India in 1941, she was determined to marry, and to marry where she chose.

'I don't like Feroze, but I love him', Indira is reported to have said of her future husband.[2] In many respects, it was indeed an attraction of opposites. Indira was a Nehru, with all that that implied. She was heir to an aristocratic family tradition, and she could not but share in the clannish Nehru pride, which has struck so many outsiders as arrogance. She had inherited from her father a patrician aloofness and sensitivity, while the strains and tensions of a troubled and lonely childhood had reinforced her innate reticence. Feroze, on the other hand, had no such inhibitions. A robust, happy-go-lucky extrovert, bursting with exuberant self-confidence, he was aggressively proud of his lower middle-class origins and made no secret of his impatience with the Nehru exclusiveness.

The romance, however, was no sudden infatuation. Indira had known Feroze when she was still a shy and awkward schoolgirl in frocks. Later, her mother's illness and death had brought them close to each other, binding her to him with the ties of gratitude and shared grief. In England they had experienced together the loneliness of foreign students and the restlessness occasioned by their desire to return home and join in the freedom struggle. According to one of Indira's cousins, Feroze had been sceptical about the survival of their relationship once Indira returned to India and to her role as Nehru's daughter; but Indira had stated emphatically that she would marry him, come what may. And she was as good as her word.

*     *     *

No warm welcome awaited Indira's homecoming. Her father was still in prison, and by April 1941 individual civil disobedience had resulted in the arrest of over 13,000 *satyagrahis*. Indira had long been awaiting an opportunity to play a political role of her own. Soon after their return Feroze and she began to take an active interest in the faction-ridden students' movement. The All India Students' Federation had by this time split into two rival organisations, one Congress and the other Communist. Indira's sympathies appear to have been with the Communist group; but she was already too aware of her responsibilities as Nehru's daughter to take a partisan attitude. In April 1941 she visited Lucknow and met representatives of the rival groups in an attempt to unite them. Though she agreed to address a meeting organised by the Communist faction, the theme of her speech was the urgent need for unity in the student movement. In December 1941 she attended the annual conference of the Communist United Provinces Students' Federation.

Nehru, by this time, had been released, and Indira had made known to him her intention of marrying Feroze. The family were taken by surprise; they had thought of Indira and Feroze as childhood friends, reading nothing further into their relationship; and Indira's reticent letters had given them no inkling of her true feelings.

The Kashmiri Pandits were, as they still are, one of the most exclusive communities in the country with a fierce racial pride. Many of them had descended from their mountain home to the plains of northern India, where they had won distinction in various walks of life; but they had continued jealously to guard their ethnic purity and traditions. The Nehrus had already shown a more liberal outlook in such matters. Both of Nehru's sisters had married outside the Kashmiri community, and the younger, Krishna Hutheesing, had gone so far as to marry a non-Brahmin.

In 1933 Jawaharlal had written to Gandhi about his younger sister's marriage:

'I would welcome as wide a breach of custom as possible. The Kashmiri community—there are exceptions, of course, in it—disgusts me. It is the very epitome of the petty bourgeois vices which I detest. I am not particularly interested in a person being a Brahmin, a non-Brahmin or anything else. As a matter of fact, I fail to see the relevance of all this; one marries an individual, not a community.'3

Indira Nehru's choice, nonetheless, encountered opposition from her immediate family. The objections arose not so much from the fact that Feroze was a Parsi as from class considerations. Both Indira's aunts had married into aristocratic and wealthy families; but Feroze was a self-made man with no private means. Even Jawaharlal, for all his socialism, found it difficult to ignore this factor. He seems to have feared that the great difference in background and upbringing would, in the long run, make for incompatibility, and that Feroze would not be able to maintain his daughter in the style of life to which she was accustomed. He felt, too, that Indira had been abroad so long that she had not given herself a chance to meet other young men in India. He urged her, therefore, not to be hasty.

Indira's mind, however, was made up, and she would brook no delay. During her years abroad, her father had sought to impress on her the virtue of being independent and of taking her own decisions. She could not now be expected to defer, in the traditional Indian fashion, to her father's wishes in a matter which so vitally affected her. Her whole education and upbringing had militated against the submissive role of an obedient Indian daughter. 'She has your strength of character as well as your ideas',4 Tagore had told her father some years ago. He might have added that she had also inherited a good deal of her mother's quiet and unobtrusive determination. Many years later, when asked about her decision to marry against her family's wishes, Mrs. Gandhi told an interviewer: 'If I know what I want, it doesn't bother me if somebody opposes it ... I go my way. And once I had made up my mind, there it was.'5

It might appear strange that Indira, hitherto so irresolute and pliable, could assert herself so vigorously. But it was a paradox essential to her character. For long periods, she might drift submissively with the current; but all the while, beneath her impassive exterior, she would be assimilating and absorbing the experiences and ideas to which she was exposed. And then, when she knew her mind, she would draw on these inner reserves of accumulated strength to act with a confidence and decisiveness that would amaze those who thought they knew her.

In this first declaration of her independence, she received support from an unexpected quarter. She later told a friend that the only person who had sympathised with her decision to marry Feroze was her orthodox maternal grandmother. 'When it came to my marrying Feroze, she was not at all orthodox,' Indira observed. 'My grandmother said that since neither Feroze nor I were much concerned with religion, she didn't see that it mattered what either of us were.'[6]

Gandhi, the supreme arbiter in all family disputes, was inducted into the controversy at an early stage, and his formidable methods of peaceful persuasion were brought to bear on the young couple. After conferring with Feroze, Gandhi reported to Nehru on 5 December: 'I had one and only one chat with Feroze, and he accepted my proposition that he would not think of marrying Indu without your consent and blessing.'[7] Soon afterwards, Nehru dispatched his daughter to Gandhi's ashram, in the hope that the Mahatma's wisdom would be a restraining influence on her. But nothing could move Indira now. According to a close relative, she appeared almost to revel in the opposition that confronted her. It was as though all the suppressed emotions and desires of her childhood and adolescence had at last found an outlet in this opportunity for self-assertion.

An article by Indira on 'Women in the USSR', which appeared in the Sunday edition of *The Bombay Chronicle* about this time, suggests that her personal desires coincided with her wider convictions about the emancipation of women in general. Echoing her mother, she wrote:

'Since I was a little child, I have watched with growing pain and horror the maze of barbaric customs and superstitions which envelop the women of India so tightly as almost to smother them. Is it any wonder, then, that out of all the stupendous achievements of the Russian Revolution, the emancipation of Soviet womanhood should seem to me one of the most striking?'[8]

\*     \*     \*

When they found Indira adamant, the family yielded gracefully enough; but public opinion still had to be faced. News of the proposed marriage leaked out to the press, and on 21 February 1942 *The Leader*, an Allahabad newspaper, made the following announcement under the headline, 'Miss Indira Nehru's Engagement':

'The marriage of Miss Indira Nehru, daughter of Pandit Jawaharlal Nehru, has been settled, it is understood, with Mr. Feroze Gandhy, brother of Miss Tehmina K. Gandhy, personal assistant to the Chief Inspectress of Schools, United Provinces. The wedding may take place shortly. A date for the ceremony will be fixed on Mr. Nehru's return to Allahabad.'9

It was only a month since Gandhi had publicly designated Nehru as his successor, and the marriage of the latter's only child could hardly fail to arouse public interest. Orthodox Hindu opinion was outraged to discover that the daughter of Gandhi's heir-apparent, and a Brahmin to boot, was to marry a Parsi. Arranged marriages were still the rule in India, even among the most emancipated families. There might be the occasional love-match within a particular community, but mixed marriages were almost unheard of.

When the news broke, Nehru was in Calcutta entertaining Chiang Kai-Shek and his wife. On his return to Allahabad, he gallantly sprang to his daughter's defence, laying aside his own reservations. In a statement to the press on 26 February, he confirmed the engagement and declared:

'A marriage is a personal and domestic matter, affecting chiefly the two parties concerned and partly their families... I have long held that though parents may and should advise in the matter, the choice and ultimate decision must be with the two parties concerned. That decision, if arrived at after mature deliberation, must be given effect to, and it is no business of parents or others to come in the way. When I was assured that Indira and Feroze wanted to marry one another I accepted willingly their decision and told them that it had my blessing.'10

'The whole nation was against the wedding,'11 Indira Gandhi later told a foreign interviewer, not without some pride. Hundreds of threatening and abusive letters poured into Anand Bhawan, although a few enlightened people sent their congratulations. Gandhi, too, received his share of poison-mail after it became known that he had given his approval to the match. 'I have seen your statement about Indu,' he wrote to Nehru, 'I like it. I receive letters concerning her marriage every day. Some are dreadful. I have destroyed all of them.'12

In a well-reasoned editorial in *The Harijan,* his weekly newspaper, Gandhi firmly rebuked his fanatical correspondents:

'I have received several angry and abusive letters and some professing to reason about Indira's engagement with Feroze Gandhi. Not a single correspondent has anything against Feroze Gandhi as a man. His only crime in their estimation is that he happens to be a Parsi. I have been, and am still, a strong opponent of either party changing religion for the sake of marriage ... In the present case there is no question of change of religion... The public knows my connection with the Nehrus. I also had talks with both the parties. It would have been cruelty to refuse consent to this engagement. As time advances such unions are bound to multiply with benefit to the society. At present we have not even reached the stage of mutual toleration. But as toleration grows into mutual respect for religions, such unions will be welcomed... My correspondencts will pardon me for not acknowledging their letters. I invite them to shed their wrath and bless the forthcoming marriage. Their letters betray ignorance, intolerance and prejudice—a species of untouchability, dangerous because not easily to be so classified.'[13]

The Parsi community, though less vociferous than the Hindus in its opposition, was also far from enthusiastic about the marriage. At the very outset, Feroze's family had politely expressed their doubts as to whether Indira would be happy with him; but Nehru had succeeded in talking them round. There remained a possibility that the Parsi residents of Allahabad might organise a hostile demonstration on the day of the wedding. To avert this danger, Nehru is said to have appealed to Feroze's mother to meet the elders of the community and conciliate them.

The marriage rites presented a further complication. The existing civil marriage laws required a renunciation of religious faith by the parties concerned. This was the procedure that had been followed for the marriage of Indira's aunt, Krishna Hutheesing; but in the present instance, though Indira and Feroze were far from religious, a formal renunciation was found unacceptable in principle. Fortunately, a non-conformist Hindu professor at Delhi University provided a way out with certain Vedic rites which, in his opinion, were valid for mixed marriages. B.K. Nehru*, one of Indira's cousins, had married a Hungarian by these unorthodox rites, and it was decided that Feroze and she should follow suit.

\*     \*     \*

The wedding had been fixed for 26 March, doubly auspicious because it was *Ram Navmi*.\*\* Anand Bhawan was filled with the peculiar air of suspense and expectancy that precedes a wedding. Presents streamed in: some, which came from total strangers, had to be returned. Indira appears to have been somewhat anxious and preoccupied. Sir Stafford Cripps, who had been sent out by the British Government to negotiate a political settlement with the Indian leaders, was a guest at Anand Bhawan about this time. 'Do have some potato Cripps',[14] Indira is reported to have pressed him with an abstracted air at the dinner table.

Another foreign visitor was Eve Curie, a French journalist and daughter of the famous scientist, who arrived on the eve of the wedding. 'She

*The present Indian High Commissioner in Britain.
**The birthday of Rama, hero of the *Ramayana*.

could have well have been born in Greece,' she commented on the bride-to-be and described her as 'slender and pale, with a pensive, classical face.'[15] She seems to have been particularly struck by the girlish enthu-siasm with which Indira made her selection from the traditional basket-full of many-hued glass bangles, picking the ones that matched her saris. 'Naturally, being glass they will break constantly,' Indira informed her, 'but then they are so cheap that one can replace them. It is fun to wear them en masse—ten or twelve together on each arm.'[16]

'In regard to Indu's wedding,' Gandhi had written to Nehru, 'it is my firm opinion that no outsiders should be invited. Some local people in Allahabad may be asked to attend as witnesses. Send out as many wedding cards as you wish. Ask everybody for their good wishes. But write frankly on the cards that no one is being troubled to attend. If you invite even one person, it will be impossible to leave out the others. Whether Indu wants such austerity or not will have to be considered. If you, too, are against it, then forget my advice.'[17] As it happened, the bridal couple themselves were all for a quiet wedding, and Gandhi's injunctions were followed. Even so, the wedding was far from small, and large numbers of people insisted on turning up from all over the country.

It was very much a nationalist wedding with several prominent Congressmen present. The lavish and often vulgar ostentation that is so typical of Indian weddings was scrupulously avoided. Most of the guests wore *khadi*, and the bride herself wore a simple, handwoven pink cotton sari, made from the fine yarn that her father had spun during his last term of imprisonment. Instead of the usual heavy jewelry, she wore fresh flowers, threaded together into armlets and ear-rings by 'Aunty Vakil' who had come to Allahabad for the occasion.

Simplicity and quiet elegance were the keynotes of this synthesis of the ancient and the modern. The ceremony itself had political overtones. Ancient policital verses from the Vedas were skilfully incorporated into the traditional frame-work. In the *Jaya-homa*, an ancient ceremony symbolic of the love of freedom and the determination to preserve it, Indira announced:

'If there are people in the four quarters of the earth who venture to deprive us of our freedom, mark! here I am, sword in hand, prepared to resist them to the last! I pray for the spreading light of freedom, may it envelop us on all sides!'[18]

The *Mantra-Abhishekha*, which followed, included a declaration of the sovereignty of the people and charged the couple with the duty of main-taining it inviolate. The mood of the ceremony swiftly changed as the couple, hand in hand, walked round the sacrificial fire seven times, thereby binding themselves in wedlock. Then came the *Pani-Grahanam* in which the bridegroom apostrophised his beloved, saying: 'Hope created the universe, love encompasses it. Love divine that reaches the heavens has taken for me a form in thee my wife, so gentle and graceful. Under thy shelter, O Love, may I attain the highest purpose of life.'[19] The political motif returned towards the end when the couple declared: 'May our projects be common and common the Assembly of our people, may our people be of like mind and purpose.'[20] The ceremony concluded with Sanskrit chants praying for universal peace.

Indian weddings are bitter-sweet occasions. Traditionally, an Indian bride bids farewell to her own home and family and takes on a new identity as part of her husband's life. An air of melancholy, more appropriate to a funeral, generally prevails in the bride's home. Indira's wedding had some innovations, but in one respect, at any rate, it appears to have conformed to the traditional pattern: the day which brought fulfilment to her was also tinged with sadness.

In her autobiography Krishna Hutheesing, Indira's incurably sentimental aunt, thus describes the bride's conflicting emotions:

'Frail and almost ethereal, she laughed and talked to those around her, but sometimes her big black eyes would darken and hold a distant and sorrowful look. What dark cloud could mar the joy of this happy day? Was it due to a longing for the young mother who was no more, by whose absence a void had been created which even on this day remained unfilled? Or was it the thought of parting from the father, a father whose very life she had been. She was leaving him now to a life that would be lonelier for him than it had ever been before. May be it was the breaking of all the old ties and the starting of a new life which brought a passing look of sadness to the young bride's eyes, for who could foretell what the future held in store for her—happiness? sorrow? fulfilment? disillusionment?'[21]

*       *       *

Two and a half centuries had passed since the Nehrus had left their Himalayan home for the plains of Hindustan; but Kashmir had continued to hold a special fascination for them. After a recent visit to the home of his ancestors, Jawaharlal had eulogised:

'The loveliness of the land enthralled me and cast an enchantment all about me. I wandered about like one possessed and drunk with beauty, and the intoxication of it filled my mind. Like some supremely beautiful woman, whose beauty is almost impersonal and above human desire, such was Kashmir in all its feminine beauty of river and valley and lake and graceful trees. And then another aspect of this magic beauty would come to view, a masculine one, of hard mountains and precipices, and snow-capped peaks and glaciers, and cruel and fierce torrents rushing down to the valleys below.'22

Indira Gandhi, too, has testified to the fascination which the mountains of Kashmir have always held for her; and it was to the romantic vale of Kashmir that the newly-wed couple came for their honeymoon. 'Wish we could send you some cool breeze from here', they wired to Nehru from the mountain resort of Gulmarg. He promptly replied: 'Thanks. But you have no mangoes.'23 In July he wired again: 'Don't hurry back. Live in beauty while you may.'24

There had been some doubt about the legality of the marriage ceremony; and so, on their way back from Kashmir, Indira and Feroze visited a princely state in western India, where they went through a civil marriage. Apparently the laws there were enlightened enough not to require the objectionable renunciation of religious faith. On their return to Allahabad, the young couple moved into a small house of their own, down the road from Anand Bhawan. But before they had time to sink into quiet domesticity, politics intervened again.

While Indira and Feroze had been preoccupied with the problems and controversies occasioned by their marriage, another confrontation— far more potent and ominous—had been brewing between the Congress and the Government. For some months, the Japanese had been knocking at the gates of India, but negotiations for a National Government to meet the threat had remained in a state of deadlock. While Nehru, with his strong sympathy for the Allied cause, had worked hard for a compromise, Gandhi had rejected the Cripps proposals as 'a post-dated cheque on a failing bank', and the Congress had followed his lead. In May 1942, the Mahatma took up the slogan of 'Quit India', calling on the British to leave the country so that a free India could stand united against the Japanese. Gandhi's logic does not appear to have impressed the Government, and he was soon thinking in terms of mass civil disobedience to support his demand. The Mahatma's plans were strongly resisted by Nehru; but as was so often the case, the latter allowed his loyalty to Gandhi to overrule his own better judgement. When the All India Congress Committee met in Bombay on 7 August to consider Gandhi's proposals, it was Nehru himself who moved the historic 'Quit India' resolution, which declared:

'The Committee feels that it is no longer justified in holding the nation back from endeavouring to assert its will against an imperialistic and authoritarian Government which dominates over it and prevents it from functioning in its own interest and in the interest of humanity. The Committee resolves, therefore, to sanction for the vindication of

India's inalienable right to freedom and independence, the starting of a mass struggle on non-violent lines on the widest possible scale, so that the country might utilize all the non-violent strength it has gathered during the last twenty-two years of peaceful struggle.'[25]

The Government, however, was in no mood to wait for the launching of the movement. In a pre-dawn round-up on 9 August, Gandhi, Nehru and the whole Congress Working Committee were arrested and dispatched by train to an undisclosed destination. This tactless and arbitrary measure was the cause of widespread national resentment. The Congress Left had long been chafing under the restraints imposed on it by the Gandhian leadership and they now seized the opportunity to lead a nation-wide insurrection against the Raj. Despite the absence in prison of the senior Congress leaders, the 'August Revolt' proved to be the most serious threat to British rule since the Great Revolt of 1857. Huge demonstrations were organised all over the country to demand the release of the imprisoned leaders; workers went on strike, and students left their colleges to form the vanguard of the movement. At first the protest was peaceful, but the authorities lost their nerve, and there was frequent police firing on unarmed crowds. This in turn provoked violent retaliation. According to the Government's own modest estimates, over 1,000 people had been killed, 3,500 wounded, and about 100,000 imprisoned by the end of November 1942.

Indira and Feroze had been present at the AICC session in Bombay. They had by now reached the parting of ways with their friends in the Communist Party. Since Russia's entry into the war the Communists had been advocating an Anti-Fascist Front with the British and were now boycotting the Quit India agitation. But for Feroze and Indira, as for Nehru, nationalism took priority over anti-Fascism, and there could be no question of ignoring the Congress call for action.

While Feroze, with other youthful militants in the Congress, went 'underground', Indira made her way back to Allahabad. These were tense days for the Nehru household. A virtual police state had come into being: there was strict censorship, and all those whose loyalty was suspected were under close surveillance. Swaraj Bhawan, the Congress headquarters, had been occupied by British troops, who were using it as a base for a campaign of repression in Allahabad and the surrounding district. The inmates of neighbouring Anand Bhawan had to endure the uncomfortable sight of a row of guns glaring at them over the garden wall; and the servants, who were constantly being challenged at gun-point by the sentries next door, lived in a state of terror. For Indira it was an opportunity to win her spurs. She had lived always on the periphery of the national struggle, sharing in its anxieties and disappointments, but unable to take her full part in it. Now, at last, she had a chance to show her mettle.

The day after her arrival in Allahabad, her aunt, Mrs. Pandit, was arrested and Indira found herself at the head of the beleaguered Nehru household; but she kept her nerve, and even harboured Lal Bahadur Shastri,* who was wanted by the police. Acting on the principle that the most obvious hiding-place would be the most secure, Shastri had concealed himself at Anand Bhawan. He kept to his room till after dark, and his food was furtively sent in to him, while Indira pretended that she was keeping a sick relative. After some time Shastri decided to move out and was arrested shortly afterwards.

Feroze, meanwhile, had made the journey from Bombay to Allahabad disguised as an Anglo-Indian soldier. With his fair complexion, a newly-grown moustache and a khaki uniform, he seems to have been entirely convincing. To avoid being recognised at Allahabad station, he had left the train at a small wayside town and hitch-hiked the rest of the way in a truck full of tommies. Their nerves appear to have been on edge, for they had almost refused to let him get off at his destination, warning him that he would be hacked to pieces by the 'damned natives'. Once in Allahabad, he went into hiding in Yehiapur, a congested, old part of the city, with tortuous, narrow alleys and by-ways. Anand Bhawan was being closely watched, and it was almost impossible for Indira to meet other Congress workers. But Feroze acted as her liaison with the underground. She met him secretly at the homes of various non-political friends and passed on to him funds and political pamphlets for the movement.

About this time Indira had her first experience of a *lathi* charge. The students of the Ewing Christian College had decided to hoist the Congress tricolour, and she was invited to attend. As the flag was raised, the police arrived and dispersed the students with their *lathis*. In the confusion that followed, the person who was holding the flag passed it to Indira as the police dragged him away. 'I was badly beaten,' she proudly recalls, 'but I didn't let it fall.'[26]

Not long after this, Indira received news that she was to be arrested. She resolved not to submit tamely. Putting together some books and clothes, she moved out of Anand Bhawan and joined Feroze and K.D. Malaviya,** who were in hiding at the home of a family friend. Here the three of them secretly operated an illegal wireless transmitter, broadcasting for the underground Congress Radio.

Indira's stay underground was brief. On September 10, 1942, she decided to address a public meeting in the centre of Allahabad. The meeting was scheduled for five in the evening and news of it was passed

*Later independent India's second Prime Minister.
**Later a member of Nehru's Cabinet, and now of Mrs. Gandhi's.

round the town by word of mouth. When she appeared at the appointed time and place, she was immediately mobbed by a large crowd which had been assembling secretly in a cinema house and neighbouring shops and houses. She had barely spoken for a few minutes when a truck-load of British troops arrived and cordoned off the meeting. Feroze, who had decided not to get involved, had been watching the proceedings from a nearby window. But the sight of a gun-barrel only a yard away from his wife's head proved too much for him, and he rushed out, yelling to the soldier to lower his gun. He was promptly arrested and thrown into a Black Maria. Pandemonium had broken out. When a police officer took Indira's arm to lead her to the waiting van, a number of Congresswomen pulled her back by the other arm. A scuffle ensued, and Indira was bruised and her clothes torn before she was bundled into the van with several other prisoners. Feroze, meanwhile, had succeeded in climbing out onto the roof of the van and was discovered shouting slogans to the crowd. He was recaptured, and the van finally drove off with its unruly cargo.

Indira could well have congratulated herself on giving the police a run for their money; but they do not seem to have held it against her. 'The ride to the jail was rather an extraordinary one,' she has observed, 'for the police in my van were apparently so moved by my talking to them that they apologised, put their turbans at my feet and wept their sorrow because of what their job compelled them to do.'[27]

Many years later, Indira Gandhi referred to her arrest as the most dramatic incident in her life. Dramatic it certainly was: but it also marked her political coming of age and the fulfilment of one of her strongest desires. Prison-going, though questionable as a political tactic, had become a form of pilgrimage for Congressmen and Indira's arrest marked the culmination of her long involvement with the national struggle. 'I had made up my mind that I had to go to prison,' she has told an interviewer. 'Without that ... something would have been incomplete.'[28] For twenty years she had looked on while her parents and other relatives had courted and faced the rigours of prison life. Now that experience was hers.

*     *     *

On 11 September 1942, at Naini Prison, Allahabad, Mrs. Pandit entered in her prison diary: 'Half an hour after lock-up yesterday there was a tremendous knocking at the outer gate and the matron came in excitedly announcing "Mrs. Indira is here."'[29] Mrs. Gandhi and her more fastidious aunt have provided between them a graphic description of the squalid barrack in which they spent the next nine months. The roof leaked, and during the monsoon the rain formed puddles on the floor and soaked the prisoners' bedding. Huge chunks of plaster fell periodically from the ceiling and littered the bedding and the floor. There was no proper sanitation: in the day the prisoners could use a small bathroom in the yard; but after lock-up they had to make do with a corner of the barrack, which had been raised a few steps from the ground to serve as a lavatory. For beds, they used what Indira has described as 'little cement tombstones.' Any object—a book, a shawl or a pair of slippers—that fell off these slabs of concrete was reduced to shreds by white ants in a matter of hours. The prisoners were subjected to frequent visitations from various unpleasant forms of insect and animal life. Bats, frogs and mice combined to make life in the barrack something of a nightmare for the more squeamish female inmates. The prisoners cooked their own food; but their rations, which came mixed with dirt and even spiders, were scarcely palatable, while clouds of acrid smoke from the damp firewood with which they were provided made cooking far from pleasant.

'Since earliest childhood,' Indira Gandhi has written, 'I had visited jails, either for trials of relations and friends or for unsatisfactory but highly treasured twenty-minute interviews ... What a world of difference there is between hearing and seeing from the outside and the actual experience. Herded like animals, devoid of dignity or privacy, we were debarred not only from outside company or news but from all beauty and colour, softness and grace. The ground, the walls, everything around us was mud-coloured, and so became our jail-washed clothes, even our food tasted gritty. Through the apertures we were exposed to the *loo** and dust-storms, the monsoon downpour and the winter cold.'30

These foul living conditions, following on the strain and exertion of the preceding weeks, seem to have told on her delicate constitution. 'Indu is running a temperature,' her aunt noted soon after her arrival. 'She doesn't look at all well.'31 Indira was determined, however, to keep busy and cheerful. 'Indu, Lekha** and I have been drawing up a plan,' Mrs. Pandit wrote on 13 September. 'I am to cook the midday meal and they will arrange the supper... The girls are planning to do a good lot of reading and Indu is going to help Lekha with her French.'32

Indira's temperature persisted, and on 23 October she received a visit from the civil surgeon, who had been asked by the Government to report on her health. He prescribed a tonic and a special diet that included delicacies like Ovaltine. 'But hardly was his back turned,' Indira recalls, 'when the Superintendent tore up the list and tossed the pieces on the floor. "If you think you are getting any of this," he said, "you are mistaken." This was surprising, for I had not asked for anything—even the Surgeon's visit was unexpected.'33

The men's prison, where Feroze was lodged, was only a stone's throw

*The scorching summer wind that sweeps the plains of northern India.
**Mrs. Pandit's daughter.

away, and occasionally the sound of young students being flogged could be heard in the women's barracks. For a month and a half Indira was refused permission to see her husband; but early in November, the Superintendent announced that husbands and wives in the same prison would be allowed a half-hour interview every fortnight. On 20 November Mrs. Pandit noted: 'Yesterday was Indira's twenty-fifth birthday. She had her fortnightly interview with Feroze and came back from the office looking very happy. In the afternoon Purnima* invited us all to tea on her side of the barrack and we had quite a good time.'[34] Not long after this, Feroze was transferred to another prison and these cheering interviews ceased.

Indira had by then settled down to a strict routine. She gave much of her time to a literacy campaign among the women convicts in the adjacent barracks, some of whom were serving life-sentences for murder. She also took a young woman and her child under her wing. She tried out her knowledge of child-care on the baby, and even toyed with the idea of adopting it, while she worked hard to educate the mother. She must have been gratified to learn later that this young mother had become a school-teacher after her release.

The political prisoners were a resourceful and imaginative lot, and they managed to keep up their spirits, in spite of their grim surroundings. On 27 November Mrs. Pandit recorded in her diary:

'The girls have been busy "decorating" our corner of the barrack. Each part has a name. Indu calls hers "Chimborazo"—Lekha's bit is called "Bien Venue" because she now has the part formerly occupied by me and which gives a view of the main gate. I am obliged to call my abode "Wall View" because it's so obvious. In the centre we have an old blue rug ... which I brought along with me in my bedding. We call the centre space the "Blue Drawing Room" and it is here we eat our meals and sit and read at night, etc. ...
'Indu and Lekha are both gifted with imagination and the evenings are seldom dull. They are planning to save up rations and have a party in the "Blue Drawing Room" soon. The menu is discussed daily with great enthusiasm. They can't decide whether to write it in French or not.
'The jail cat named by Indu—Mehitabel—has had four kittens and Indu and Lekha are quite excited. Our ration of milk now has to be shared with the new arrivals and the mother.
'The girls have a habit of giving names to everything; the lantern, table, bed, even the bottle of hair oil which has recently lost its top, as the result of a fall. It is now referred to as "Rupert—the headless Earl". The

*Purnima Banerji, a fellow Congresswoman who was in the same barracks.

lantern is "Lucifer". I find it very difficult to remember the various names, but apparently the girls have no such trouble and get a terrific amount of amusement. After lock-up they read plays, each taking a part. I am the audience. It is amusing.'[35]

'The girls invited Purnima to supper in the Blue Room after lock-up', Mrs. Pandit wrote on New Year's Eve. 'They have been saving rations for days and planning a meal. Unfortunately our table-cloths have become grey with constant washing and our crockery and cutlery are limited to one plate and one fork each. We have a knife between us— nevertheless we managed to turn out an attractive meal and a change from the things we eat.'[36]

In an effort to bring some colour into their drab environment, Indira and her cousin had acquired some flower-pots from the matron and planted some seeds. Their miniature garden was soon blooming. 'Our flowers are looking up', Mrs. Pandit rejoiced on New Year's day, 1943. 'The morning glory is climbing well and there are several deep blue and mauve flowers. We have some pansies and nasturtiums also and a row of cosmos which stand against the wall and look quite pretty. The lark-spurs and several other flowers have not done at all well in spite of care from Indu and Lekha.'[37]

Soon summer was upon them, and the flowers had withered in the heat. Some months back, Indira had been promoted to the status of an 'A Class' prisoner which entitled her to sleep out in the yard. But according to her aunt, she refused this discriminatory privilege and endured the stifling heat indoors with a friend who had Second Class status.

For Indira, an Indian summer had always meant mangoes, her favourite fruit. Though her father was in prison, he had not forgotten her passion for mangoes and arranged for a basket-full to be sent to her as soon as the season began. Unfortunately, the fruit was intercepted by the gaoler. 'The Superintendent came and thanked me for the very delicious fruit which had been sent,' she remembers. 'And he didn't even have the grace to give us one small piece!'[38] The Superintendent's manners appear to have improved subsequently, and a fruit parcel from her aunt Krishna did eventually reach Indira shortly before her release. 'Indu wrote to me that she had received the fruit sent by you', Nehru reassured his sister, 'She was quite excited about the Alphonsos, and smelt them and touched them and almost hugged them. She loves mangoes and getting good fruit, and especially good mangoes, after long being deprived of them, was an exhilarating experience.'[39]

'No one who has not been in prison for any length of time,' Indira Gandhi has written, 'can ever visualise the numbness of spirit than can creep over one when, as Oscar Wilde writes, "each day is like a year, a year whose days are long", when day after day is wrapped in sameness and in spite and deliberate humiliation.'[40] Even so, the monotony of prison life was enlivened by the occasional drama.

Mrs. Gandhi has recorded that she and the other prisoners were awakened one night by a blood-curdling scream from the yard. They looked out to find Zohra, 'the nastiest and the most unpopular of the wardresses', confronted by a large cobra. The snake was about a yard away from their barred window, coiled under a clock which the wardress was required to punch on her rounds. Zohra, described by Mrs. Pandit as 'a deadly female', appears to have met her match. Torn between her fear of the snake and the prospect of losing her job, she shouted for help to the phlegmatic sentry outside the prison wall. For a long time she was unable to impress upon him the urgency of the situation. He insisted on being given specific details about the exact location of the snake and its length and breadth. 'Have I got a tailor's tape to measure it from head to tail?' Zohra is reported to have remonstrated. She finally prevailed on him to call the matron, who lived almost half a mile away. The matron in turn had to go to the Superintendent's house and wake him, after which they went together to the main office to fetch the prison keys. 'By the time this little procession entered our enclosure,' writes Indira, 'we had long since fallen philosophically asleep and the snake had glided away.'[41]

On another occasion, the prisoners narrowly escaped being trapped in a fire. A number of Allied air-force personnel had been stationed in a nearby cantonment. A Canadian airman is reported to have been en-amoured of the gaol Superintendent's attractive daughter and was in the habit of flying low over her house. One day, while he was thus displaying his skill, one of his wings touched a telegraph wire and burst into flames. While the prisoners watched, heart in mouth, the plane came hurtling down towards them at a terrific speed, narrowly missed the prison wall and crashed into an untenanted house nearby.

As news filtered through about the collapse of the August Revolt, the prisoners were convinced that the country would have to wait several years for independence. In the meanwhile, they expected to remain at Naini and lightly joked about this dismal prospect, much to the as-tonishment of the Irish matron, who could not understand such levity. Their calculations, however, proved unduly pessimistic. On 5 May, Indira and her aunt were summoned to the Superintendent's office and informed that they would be released, provided they complied with an externment order confining them to the hill-station of Almora. Although they both refused to give any such undertaking, they were released on 13 May. A fortnight later, Mrs. Pandit was back in prison for refusing to comply with the externment order. There was no warrant, however, for her niece who was in hospital with a bad attack of 'flu and a high fever.

Indira Gandhi had spent nine months in prison. Compared with her father's total record of nine years, it was not a long period. Nevertheless, it had been necessary for her own fulfilment and an important part of her political apprenticeship. As she later asserted, it had toughened her character. 'The reaction in me was to seal in my mind', she has told a journalist, 'so that while I was in prison, I didn't consciously feel that I was missing anything. Some of the other prisoners would talk about food and say: "Oh, I wish I could have some lobster", or this or that. But I didn't miss a thing. It was only when I left prison that I suddenly found I had cut off my emotions and intellect, and I had been living only at a surface level.'[42]

For Nehru prison life, with all its privations, had been a form of enforced leisure. The greater part of his time in prison was served in solitary confinement, and cut off from the distractions of the outer world he was able to give free rein to his intellect and imagination. His years in prison were probably the most fertile period in his intellectual life; it was there that he developed his political ideas and wrote his best books. His daughter, however, was of a different turn of mind. She was a doer, not a thinker, always more at home in the world of action. Isolation from that world, however resolute her stoicism, must have imposed a great strain on her. 'My unexpected release was like coming out of a dark passage,' she has recorded. 'I was puzzled with the rush of life, the many hues and textures, the scale of sounds and the range of ideas. Just to touch and listen was a disturbing experience and it took a while to get adjusted to normal living.'[43]

In August 1943 Feroze was also released and his wife and he were reunited. He now settled down to the business of earning a living, working as an insurance agent and writing articles on his travels abroad for various periodicals. A year later Indira gave birth to her first son, Rajiv. 'To a woman, motherhood is the highest fulfilment,' she later wrote. 'To bring a new being into this world, to see its tiny perfection and to dream of its future greatness is the most moving of all experiences and fills one with wonder and exaltation.'[44] She had looked forward eagerly to having children of her own and was determined that nothing should go wrong. She took every precaution, observed a strict diet and regular hours, and religiously performed the pre-natal exercises. Despite her frail constitution the delivery proved extremely easy. Mrs. Gandhi is reported to have told a male Cabinet colleague many years later: 'I just felt hungry and I asked for a piece of toast. As I was eating, Rajiv came out. I was so sorry I couldn't finish my toast!'[45]

# CHAPTER V

# FIRST LADY

THE SUMMER of 1945 found the British Government convinced at last of the necessity of coming to terms with the Congress, and Nehru, along with some other members of the Congress Working Committee, was released. In the talks that followed, the Congress found itself at a serious disadvantage. For almost three years the Party had been banned, with its leaders in prison and its organisation disrupted. The Muslim League, meanwhile, had taken advantage of the resultant political vacuum to win a mass following for itself. Now the League, with its claim to speak for the Muslims of India, was allowed a virtual veto by the Viceroy on any constitutional change. Jinnah was by this time determined on the creation of a sovereign Pakistan, and the Congress found itself hard pressed to maintain the unity of the sub-continent.

There followed a year of tense political bargaining, while the British Cabinet Mission sought in vain to square the circle and reconcile the demands of the Muslim League with the integrity of the country. By the middle of 1946, however, a deadlock had been reached, and the League launched direct action to achieve its objectives; the Great Calcutta Killing of August 1946 was the first of a series of horrific waves of communal violence. Britain, for her part, having decided—primarily for financial reasons of her own—to quit India, was determined that the transfer of power should be effected with all possible speed.

It was in this hour of crisis that Jawaharlal Nehru assumed the 'crown of thorns' in September 1946 as head of the Interim Government. At the same time, Feroze Gandhi succeeded his father-in-law as Managing Director of *The National Herald*, a Lucknow newspaper, which had been founded by Nehru and had been, by and large, his political mouthpiece. Feroze now moved with his wife to Lucknow, the capital of the United Provinces. He was to find his new job a difficult one, as *The National Herald* had been dogged by financial misfortune ever since its inception. He hoped, nevertheless, to bring out a Delhi edition and worked hard to put the paper on its feet. 'Feroze had the common touch', Chelapathi Rau, Editor of *The National Herald*, has commented. 'He often worked in the press day and night. He loved machines; he did not mind the ink and soot. This endeared him to the workers.'[1] One wonders, however, if these qualities endeared him to his wife.

Indira and Feroze had much in common, not least their political radicalism. But with the passing of time, their temperamental differences were becoming increasingly pronounced. Rather stout and flushed in the face, with a brash and hearty manner and a mischievous—and often bawdy—sense of humour, Feroze made friends wherever he went. Indira, with her patrician refinement and reserve, seems to have found it difficult to share the more Bohemian side of his life. Despite the genuine affection they retained for each other till the very end, Feroze and Indira found their separate worlds gravitating ever further apart. As the years passed, they would drift from each other, she to her father and public life, and he to his own career and the friends with whom he was comfortable. Nehru, had been living alone in the capital, grappling with the enormous problems involved in the impending transfer of power; and Indira now began to spend most of her time with him in Delhi. While there was as yet no estrangement with her husband, it was becoming increasingly clear that her father came first.

It has sometimes been suggested that Indira Gandhi's decision to live with her father was politically motivated and that she wished to be near the seat of power; but such an interpretation seems both uncharitable and unlikely. Quite possibly, she was bored by the small-town monotony of life in a provincial city and missed the bustle and excitement of the Nehru household. It is also quite likely that, with her strong psychological need to be respected as a personality in her own right, she would not for long have acquiesced in the subsidiary, domestic role of an average wife. This desire might have led her—as it later did—to carve out an independent place for herself in public life. By its very nature, however, it could not have prompted her to flee the constraints of matrimony, only to subject herself afresh to the demands of filial obligation. For hers was an essentially independent nature that would not be satisfied with reflected glory, whether her father's or her husband's; and she had shown conclusively by her determination to marry Feroze only a few years back that the trappings of social approval and official status meant little to her when they involved the compromise of her independent will.

Nobody has ever questioned the existence of a deep emotional link between father and daughter, and it is to this attachment that one must look for an explanation of what was for Indira a gesture of self-effacement. It must have appeared unthinkable to her that Nehru, a lonely, middle-aged widower, weighed down by affairs of state, could be allowed to live alone, neglected and uncared for. It was obvious that he needed someone to protect him from over-work and from the importunate demands of supplicants and go-getters, to watch over his health and diet, and to share his few moments of relaxation. His sister, Vijayalakshmi Pandit, had already embarked on the first of a series of diplomatic missions, and there was nobody else who could give him the necessary care and companionship except his daughter. It was not unnatural then for Indira to have been moved by his loneliness and exhaustion—especially during this period of crisis—into feeling that her place was by his side, performing the functions that would have been her mother's had she lived. Shanta Gandhi, the old friend of her Poona and London days, recalls that her anxiety about her father had troubled her even at the time of her marriage. Now, when the first flush of youthful romance was wearing thin, this anxiety must have assumed ever more compelling dimensions.

This response was not in any sense the result of a traditionalist view of her duty as a daughter. 'If you are attached to a person', Mrs. Gandhi told the author, 'you want to help that person, regardless of the relationship. Of course, if you are related, normally you are more attached. I helped my father because I thought he needed help, although at some periods other people were rather annoyed; they thought I was wasting my life . . . by doing these small jobs for him. But I just felt that he had a real need.'[2]

\*     \*     \*

It was in Delhi, in December 1946, that Indira gave birth to her second son, Sanjay. This time there were serious complications. On the evening of 14 December, Lady Cripps called at the small official residence then occupied by Nehru and asked Indira to go shopping with her. 'There isn't anyone who knows just what's right for me the way you do', she is said to have pleaded.[3] Indira, though in an advanced stage of pregnancy and feeling faint, agreed to accompany her. The result was a premature confinement late the same night. Feroze and her aunt Krishna rushed her to hospital without waking Nehru. The baby was safely delivered; but Indira had a difficult time and her health received a serious set-back. Nevertheless, political developments during the next two years were to place a heavy strain on her capacities.

On 15 August 1947, India became independent, and Jawaharlal Nehru was sworn in as her first Prime Minister. Indira Gandhi has recalled that it was one of the proudest and most exciting moments in her life. She had grown up with the struggle for freedom and had played her own part during its crucial, final years; and now she was beside her father amid the pageantry that marked the ceremonial transfer of power. Independence was celebrated all over the country with jubilant rallies and processions. But the new nation, though conceived in the spirit of Gandhian non-violence, was born in the blood and tears of millions.

By the end of 1946, the British had virtually conceded the Muslim League's demand for Pakistan. The League had boycotted the Constituent Assembly convened in December 1946, and the 'War of Succession' had shifted to the streets. It had been the beginning of a civil war in which no quarter was asked or given. Nehru did not exaggerate when he said after a visit to the affected areas: 'I have seen ghastly sights and I have heard of behaviour by human beings which would disgrace brutes.' Demoralised by this holocaust and by the fear of worse to come, the Congress leadership, with the exception of Gandhi, had lost its will to fight and had moved rapidly towards acceptance of partition as the necessary pre-condition of independence.

If the makers of partition had imagined that the canker of communal violence could be removed by a surgical operation, they were soon to be disillusioned. Independence was the signal for the erruption of communal violence on an unparalleled scale in both the successor states. By comparison, the pre-partition riots appeared as minor disturbances. In both countries, panic gripped the minority communities and a massive two-way exodus began, as an estimated total of 12,000,000 refugees—Hindus and Sikhs from Pakistan and Muslims from India—fled across the newly carved border. It was a traumatic experience from which neither country has yet recovered.

In India, Nehru worked desperately to prevent economic break-down and to preserve the secular character of the new state. But atrocities in one country inevitably interacted on the other, triggering off fresh massacres. Early in September 1947, riots broke out in Delhi, as Hindu and Sikh refugees from West Pakistan avenged themselves savagely on the large Muslim community in the Indian capital. After Gandhi, Nehru had always ranked as the most staunch champion of India's Muslim minority, and it was to him that the Muslims now looked for protection. Unmindful of his personal safety, he went about unguarded, rescuing people from violent mobs.

Indira Gandhi was with her children in Mussoorie—a nearby hill-station—when the Delhi riots erupted. The first indication she received that all was not well was a cryptic message from her husband asking her on no condition to return to the capital. 'Like all young wives, I began to get suspicious,' Mrs. Gandhi has confessed, 'and I thought this was one reason why I should come immediately.'[5] It was then that Feroze tele-phoned and told her the facts. He should, however, have known his wife better. The grim picture he painted, far from deterring her, presented a challenge to which she responded with typical enthusiasm. Taking the children with her, she caught the next train to Delhi.

The journey was an eventful one, and Indira witnessed a number of violent incidents on the way. The climax, however, came at Shahdara, a small station on the outskirts of Delhi, when she looked out of the window to see a man about to be lynched by an angry crowd on the platform. She leapt out at once, and harangued the mob till the train was ready to leave, thereby saving the man's life. 'I would have done a great deal more,' Mrs. Gandhi has assured a foreign journalist, 'except that I myself was in the process of dressing.'[6]

These were the darkest days of Nehru's life, as his most valued ideals were swept aside in a hysterical orgy of violence. He must have been grateful for the quiet sympathy and support of his daughter. Indira had not yet recovered from the effects of her second confinement, and her health was still poor; but by all accounts, she was an enormous help to her father.

Following the break-down of law and order in the capital, a number of people belonging to various communities had taken refuge at the Prime Minister's residence, convinced that it was the only safe shelter in a city given over to murder, rape and plunder. Despite the security risk involved, Indira allowed them to stay, much to the chagrin of some government officials. Later some of these refugees were taken onto the Prime Minister's staff and repaid their debt by serving Nehru, and later his daughter, with unfailing devotion and loyalty.

Although it was a small house, two rooms were set aside for the use of refugees, the rest of whom camped out on the lawn in tents. The riots had created an acute food shortage in the city, but Indira was an efficient and resourceful housekeeper, and her homeless guests did not go hungry. Finding the larder empty one day, she is said to have commandeered the services of her husband and a friend to capture some goats from an abandoned herd grazing nearby. On another occasion, she discovered a stranger with a knife hiding in one of the bathrooms. Her composure unruffled, she is reported to have taken away his knife, dragged him out and handed him over to the police.

Amid the savage carnage there were also acts of individual heroism, as people risked their own lives to rescue the victims of mob violence. Nehru's physical courage has already been noted, and his daughter, too, did not flinch when the occasion arose; on the contrary, danger appears to have brought out the best in her. 'I don't go in search of danger,' Mrs. Gandhi has said, 'but if it's there, I just meet it.'[7] This approach was well illustrated by an incident which occurred when she was being driven through the streets of riot-torn Delhi. Seeing an old man being pursued by an armed crowd of about two hundred people, she immediately halted the car, jumped out and put herself between the victim and his assailants. 'What do you think you are doing? Who are you?' the mob asked. 'It doesn't matter what my name is,' she replied coolly, 'but I want to know what *you* are doing. I know what I'm doing. I'm saving this man.' 'You can't save him,' they shouted. 'We are going to kill him, and if you stand there we'll kill you too.' But Indira stood her ground boldly. 'If you want to kill me,' she dared them, 'you may certainly do so, but I don't think you have the courage.' Fortunately for her, she was right. 'There is nothing that frightens a bully mob more than somebody not being afraid,' Mrs. Gandhi has observed with satisfaction, referring to this episode. 'No weapon is needed, except the fact of genuinely not being afraid.'8

*     *     *

Gandhi had arrived in Delhi in September 1947 after a long stay in partitioned Bengal, where his healing presence had worked wonders in quelling communal violence. Neglected by many of his former followers, he watched in anguish while the fragile edifice of non-violence fell in fragments around him. Indira Gandhi has recorded that it was now, in the twilight of his life, that she came really close to the Mahatma. She had always been dear to him as the daughter of Jawaharlal and Kamala; but now he began to respect her for herself.

On hearing reports of Indira's daring exploits, Gandhi sent for her and asked her to do relief work in the Muslim quarter of Delhi. 'I have asked several others,' he told her, 'and they have replied, "Yes Bapu." But I know they are still hesitating.'9 It was a dangerous and exacting mission; but it was the sort of challenge that Indira, despite her ill health, could never resist. She worked hard in the riot-torn areas, rushing help to threatened families and reassuring the terrorised Muslim community. Whenever possible, she reported to Gandhi on the situation.

Finding that police action was making little headway, Indira tried a Gandhian approach to the problem. She got the Hindus and Muslims respectively to name a few individuals in the rival community who had remained uninfected by the communal virus and continued to enjoy their trust. The individuals thus selected were then persuaded by her to meet and discuss their problems. The operation proved successful once the initial reluctance had been overcome, and the area of fraternisation progressively expanded.

By October the Delhi riots had subsided and communal harmony had, for the present, been restored. Indira, exhausted and on the verge of collapse, was dispatched by Gandhi to Lucknow for a well-earned rest. 'Now I know your education and your years abroad have not been wasted', the Mahatma complimented her before she left.10

On 29 January 1948, Indira, accompanied by her three-year-old son, her aunt Krishna and one of her female cousins, called on Gandhi. They found him basking in the mild winter sunshine, with a Bengali straw-hat perched on his head. 'Hello, have all these princesses come to see me?' he quipped when he saw the Nehru women. The Mahatma was in a relaxed mood, and he chatted merrily with his visitors avoiding political topics, while little Rajiv played with his feet, decorating his big toe with a chain of flowers. When the visitors remarked on his hat, he joked: 'An elegant Burmese hat is on its way. Shall I not look very handsome in that hat?' At last he told them: 'You girls, all of you vanish now, otherwise people waiting outside will curse you.' 'Little did we guess,' Indira has written, 'that we would never see his wide toothless smile again, nor feel the glow of his protection.'[11]

The day after this visit, the apostle of non-violence died a martyr's death, assassinated by a Hindu fanatic. The nation was plunged into a grief that knew no distinction of caste or religion, and the like of which has never been witnessed for the passing of any Indian leader before or since. Nehru himself was inconsolable. Ever since Motilal's death, Jawaharlal had found in Gandhi a father-figure and had leaned on him for strength and guidance. Now he was bereft at one stroke of a leader, a father-figure and his closest confidant; and as Prime Minister he felt a personal responsibility for having failed to protect the country's 'most treasured possession.'

In an unprepared broadcast, his voice breaking with emotion, Nehru told the nation:

'The light has gone out of our lives and there is darkness everywhere. I do not know what to tell you and how to say it. Our beloved leader, Bapu as we called him, the Father of the Nation, is no more. Perhaps I am wrong to say that. Nevertheless we will not see him again as we have seen him for these many years. We will not run to him for advice and seek solace from him, and that is a terrible blow, not to me only but to millions and millions in this country... The light has gone out, I said, and yet I was wrong. For the light that shone in this country was no ordinary light. The light that has illumined this country for these many years will illumine this country for many more years, and a thousand years later, that light will still be seen in this country and the world will see it and it will give solace to innumerable hearts.'[12]

'Each person's understanding of Gandhiji is a measure of his own change and growth,' Indira Gandhi has observed. 'Whilst he was alive, many of my age group found it difficult to understand him. Some of us were impatient with what we considered to be his fads, and we found some of his formulations obscure. We took his Mahatmahood for granted, but quarrelled with him for bringing mysticism into politics.'[13]

Like other youthful members of the Congress Left, Indira had objected vehemently to the more conservative and obscurantist aspects of Gandhi's thought. Indeed, as she later confessed, her vocal protests had been the cause of friction with her father, who had felt that she was being disrespectful. Nevertheless, even while she argued with the Mahatma, she had marvelled at his patience and tolerance. And towards the end, she had grown to understand him better. In particular, she had been impressed by his extraordinary understanding of the mind of the Indian masses, of their feelings and aspirations, and by his role as a social reformer, especially as a champion of the rights of women and Untouchables.

From her early childhood Indira had thought of Gandhi as a member of her intimate family circle, and his death was a personal loss for her. Her own emotions apart, she must have realised how much it had increased her father's dependence on her. Nehru would henceforth be 'a lonely eagle in a flock of pigeons', temperamentally alien to the pygmies who surrounded him. Now more than ever, he needed care and companionship; and any ideas Indira may have had of making a home of her own with her husband and children must have receded into the background.

\*      \*      \*

'What a gentle word is domesticity!' Indira Gandhi wrote, but went on to ask: 'What form does it take when it involves my father, a being so versatile—at once volatile and calm, politician and poet, who finds himself equally at home in the richest palace or the poorest hut, who loves the jolting, the sweat and the tumult of immense crowds no less than the quietness and solitude of the Himalayas?'[14]

Acting as hostess, housekeeper and companion to a person of as many facets and moods as Nehru must indeed have been an overwhelming experience, with exhilaration and exhaustion, excitement and depression, alternating at a breakneck pace. Despite her strong attachment to him, Indira's contact with her father had so far been intermittent, continually interrupted by the long separations imposed by the Independence movement, and later by her education abroad and her marriage. To live by his side as a permanent companion and confidante must have been a new and stimulating adventure.

Soon after he took office as Prime Minister, it was decided that Nehru should move to Teen Murti House, formerly the official residence of the Commander-in-Chief of the British Indian armed forces. It was a palatial mansion, built in the golden and red sandstone of Lutyens's Delhi, with long rambling corridors, large reception-rooms and spacious grounds, which included a picturesque, medieval stone pavilion perched on top of a small artificial hill. When Indira first came to inspect it, her heart sank. Glaring disapprovingly at her from the walls were life-size portraits of former guardians of the British Empire, cold and severe in their bemedalled uniforms. 'I felt they were watching every movement, criticising every unspoken thought,' she has written. She decided that prompt action was called for. The generals were unceremoniously taken down from their places of honour and dispatched, rather appropriately, to the Defence Ministry. But Indira's problems did not end there. 'Their removal made the rooms seem larger and the walls seemed to stretch in their stark bareness,' she has lamented. 'Such enormous rooms, such long corridors! Could this ever be made livable, could it ever have any semblance of a home? I need not have worried. What house can resist fast-growing boys full of healthy noise and mischief and a host of animals?'[15]

The house which had once appeared so forbiddingly empty soon burgeoned with a wide variety of animal life. Apart from dogs, both pedigreed and strays rescued from the streets, parrots, pigeons, squirrels, deer and various other small animals, the growing Nehru menagerie included such exotic creatures as Himalayan pandas and tiger cubs. Not surprisingly the mistress of the house faced problems rarely if ever encountered by other First Ladies. 'Whatever other experiences we might share,' she observed, 'I wonder how many of these ladies have had to chase a panda through their living rooms or to sit up nights with a sick tiger?'[16]

The family zoo appears to have claimed much of Indira's time and attention. 'We arranged a corner for Bhimsa (the panda) in the children's bathroom,' she has written, 'but somehow I could not house-train him and he always climbed onto the towel-rack to do his business, besides racing all over the house.'[17] Even her patience had its limits, and Bhimsa was eventually exiled to an enclosure in the garden, where he was later joined by a mate and settled down happily to the business of raising a family. The panda family were particular favourites of Nehru's and he visited them regularly, morning and evening; when he was ill they called on him informally in his bedroom.

While Nehru loved his animals, it was his daughter who had to attend to them. When one of the tiger cubs fell ill, Indira sat up with him for five nights in succession. The cubs are reported to have terrified most of the Prime Minister's visitors, and they were soon too large to be kept loose in a house which had so much coming and going. Two were presented to the Lucknow zoo, while the third and most distinguished went to Marshal Tito in Belgrade. Sanjay's baby crocodile met with the same fate. 'It bit everybody except me,' he is reported to have said. 'But when it bit Mother it had to go.'[18]

\*     \*     \*

'I hated the thought of housekeeping,' Indira Gandhi has told a British interviewer about her early days as mistress of Teen Murti, 'and what I hated most was to be hostess at a party, as I always disliked parties and having to smile when one doesn't want to. But if one has to do a thing, one might as well do it well, so I grew into it.'[19]

According to various intimates of the Nehru circle, Mrs. Gandhi has always had a sense of humour and a spontaneous charm that makes her excellent company for the select few whom she knows and likes. But large, formal gatherings appear in these earlier years to have had a freezing effect on her, bringing to the fore all her shyness and reserve. 'When I came to Teen Murti House, I was always finding excuses to stay away from parties,' she has confided to a young interviewer. 'I hated socialising and making small-talk. I would say, "I'll make the arrangements", and having done so, would then disappear upstairs. It took me a long time to get over this. But I had to learn to enjoy it, so I did.'[20]

Her aunts, of course, had always dismissed her as socially inept, because she had failed to conform to their own stereotype of a sophisticated young debutante. Indira Gandhi may have lacked the suave veneer of a seasoned socialite, but she was to prove herself an efficient housekeeper and a natural and attentive, if not scintillating, hostess. Nehru enjoyed entertaining, and his daughter had to cope with the constant influx of celebrities who visited Teen Murti House. Like other official hostesses, she found herself entangled in the web of protocol. 'It is like walking on a tightrope,' she commented, 'to adhere close enough to the formal side of protocol, so as not to offend even the most particular of dignitaries and yet manage not to stifle the human element.'[21] She seems, nonetheless, to have been remarkably successful at maintaining the requisite balance. The Prime Minister's residence was noted for its air of informality. Though protocol required that visiting heads of state should move to the presidential palace after spending a couple of days as the Prime Minister's guests, most of them are reported to have done so with marked reluctance.

An episode which occurred during the visit of the Dalai and Panchen Lamas in 1957 is revealing of the relaxing effects of Teen Murti House. In the course of an official luncheon in their honour given by the Prime Minister, the two chief guests were reported missing. A search was organised, and eventually Indira Gandhi discovered the truant incarnations of the Buddha in a remote corner of the garden, playing at being Red Indians in a wigwam which had been set up by Rajiv and Sanjay. The Tibetan visitors, we are told, assured their bewildered hostess that it had been the happiest day of their lives, confiding to her that as children they had been denied any opportunity to play games. The presence in the house of two high-spirited young boys undoubtedly contributed to the lighter side of official life. When Major Gagarin, the Soviet astronaut, was staying at Teen Murti House as Nehru's guest, young Sanjay is reported to have caused some embarrassment when he remarked irreverently: 'He had to go into space or he would have been liquidated.'[22]

Nehru's avid interest in foreign affairs and his wide, international contacts brought to New Delhi a never-ending stream of world statesmen—Krushchev and Bulganin, King Saud of Saudi Arabia, President

Nasser, Chou-En Lai, Marshal Tito, President Eisenhower, the Kennedys and many others who had little in common except their admiration for India's Prime Minister. Many of them stayed at Teen Murti House as Nehru's guests; and although their tastes and requirements were as varied as their politics, their hostess was equal to the task. With a scrupulous eye for detail and an intelligent capacity for making people comfortable, it was she who personally checked the various fixtures in the guest-rooms and selected the official gifts for visiting dignitaries. According to Marie Seton, a frequent visitor at Teen Murti House during this period, Indira had a 'do-it-yourself' attitude to her duties; when Miss Seton first met her, she was busy personally wrapping about a hundred gifts for junior members of a visiting Russian delegation.

By far the most taxing part of her functions seems to have been the planning of menus. Apart from the food taboos of various Indian communities, Indira had to anticipate the fads of a wide cross-section of nationalities. 'There are endless combinations and mutations!' she complained. 'There are meat-eaters who are vegetarians on certain days of the week—there are vegetarians who eat eggs, others eat fish as well, and one distinguished guest, who declared himself a vegetarian, ended up by eating everything except chicken!'[23]

Indian food habits were bad enough, but even more unpredictable were the tastes of Nehru's foreign guests. Twenty minutes before a formal lunch, Indira was informed that the King of Saudi Arabia was on a special diet prescribed by his physician. She performed the impossible and had the special food ready in time, only to find that the Arab potentate, having made short work of his own food, attacked the rest of the menu with undiminished gusto.

For all the efficiency of the Nehru household, circumstances inevitably precipitated the occasional crisis. Indira Gandhi has described a hot summer evening when a party, which had been arranged out on the lawns after due consultation with the meteorological department, developed into a nightmare reminiscent of the Black Hole of Calcutta. A sudden thunderstorm sent the guests scurrying indoors where the heat was so stifling that a couple of them fainted. This mishap, however, appears only to have whetted the appetite of the others, with the result that the food ran out before all the guests had arrived. *Pakoras*, nuts and dried fruit had to be hastily improvised.

On another occasion, during a Buddhist Conference in Delhi, Nehru gave a luncheon for the delegates, a large number of whom were Buddhist monks. At the last minute, Indira's attention was drawn to the fact that the monks were required by religious custom to eat their last meal before midday, while the other guests would not be free till 1.30 in the afternoon. She resolved the muddle in the only way possible and entertained the delegates in two batches—seventy-five monks at 11.30 in the morning and a hundred others two hours later.

Indira also had to keep up with her father's many whims and fancies. 'Almost every time my father goes on a journey in India or abroad,' she wrote, 'he finds recipes or customs of which he approves and which we have to adopt.' After dining at Buckingham Palace, for example, Nehru decided that the royal custom of serving milk and sugar before coffee should be introduced at Teen Murti. As his daughter pointed out: 'This is often bewildering to our guests, who look around furtively to see if they have somehow mislaid or forgotten to take the coffee.'[24]

Perhaps the most prominent feature of Indira's housekeeping was the thrift and discipline which she had learnt at an early age and which now moderated her father's more lax and extravagant habits. Waste of any kind she abhorred; and anything that was not perishable—ribbons, gift-wrappings and all sorts of other objects—was stored away for future use. The large domestic staff soon learnt that, while sympathetic and helpful in cases of genuine need, their mistress was far from indulgent. The family cook is reported to have once asked Nehru for some money to enable him to visit his family in Simla. The Prime Minister, we are told, promptly produced his purse and handed him Rs. 60. On the cook's return from Simla, however, Nehru took him aside and asked him not to say anything to his daughter about the money he had received. 'She might deduct the amount from your salary!' the Prime Minister warned him with a smile.[25]

*          *          *

It is customary to regard the 1950s as the golden age of India's foreign policy, as her Prime Minister, the recognised apostle of non-alignment and peaceful co-existence, presided over the councils of the emerging 'Third World' and mediated between rival power blocs. Nehru's involvement with world affairs had a long history reaching back to the 1920s. Before Independence the lengthy foreign policy resolutions which the Congress adopted, largely at Nehru's behest, had been little more than pious academic exercises. But now, combining the offices of Prime Minister and Minister of External Affairs, Nehru was able to determine India's foreign policy to an extent where it became virtually an extension of his own personality. His policy of non-alignment—not to be confused with neutralism—was conceived as a dynamic instrument which, by peacefully combating colonialism, old and new, and by widening the area of international detente, would secure for India a world status far higher than that to which her military and economic resources might otherwise entitle her.

Nehru's foreign policy necessarily involved close and continuous contacts with a wide cross-section of nations and their leaders. While New Delhi was the scene of a series of State visits, Nehru himself became something of a globe-trotter. His daughter was often his companion on this Odyssey which covered every continent and almost every country of any importance. To cite a few of the more notable instances—she was present when Nehru addressed the U.N. General Assembly in November 1948 and pleaded strongly for an end to colonialism and racism; in 1948 and 1949, she accompanied him to the Commonwealth Prime Ministers' Conference, where a new formula was hammered out to enable India to remain in the Commonwealth as a republic; when Nehru visited the United States for the first time in 1949 in search of food aid, she was with him again, sharing his disillusionment with the political strings that the Americans sought to attach to their aid and his distaste for what he considered their *nouveau riche* materialism; she went with him to Karachi in April 1950 for talks with Liaqat Ali Khan, the Pakistani Premier, on the critical refugee problem; later in 1954 she accompanied him to Red China, and in 1955 to the Bandung Conference and the Soviet Union.

These tours, and many others, make her one of the most widely travelled people in the world. What was unique, however, was the opportunity she had to observe the finer points of summit diplomacy from the inside. Her presence was quiet and unobtrusive, but she had a shrewd and perceptive eye for details that had political significance, and few things escaped her attention. After Krushchev and Bulganin visited India in 1956, she told a friend that she had been struck by the way in which Krushchev kept pushing ahead of Bulganin when they passed through a doorway and kept cracking jokes at the latter's expense. It was a shrewd premonition of Krushchev's subsequent assumption of supreme power.

Indira Gandhi's intimate contact with world statesmen enabled her to establish a personal rapport with many of them and to assess them as flesh-and-blood human beings, as prone to irrational emotion and prejudice as the people they led. At Elizabeth II's coronation, she found herself seated beside Winston Churchill. 'Isn't it strange.' he asked, 'that we should be talking as friends when we hated each other such a short while back?' 'We didn't hate you, Sir Winston,' she promptly replied. 'But I did!' he exclaimed, and then hastened to add, 'But I don't now.'[26]

Indira kept well in the background and was careful not to push herself when she travelled with her father. Avoiding the formal functions which Nehru had to attend, she would spend her time at theatres, concerts and art galleries, and fraternising with local artists and intellectuals to whom she would arrange to be introduced. But although in these earlier years she shunned the official limelight, she could when the occasion arose talk intelligently and persuasively on political subjects. She was far from being a passive and colourless appendage trailing her father around the world; and on more than one occasion she is known to have exerted a restraining and moderating influence on Nehru's more volatile and emotional nature. At the Bandung Congress she sat behind her father, conscientiously taking notes of the proceedings. When Nehru, in a temper, was about to walk out in protest against an anti-Communist resolution moved by the Ceylonese Premier, Indira was heard admonishing her father sharply and telling him to control himself.

Even in the early fifties, Indira, for all her retiring and self-effacing ways, had become something of an international figure, though at this stage she was admired more for her elegance and grace than for her political insight. After her visit to Red China with Nehru in October 1954, a British journalist, giving an eye-witness account of a women's reception in her honour, wrote: 'When Indira Gandhi entered the clinically furnished room, there among the massed blue boiler suits of ideological orthodoxy and the square bobs of liberation, she resembled in some way a lotus flower that had been planted in a bed of broccoli.'[27] Her bourgeois feminity notwithstanding, Indira is believed to have made a favourable impression on the Chinese leadership and to have established a particularly good rapport with Chou-En Lai. She in turn was greatly impressed by the visible signs of revolutionary progress in a country whose problems had been as gigantic as India's. 'The country throbs with energy towards a single end,' she commented approvingly after returning home.[28] At the same time, she is believed to have had premonitions of a future Sino-Indian conflict and to have counselled her father to reach on agreement on the Sino-Indian border while the climate was favourable.

The most successful of her early visits abroad were undoubtedly those to Soviet Russia, where she was able to lay the foundations of a friendship which has proved remarkably enduring. Her first visit to the Soviet Union was made in a private capacity—for once without her father—in the summer of 1953. She toured extensively, not only in European Russia, but in Georgia and the Central Asian Republics. K.P.S. Menon, then India's Ambassador to the U.S.S.R., has described her enchantment with Tbilisi, the Georgian capital. She was so intoxicated, he says, by the view from her room of the city's lights that she stayed up till three in the morning. 'I don't get drunk on wine,' she told Menon the next day, 'I get drunk on other things.'[29] She is reported to have been greatly taken with the discipline of Soviet life and the phenomenal growth of Soviet technology, and was particularly impressed by the modernisation of Soviet Central Asia. Her visit confirmed and strengthened a genuine and lasting, if uncritical, admiration for the Soviet Union.

Two years later Indira was back in Soviet Russia, this time with her father. She seems already to have become something of a cult heroine with Soviet women. In the course of his visit, Nehru received a spate of telegrams from Russian mothers asking his permission to name their newly born daughters after his own distinguished daughter, whose 'quiet and dignified manner' and 'winsome smile' had won their admiration. Nehru graciously agreed, and the result was a generation of Soviet Indiras, some of whom still correspond with their Indian prototype.

Commenting on Indira Gandhi's visit to the Soviet Union, Frank Moraes, a leading Indian journalist, wrote:

'She has grace, charm, and when the mood moves her, vivacity which is the more attractive for being completely natural and not mannered. Perhaps her naturalness, restrained but alive, found an answering echo in the hearts and minds of the Soviet people, so long inured by regimentation in thought and behaviour.

'Mrs. Gandhi has proved once again that she is the ideal helpmate of her father, broadening not merely minds but opening hearts to a way of life different from theirs.'[30]

\*     \*     \*

Indira's activities during this period were by no means confined to the drawing-room role of her father's hostess and travelling companion. She also took an active and prominent part in the activities of various welfare organisations in the capital. In a country like India, where social welfare is organised largely on an honorary and charitable basis by untrained amateurs, one finds two kinds of social workers—the great majority of go-getters and publicity-hunters, whose main object is their own advancement, and the very few who feel a sincere commitment to ameliorating poverty and distress. Indira Gandhi, according to those who worked with her, was in the second category. While the anxieties and tensions of her childhood had led her to throw up a defensive wall around her emotions, they had also enhanced her capacity for understanding and identifying with other people's misery. However, much she might avoid any display of emotion, she remained acutely sensitive to real suffering whenever she saw it. Though wary of being imposed upon or exploited, she could identify herself passionately and consistently with a genuine victim of injustice or misfortune.

The best instance of this is a case which she herself has described. During the critical days that followed Partition, Indira had spent her mornings meeting groups of refugees and hearing their tales of woe. In the course of these gloomy sessions, she came across a twenty-year-old, orphaned girl who had as a child lost both legs in a railway accident. The only way she could move was by dragging herself on her hands, with the result that her body had grown misshapen. Indira was deeply moved by her plight and resolved at once to provide her with artificial legs, only to discover that this was far from easy in the India of 1948. After making many enquiries, she found that the only institution in the country which could provide this service was the Artificial Limb Centre at Poona, which catered exclusively to the armed forces. It took her several months, she says, to persuade Sardar Baldev Singh, the Defence Minister, to make an exception in this case. 'Several visits to Poona were required,' Indira has recorded, 'and many painful months of patient endurance which were interspersed with fits of depression—dark moments when she felt it wasn't worthwhile to persevere and when she sought me out for reassurance. At last her body had been coaxed into normal shape and she was not only fitted with the final pair of legs but had learned to use them with the greatest self-assurance. She came to show off a little and to announce her engagement, her face transformed, glowing, positively scattering the gold dust of her happiness on all who happened to be near.'[31]

Indira Gandhi's position beside Nehru made her an obvious choice as patron of charities and welfare institutions. Her own qualifications, however, were by no means negligible. Carefully fostered by both her parents, her social conscience had manifested itself when she was still a little girl. Subsequent years had given her practical experience of the abject condition and apathetic attitudes of India's poor, and had enlarged her desire and capacity for organising other people. Of the myriad organisations with which she was associated, those to which she gave her special attention and patronage were the Central Government's Social Welfare Board, of which, she was Vice-Chairman from 1953 to 1957, the Bal Bhawan Board* and the Children's National Museum, and the Indian Council for Child Welfare of which she was President and is now Life-Patron. She was also active in two Allahabad foundations which comemorated her mother—the Kamala Nehru Memorial Hospital and the Kamala Nehru University. Child Welfare work, however, was closest to her heart, owing perhaps to her own unhappy childhood. She became Vice-President of the International Council for Child Welfare, and in July 1958 led the Indian delegation to the first World Child Welfare Congress.

Indira Gandhi's involvement with these organisations did not, as with most other 'committee women,' institutionalise her social conscience or stifle the spontaneity of her responses. On one occasion, while shopping at Connaught Place, she was pestered in the usual fashion by a little boy selling combs. 'He followed me, sticking them again and again under

*Bal Bhawan was a children's recreation centre in New Delhi.

my nose...' she has recalled. 'I kept stumbling over him. Finally I lost
patience and exclaimed: "For God's sake!... All right, I'll buy a comb!
But why aren't you in school?"' The boy replied proudly that he earned
Rs. 2 a day, which was more than any of his school-going friends could do.
'But when you grow up two rupees won't seem very much,' Indira remonstrated. 'Your friends may be able to earn much more after going
to school.' When he explained that his grandmother would not hear of
his going to school because the family needed the money he earned, she
insisted on going home with him to meet the old lady: 'I put him in my
car, and the first thing I knew, I was in a narrow lane and found myself
engulfed by dozens of grandmothers!'32 From this unexpected visit
originated the idea of *Bal Sahyog*, a centre for training destitute children
in handicrafts and other useful trades. Founded by Indira at Teen Murti
House in September 1954 with about fifty children, it is now a large
institution with premises of its own at Connaught Place, which, of course,
is where it all began.

*    *    *

In an article published in August 1957, Indira Gandhi wrote: 'Situated
as I am, it is perhaps inevitable that I should be asked a great many
questions. But the most frequent is "How do you do it?"' After describing
her manifold activities, she concluded, with a trace of vanity: 'Have I,
in this random meandering, answered the question "How", or have I
merely provoked another one, "When"?'33 When asked this question
by the author, Mrs. Gandhi replied: 'I don't think I ever allowed public
activities to interfere with anything that was important on the domestic
side on any day or any occasion. I was always there if the children needed
me... I think the more you do, the more you are forced to organise
yourself... you organise it in such a way that things fit in much better.'34
Her capacity for organising herself seems to have been so efficient
that her family life, and especially her relationship with her sons, did
not suffer on account of her official and social duties. 'To a mother her
children must always come first,' she has written, 'because they depend
on her in a very special way. The main problem in my life was, therefore,
how to reconcile my public obligations with my responsibility towards
my home and my children.'35
She has recorded that a woman who visited her when her sons happened
to be down with some childhood ailment remarked: 'Children always
have something or other. That's why I'm glad I don't have any.' 'How
could I explain to her,' wrote Indira, 'that the joy of having children far
outweighs the worry and trouble?'36 She was determined that her children
should not experience the insecurity and loneliness of her own childhood. When Rajiv and Sanjay were babies, she did not like the idea of

their being cared for by nursemaids, and she did as much for them herself as she could. The Mothers' Award, which she received in the United States in 1953, appears to have been well deserved. According to one of her cousins, she was extremely well informed on the subject of child care and saw to it religiously that her children were given a balanced diet and regular sun-baths and vitamins. Later, when the boys reached school-age, she tried to plan her engagements during school hours, so that she could be free when they came home. Later still, when they left for boarding school, she planned her travelling during term and was with them during their vacations.

'It is not the amount of time spent with the children that matters as much as the manner of spending it,' she wrote. '. . . No matter how busy I have been, or how tired or even unwell, I have taken time out to play and read with my sons.'[37] The boys themselves certainly do not appear to have felt neglected. When Sanjay was still very little, the mother of one of his friends, a wealthy socialite who spent her day playing bridge, remarked rather tartly to Indira that with all her other activities she must have very little time for her children. Stung by the remark, Sanjay replied on his mother's behalf that, although she was very busy doing important things, she spent more time playing with him than the visitor did with her own son.

'Real love is not that which gives in to the child's whims,' Indira has written, 'but which can also discipline and teach whenever necessary.'[38] She herself acted strictly in accordance with this maxim. When Rajiv was three, the arrival of a baby brother, coinciding with his removal from the familiar Allahabad environment, produced in him a temporary emotional disturbance. 'I was far from well,' Indira wrote, 'and I found his tantrums very irritating. Scolding only made it worse, so I tried reasoning. I told him that much as I loved him, his shouting disturbed me.' Pointing out a fountain in the garden, she told him that when he wanted to cry or shout he should go and do it there. Her experiment in child psychology was successful: 'After that, at the first sign of tears I would whisper "fountain" and away he went. In the garden there was much to distract his attention and he soon forgot his troubles!'[39]

Some years later, when Rajiv was to have an operation and the surgeon was assuring him that it would not hurt, Indira Gandhi interrupted and bluntly told her son that there would be considerable pain and discomfort for a few days after the operation and that he must be prepared to bear it. Weeping and complaining, she said, would make no difference, except perhaps to give him a headache as well. 'Rajiv, never once cried or complained, but bore the pain smilingly,' she has commented proudly. 'The doctor said he had never had such a good patient, even amongst older people.'[40]

Indira's family responsibilities were not limited to her children. The person who required, perhaps, the most care was her father. Generous, impressionable and tolerant, Nehru was an easy prey for the multitude of sychophants and go-getters who swarmed through the gates of Teen Murti House early every morning when *Panditji*—as he was affectionately known—was available to his people. Less trusting and gullible than her father, Indira was a formidable obstacle to these rapacious courtiers. She complained legitimately in an article: '...much of his time is taken by people's personal problems and by matters which could be dealt with by the people in charge of departments more directly concerned... If the people were more considerate of my father's time, it would be possible for him to have a little leisure which is so essential.'[41] She guarded Nehru with firm, and sometimes ruthless, efficiency. This inevitably made her unpopular in certain circles, and she acquired a reputation for being unduly domineering and possessive of her father. She was undoubtedly the decisive influence in his personal life during this period, planning everything from his holidays to the friends he met. This state of affairs is said to have greatly incensed her aunt, Vijayalakshmi Pandit, who complained loudly and vociferously that she was being kept away from her brother.

According to one of Indira's cousins, though she was devoted to her father and looked after him conscientiously, her manner, both with him and with her sons, was cool and undemonstrative, reflecting an inability to express her emotions freely. 'She never came to *Mamu's* (Uncle's) room,' says her cousin. 'I remember that even after his stroke*, he had to walk down the long corridor from his room to hers when he came home from office.'[42]

\* \* \*

'One does not wear one's heart on one's sleeve,' Indira Gandhi is reported to have told Satish Gujral, a well-known artist, who had painted her as a tragic figure and wanted to know why she hid her feelings behind a mask.[43] Perhaps one reason for the severe manner and high-handed behaviour of which some people complained was the emotional stress which she was undergoing at this time, but which she rarely confided to anyone, however close. As noted earlier, despite her genuine affection for her husband, her father's needs had claimed priority; but the choice was not easy and inevitably generated deep-seated tensions and conflicts.

In 1950, Feroze Gandhi had been elected to the Constituent Assembly and had joined his wife in Delhi at Teen Murti House. Re-elected to

*Nehru's first heart attack in January 1964, which marked the beginning of the end. He died five months later.

Parliament in 1952 and again in 1957, he soon won a reputation for being one of the most independent and irrepressible Congress back-benchers and, as a member of the Congress Socialist Forum, a leading light of the Congress Left. He emerged as a national figure in 1955, when he exposed the corrupt dealings of the privately-owned Bharat Insurance Company and contributed thereby to the nationalisation of life insurance. He was also the darling of the Indian press, owing to his part in the passing of an act which gave newspapers legal immunity for accurate and bona fide reports of parliamentary proceedings. With his lively sense of humour, his devil-may-care attitude to people in authority and his unquestioned integrity, Feroze was a popular figure with both Congress and Opposition M.P.s. The famous 'corner' over which he presided in the Central Hall of Parliament House soon became some-thing of an institution, drawing parliamentarians and press-men of various shades of political opinion. Even more significant was the wide reputation he enjoyed among the masses as a champion of the under-dog; people who had been wronged could always be sure of a sympathetic hearing and prompt action when they took their grievances to him.

For a self-made man, who had all the qualifications for political success in his own right, the privilege of being the Prime Minister's son-in-law, far from being an asset, was a constant irritant and constraint, especially when it involved living at Teen Murti House. While Feroze admired Nehru's greatness and was in general agreement with his political ideology, he is believed to have disapproved of the cult of personality around Nehru and of the Prime Minister's capacity for suffering fools and scoundrels in high places. Feroze was no respecter of persons and could not refrain from sniping at some of the top brass in the Cabinet and the party leadership. In these circumstances, his position as the Prime Minister's son-in-law was an embarrassment both to him and to those who were the butt of his attacks. Also, living at the Prime Minister's official residence, it was not possible for him to receive freely the wide variety of politicians and petitioners with whom he mixed. This difficulty was overcome, to some extent, when he took an M.P.'s flat, where he set up his office and received his visitors. But this double existence can only have increased the strain on his relationship with his wife.

'My husband was not the sort of person who wanted me to sit around the house,' Mrs. Gandhi has assured the author.[44] But while Feroze Gandhi did not grudge her a career of her own, he did, by all accounts, resent the implications of her role as her father's hostess and was certainly not willing to play Prince Consort to her First Lady. Awkward situations inevitably cropped up, creating friction and embarrassment all round. For one thing, Feroze was often not invited to functions which Indira attended with her father, and when invited was given a much lower seating than his wife; for another, he had to endure the frequent, and for him tedious, official receptions, luncheons and dinners which were so much a part of life at Teen Murti. It cannot have been easy for an independent young man with tastes and interests of his own to live permanently in the shadow of his father-in-law and without the privacy and freedom of a home of his own.

Krishna Hutheesing, Nehru's sister, has written rather patronisingly of Feroze:

'There is no doubt that his reactions to life at the Prime Minister's House were due in part to his background, which was so different from Indira's. He came from a middle class Parsi family of modest means. He may have felt ill at ease in the midst of social formalities. Such unimportant things as the order of precedence laid down by protocol became a complex with him.'[45]

Feroze's resentment, however, flowed from deeper sources than the minor irritants of protocol. A man who marries for love, only to find that his wife prefers her father, cannot be expected to react in a rational and good-humoured way. Though aware of the emotional strain that Indira was also experiencing, Feroze seems to have felt a certain amount of bitterness, which expressed itself—sometimes not in the best taste— in relatively trivial matters. For instance, when Krushchev and Bulganin addressed a public meeting in Delhi during their 1956 visit, Indira attended with her father, while her husband along with some M.P.s was refused admission by bungling security officers. Feroze is reported to have been livid and raised the matter in Parliament, extracting an apology from Nehru on the floor of the House. On another occasion, when the Prime Minister admonished the delegates at a meeting of the All India Congress Committee for bringing along their wives and children, he is said to have been interrupted by his son-in-law, one of the members, who announced amid laughter: 'It wasn't I who brought my wife here,' referring, of course, to Indira's presence beside her father.

An old acquaintance of the Nehrus remembers being asked informally to lunch by Indira and her father. On entering the dining-room with them, she found Feroze seated already at one end of the table. Apart from a cursory nod, he ignored the guest and concentrated on his food, pausing every now and then to contradict his father-in-law's opinions on virtually every subject from the merits of the food to the state of the country. The atmosphere was explosive, the uncomfortable visitor recalls, even though Indira tried valiantly to steer the conversation into safe channels and kept directing long, pleading looks at her husband in an effort to restrain him. After finishing his meal, Feroze, without waiting for the others, rose abruptly, excused himself and left.

It must indeed have been a trying time for both husband and wife, as feelings not easy to suppress simmered near the surface, threatening at any moment to boil over in an unpleasant and embarrassing quarrel. But according to Nehru's niece, the person who suffered the most was Nehru. Though he had never tried to interfere in Indira's married life, her unhappiness upset him, and he must have felt indirectly responsible. When his niece came to him some years later with her own marital problems, he told her: 'For God's sake, whatever you do, don't make the mistake Indu did. She couldn't make up her mind one way or the other, and it only caused more suffering all round.'[46] But for Indira, whose feelings were so evenly divided, there could be no easy solutions.

In a country where gossip travels like wild-fire, it is not surprising that there was much speculation about the future of Mrs. Gandhi's marriage. Many people confidently expected a divorce, blaming either Feroze's rumoured infidelity or Indira's lack of wifely consideration. When the Government introduced a Hindu Marriage Bill, for the first time permitting divorce among Hindus, some hostile Jan Sangh members went so far as to insinuate that its purpose was to free the Prime Minister's daughter from her *mesalliance*. There is no evidence, however, to suggest that either of the two parties directly concerned ever seriously considered divorce as a solution. The ties that bound them, like the barriers that kept them apart, were too complex and involved to admit of so simple an answer. Meanwhile, they both sought an outlet for their emotions in public life.

\*      \*      \*

# CHAPTER VI

# BEHIND THE THRONE

'LIFE DOES not run according to our desires or expectations,' Indira Gandhi wrote with some regret, 'and when India became free, I was catapulted into a new life and involved in new responsibilities which have grown considerably with the years. At first it was only a question of setting up a home for my father in New Delhi and coping with the social obligations of the Prime Minister's House. But gradually, circumstances and my own intense interest in the path which the country was trying to follow, drew me deeper into public affairs.'[1] Placed where she was, it would have been impossible for a person with even a modicum of political awareness to remain aloof from the complex and devious processes of lobbying and decision-making that are characteristic of Indian politics.

In a country where politics remain predominantly personal and factional, the decision-making process, for all its bureaucratic forms, was susceptible to the pressures of an infinite plurality of groups and individuals, representing various regional, linguistic, caste and communal interests and, more often than not, simple self-interest. At the centre of the tangled web of institutions and associations through which decisions were made, processed, and occasionally implemented, stood the Prime Minister. Unlike his British prototype, he was not merely the leader of the ruling party, responsible to Parliament and the party organisation. While the ruling party remained essentially a 'broad-bottom' coalition of local factions and pressure groups, welded together by a combination of self-interest and charismatic leadership, parliamentary government and joint Cabinet responsibility existed more in theory than in practice. Instead, the Indian political system relied for its stability on the existence of an undisputed leader who could bring to the office of Prime Minister many of the attributes of the American presidency and medieval Indian monarchy. In keeping with a cultural tradition in which the individual tends always to be greater than the organisation, the Prime Minister was a charismatic, All-India figure, deriving power and legitimacy as much from popular adulation as from his parliamentary majority. In a society which was traditionalist and semi-feudal at the core, dominated not by national issues but by the narrow particularism of local and caste affiliations, the Prime Minister's chief function was to draw together these diverse threads into a workable national consensus.

In Nehru, independent India had a charismatic leader whose popularity and pre-eminence, both in the Congress and in the country, remained unchallenged for over a decade, until the Sino-Indian War finally broke the spell. Nehru's conservative provincial lieutenants might discreetly shelve the more radical of his policy formulations—a fact to which the Prime Minister himself preferred to turn a blind eye—but his authority as undisputed leader in party and governmental affairs was never questioned when he chose to exercise it. Politicians, bureaucrats, industrialists, journalists and diplomats assembled at Teen Murti as at a princely *durbar*, jostling each other for *Panditji's* ear. Some wished to secure his support for their projects, others to complain about their rivals, or merely to know his mind so that they could be on the winning side.

For Nehru's daughter it was an exhaustive education in the subtle workings of the Indian parliamentary system. She had already been apprenticed in the politics of nationalist struggle; now she had a unique opportunity to study the more complex, if less inspiring, politics of governance. It was an education that any political tactician might envy; and Indira learnt quickly—and often better than her father—to assess people and situations, sifting the wheat from the chaff and the possible from the impractical. She did not long remain a neutral observer in the political dramas that were being enacted around her. With her lively interest in public affairs, her shrewd political insight and her strong emotional hold over her father, she had emerged by the middle 'fifties as a factor to be reckoned with in the political power structure. Michael Brecher, the most authoritative of Nehru's biographers, described her as the Mrs. Woodrow Wilson of India, scrutinising and controlling Nehru's schedule, his appointments and the papers put up to him.[2]

\*          \*          \*

Indira's position beside her father was reinforced by her alliance with the two men—themselves believed to be rivals—in whom he reposed at this time the greatest confidence and trust—M.O. Matthai, the Prime Minister's Principal Private Secretary, and Krishna Menon, Union Defence Minister and Nehru's most intimate friend. Matthai, an adventurer from Kerala, appeared on the political scene as suddenly as he was to vanish from it. Shortly before Independence, he is reported to have arrived at Anand Bhawan with few possessions other than a single-minded devotion to Nehru and a determination to serve him in any capacity. His rise was meteoric, and Nehru soon developed for him the uncritical affection to which he was so prone. At a time when the Prime Minister's Secretariat had not yet been established as a regular department, staffed by professional civil servants, Matthai at his zenith acted as a de facto Deputy Prime Minister, managing all the Prime Minister's most confidential files and correspondence, influencing his decisions and conveying his instructions. His favour was assiduously courted even by top Cabinet ministers, and, after Nehru himself, he became the most sought after man in the capital, a position which appears to have gone to his head and undermined his better judgement. Matthai is believed to have consistently pushed Indira Gandhi into the limelight, encouraging her to play a more active political role. He was to find, however, that she was nobody's puppet. When serious allegations of corruption were made against Matthai—and publicised among others by Feroze Gandhi—Indira, with sound political sense, did not hesitate to dissociate herself from him and is believed to have persuaded her father to relieve him of his duties. It was a practical and unemotional approach which would be characteristic of her future political relationships and which contrasted strongly with her father's more sentimental and easy-going nature.

Indira's relationship with Krishna Menon, though it was to end on a similar note, was on a different plane. Both she and her husband had been taken under Menon's wing during their student days in England, and he had since continued to take an avuncular interest in them, reportedly mediating in their marital differences. When he returned from his posting in London as independent India's first High Commissioner, Krishna Menon moved into Teen Murti House as Nehru's guest. Indira's reactions are not known: but when Nehru appointed Krishna Menon Defence Minister, she is believed to have insisted that it would be improper for a Cabinet minister to live with the Prime Minister. A compromise was effected and Krishna Menon moved to an independent house across the road from Teen Murti, where he continued to be a daily visitor. If this report is accurate, it was another display of political common sense on Indira's part. Krishna Menon, owing partly to his pro-Communist orientation, was considered something of an upstart and an outsider in orthodox Congress circles, and there had been a good deal of jealousy at his elevation to the Cabinet. Indira may well have felt that her father was demonstrating his partiality in too marked and public a fashion.

Krishna Menon, for all his brilliance and innate generosity, was a man of many idiosyncrasies, and an episode recorded by Marie Seton indicates that Indira was occasionally irritated by them and thought he was being boorish. In September 1957, he persuaded her, against her own inclination, to attend an official dinner that he was giving in honour of a visiting British official. Having got her there, he left it to her to entertain his official guests, by whom she was thoroughly bored, while he himself spent the evening in a huddle with his own intimate coterie. Indira Gandhi, we are told, was furious.

Her relations with Krishna Menon continued to have their ups and downs in the following years. She is reported to have told a woman journalist early in 1960 that she had stopped discussing Krishna Menon with her father 'because he won't listen to me on that man.'[3] By the end of the year, however, a reconciliation is believed to have taken place. When Indira accompanied Nehru to the United States in November 1961, during the Sino-Indian confrontation, she is reported to have loyally defended Krishna Menon against American criticism, even when it came from as high a source as President Kennedy. Krishna Menon, for his part, staunchly and consistently supported Indira's participation in politics and was always canvassing support for her from the Congress Left.

*          *          *

Although there was a tendency to regard Indira Gandhi as her father's political shadow during these earlier years, this was by no means the case. Nehru had no doubt been the main formative influence on her political thinking; but their views were far from identical and their differences were often hotly debated. According to Chelapathi Rau, who witnessed some of these arguments, 'they were the freest and fairest of exchanges with a touch of humour'.[4] While Indira was tactful enough to maintain friendly relations with the Old Guard of the Congress, she also had close contacts through her husband with members of the Congress Socialist Forum or 'Ginger Group', who were strongly critical of the conservative party 'bosses' and of Nehru's leniency towards them. Mrs. Gandhi, though never a member of the Socialist Forum, is believed to have sympathised with some of its objectives, and in January 1959 she is reported to have joined her husband in signing a manifesto of the Ginger Group which attacked the party leadership for not implementing socialist policies, 'It is impossible for people with definite views not to disagree.' Indira Gandhi later commented, 'I naturally disagreed with my father on many things, although this was more marked when I was younger. Later we came much closer together and he depended a great deal on me, and I think he valued my judgement on people and affairs.'[5]

Asked whether her role as her father's political companion and heir would have been easier had she been his son and not his daughter, Mrs. Gandhi admitted: 'I think there would probably have been more difficulties, because ... I could not really have remained with him and helped him in the way that I have. I would have had to make a living... That would have created an entirely new situation. I think the political world also would have been much more sensitive to the situation and wary of it.'6

Whether or not Nehru deliberately groomed his daughter as his political heir is a question which has been long debated, but which must remain unanswered in the absence of more authoritative evidence. He was certainly not averse to the idea, and Mrs. Gandhi's position as his daughter provided her with unique opportunities and advantages. For one thing, it freed her from the political limitations imposed on her sex by Indian tradition. While a number of Indian women have secured seats in legis-latures and other political offices, the overwhelming majority have risen not by their own initiative or merit, but through male patronage, the price of which has been their own independence, and often self-respect. While Nehru's position ensured for his daughter a high status in the political world, and protected her from the more embarrassing and humiliating pressures experienced by other women politicians, it did not, as far as one can see, compromise her independence of thought or action; for Nehru was nothing if not tolerant of dissent, especially when it came from his daughter, and was also a genuine believer in the equality of the sexes. At the same time, Mrs. Gandhi's position as Nehru's official hostess and companion made it appear only natural, even to critical observers, that her assistance should extend to his political obligations. While India's traditionalist masses saw and admired her as a model daughter doing her duty by an ageing and widowed father, educated public opinion, though more cynical, did not react with the vehement charges of dynasticism and nepotism that similar prominence given to a male heir would certainly have provoked. In these circumstances, Indira Gandhi could achieve the apparently im-possible—she could remain inconspicuously but permanently in the public eye without attracting adverse comment, and she could build, unobtrusively but consistently, a national image and standing for herself in Indian politics without compromising her independence as a woman.

This is not to suggest that it was smooth sailing all the way. The fact that Indira's political influence was both intangible and all-pervasive could be a disadvantage when critics of the Government, who were unwilling to attack the Prime Minister directly, found in his daughter a convenient whipping-boy and visited on her the more controversial decisions of her father. In such instances, Indira's responsibility was greatly exaggerated, for Nehru as Prime Minister was subject to many other pressures and influences and had, in any case, a mind of his own. When Sheikh Abdullah, 'The Lion of Kashmir', was arrested for the second time early in 1958, an ardent female champion of Kashmiri self-determination, who was also an old friend of the Nehrus, is reported to have arrived at Teen Murti House hysterical with anger. Bursting in on Indira, who lay ill in bed, she demanded justice for the Sheikh. Calling Nehru's daughter the country's evil genius, she slapped her across the face and stormed out of the house, while the Prime Minister's staff stood by in stunned horror. Whatever Indira's private feelings, she reacted with admirable dignity and magnanimity. No action was taken against the hot-tempered visitor, and she continued to be allowed free access to Teen Murti House.

*          *          *

In February 1955 Indira Gandhi made her debut on the national political scene as a member of the Congress Working Committee, the party's high-powered national executive. She herself describes the event as 'unexciting'. She was in bed with 'flu when U.N. Dhebar, the Congress President, and Lal Bahadur Shastri came to ask if they could nominate her as a member. 'I came out all wrapped up in woollies,' Mrs. Gandhi told the author. 'They insisted. I cannot say I resisted too much.'7

It was a post for which she was psychologically and politically well prepared. 'I had been working for the Party all along,' she recalls, 'except for a very few years—three or four—when my children were very little.'8 Her social welfare activities must also have impressed upon her that social and charitable work, however well-intended, could not of itself solve monumental social and economic problems without political action.

As far back as 1945, Govind Ballabh Pant, the U.P. Congress leader, had asked Indira to stand for election to the provincial legislature and had even appealed to Gandhi to persuade her to agree. But she had firmly rejected this and subsequent proposals that she should be in Parliament, on the ground that it would not be proper in view of her father's position. Legislatures, in any case, were not her milieu. Still painfully shy of public speaking, she was at her best with small groups of Congress workers; and it was to work in the party organisation that she applied herself. Though eschewing the glamour and publicity of parliamentary oratory, her work at the grass-roots level, aided by the Nehru charisma, would win her a substantial following among the Party's rank and file.

India's first general election in 1951 has been described as a one-man affair, with Nehru as the star performer of the Congress campaign. His daughter, while herself refusing to contest, canvassed widely for the party and often filled in for Nehru. Later she was active in the Congress election campaigns in 1957 and 1962. Initially her audiences were small, but her mass appeal steadily increased. Her perseverance, no doubt, had much to do with her success. She recalls with amusement a remote village in the Punjab where she insisted on making a pre-dawn election speech:

'It was a cold and misty January morning with a sharp breeze and at 6 a.m. still quite dark. Not a soul was in sight. All doors and windows seemed to be tightly secured. However, there was a *takhat* (platform) and a microphone and some *durries* (carpets), wet with the heavy dew. Hansrajji* felt that we had done our duty by coming and we could now drive on to the regular programme with a clear conscience. However, much to his embarrassment, I insisted on giving a speech whether there was anybody to listen or not. Almost with my first word, windows started banging open and tousled heads appeared. Immediately afterwards the entire village poured out from the warmth of their houses, wrapped in blankets and *razais* (quilts), some with *dattun*** sticks and some with tumblers of steaming tea... Raizadaji remembered this as the most extraordinary meeting he had witnessed in his long life and spoke of it every time we met thereafter.'9

When she was not electioneering, Indira Gandhi was active in the Women's Department of the All India Congress Committee, working so hard that Nehru wrote to the Secretary of the Women's Department, expressing concern about his daughter's health and asking her to reduce the burden. Unlike her mother, Indira was never a feminist leader. Whereas Kamala Nehru had passionately urged women to assert their equality and revolt against traditional restraints, Indira Gandhi exhorted them to make small savings, to feed their children on a balanced diet, and to grow more vegetables in their gardens. Secure in her own status as an educated and emancipated young woman, she appears to have felt little compulsion to take up arms in the cause of female emancipation in general. Her attitude to women's problems was conventional, and she was fond of citing to them the example of Sita, the archetypal symbol of feminine self-sacrifice and, by any modern feminist standards, the victim of male chauvinism. This approach, surprising in the daughter of Kamala Nehru, might well have been the result of Mrs. Gandhi's consistent reluctance to be identified with any particular group or sectional interest and of her desire to make her appeal as wide and national as possible.

The existence of a separate women's wing has been found in most political parties—and the Congress is no exception—to restrict the rise of women to positions of party leadership, siphoning them instead into those channels of constructive work with which their male colleagues prefer not to be burdened. Indira Gandhi, however, was no ordinary

*Raizada Hansraj, a senior Punjab Congressman.
**The bark of a tree, used to brush teeth.

Congress worker, and her unique position ensured that the Women's Department of the A.I.C.C. would not be her political graveyard. She was soon prominent in the higher echelons of party leadership: in 1957 she topped the list—leaving even Nehru far behind—in elections to the Congress Central Election Committee, which was to scrutinise applications for party nomination in the impending general election; and in February 1958 she took her father's place as a member of the powerful Congress Parliamentary Board.

At the same time, she did not scorn less prestigious offices when she felt she could be useful. In September 1956 she took on the Presidentship of the faction-ridden Allahabad Congress Committee, hoping to restore Congress unity in her home-town, only to resign it three months later when she found that factionalism persisted. She also served as President of the All India Youth Congress and as a member of the Party's sub-committees on Economic Planning, Small Savings and Congress Workers' Training. Occasionally, she spoke in various party forums on uncontroversial subjects such as the role of women and youth in constructive work, the need for national integration, and child welfare. In January 1958 she was an active participant at the annual session of the Party, where she presided over the Congress Women's Convention and made a speech in the Congress plenary session, strongly backing the Algerian freedom-fighters and condemning French atrocities.

Though she avoided controversy and was tactful and considerate with political colleagues, she was, even at this stage, a stern disciplinarian when people failed to conform to her own standards of efficiency and punctuality. The long-winded and bombastic verbal perorations of her elders appear to have bored and irritated her, and she did not hesitate to cut them short, even when the offender happened to be her father. At the Nagpur Congress session in January 1959, Mrs. Gandhi allowed Nehru exactly five minutes to address a women's meeting over which she was presiding. 'Your leader just told me,' he confided to his audience, 'that I should speak for only five minutes, because she was afraid that I might go on speaking and take all the time. It is quite correct—I often speak a lot.'[10] Having conceded this, he proceeded nonetheless to exceed his time by another five minutes.

\*       \*       \*

In 1959, at a party meeting presided over by his daughter as President of the Indian National Congress, Nehru humorously observed that at first Indira Gandhi had been his friend and adviser, then she had become his companion, and now she was his leader. How this came to be is described in two conflicting reports.

According to Mrs. Gandhi's own account, publicly corroborated by Nehru, she did not covet the post of party president, nor did her father have anything to do with her election to it. 'I was terrified,' she has told a British interviewer. 'I was really scared stiff, and I am sure my father didn't like it.' The proposal, she said, was put to her by G.B. Pant, then Union Home Minister, in January 1959, and she replied at once that it would depend on her father's reaction. 'It has nothing to do with your father,' Pant told her. 'It is for you to decide.' Her father, apparently, gave her the same reply, 'but I thought I saw disapproval in his expression.' After much persuasion, she gave her consent, but soon had second thoughts and told U.N. Dhebar, the outgoing President, that she had changed her mind. She recalls: 'He said the one thing which he knew. . . would have effect. . . : "All the newspapers are saying that you can't do it. Now, are you going to allow them to get away with this?" I said: "All right".'[11]

According to the rival version, also widely supported by people involved, Nehru pulled the strings from behind the scenes, as his own father had done for him in 1929. At a special meeting of the Congress Working Committee, the Prime Minister is said to have brushed aside every other name proposed, while dropping the members broad hints that the Party needed a young person for a change, possibly even a woman. Finally, A.S. Raju took the cue and suggested Indira Gandhi. 'What a good idea!' the Prime Minister is said to have exclaimed. 'I'm surprised we didn't think of it earlier'. The proposal was at once taken up by Dhebar and most of the other members, despite opposition from those who favoured the claims of Nijalingappa, the Mysore Chief Minister, who had been tipped for the post. According to a leading Indian journalist, Pant, far from favouring Mrs. Gandhi's nomination, opposed it on the ground that her health was too fragile, an argument which was supported by other members until Nehru interrupted to say that his daughter was healthy enough and, indeed, 'healthier than some of the members present.'[12]

In the absence of documentary evidence, it is impossible to pronounce judgement upon these two accounts which contradict each other in almost every particular. One thing is certain, that however much Nehru may have wished to make his daughter Congress President, even he could not have forced her on the Party had she not already built a wide enough political base for herself. And even if one allows for the usual amount of sychophancy, Indira Gandhi's nomination was well received by the Party's rank and file and by public opinion at large, though it naturally disappointed rival contenders.

Nehru conceded at a press interview: 'Normally speaking, it is not a good thing for my daughter to come in as Congress President when I am Prime Minister.'[13] He appears, nonetheless, to have been proud

of her and paid her a handsome tribute at a meeting of the Congress
Parliamentary Party soon after her election:

'It is superfluous for me to say that Indira is my daughter and that
I have love for her. I am proud of her good nature, proud of her energy
and work, and proud of her integrity and truthfulness. What she has
inherited from me I do not know. Maybe she has inherited these
qualities from her mother.'[14]

At forty-one, Indira Gandhi was not the youngest president in Congress
history—both her father and Subhas Chandra Bose had been younger
when they assumed that office—but she was certainly well below the
average age. She was the fourth woman, and the third member of the
Nehru family in three successive generations, to occupy the post. In
February 1959 Dhebar formally installed her as his successor at a function
in New Delhi attended by the Prime Minister and other Congress leaders.
According to one of her cousins, Mrs. Gandhi, though nervous at having
to make a speech, was happy and proud. Perhaps her thoughts travelled
back three decades to the Lahore Congress, when she had watched with
excitement as her grandfather handed over the Congress presidency
to her father. In a brief and disarmingly simple speech, she asked the
Party to treat her as an ordinary worker, quoting amid laughter some
lines from a Hindi song:

'We are the women of India,
Don't think us flower-maidens,
We are the sparks in the fire.'[15]

*          *          *

The new President's youth and sex, her Leftist image and her special
access to the Prime Minister aroused optimism that a new wind was
blowing through the Congress corridors and would sweep out at last
the Tammany Hall 'bossism' of the Party's conservative, septuagenarian
leaders. Through no fault of Mrs. Gandhi's, however, 1959 would mark
no historic advance such as that of 1929, when Nehru as the new President
had proclaimed the Congress objective of complete independence.
The office of Congress President had been considerably devalued since
Independence, owing to the inevitable shift in the political centre of
gravity from the organisational to the legislative wing of the Party.
Since Purshottamdas Tandon's abortive attempt in 1951 to assert the
independence of the Congress presidency, the party president, once
the chief executive of the nationalist movement, had been no more
than the Prime Minister's deputy in party affairs. Even more significant
was the fact that the Congress President was powerless without the

cooperation of the provincial Congress bosses, who ultimately controlled the Party machinery.

The foremost challenge to Mrs. Gandhi's abilities as Congress President was the implementation of the controversial resolution on co-operative farming adopted by the recent Nagpur Congress, which had laid down joint co-operative farming as the future model of Indian agriculture. The operative part of the resolution called on State Governments to impose ceilings on agricultural holdings, abolish all intermediaries, and redistribute the land thus acquired to co-operatives of landless labourers. Though in retrospect the scheme might appear far from revolutionary, large landed interests in the Congress and in Opposition attacked it as a back-door attempt at collectivisation. If the Nagpur resolution was not to be filed and forgotten like so many other socialistic resolutions passed by the Congress, it was obvious that the Party would have to break with its old methods of functioning, start building trained and ideologically committed cadres and welcome the assistance of other progressive forces. This the Party leadership was clearly not willing to do. A.S. Raju, one of the General Secretaries of the Congress, said publicly that the party's High Command had backed Mrs. Gandhi for Congress President because it wanted to check 'the drift towards rightist trends of thought.'[16] Such rhetoric notwithstanding, the High Command's commitment to socialism was far from sincere, and in the course of the next few months, Indira Gandhi, like her father before her, learned to make her compromises.

Her own approach to the problems of party organisation was energetic, practical and down to earth. At her first press conference, she said: 'The nation is in a hurry and we can't afford to lose time. My complaint against the Congress is that it isn't going as fast as the people are advancing. And that can be fatal for a political organisation.'[17] Questioned by a Left-wing weekly as to how she proposed to deal with factionalism in the Congress and galvanise provincial Congress units into implementing national policies, she spoke of allotting specific targets to individual party members who would be held accountable, instead of entrusting vague and pretentious objectives to a Provincial Congress Committee as a whole. She also agreed on the need for joint work for common objectives by Congressmen and members of other like-minded parties. While ruling out any co-operation with the semi-fascist Jana Sangh, she expressed her willingness to co-operate with the Communist Party in the task of national reconstruction, even though its 'outlook and methods,' she said, were 'different' from those of the Congress. She made it clear, however, that these were her personal views and, as far as one can see, they remained so.

Though Mrs. Gandhi was unable to canvass much support for her ideas in the party, she does appear to have tried. In March 1959, she sternly told a Conference of Provincial Congress Committee Presidents and Secretaries:

'It must be made clear that the persons who do not see eye to eye with the objectives of the Congress and its economic programme and are not in a mood to keep pace with the progressive section, who are determined to work for the establishment of democratic socialism, should have no place in the organisation. We are at the parting of ways and the Congress would certainly not weaken itself by dissociating from them.'[18]

A month later, she appealed in a circular letter to Congress M.P.s:

'The task of building up a powerful cooperative movement must be taken in hand immediately... Though there have been protests from some vested interests against co-operatives and co-operative farming, it is good to note that the country as a whole has accepted our policy. It is now the duty of every Congressman, and more so of Congress legislators, to go down into the villages and to spread the message of the efficacy and usefulness of the co-operative way.'[19]

Recognising the necessity for trained cadres to implement the Nagpur resolution, the new President made a modest beginning by opening a small training centre for Congress workers at Madras; but the scheme being voluntary, it was not surprising that the response was negligible. She also attempted as far as she could to infuse younger blood into the party leadership and to increase the participation of women, setting up a 21-member women's advisory committee for this purpose. To bring Congressmen into closer contact with the masses, she laid great stress on *padayatras* (walking-tours), herself setting a strenuous example.

During her first three months as Congress President, Mrs. Gandhi travelled continuously and extensively, visiting almost every province in the country. Her meetings attracted an unusually large number of women and youth, and her speeches invariably struck a radical note. In Kanpur, for instance, she told her audience that she was in the Congress, not because of her family associations, but because it was socialist, and warned that the criterion for the selection of party candidates in the next general election would be present work, not past service to the nationalist movement. But when outsiders criticised the Congress, she reacted with fierce party loyalty. To a Bombay press reporter who urged the reduction of ministers' salaries and cited Mahatma Gandhi's views on the subject, she replied angrily: 'Even Gandhiji's living was not so simple and cheap as is commonly believed. Several times he stayed with us, and I could not form the impression that his living was economical.' She added with surprising naiveté: 'Since the ministers in India work harder than their counterparts in the rest of the world, their present salaries are quite justifiable.'[20]

On 15 August, in her Independence Day message as Congress President, Indira Gandhi, drawing one of her favourite analogies, told the nation: 'In mountaineering, the higher one climbs, the more hazardous the journey and the narrower and steeper the trail. So it is in the life of a nation. As our aims become more clearly defined, our path becomes more difficult. Progressive measures knock against vested interests and all kinds of conflicts arise. This should not dishearten us or force us to give up the climb...'[21] She herself appears to have found the going rough by this time. The levers of power remained firmly in the hands of the party bosses and she, after all, was their nominee. There was little she could do to alter this state of affairs with the limited time and resources at her command. And so the Congress, for all her radical exhortations, refused to climb the slope, and the Nagpur resolution, like so many others, quietly lapsed.

While unable to alter significantly the party's structure or approach, Mrs. Gandhi did manage, for all her inexperience and shyness, to make her mark on the party meetings over which she presided. She was a strict chairman, keeping speakers to the point and not allowing them to exceed their time. In May 1959, presiding for the first time over the All India Congress Committee, she emphasised in her preliminary remarks the need for swift implementation of the Nagpur resolution. 'The more it is delayed,' she warned, 'the more difficult it will become to implement it.'[22] Then, getting down to brass tacks, she asked for immediate volunteers for the Madras training centre. When some members tried to turn the ensuing debate into a discussion on the merits of co-operative farming and the need for training workers, she interrupted repeatedly and forcefully, asking them to confine themselves to the immediate issue—the raising of volunteers. But it was all water off a duck's back, and her appeal for a hundred volunteers brought in only six names—an indication of the strength of the landlord class in the Congress and of the indifference and even hostility in the party to the resolution it had passed with so much flourish scarcely four months back.

When Mrs. Gandhi presided over the next A.I.C.C. session in September, a right-wing weekly described the attitude of the members as being 'very much like the curiosity of old boys in a freshly-appointed school-mistress.' But the mistress of the Congress house was determined not to be bullied and told recalcitrant and unruly members: 'If you don't like it, you can leave your positions and go out.' Her scolding is reported to have provoked one incorrigible delegate to rise and ask her: 'Who are you to tell us to get out of the Congress? Does the Congress belong to you or to your father?'[23]

Her duties as Congress President appear to have given Mrs. Gandhi increasing self-confidence, and the shy and retiring young hostess of Teen Murti was developing rapidly into an assertive and imperious woman who could no longer be dismissed or ignored with impunity. This, of course, was not to the liking of some Congressmen, who complained that power was going to her head and that her manner was arrogant and high-handed. The methods and outlook of most Congress faction-leaders, however, were devious and obstructive enough to infuriate any younger and more committed person; and Indira Gandhi can scarcely be blamed for succumbing occasionally to her impatience and irritation.

*        *        *

One reason, perhaps, why Mrs. Gandhi was unable to make a greater impact on the party organisation was her pre-occupation with the Kerala crisis, which deflected her energies from more real tasks. In 1957 the State of Kerala—which had a record for both the highest literacy and the greatest poverty and exploitation in the country—had elected a Communist Government to power, the first non-Congress government in post-Independence India and the only Communist government in the world to achieve power through parliamentary elections. It was a unique experiment and many observers expected great things of it. The Communists' determination, however, to carry through certain moderate and essential reforms, which were long overdue, soon brought them into conflict with strongly entrenched conservative forces. The Communist policy of promoting Untouchables and other low castes aroused the ire of privileged caste groups, while the Kerala Agrarian Relations Act encroached upon the vested interests of the landlord class. Matters came to a head when the Kerala Education Act sought to regulate the notoriously corrupt private management of educational institutions, thereby infuriating various religious endowments, and especially the wealthy and powerful Catholic Church. By the beginning of 1959, all these disgruntled elements were banding together in a united front that aimed at ousting the Communist Ministry. The Kerala Congress, anxious to return to power, was straining at the leash for permission from the Central leadership to join this unholy alliance, even though the previous Congress Ministry had attempted a similar educational reform and the Communist land reforms were in line with official Congress policy.

In April 1959, the new Congress President visited Kerala with instructions from her father to study the situation and report back to him. The Kerala Communists, in an open letter to Mrs. Gandhi, welcomed her to the State and appealed to her not to be misled by opportunistic local Congressmen. Referring to the agitation of various communal organisations, with indirect Congress backing, against the Government's agrarian and educational legislation, it asked whether 'the policy of isolating and annihilating the Communist Party was the aim of the Congress throughout India.' The letter concluded: 'We hope that you will seriously consider the repercussions such an agitation, challenging a law passed by the legislature, by a section of the people affected by the law, will have throughout India. For it will mean that any sectional interest can challenge and try to defeat any progressive legislative measure by unlawful, threatening methods.'[24]

In view of Mrs. Gandhi's reputation as a Left-winger and her recent statements regarding possible co-operation with the Communists, she might reasonably have been expected to moderate the tactics of the Kerala Congress. But considerations of party loyalty appear instead to have prevailed with her. In a strongly worded reply to the Communist letter, she defended the Kerala Congress and attacked the Communists along a wider front for 'fomenting strikes and backing demands which have no justification' in other parts of the country. She even questioned the patriotism of the Indian Communist Party, saying: 'China is trying to draw India into the cold war. But not one Communist voice is heard that if China starts a war against us, the Communists would be for India.'[25]

Nehru is believed to have been unhappy about the participation of the Congress in the Kerala agitation; but his daughter is reported to have advised him that withdrawal from the agitation would mean the end of the Congress in Kerala. Following her return to Delhi, she made public statements to the effect that she saw nothing wrong with the Opposition in Kerala agitating against the Government's agrarian and educational legislation. In a press interview on the eve of the A.I.C.C. session, she defended the Congress coalition with the Ganatantra Parishad—a party of princes and big landlords—in Orissa, but complained that 'one real difficulty in collaborating with the Communists is that their approach is much too rigid and their insistence is always on all joint efforts being planned to fit into the Communist scheme of things.'[26] A month later, at a public meeting in Madras, she went so far as to say: 'I personally feel that the major danger for India is from Communism. Educated people in India realise this danger.'[27]

This militant anti-communism, contrasting so strongly with her earlier and later postures, can only be explained by Indira Gandhi's essentially pragmatic political outlook. Politics for her would always be the art of the possible. At a time of Sino-Indian tension, the Indian Communists were convenient whipping-boys and Congressmen were keen to cash in and retrieve the fortunes of their own party in Kerala. The Congress President's impotence when opposed by the party bosses has already been noted. Mrs. Gandhi might well have felt that, rather than plunge into an unequal struggle with them and expose herself to the charge of disloyalty to her own party, she would do better to swim with the tide and make the best of a bad job. She may also—though there is no evidence for this—have been encouraged by hints of the impending split in the Communist movement itself, between the Peking-oriented Left Communists, led by E.M.S. Nambudripad, Chief Minister of Kerala, and the pro-Moscow Right Communists, who had always been closer to the Congress Left.

At the beginning of June, direct action in Kerala began when the Congress High Command authorised the Kerala Congress to launch 'a peaceful, non-violent and constitutional movement' against the Communist Government. But the movement did not long remain peaceful. Ignoring the advice of Nehru and his daughter, the local Congress joined with the Catholic Church and Mannath Padmanabhan, the Nair leader, in violent picketing and other forms of intimidation, which included attempts to occupy Government offices by force. Despite the Kerala Government's restrained handling of the situation, the agitation soon became violent and civil war in Kerala seemed a distinct possibility.

Amid reports of violent incidents, for which its own followers and their communal allies were responsible, the Central Congress leadership began to demand presidential intervention in Kerala on the ground of a break-down of law and order. On 25 July, after talks with Rajendra Prasad, President of the Republic, Mrs. Gandhi told the press: 'Central action in Kerala is already long overdue... If the Constitution has no remedy for the people of Kerala, the Constitution should be amended.'[28] Under fire, she later retracted this plea for changing the Constitution and admitted that she had expressed herself badly. Nehru, unlike his daughter, is believed to have had reservations about the legitimacy and merits of such drastic action; but, as with the Sino-Indian border dispute, he gave in to the 'hawks'.

On 31 July, the President of India issued a proclamation dismissing the Communist Government of Kerala and bringing the province temporarily under Central rule. A popular and democratically elected State government had thus been ousted by the Central Government for failure to cope with a violent and unconstitutional agitation waged by the Centre's own followers and their motley allies. This Alice-in-Wonderland drama was not a healthy precedent for Indian democracy, and it alarmed many non-Communists, including members of the Congress Left. At a meeting of the Congress Parliamentary Party on 2 August, Feroze Gandhi, the Congress President's husband, emerged as the strongest critic of the leadership for 'getting mixed up' with communalists, casteists and other vested interests in Kerala.

The dismissal of the Kerala Government was followed by political manoeuvring for a united front against the Communists in the fresh elections that were due to be held in the province. Mrs. Gandhi took a leading part in these negotiations, euphemistically describing the front as an 'understanding', not an alliance. On 8 December, she inaugurated the united front's election campaign, and she must have been pleased when the Congress strategy paid off in the elections of February 1960. The Communists polled the highest percentage of votes—44 per cent as against 35 per cent in the 1957 elections, an index of their increased popularity with the electorate. The Congress vote, on the other hand, declined from 37 per cent in 1957 to 34 per cent in 1960—10 per cent less than that of the Communists. Nevertheless, owing to the vagaries of the 'Anglo-Saxon' electoral system, the Congress-led united front won a comfortable majority in the legislature and formed a coalition government.

*       *       *

Possibly the most constructive feature of Mrs. Gandhi's term as Congress President was the strong emphasis she placed on international affairs, and especially on Congress solidarity with anti-colonial movements in other countries. She set up a National Committee for Algeria to mobilise support for the Algerian freedom struggle and was one of the founders and Patron-in-Chief of the Indian Council for Africa, a non-official organisation which aimed at closer contacts with African Nationalists. It was largely owing to her initiative that the Congress Working Committee passed a resolution condemning racialism in South Africa and British Nyasaland and calling on Indian settlers in Africa to support the demands of the African peoples.

The most pressing foreign policy issue at this time was that of relations with China. By 1959 the 'Rape of Tibet'—as many Indians called it— followed by the escalation of a relatively trival border dispute, had put an end to Sino-Indian amity and created an atmosphere of extreme jingoism that threatened to wreck Nehru's foreign policy. Mrs. Gandhi's militant opposition to the Kerala Communists did not colour her better judgement on Sino-Indian relations. Addressing the A.I.C.C. in May 1959, she expressed sympathy for the Tibetan people and welcomed the granting of asylum to the Dalai Lama; but she also reiterated India's desire for friendly relations with China. She was by no means unmoved at the plight of the Tibetans and was instrumental in setting up an all-party Central Relief Committee for Tibetan refugees; but at the same time, she stated publicly that Tibet was China's internal affair and that

there was nothing India could do by way of intervention. At the next
A.I.C.C. meeting in September, she referred again to Sino-Indian
relations and counselled Congressmen 'to maintain a dignified and
decorous attitude, instead of indulging in vituperative language.'[29]

The right-wing opposition and its fellow-travellers in the Congress
had by this time seized upon Nehru's China policy as a popular stick
with which to beat the Government and goad it into extreme and, as
later developments showed, disastrous action. Aware of this danger,
Mrs. Gandhi sprang to her father's defence. She wrote in November
1959 to Provincial and District Congress Committee Presidents.

'...we must realise that strength lies, not in anger or excitement,
but in cool thinking and firm action, and above all in unity... It
is strange that when even the leading newspapers of England and
America are praising our Prime Minister for his firm stand as well as
his restraint, some of our own people should be so hysterically critical of
our foreign policy... Public opinion must be mobilised towards a
positive and unified effort to strengthen the hands of the Prime Minister
who has already appealed to the nation to be prepared but calm.'[30]

To an American journalist, she spoke more freely, revealing a
statesman-like insight that recent research has vindicated: 'I think
Chinese policy is partly motivated by their desire to consolidate Tibet
and the frontier with India. They strongly disapprove of our giving
sanctuary to the Dalai Lama. The Chinese call us American satellites...
I think the Chinese felt the need to consolidate their hold on the border
since we were politically "unreliable".'[32]

*           *           *

It was a strenuous year for Mrs. Gandhi, and towards the end the
strain seems to have told on her health and she developed an acutely
painful kidney ailment. Nevertheless, she had new problems to face.
In September 1959, following widespread rioting, the Congress High
Command decided to reopen the question of the bifurcation of bi-lingual
Bombay State into its Gujerati and Marathi-speaking areas. Mrs.
Gandhi was commissioned by the Congress Working Committee to tour
the State and report back after consulting local party committees.

Long before Independence, the Congress had committed itself to the
principle of linguistic provinces, in place of the existing administrative
units created by the haphazard processes of British annexation. The
nationalist movement had thus been able to mobilise the support of
various linguistic and regional pressure groups; but after Independence
the Congress in power had had second thoughts, fearing that the linguistic
reorganisation of States might encourage fissiparous tendencies. The

Union Government had, however, already been compelled under popular pressure to apply the linguistic principle in reorganising the old Madras Presidency and the princely state of Hyderabad. It was on the cards that Bombay, sooner or later, would have to follow suit.

While Nehru continued to hope that it might yet be possible to preserve Bombay as a composite, bi-lingual province, his daughter, after a hectic six-day tour of the Marathi-speaking areas—in the course of which she addressed no less than a hundred and fifty meetings—returned convinced that the Congress would seriously jeopardise its political future unless it conceded the linguistic demand, which was undoubtedly popular and had the support of the entire Opposition. She appointed a high-powered committee to report on the matter and, when it endorsed her view, the Congress Working Committee adopted a resolution authorising the partition of Bombay. Some months later, after Parliament had passed the necessary legislation, Sanjiva Reddy, Mrs. Gandhi's successor as Congress President, confirmed that she had been 'mainly responsible for bringing about a happy understanding between the different elements, so that the new States of Gujerat and Maharashtra could be ushered in an atmosphere of harmony.'[32]

When the Congress met for its annual session in January 1960, Indira Gandhi, ill and exhausted, had decided to stand down from the presidency, instead of completing the normal two-year term. 'There is no dearth of factionalism and petty group quarrels,' she told the A.I.C.C. in her valedictory address. 'It is therefore well that we don't get swept away either by our complacency at our very real achievements or despair at the criticism levelled against us by the Press or the Opposition.' She graciously assured the members: 'For me personally this year's work has been sometimes exhilarating, sometimes exasperating, but always interesting.'[33] Asked at a press interview about her plans for the immediate future, she replied: 'Hospitalisation'.[34]

\*     \*     \*

While his wife had been busy grappling with the problems of being a party leader, Feroze Gandhi had been acquiring a reputation as a political giant-killer with an infallible nose for corruption and mal-administration in high places. In December 1957 he had exposed in Parliament the collusive dealings of high officials in the State-owned Life Insurance Corporation with Mundhra, a private businessmen, which, Feroze alleged, had amounted to a conspiracy to defraud the policy-holders. 'I am a champion of the public sector,' he had told Parliament in a blistering attack on the L.I.C. management. 'I was one of those persons who championed life insurance nationalisation. But I am not ashamed to face an inquiry. I would like the public, the Government and members of Parliament to know that if in the public sector such a thing happens, we are prepared to face an inquiry and get to the bottom of it.'[35] The Mundhra Affair had soon mushroomed into a major public scandal, leading to a public judicial inquiry and eventually to the resignation of T.T. Krishnamachari, Nehru's able Finance Minister and close confidant. Feroze, who had managed to collect most of the evidence from secret Government files and was the driving force throughout, had emerged as something of a popular hero.

His role in the Mundhra Affair cannot, however, have increased his popularity at Teen Murti House. Perhaps Mrs. Gandhi had her irrepressible husband, among others, in mind when she told the A.I.C.C. in May 1959:

> 'There is a tendency on the part of Congressmen to make references to their own lapses and indulge in self-criticism in public time and again. Carried to excess, this practice, however, creates a lot of misunderstanding and confuses the public mind. A general impression is created that the evils of corruption and degeneration are widespread and deep-seated among Congressmen... It does harm rather than good to the organisation. Though Congressmen are expected to analyse their own weaknesses, this should not be carried too far.'[36]

Feroze Gandhi seems to have recognised the impropriety of living under the Prime Minister's roof while making scathing public attacks on the inner workings of a Government department. In 1958 he moved to his own house, though he is reported to have maintained friendly contacts with the Nehrus and often joined them for meals at Teen Murti.

Feroze's interests were by no means confined to politics, and he is reputed to have been a man of robust and versatile talent, though he lacked the sophistication of the Nehrus. He was particularly adept at various manual crafts, such as carpentry, lacquer-work, printing and gardening. He was also a devoted father, and it is from him that his sons are believed to have derived their interest in machines and technology. Living alone, however, he over-worked himself relentlessly, and the result was a heart attack in 1959. His illness appears to have effected a reconciliation with his wife, who nursed him conscientiously, despite her heavy schedule as Congress President. Together they snatched a month in Kashmir—the scene of their honeymoon—while Feroze convalesced.

In September 1960, after mediating successfully in a strike of Central Government employees, Feroze Gandhi had his second and final stroke. With characteristic self-neglect, he ignored the symptoms for two days, and then, though in great pain, drove himself to the hospital where he finally collapsed. Indira was in Kerala, presiding over a women's convention. It had been a successful visit, and the flight back to Delhi found her in an elated mood. According to one source, however, the thought crossed her mind that whenever she had felt so pleased with the world, something calamitous had always occurred to blight her happiness. When the plane landed in Delhi at eleven at night, she was met by an emissary from her father and informed that Feroze was in hospital with a massive heart attack. She drove straight to the hospital and sat up all night by his side. Early the next morning, he died.

'I was actually physically ill,' Mrs. Gandhi has said, recalling her emotions. 'It upset my whole being for years, which is strange, because after all he was very, very ill and I should have expected that he would die. However, it was not just a mental shock, but it was as though somebody had cut me in two.'[37] Believing that her father's needs were more urgent, she had given them priority, expecting perhaps to spend more time with her husband when Nehru was no more; but fate had decided differently.

Feroze's last rites were a compromise between Hindu and Parsi custom. He had expressed a desire to be cremated, and so, after the Zoroastrian prayers had been said, the body was cremated according to the traditional Hindu rites, amid the chanting of Vedic hymns. The funeral cortege, which included the Prime Minister and the President of the Republic, is reported to have been two miles long. As the procession wound its way through the capital from Teen Murti to the cremation ground, thousands of people lined the route. Nehru is said to have exclaimed with genuine surprise that he had no idea that his son-in-law had acquired so large a following.

Feroze Gandhi had been struck down in the prime of life—he was forty-eight—on the threshold of a bright political future. His wife later told Marie Seton: '...if Feroze had to die, he died at the moment of fulfilment for himself. He might not have succeeded if circumstances had thrust him further—into the Cabinet, for example. Too much would have been expected of him.'[38] But Feroze's old political associates— some are now Mrs. Gandhi's loyal supporters—firmly maintain that Feroze Gandhi, though consistently underrated by the Nehru family, had all the makings of a successful Prime Minister and, had he lived, would have led India after Nehru.

*     *     *

By the beginning of 1961, Indira Gandhi was back in active politics, with her health considerably restored. In January she stood for the first time for election to the Congress Working Committee—previously she had been a nominated member—and topped the list with 331 votes, while Y.B. Chavan, a veteran Congress boss, trailed far behind with 250. Indeed, only four delegates did not vote for her, a fact which aroused her curiosity. 'Had a hundred people not voted for me, it wouldn't have bothered me at all,' she has told the author, 'but I was wondering who these four were!'³⁹ She also returned to the Congress Parliamentary Board and was appointed to the Party's Central Disciplinary Action Committee. She was a member of the Congress Central Election Committee for the 1962 general election, and campaigned strenuously for the party, often taking the place of her father who was now too old for active campaigning. In April 1963 she was appointed to yet another committee for screening non-Congress legislators who wished to join the Party.

From time to time she spoke in party forums. It was she who usually moved the official resolutions on foreign affairs, strongly emphasising in her speeches Congress solidarity with other anti-colonial movements. Her favourite theme, however, was that of national integration. As Chairman of the Congress National Integration Committee and a member of the Union Government's National Integration Council, she consistently attacked communalism, especially that of the majority community, and spoke up for minority rights. When Hindu-Muslim riots broke out in Jabalpur in February 1961, she rushed to the spot as the representative of the Congress Working Committee and is reported to have visited every street on foot to assess the damage and restore confidence.

Abroad, too, Mrs. Gandhi was emerging as a personality in her own right. A whirlwind series of goodwill missions and lecture tours took her—often without her father's eclipsing presence—to the United States, Mexico, Eastern and Western Europe, Africa, the Middle East, Japan and the Soviet Union. In November 1960 she received Yale University's Howland Memorial Prize for distinction in the field of Government; and in the same year, she joined the Indian delegation to the UNESCO Conference in Paris and was chosen a member of UNESCO's Executive Board.

Her visits to African countries, with their influential but unpopular Indian communities, were particularly significant in view of her own long-standing sympathy for African nationalism. In the summer of 1961 she was sent to Kenya as Nehru's emissary to establish contact with Kenyatta, who had recently been released. She got on well with the African leader and is reported to have joined him in a Kikuyu tribal dance. In December 1963, she returned to East Africa to participate in the Independence Day celebrations of Kenya and Zanzibar. In a controversial public statement, she criticised East African Indians for segregating themselves from the Africans and warned them that they must identify themselves with local needs and aspirations if they wished to survive. Her advice was sensible and far-sighted, especially in the light of later developments, but was rudely brushed aside at the time. In an angry rejoinder, the Kenya Indian Congress dismissed her criticisms and deplored 'the tendency of visitors from India to criticise and preach to the people of Indian origin here, forgetting that their words can be torn out of context and misused by irresponsible and reckless politicians of the lower ranks to curry favour with the masses.' 'What Indians in East Africa need,' the statement continued, 'is understanding of their present difficulties by friends and impartial observers and not sermons and pompous advice, which only serve to encourage antagonism and derision on the part of Africans towards Indians.'[40]

Mrs. Gandhi's visit had coincided with the African safari of Chou En-Lai and other Chinese leaders, the effects of which she loyally tried to counteract. In Addis Ababa, for instance, she scolded local Indian merchants for trading in Chinese goods and thus providing indirectly the arms which threatened their homeland. 'What would be your future here if India goes under?' she asked them. 'Would anybody in this country treat you with respect?'[41] She succeeded in extracting from them a pledge to boycott the lucrative China trade.

*          *          *

Sino-Indian tension had been steadily mounting since the first border incidents in 1959. A minor territorial dispute, involving a largely un-populated Himalayan no-man's-land, was escalating out of all propor-tion under the pressure of mutual suspicion and misunderstanding. While the Chinese nursed exaggerated fears of Indian designs, backed by the West, on Tibet, the Indian Government, owing partly to its own folly and partly to chauvinistic pressures, was trapped in the toils of its own dogmatic and inflexible posture regarding a disputed border, which had neither been delimited by treaty nor demarcated on the ground, and which might have been negotiated peacefully in a spirit of compromise. Nehru's somewhat subjective reactions to what he consider-ed Chinese ingratitude and bullying had by the end of 1961 overcome his earlier and more rational commitment to Sino-Indian friendship as the corner-stone of his foreign policy. The launching of the reckless 'Forward Policy' which aimed at pushing Indian patrols and posts into Chinese-held territory claimed by India, had set the country inevitably on a collision course. On 20 October 1962, when the Chinese embarked on a massive punitive expedition, the moment of reckoning had arrived.

As a member of the Government's National Defence Council and Chairman of the high-powered Central Citizens' Council, Indira Gandhi played a key role in leading the civilian war effort, working with great zeal to mobilise public energies and restore sagging morale. 'I hardly see her to talk to these days,' her father is reported to have said, looking rather forlorn. 'She is so busy.'[42]

When the Government launched a campaign for public donations of gold for the purchase of arms, Mrs. Gandhi made what the *Times of India* described as 'a golden gesture.'[43] Walking across to the donation booth at Teen Murti, she handed in all her gold jewellery, which included, among other childhood mementos, the little trinkets she had used for the weddings of her dolls. She was particularly active among women, exhorting them to donate their jewellery and volunteer for various civilian jobs on the home front and reminding them of the proverbial Sita, who had sacrificed all to follow her husband into the wilderness. Addressing various public meetings, she struck a note of militant nationalism. To Western proposals, backed by some Indian politicians, that India should buy Pakistan's support in exchange for Kashmir, she replied fiercely: 'Let us tell these politicians that, whether it is Kashmir or Ladakh, every inch of land is the land of India. Not an inch of this land will be given to anybody under any pressure whatsoever.' At the same meeting, she warned against the propaganda of the right-wing opposition and said: 'Those who seek to divert us from our struggle to create a socialist society... are as great enemies as the Chinese.'[44]

Mrs. Gandhi's war activities were not confined to speech-making. She paid several visits to Himalayan forward areas in both the Ladakh and North East Frontier sectors, carrying donations of woollen clothes and other necessities to the ill-equipped, exhausted and frost-bitten Indian army. She also visited the threatened north-eastern province of Assam and attempted to restore public morale, which was crumbling amid fears of imminent Chinese occupation.

Her most daring exploit was her air-dash to Tezpur, the military and civil headquarters of the North-East Frontier Agency, on 21 November. It was a moment of grave national panic. Indian defences had collapsed, the Chinese were within thirty miles of Tezpur, and there was nothing to prevent them, had they so desired, from pushing on to the plains of Assam in a full-scale invasion of the country. In Tezpur itself, the Chinese were expected at any moment, and military headquarters had made a precipitate exit. The District Commissioner had also fled, the local towns-people were following suit, and there was a complete break-down of civil administration. Braving the prospect of finding the Chinese army at Tezpur, Mrs. Gandhi arrived on the scene to assess the situation and reassure the bewildered civilian population. The Chinese, fortunately, did not turn up. On the same day, the war came abruptly and unexpectedly to an end when China announced a unilateral cease-fire and withdrawal, confirming that her objective had been limited to punitive action against India's forward policy. Ten days later, Chinese forces scrupulously withdrew behind the November 1959 line of actual control. They had made their point, and the Indian Government, for all its bitter humiliation and indignation, had to resign itself to the inevitable.

One of the most startling effects of the war was its impact on Nehru, both physical and political. 'I think he collapsed,' Krishna Menon has observed, 'It demoralised him completely because everything he had built up in his life was going.'[45] Nehru had weathered the political crisis, paying the price of Krishna Menon's resignation, but things could never be the same again. As a result of the war, Indian politics moved noticeably to the Right, and Nehru's policies both at home and abroad, came in for increasingly open criticism from opponents in the Congress and outside. In a country where feudal analogies are never far from the mind, the twilight of Nehru's career was seen to resemble the last days of a Mughal emperor whose sons and provincial satraps were waging already a fratricidal war of succession. And in these last eighteen months of Nehru's life, his imperious daughter appeared to some observers to be playing the role of Empress Nur Jehan, who had maintained the supremacy of her declining husband's throne by shrewdly playing off rival princes and factions.

# CHAPTER VII

# THE SUCCESSION

EVER SINCE the death of Sardar Patel in 1950, Nehru had towered over the Indian scene like an ageless colossus. He had never said 'L'État C'est Moi', nor had he acted upon that principle, despite the temptations of his position; even so, Nehru, both at home and abroad, had become synonymous with India, and a future without him was hard to imagine. To the Indian masses Nehru may have appeared immortal; but when in 1959 he had celebrated his seventieth birthday, the country's educated élite had begun to speculate seriously about the political future. When even the most powerful of Nehru's colleagues lagged so far behind him in the public esteem, there could be no obvious successor, though there were several contenders. Among them Welles Hangen in his survey, 'After Nehru Who?', included Indira Gandhi, along with Morarji Desai, Y.B. Chavan, Kamaraj, Lal Bahadur Shastri, Jagivan Ram, Krishna Menon, S.K. Patil and General B.N. Kaul. 'Her father's active backing would remove many obstacles from Mrs. Gandhi's path,' Hangen wrote. '. . . It is her misfortune that she will lose her most precious key to power the moment she needs it most—when her father's passing has left an empty room at the top. Without the key, I doubt that Indira Gandhi can open the door to that room unless, of course, it were battered down for her by as yet unseen forces dedicated to the Nehru legend and its political trappings.'[1]

Hangen's pessimism, based as it was on the political and journalistic gossip of New Delhi drawing-rooms, overlooked the fact that Indira Gandhi, though a gate-crasher in the eyes of top Congress bosses, was already, unlike most of her rivals, a popular figure of All-India standing. In winning this position, she had, of course, been aided by the 'Nehru legend', but also by her own perseverance and persistence. Vijayalakshmi Pandit, by no means uncritical of her niece, told an American journalist in March 1964: 'Indira has risen by sheer value of her worth and the work she has done. Of course, she has the advantage of being her father's daughter, as I had the advantage of being his sister. But once that's been accepted, you cannot pin that to a person for ever. She has really worked hard all through these years, and it's absolutely in the fitness of things that she has reached the position she has today.'[2]

In the aftermath of the China War, the succession began to be debated openly where previously it had been discussed in muted whispers. Nehru's physical powers were failing rapidly and visibly, and reports circulated that his daughter, believed by some to be *de facto* Prime Minister already, was being groomed to succeed him. Nehru himself firmly, and often irritably, denied any such intention; but the rumours persisted, feeding on attempts by some Nehruites to induct Mrs. Gandhi into a strategic position in the political hierarchy.

In March 1962 authoritative reports had appeared in the press that she was being requested to return to the post of Congress President, and this attempt is said to have been repeated in the following year. Nothing, however, came of these moves, owing partly to the opposition of certain party bosses, and partly to her own reluctance to assume new responsibilities at a time when her presence was so necessary beside her ailing father.

In the changed political context, the Congress Presidentship was assuming new importance. Following the Kamaraj Plan in August 1963, a new duumvirate of the Prime Minister and the Congress President came into being and political commentators noted that the period of a unifocal centre of power had come to an end. Under the Kamaraj Plan—named after its powerful author, Kamaraj Nadar, Chief Minister of Madras— six leading Cabinet ministers and six provincial Chief Ministers were asked to resign their governmental offices and apply themselves to organisational work for the Party. Among these were Morarji Desai, Jagjivan Ram, Lal Bahadur Shastri and S.K. Patil, all contenders for the succession. Kamaraj himself resigned his Chief Ministership to take up the Congress Presidentship, a post which he would occupy for the next four years as an enigmatic and laconic *Eminence Gris*, the maker of Prime Ministers, though not one himself.

The Kamaraj Plan was widely interpreted as a brilliant coup by Nehru, aided by Kamaraj, to remove at one stroke all the more factious and tiresome of his colleagues, thereby restoring his own waning power. In retrospect, it has been suggested that the plan also aimed at clearing the decks for Mrs. Gandhi by depriving all her rivals of their ministerial patronage and power, and Morarji Desai, in particular, of his advantage as the top-ranking Cabinet minister after Nehru. A year after the Plan, Desai was recorded as saying that its motive had been to pave Mrs. Gandhi's way to the Prime Ministership. Nijalingappa, who had been superseded by her for Congress President in 1959, noted rather belatedly in his diary on 15 July 1969—by which time Mrs. Gandhi and he were engaged in a public duel—that Nehru 'was always grooming her for the Prime Ministership, obviously and patently.'[3] S.K. Patil, crediting Nehru with powers that reached beyond the grave, told an Indian journalist in January 1970: 'Nehru would have seen to it that she became Prime

Minister after his death, but he realised that she needed to be groomed and therefore selected Shastri for an interim period.'4

Such hindsight cannot, however, be considered authoritative. It is quite possible that Nehru used the Kamaraj Plan to send his would-be successors back to the country and test their strength; but it is highly improbable that he hoped in their absence to smuggle his daughter into a strategic position. 'Had this been in my father's mind,' Mrs. Gandhi has pointed out, 'surely he would have wanted me to be elected to Parliament. However, whenever the suggestion was made he agreed that I should not go into Parliament.'5 The blatant dynasticism with which Nehru has retrospectively been charged is alien to all that one knows of both his character and his political judgement. He was certainly proud of his daughter's public standing and would no doubt have liked to see her in an important position; but according to his sister, Vijayalakshmi Pandit, his ambitions for Mrs. Gandhi went no further than a Cabinet post. Nehru's own wishes apart, he was enough of a politician to know that the country would never have accepted an immediate dynastic succession. In so far as he favoured any potential successor, it appears to have been Lal Bahadur Shastri. And to suggest that Shastri was merely expected to keep the seat warm for Indira Gandhi is to credit Nehru with supernatural foresight.

In January 1964 Nehru's stroke at the annual session of the Congress in Bhubaneshwar signalled the beginning of the end. Though he lived for another five months, he never fully recovered from its paralysing effects. The seriousness of the Prime Minister's illness was kept a closely guarded secret, so that the Congress leadership could sort out its political implications undisturbed by public pressures. Mrs. Gandhi, recently returned from East Africa, nursed her father, keeping a strict watch on all who sought access to him. Despite her anxiety, she managed to keep up a normal front and participated in the Congress proceedings. She stood for re-election to the Congress Working Committee, again topping the list, and made a spirited speech in the open session in defence of India's non-alignment. She is reported to have remarked humorously at the open session that Biju Patnaik, the Orissa Congress boss, was responsible for Nehru's illness, a reference to the strenuous schedule which Patnaik had arranged for Nehru in order to derive the maximum political benefit from the Prime Minister's presence in Orissa. But when Patnaik, anxious not to disappoint the crowds he had collected, callously tried to get Nehru to visit the open session, Mrs. Gandhi is said to have been firm, and the doctors supported her.

Meanwhile, rumours circulated that Indira Gandhi was about to enter the Cabinet as her father's assistant and Minister for External Affairs. Patnaik and Kamaraj, backed by some Congress Chief Ministers, are reported to have put the proposal to Nehru; but nothing came of it. Patnaik later said that Nehru had rejected the idea and told him: 'You don't understand. In the Citizens' Council she can establish a national image with all the people who rule India.'[6] Some years later, Kamaraj told an Indian journalist that Mrs. Gandhi herself had been willing, but that Nehru, after some reflection, had replied: 'No, not yet. Indu probably later.'[7] Kamaraj claimed that it was then that he had promised himself that he would one day make Indira Gandhi Prime Minister.

The only immediate result of Nehru's stroke was that Lal Bahadur Shastri returned to the Cabinet—the only 'Kamaraj-ed' minister to do so—to assist the Prime Minister as Minister without portfolio. While this undoubtedly boosted Shastri's prestige and his prospects for the succession, the arrangement does not appear to have worked smoothly. According to some sources, the ailing Prime Minister had been bullied by the 'Syndicate'* into restoring Shastri to the Cabinet against his own inclinations. It was also rumoured that there was considerable friction between Mrs. Gandhi and Shastri, and the latter's family are said to have been openly critical of Nehru's daughter. Shastri himself seems to have hinted that he was being by-passed in important matters at Mrs. Gandhi's instance, and was fond of telling people: 'I am only a glorified clerk.'[8] There may well have been an element of truth in these reports. Shastri, after all, had started his career in Allahabad as a virtual retainer of the Nehru family, running political and domestic errands for them, receiving their guests at the railway station, and performing various other household and clerical duties. His political advancement had been due entirely to Nehru's patronage. Against this background, the Nehrus might well have resented attempts by this loyal henchman of the Allahabad days to act above himself and try on his dying master's crown.

In a sample survey carried out in the early months of 1964 by the Indian Institute of Public Opinion on the question 'After Nehru Who?', Indira Gandhi ranked third in order of preference, after Shastri and Kamaraj but before Morarji Desai. She, however, disclaimed any political ambitions for herself. On 18 April, en route to the New York World's Fair, she told press reporters in Hong Kong: 'I do not want to be in the Government'; and added that she had already refused several requests to become Foreign Minister.[9] In an interview for American television on 18 May 1964, less than a fortnight before his death, Nehru refused to answer the question that was on everyone's mind. 'If I nominated somebody,' he explained, 'that is the surest way of his not becoming Prime Minister. People would be jealous of him, dislike him.' Acting perhaps on this logic, he said it was highly unlikely that his daughter would succeed him and that he was certainly not grooming her for anything. In the same

*See Page 128.

interview, Mrs. Gandhi commented on her father's remarks: 'I think he is right in what he said, in that I have no such idea... Different types of people want different things—it is just not what I want for myself.' Asked whether she would accept the Prime Ministership if it was thrust upon her, she answered firmly: 'It can't be thrust upon me if I don't want it.'[10]

In a country where overt ambition is frowned upon, and where an age-old tradition of worldly renunciation—observed more in hypocrisy than sincerity—requires that the office must seek the individual and not the reverse, Indira Gandhi's protestations were received with a certain amount of scepticism and cynicism in political circles. Her reluctance, however, may well have been more genuine than some people believed. Ambition and diffidence, assertiveness and reticence, had been inseparably interwoven in her character ever since the days when a painfully shy and introverted school-girl had dreamt of leading her people like Joan of Arc. While one part of her personality sought fulfilment in political leadership, the other might well have craved the greater intimacy, peace and security of private life.

*       *       *

In these last months of Nehru's life, his daughter, though suffering from a painful slipped disc, nursed him dutifully, trussed in an orthopaedic collar which, according to one observer, evoked a striking resemblance to Queen Elizabeth I, her aquiline features framed by a ruff. On 28 May, after a second stroke, death finally overtook Nehru. In an unsuccessful attempt to save him the doctors had decided on a blood transfusion, and his daughter, who belonged to the same blood group, had insisted on being the donor.

For fifteen years, Indira Gandhi had been her father's constant companion, her life centred round his, his giant presence filling even Teen Murti House. She had known loneliness and insecurity before, and she had learned as a young girl to be independent; but her father, powerful and devoted, had always been there behind her, the sheet-anchor of her life and a constant support when she was in doubt or distress. The late Prime Minister's followers and friends might assure her of their continuing support; but she must have known from experience that such loyalties could be notoriously fickle and would not, in most cases, survive the self-interest they masked. Nor could she depend on the Nehru clan, with most of whom she had never been intimate. Now she would have to fend for herself in a man's world, dependent on her own resources, her own friendships and her own wits. For the first time in her life, she stood alone in the world, a widow with two adolescent sons who were too young to fight her battles for her.

The emotional impact of her father's death and all its implications must have been enormous, however much she may have anticipated it; but by all accounts she bore it with fortitude, and her composure was remarkable. According to an eye-witness report by Marie Seton: 'Although her face, drained of all colour, was sorrowing, it was not that of a person devastated in the face of death.'[11] Calm and methodical, she took in hand all the arrangements, funereal and political, that had to be made. With scrupulous regard for Hindu custom, she went about the house removing all the pictures and objets d'art from their walls and shelves. When a foreign woman reporter tried to take a close-up of her, she snapped out fiercely: 'You cannot do things like that here. Go out to the verandah!'[12]

Among the large crowds of mourners who gathered at Teen Murti were the politicians, their minds exercised more by their own rivalry than by grief for their departed leader. While Morarji Desai went about giving orders, in an attempt to assert his supremacy and take over the arrangements, Kamaraj stood in silence, the proverbial strong-man, taking in everything but divulging nothing. Mrs. Gandhi, meanwhile, is reported to have withdrawn into an inner chamber with Shastri, T.T. Krishnamachari and Gulzarilal Nanda, the top-ranking member of the Cabinet, to discuss plans for carrying on the Government.

Later, after enquiring with characteristic consideration whether the late Prime Minister's staff had been fed, Mrs. Gandhi kept a night-long vigil beside her father's body. According to her aunt, she broke down temporarily the next morning; but she had soon recovered sufficiently to instruct the staff, who had been up all night, to go back home and return for breakfast after they had washed, shaved and changed their clothes. 'My father never liked slovenliness in life,' she is reported to have told them. 'He would not like it after his death.'[13]

The funeral procession to the cremation ground at Rajghat included, among other dignitaries, Mountbatten and Douglas-Home, the British Prime Minister, Kosygin from the Soviet Union and Dean Rusk from the United States. At the head of the motorcade which threaded its way through a vast concourse of mourning humanity, Mrs. Gandhi drove in an open car, accompanied by her aunts, Vijayalakshmi Pandit and Krishna Hutheesing, and her son, Sanjay. Rajiv Gandhi, who was at university in Cambridge, had not been able to return in time.

'I wish to declare with all earnestness,' Nehru had written in his Will, 'that I do not want any religious ceremonies performed for me after my death. I do not believe in any such ceremonies, and to submit to them, even as a matter of form, would be hypocrisy and an attempt to delude ourselves and others.'[14] Nevertheless, his body was cremated according to the traditional Brahminical rites amid the chanting of Vedic prayers.

Indira Gandhi was blamed on this account for ignoring her father's instructions, either because of her own religious preferences or because she wished to avoid shocking Hindu orthodoxy. It is well to remember, however, that Nehru had made his Will in 1954, ten years before he died, and that his own last wishes may not have been so radically opposed to the rites Mrs. Gandhi sanctioned. Nehru, like his daughter and other agnostics who have received a religious upbringing, had remained curiously ambivalent in his attitude to religious ritual. Religion was intellectually repugnant to him and he openly rejected it in his writings; but as he himself confessed, he had never completely escaped from the subtle grasp of his Brahminical Hindu background. Visitors to Teen Murti recall that religious ceremonies were regularly performed at the Prime Minister's House during Hindu festivals and sacred days, ostensibly at the desire of Nehru's female relatives, but with his own willing consent. And during his last days, Nehru is reported to have submitted meekly to the ritual ministrations of the family *pandit*.

On the thirteenth day after the funeral, Nehru's ashes were taken by special train from Delhi to Allahabad for the customary immersion in the sacred Ganges. The five hundred mile journey lasted twenty-four hours, and large crowds waited at wayside stations to get a glimpse of Indira Gandhi as she sat stoically, exposed to the scorching summer heat in a decorated, open carriage, beside the urn that bore her father's ashes. A lonely figure, clad in traditional white mourning, she stared with frozen immobility into an uncertain future.

*       *       *

Many political observers, both at home and abroad, had doubted the capacity of the Indian political system to survive Nehru's death and had forecast some sort of cataclysmic break-down. The extent of this alarmism was indicated by the wild rumours of a military coup when General Chaudhuri, the Army Chief of Staff, moved reinforcements into the capital to cope with the mammoth crowds at Nehru's funeral. In the event, while Nehru's passing did have far-reaching political implications, nothing very dramatic occurred and the transition was smooth.

Preparations for the succession had begun well before Nehru's death. By 1963 Lal Bahadur Shastri and Morarji Desai had already emerged as the leading contenders. Desai, however, proved to be his own worst enemy. His authoritarian manner and puritanical outlook had made him generally unpopular in party circles, and he was widely regarded as a somewhat dangerous whited sepulchre. In October 1963 the all-powerful 'Syndicate' had been formed. It was an exclusive caucus of State Congress bosses, including Kamaraj, Atulya Ghosh, Sanjiva Reddy, Nijalingappa and S.K. Patil, and its chief purpose was to keep Morarji Desai out of power. Shastri, unlike his rival, was tactful, tolerant and unlikely to challenge the collective leadership at which the Syndicate aimed. By the time of Nehru's death, therefore, Shastri was the favourite candidate of both the Syndicate and Kamaraj, the Congress President, and as such his election seemed assured.

There remained, however, the unpleasant possibility that Desai, with his usual stubbornness, would refuse to bow to the inevitable and would instead force a contest. Though in accordance with democratic practice, such a contest would, it was feared, violate Congress traditions of unanimity and bring to a head the latent factionalism in the ruling party. Various attempts were therefore made to secure a unanimous election, among them a still-born move to draft Indira Gandhi as a compromise candidate.

For the Congress Left, faced with the fanatical obscurantism of Morarji Desai and the more moderate conservatism of Shastri, Indira Gandhi, as the heir to Nehru's socialism, seemed to offer a more progressive alternative. At an early stage, K.D. Malaviya, a leading Nehruite, appealed to her to enter the lists, but was told firmly that she was not a candidate. This did not, deter Jagivan Ram, who, in a subtle attempt to put Shastri in the wrong, sent emissaries to Shastri and Desai, proposing that they both withdraw in favour of Mrs. Gandhi and thereby preserve party unity.

An Indian journalist has recalled having told Shastri prior to Nehru's death: 'People think you are such a staunch devotee of Nehru that you would yourself propose Indira Gandhi's name after his death.' Shastri, however, replied with a smile: 'I am not as much of a *sadhu* (ascetic) as you imagine me to be.'[15] Nevertheless, in reply to Jagjivan Ram's suggestion, Shastri shrewdly offered to withdraw for the sake of unanimity, provided Mrs. Gandhi's nomination was also acceptable to Morarji Desai. On the night of the 1st June, after a visit, appropriately, to Nehru's cremation site, Shastri is believed to have called personally on Mrs. Gandhi to suggest that she should become Prime Minister.

But as Shastri must have foreseen, Morarji Desai would have none of it. He refused absolutely to withdraw, questioned Mrs. Gandhi's capacity to govern the country and asserted that he would rather see Shastri as Prime Minister. The Syndicate, too, reacted sharply to the idea and even threatened to support Morarji Desai, rather than accept Indira Gandhi. Besides her lack of administrative experience, they cited against her the imperious manner which had once caused Sanjiva Reddy to remark when he was Congress President that she ordered him about like a *chaprasi* (peon).

Though aware of the manoeuvres being made on her behalf, Mrs. Gandhi herself remained discreetly in the background. The shock of her father's death was still fresh, we are told, and she needed time to recover. Meanwhile, there was much to keep her occupied; as Chairman of the Nehru Memorial Trust, she had to take in hand the conversion of Teen Murti House into a museum and library dedicated to her father's memory, a task near to her heart. She must also have recognised the heavy political odds against an immediate dynastic succession. Jagjivan Ram later commented that 'she was not very keen about the post and was very doubtful that either Morarji or Shastri would withdraw.'16 D.P. Mishra, the powerful Chief Minister of Madhya Pradesh, confirmed this in an interview with the author. 'After Panditji's death,' he recalled, 'I went to Indiraji to ask her if she wished to stand. She said no. Because people had accused Nehru of grooming her and this would confirm it. When I persisted, she was irritated and said: "If you don't believe me, I will write it down on paper!"'17

While refusing, therefore, to stake her own claim, Indira Gandhi joined the Left in backing Gulzarilal Nanda, who had been temporarily sworn in as Acting Prime Minister. She later told a foreign writer: 'Nanda came to me and said he would like to continue for at least a month. He seemed so terribly keen that I made a special effort to wrench myself from the numbness that I felt and said to Kamaraj and others, "Why not let him continue for a month or so; there can be no harm in this, and he is so keen." They bawled me out for suggesting that sort of thing.'18 Perhaps their irritation arose from the suspicion that her concern for Nanda was not entirely disinterested: in some circles, the idea that Nanda should continue as a 'lame-duck' Prime Minister was seen as a shrewd ploy to stall Shastri's election and pave the way for Indira Gandhi's succession a few months later when the dust had settled.

Be that as it may, Kamaraj and the Syndicate, with the active support of provincial Congress Chief Ministers, had their way: Morarji Desai withdrew and Shastri was elected unopposed. Following his election, he paid a call on Nehru's daughter. 'Actually, *you* should have been here,' he told her. 'I quite honestly thought it was the biggest joke,' Mrs. Gandhi has told a foreign interviewer. 'I thought it was very funny.'19 But according to one source, when R.K. Khadilkar, a Leftist M.P., asked her why she had declined the Prime Ministership, she replied frankly that no one had offered it to her.

*          *          *

The passing of Nehru's unique charismatic leadership was bound to leave its mark on the political power structure. Nehru as Prime Minister had been supreme both in Party and Government; but his successor, it was obvious, would be no more than the first among equals. In party affairs Shastri had to share power with the Congress President and the Syndicate; and in the Cabinet, too, individual ministers began to exercise greater independence within their respective spheres. Most important, perhaps, was the greatly increased political leverage of the State Chief Ministers, who had played such a crucial role in the succession process, and the effects of this development on Centre-State relations. Shastri—initially, at any rate—accepted the limitations of his position. By temperament he was well fitted for the politics of consensus that the new balance of power required, and his talent for compromise was reflected in the composition of his Cabinet. While G.L. Nanda retained second place as Home Minister, Indira Gandhi was brought into the Cabinet as Minister for Information and Broadcasting, ranking fourth among her colleagues.

Shastri must have foreseen the possibility of Nehru's daughter acting as a nucleus for opposition within the party. He had therefore decided to include her in his team and benefit from her presence as a symbol of continuity. He is even believed at first to have offered her the coveted post of Foreign Minister, which she is said to have declined as being too demanding at a time when her energies were also required by the Nehru Memorial. Indira Gandhi's entry into the Cabinet was welcomed by public opinion in general and by the Congress Left in particular. *The Socialist Congressman* commented in an optimistic editorial on 'Indiraji's New Role':

> 'The nation is grateful to Nehru not only for all the great services he rendered to India, but also because he has left behind Indira Gandhi as his symbol. She inspires respect and is the nation's hope. Her acceptance of a post in the Cabinet ensures that the new team will always be on Nehru lines. Together with Shastriji and Nandaji, she will ensure that Nehru's policies are carried forward and that India will uninterruptedly march to the socialist goal.'[20]

Significantly, the same editorial observed: '... in the public mind it is taken for granted that her present portfolio, important as it is, will soon be replaced by even greater responsibilities.' Shastri, however, did not take the hint. Following Nehru's example, he had at first retained the portfolio of External Affairs for himself, until a heart attack compelled him to part with it a month later. Mrs. Gandhi was the obvious choice for the post, and would probably have been ready by then to accept it. But Shastri, though urged by some of his colleagues to offer it to her, did not do so and gave it instead to Swaran Singh, an uncontroversial figure.

In August 1964, Indira Gandhi was elected for the first time to the Indian Parliament. Reluctant to face a strenuous election campaign so soon after her father's death, she had opted for a seat in the *Rajya Sabha,* the indirectly elected second chamber. Her performance in Parliament was, by all accounts, unimpressive, and she rarely spoke in that forum, or for that matter at Cabinet meetings. Nevertheless, she proved a successful minister, despite her lack of administrative experience. According to a retired senior official who worked under her: 'Although she wasn't really interested in Information and Broadcasting—she wanted External Affairs—she was keen to make something of it.' One of her first actions was to constitute the Chanda Committee to recommend structural changes in the Government-owned mass media. In the interim, she herself introduced various minor reforms. All India Radio was told that programmes should be liberalised and more controversy and dissent permitted. She was always sympathetic to the grievances of staff artistes, and she issued instructions that the antiquated fee structure for guest artistes and commentators should be revised. She was also instrumental in establishing the Press Council of India as a self-regulatory mechanism for enforcing a code of conduct for journalists and curbing monopolistic and restrictive practices in the newspaper industry. 'Where most of the large newspapers,' she explained, 'are not only in a foreign language but emanate from cities which are unrepresentative of the vast majority of our population, there is the grave danger that the viewpoint and self-interest of an exceedingly small section of society may be presented authoritatively as the voice of the people.'[21]

As might have been expected, Mrs. Gandhi refused to be bound by the 'steel frame' of the bureaucracy, and she did not hesitate to take advice from intellectuals outside the Ministry, a habit which is said to have irritated some civil servants. Nor did she confine herself to the ranks of the professional civil service in making selections for important posts. In several instances, and notably in her appointment of Dr. Narayana Menon, an eminent musicologist and broadcaster, as Director-General of All India Radio, she succeeded in overcoming strong resistance from the civil service and the Union Public Service Commission. Summing up her tenure as Minister for Information and Broadcasting, a former official comments: 'She gave a lot of time to doing things which weren't part of her duties, because she was mainly interested in building her public image. But although she wasn't there very much, and we didn't see as much of her as we had of previous ministers, at least there was no nepotism. She never interfered with promotions, etc., in order to favour people, and that was a welcome change.'

\*          \*          \*

Within three months of her father's death, Indira Gandhi had vacated Teen Murti House, leaving behind her the memories of fifteen years. Life at Teen Murti had been strenuous and often exhausting, but never dull or commonplace, and always there had been her father. Now, taking with her a few devoted members of Nehru's domestic and clerical staff, she moved to the relatively modest, four-bedroom official residence which had been allotted to her as a Cabinet minister. Here she began life afresh, living alone while her sons completed their education in England. There was nothing to distinguish I, Safdarjang Road from the rows of white-washed British Colonial villas that stand in their neat gardens along the spacious avenues of 'official' Delhi. But with her impeccable taste, Indira Gandhi had soon created around her an intimate and exquisitely furnished home, where she could indulge at last her craving for privacy. While the grander and more courtly traditions of palatial Teen Murti were perforce abandoned, mostly without regret, one survived in tact— the morning *durbar*. Between eight and nine in the morning Indira Gandhi's home, like Nehru's, was open to the public, which included politicians, social workers, students, peasants, and even tourists. Political lobbying, applications for jobs, petitions for the redress of grievances, or simply *darshan* (blessings) from Nehru's daughter, were all part of this regular morning ritual which symbolised Mrs. Gandhi's continuing role as a national leader and Nehru's political heir.

If Shastri had thought to neutralise Indira Gandhi as a political force by including her in his Cabinet, he must have been disappointed. While she accepted and retained her ministerial office, probably for its strategic importance, and modulated her public statements within the bounds of Cabinet and party loyalty, it was an open secret in political circles that Mrs. Gandhi was far from contented either with her own position in the official power structure or with the direction of Government policies.

Owing partly to the new balance of power and partly to Shastri's own lack of decisiveness, Government policy was appearing increasingly as one of drift and patchwork compromise. This was particularly striking in the handling of the food problem in 1965, when Shastri's surrender to the traders' lobby and the Chief Ministers of 'surplus' States led to the shelving of proposals for statutory food rationing, the abolition of food zones, and the creation of a State Food Trading Corporation, and this despite the danger of famine. The same indecision manifested itself during the stormy language crisis early in 1965 and in the makeshift compromise formula that eventually emerged. Both issues demonstrated the increased influence of commercial and regional-linguistic pressure groups in the post-Nehru period.

On these and other issues, Indira Gandhi, though careful not to alienate the Centrists, identified herself increasingly with the Left. Addressing a Socialist Convention of Congressmen in September 1964, she warned the delegates against 'the danger of the Congress sliding away from the socialist path' and reminded them that only the rank and file could stop 'the present drift' and 'rescue the party from those who do not believe in its policies.'[22] In January 1965, at a press conference in Calcutta, she admitted frankly that virtually nothing had been done to implement the Bhubaneshwar Congress's resolution on Democracy and Socialism. She went on to say: 'A small but powerful group of persons, well entrenched in the party's leadership, is always willing to raise its hands in favour of any resolution supported by the majority, but in practice they see to it that the decisions not to their liking are not implemented.'[23] These remarks are believed to have greatly incensed some of the party's Old Guard, and resulted shortly after in an abortive attempt at the Durgapur Congress session to pass a resolution in the Working Committee censuring Mrs. Gandhi for her statements.

In private interviews Indira Gandhi was even more outspoken. According to Kuldip Nayar, a leading journalist, when he interviewed her in November 1965 she made no secret of her contempt for the Government and cited many instances of how 'India had swerved from the right path.'[24] According to the same source, she was particularly annoyed by Shastri's decision to drop T.T. Krishnamachari, a loyal Nehruite and one of her confidants, from the Cabinet. Her dissatisfaction with the Shastri regime drew her close to Kamaraj, the Congress President, who was also growing restive as the Prime Minister chose increasingly to by-pass him. In a speech at Coimbatore in August 1965, Mrs. Gandhi, while omitting any reference to the Prime Minister, said of Kamaraj, who was present: 'We have been fortunate that we have at the head of our organisation a man of the people and a man who understands the problems of our organisation and of our country. It is because of his clear and sound leadership that our organisation has been able to weather many storms and has emerged with greater unity and strength.'[25]

Indira Gandhi's role in the Shastri Government was by no means limited to negative criticism. Despite her exclusion from the portfolio of External Affairs, as a member of the Emergency Committee of the Cabinet—its inner circle—she had an important voice in the making of Indian foreign policy. The Shastri Government, for its part, had the benefit of the diplomatic contacts she had built up over the last two decades. In July 1964 she represented India at the Commonwealth Prime Minister's Conference in London, and this was followed by a series of goodwill tours which took her in the course of the next seventeen months to France, Yugoslavia, Burma, Mongolia, the U.S.A., Canada, the Soviet Union and Italy, where she received from President Saragat the Isabella d'Este Award for achievements in the field of diplomacy.

Mrs. Gandhi's visits to the Soviet Union during this period were particularly important and attracted wide publicity. Her visit in October 1964, shortly after the fall of Krushchev, took place at a time when the changes in the Soviet leadership had raised fears in New Delhi of a Sino-Soviet rapprochement to the detriment of India's interests. It was significant, then, that Indira Gandhi was the first foreign dignitary of any importance to visit Russia after Krushchev's removal and that she had been invited in her official capacity. She was warmly received in Moscow and returned with categorical assurances from the new Soviet leadership that Russian economic and military aid to India would continue as before. At a press conference on her return, she told newsmen that the reasons for Krushchev's fall were purely personal and that there was no reason to fear any change in the Kremlin's policies towards India and China. In February 1965 she revisited the Soviet Union, this time with the even more delicate task of allaying Soviet apprehensions that India's policies at home and abroad were moving to the Right under Shastri. Again her mission seems to have been successful, and she is reported to have received in Moscow courtesies normally not extended even to visiting heads of government.

At home, meanwhile, Mrs. Gandhi was demonstrating that in an hour of crisis she could act boldly and with a shrewd sense of political timing. Early in 1965, during her absence abroad, the language problem had come to a head with large-scale rioting and police firing in the southern State of Madras, as the Tamil-speaking population of the province gave violent expression to their fears regarding the imposition of Hindi as the official language. The tremors of the Madras riots were felt all over the country and led to the resignation of two southern members of the Central Cabinet. On her return from Moscow, Mrs. Gandhi promptly suggested that Central leaders should visit Madras; and when nobody else responded, she herself took the initiative and arrived dramatically upon the scene. While she was unable to address a public meeting or to visit Coimbatore, the most disturbed district, owing to the Madras Congress Government's lack of co-operation, her presence in Madras City and her talks with local leaders helped to allay Tamil suspicions. She returned to Delhi with a strong plea for bold and positive action, and if necessary legislation, to reassure the people of the South that Hindi would not be forced upon them. Such guarantees to regional linguistic groups could not fail to be unpopular in the northern Hindi-speaking belt, and especially in U.P., Mrs. Gandhi's home-state. Even so, in the months that ensued before an acceptable formula emerged, she was one of the few northern leaders to throw their full weight on the side of conciliation and compromise.

Despite her ministerial duties, Mrs. Gandhi had continued to take an active interest in the Congress organisation, and particularly in the work of the youth and women's sections. She travelled widely through the country, mediating in factional disputes and calling for moderation and tolerance on the thorny language issue. Her speeches were invariably replete with shining references to her father and his dream of a Socialist

India. Political analysts might point out that the seeds of many of the country's ills had been sown in Nehru's lifetime; but at a time of intensifying economic hardship and political fragmentation, it was not surprising that the large crowds that came to hear Nehru's daughter felt nostalgia for the relative prosperity and stability of the Nehru era, when *Panditji*, a benign father-figure, had watched over his flock. And for many people Nehru's daughter represented not merely a dying legend, but a hope for the future.

Following closely upon her intervention in the language crisis, Mrs. Gandhi exploits during the Indo-Pakistan War of 1965 were to win her the title of 'the only man in a Cabinet of old women.' She was in Srinagar on a brief visit when Pakistan launched its armed infiltration, and she refused to leave until the situation had stabilised. Her presence in the Kashmiri capital helped to maintain Indian morale during the initial period of confusion and uncertainty. Addressing a public meeting in Srinagar, she declared that India considered the Pakistani infiltration nothing less than an invasion on the 1947 model and reiterated that Kashmir was an integral part of the country and that not an inch of it would be surrendered. Later, when full-scale war broke out between the two countries, Indira Gandhi was a frequent visitor at various forward positions. According to a foreign journalist, she even resorted to deception in order to visit the Haji Pir pass, the scene of heavy fighting in the Kashmir sector. A senior Air Force officer had vetoed the idea as too dangerous; but Mrs. Gandhi was not to be deterred. She got a member of her staff to engage the officer in conversation, while she boarded a nearby helicopter and took off unobserved for the front. When the officer turned round moments later and enquired anxiously: 'Where is Mrs. Gandhi?', he was told to his dismay: 'Up there in the helicopter.'[26]

*        *        *

On 10 January 1966, within a few hours of signing the controversial Tashkent Agreement with Pakistan, Lal Bahadur Shastri died in the Soviet Union after a sudden heart attack. His death came at a moment when his popularity had reached a new and unexpected peak. Although he had lacked conspicuously the Nehru charisma, and his diminutive height had made him an obvious butt for the humour of India's élite, he had from the outset commanded respect as a well-meaning and honest man, 'the salt of the earth.' And during the Indo-Pakistan War the country had rallied round this incongruous, bird-like figure who inspected the nation's troops with a gentle smile and directed the war effort without any attempt at war-like rhetoric. While the war was by no means a decisive victory for India, the country's forces had registered important gains both in West Pakistan and in Kashmir, thereby boosting national pride after the ignominious military collapse of 1962. In the course of the hotly contested diplomatic war that followed at Tashkent, Shastri had appeared as a sort of David, standing up with quiet dignity to Ayub Khan's Goliath, and winning the respect and affection even of his adversary. While Nehru's death had been expected for some months, Shastri's came as a bolt from the blue. His drawbacks and limitations were forgotten for the moment, and he was widely mourned as a man who had worn himself out in the service of the nation.

Shastri, it seems, had foreseen an early end for himself and had speculated with surprising accuracy about its political consequences. According to Kuldip Nayar, his Press Secretary, he once remarked that if he were to die within the next year or so Mrs. Gandhi would succeed him, but that if he lived another four or five years Y.B. Chavan, then Defence Minister, would be his successor. However tempting it might be to postulate the inevitability of Indira Gandhi's succession to the Prime Ministership, there can be little doubt that while Shastri lived, she could not have advanced further towards that goal. She would certainly have continued in his Cabinet, and her voice would have continued to be heard with respect, especially when she pointed to the obvious gap between Congress promises and Government performance. But it is highly unlikely that she could ever have proceeded beyond that to challenge Shastri's primacy. Shastri's unexpected removal from the political scene, however, opened up new vistas for which Mrs. Gandhi's background and training, if not her own ambition, had long prepared her.

It is almost axiomatic to say that had Indira Gandhi not been Nehru's daughter, she would not in the first instance have become India's Prime Minister. Her parentage, no doubt, was a great asset in a country where heredity still commands reverence. But having said that, one must add that she had other qualifications, deriving partly from the advantages of birth and partly from her own abilities and efforts. She had a clean public record, the Nehru mass appeal and an All-India image, and these were important assets in an election year. At a time when the language controversy was still simmering, she could claim to represent the highest common denominator. While U.P., the largest and most populous of India's provinces, was her home-state, and she had a substantial following in other Hindi-speaking provinces, she was also popular in the south, owing to her intervention during the language riots. As Nehru's daughter and a consistent opponent of Hindu chauvinism, she provided the best guarantee for the security of Indian Muslims and other minorities. She was forty-eight—young by Indian standards—and had a modern and technology-oriented outlook. She also had wide international contacts, which could be valuable at a time when food and foreign exchange were scarce.

A foreign jounalist commented on Mrs. Gandhi's prospects: 'She is India's best bet. Look at the others and you know it has to be her.'[27] As important as her own assets, were the fatal flaws of her possible rivals— Desai's authoritarianism, Nanda's obscurantism and the limited, regional identity of Kamaraj and Chavan. The most decisive factor in her favour, however, was the decision of the Congress President to back her. Kamaraj's choice appears to have been dictated by two main considerations. In the first place, Mrs. Gandhi, being a woman, could be expected to be more pliable and dependent on the 'King-maker' than the other contenders. And secondly, she was the candidate most likely to defeat Morarji Desai—still the *bête noire* of Kamaraj and the Syndicate—in a contest.

Although it was Kamaraj who masterminded Mrs. Gandhi's succession strategy, he was careful to remain in the background and to project her as the choice of a majority of the party. She herself was equally careful not to appear unduly eager and to hold back until the demand for her had gathered momentum. The morning after Shastri's death, Nanda, again Acting Prime Minister, called on her to seek her support for his continuation. While avoiding any commitment, she assured him that that she herself would not be a candidate. On the evening of the same day, she visited Kamaraj and reported her conversation with Nanda. 'Just leave things as they are,' he is reported to have told her.[8] Two days later, she met Chavan, a rival contender. The two are reported to have struck a reciprocal deal to the effect that each would support the other if he or she received greater backing from the other leaders. Mrs. Gandhi, by this time, had made it clear that she was available if the party wanted her. On 12 January, Mohanlal Sukhadia, Chief Minister of Rajasthan, while proposing her name to Atulya Ghosh, a member of the Syndicate, said that 'her mind was in a fluid condition' and that she 'left it in the hands of the Congress leaders.'[29] The next day she herself told D.P. Mishra, Chief Minister of Madhya Pradesh; 'If there is near unanimity and Kamaraj asks me, I would stand.'[30]

The resistance of the Syndicate, however, had yet to be overcome. Though determined to keep out Morarji Desai, these gentlemen were by no means favourable to Mrs. Gandhi, citing against her a lack of administrative experience, Leftist leanings, youth, poor health and an arrogant manner. While attempting to convince the Syndicate that they must back Indira Gandhi if they wanted to exclude Morarji Desai, Kamaraj, acting through D.P. Mishra, mounted strong pressure in Mrs. Gandhi's favour through the collective weight of the Congress Chief Ministers. The latter had already played an influential role in the previous succession and were now in an even better position to influence the decision of the Congress Parliamentary Party, officially the sole deciding body. In a few weeks' time one third of the Rajya Sabha was due to retire for re-election by the State legislatures which were controlled by the Chief Ministers. The Chief Ministers would also have an important say in the nomination of Congress candidates for the general election that was due in a year. Owing to Mishra's efforts, eight Chief Ministers met on 15 January and issued a public statement supporting Mrs. Gandhi. On the same day, four more Chief Ministers added their support, making an impressive total of 12 out of 14 Chief Ministers for Mrs. Gandhi. While the Chief Ministers knew Kamaraj's mind, there is no reason to believe that they were browbeaten by him. 'Kamaraj helped us to make up our minds', Nijalingappa, Chief Minister of Mysore, later observed.[31] Kamaraj himself commented: 'I allowed them to talk things out: I knew they would come round to the view that Mrs. Gandhi was the best choice.'[32]

The Chief Ministers' announcement marked a dramatic turning point in the succession struggle. The backstage negotiations on Mrs. Gandhi's behalf had been conducted with such discretion that her name had as yet received little notice in press speculation about the succession. The names most mentioned had been those of Nanda, Morarji Desai and Kamaraj himself, while Indira Gandhi and Chavan had figured en passant as mere possibilities. The Chief Ministers' decision, however, seemed to have clinched matters in Mrs. Gandhi's favour. On the evening of the 15th, large crowds gathered at her residence to congratulate her, while her staff began preparations for the expected victory celebration. Nevertheless, even at this stage, Mrs. Gandhi refused to make a public announcement of her candidature and skillfully parried leading questions from the press. The only information that newsmen could elicit from her was that she would do whatever the Congress President required of her. 'He has asked me to stay at home until he calls me,' she added with a smile. A foreign correspondent asked: 'How does it feel to be the first woman Prime Minister of India?' 'I am not a feminist at all', she replied. 'I am doing a particular job and would do it wherever I am placed.'[33]

There remained the determination of Morarji Desai to force a contest on the Congress Parliamentary Party. He had already withdrawn once for the sake of unanimity and nothing could induce him to repeat the performance for 'this mere chokri*,' as he is said to have termed his rival. It was not only a matter of pride; a second withdrawal would have meant political suicide and the loss of his following. Both sides now began feverish canvassing in preparation for the crucial meeting of the Congress Parliamentary Party on the 19th January, when a new leader would be elected. Desai launched an open campaign and personally telephoned as

*Slip of a girl.

many Congress M.P.s as he could. He also issued a manifesto which criticised the Congress Chief Ministers and organisational bosses for trying to impose their nominee on the legislative wing of the party and urged Congress M.P.s to exercise their democratic right to choose their own leader in a free vote.

Mrs. Gandhi, by contrast, never formally announced her candidature and disdained to canvass for herself. 'My beliefs and convictions are well known to my fellow party members,' she announced. 'There is no need for a reaffirmation on my part.'[34] Her supporters, nonetheless, were active on her behalf, and the Indira bandwagon soon gathered momentum. At the instance of provincial Congress bosses, M.P.s were asked to meet in provincial groups and pass resolutions in her favour, and a large number did so. Many who were reluctant to come out so openly were persuaded to give a private written pledge. Naturally, there was much horse-trading and hard bargaining behind the scenes. Jagjivan Ram, who claimed a following of eighty Untouchable M.P.s, is believed to have offered himself to the highest bidder. 'I have yet to make up my mind,'[35] he told the press on the 16th January. While Desai apparently refused to make him any prior commitment of a Cabinet post, Kamaraj is said to have given him the necessary assurance on Mrs. Gandhi's behalf, and Jagjivan Ram promptly switched sides. Kamaraj is also reported to have conceded the Syndicate's demand for the inclusion of two of their nominees in Mrs. Gandhi's future Cabinet. A strange feature of the second succession, and one which embarrassed both candidates, was the unsolicited intervention of the Opposition in the contest. While Dange, Chairman of the Communist Party of India, issued a statement supporting Mrs. Gandhi, the Right-wing opposition first argued for the continuance of Nanda and then backed Morarji.

An eleventh hour endorsement of Mrs. Gandhi's candidature by Vijayalakshmi Pandit is believed to have influenced some wavering M.P.s in U.P., the Nehru home-state, where C.B. Gupta, President of the U.P. Congress, was staunchly backing Morarji Desai. Nehru's sister, now an M.P. from U.P., had previously been considered a firm supporter of Desai's. But on 18 January, after an interview with her niece, she told the press in an open display of dynastic sentiment: 'It is a certainty that Mrs. Indira Gandhi will be India's next Prime Minister. We Nehrus are very proud of our family. When a Nehru is chosen as Prime Minister, the people will rejoice.' She added patronisingly: 'Mrs. Gandhi has the qualities. Now she needs experience. With a little experience she will make as fine a Prime Minister as we could wish for... She is in very frail health indeed. But with the help of her colleagues, she will manage.'[36]

*          *          *

As the day of the contest dawned, Indira Gandhi embarked on a symbolic pilgrimage. The cold winter mist had not yet lifted when she drove to Rajghat to visit the cremation sites of Mahatma Gandhi and Jawaharlal Nehru, and thence to the Nehru Museum at Teen Murti, where she stood in silence before her father's portrait. Thus fortified, she made her way to Parliament House, where the Congress Parliamentary Party was meeting to choose, as an Opposition leader put it, between monarchy and puritanism. Her mood was pensive, even wistful; but she did not confide her emotions to her entourage. Later she wrote to her son Rajiv that running through her mind had been the lines of Robert Frost's poem, 'How hard it is to keep from being King, when it's in you and in the situation.'[37] She might also have felt some apprehension for the outcome of the election. Her victory seemed assured; but professions of support were not always reliable, and a secret ballot could spring its surprises.

Large crowds had massed around Parliament House, a circular, baroque structure, built in the red and gold sandstone of Lutyens's Delhi. Cheers of 'Lal Gulab Zindabad!'* greeted Indira Gandhi as she alighted from her car. An austere and dignified figure, she had worn for the occasion a simple white khaddar sari and a beige Kashmiri shawl, upon which was pinned a single red rose, the emblem of Jawaharlal Nehru. Having greeted the crowd, she made her entry into the high-domed Central Hall of Parliament, where she received a standing ovation from the assembled Congress M.P.s, twenty-six of whom had been summoned from hospital beds for the occasion. While the cameras clicked, Mrs. Gandhi warmly greeted Morarji Desai—his response was cool—and then took an inconspicuous seat in the seventh row.

Beneath the larger-than-life portraits of those who had led the Congress and the nation, the proceedings began. From the galleries above, Opposition members, the press and various dignitaries looked on. The procedure was slow. First both candidates were duly proposed and seconded. Then, one by one, the 526 Congress M.P.s present rose and cast their votes by secret ballot. By the time the counting began, pangs of hunger and thirst were added to the suspense of the occasion. The meeting had begun at eleven in the morning, and it was three in the afternoon when the result was announced. Indira Gandhi had defeated Morarji Desai by a comfortable majority of 355 votes to 169.

If the Congress élite in the Central Hall had grown restless and impatient by this time, the crowds outside were no less so. When, at last, Satyanarayan Sinha, Minister for Parliamentary Affairs, appeared on the portico to announce the result, someone shouted: 'Is it a boy or a girl?'

---

*'Long Live the Red Rose'.

'A girl', came the reply.[38] The crowd began to chant, 'Jawaharlal Nehru Zindabad!' Their charismatic leader had been reborn.

Inside the Central Hall, there were scenes of jubilation as those who had voted for the winner, and many who had voted against her, vied with each other in felicitating and garlanding her. When the initial excitement subsided, the speeches began. Kamaraj spoke first, followed by Nanda. Then came Morarji Desai, who offered his full co-operation 'consistent with my self-respect and the interests of the country.' In an oblique reference to the succession struggle, he expressed the hope that 'an atmosphere of fearlessness will be created and cultivated' in the Congress.[39] Indira Gandhi spoke last, beginning, significantly, in Hindi and concluding with a few words in English. Her speech was short, and its central point was the need for party and national unity. 'I have every hope,' she declared, 'that with unity we shall be able to tackle the difficult problems facing us. I want to thank Mr. Morarji Desai, in particular, for pledging himself to work for unity. Elections are a normal feature in politics. Once elections are over, however, it is only fit and proper that differences should be forgotten and that we should all work together, especially at a time like this... when the country is facing so many difficulties... I thank both those who voted for me and those who voted against me... I hope all of you will fully support me and take the country forward.'[40]

Emerging into the afternoon sunshine, Indira Gandhi stood with folded hands, acknowledging the cheers of the crowd, while the weary Congress legislators streamed out behind their new leader. Some had known her as a helpless, four-pound baby and found, perhaps, some irony in the fact. While cheering crowds pelted her with flowers and garlands, Mrs. Gandhi drove in triumph in an open car to the presidential palace, where Dr. Radhakrishnan received her and invited her to form a government. The lonely adolescent with her dreams of leadership had arrived.

# CHAPTER VIII

# STRUGGLE FOR SURVIVAL

'I OFTEN wonder,' wrote Welles Hangen, 'why anyone would want to be prime minister of India. What could be more difficult than running the world's most populous democracy by a combination of persuasion, pressure and pugnacity? The pay is modest ... satisfactions are few, and there is no security. The burdens that come to rest on the shoulders of India's prime minister dwarf the Himalayas.'[1] To this one might add the dictum commonly attributed to Nehru that the Prime Ministership of India was like riding a tiger: once one got on, one couldn't get off.

Faced with this alarming prospect, Indira Gandhi might well have had misgivings about the perilous seat to which circumstances, acting upon her own propensities, had brought her. In an interview with an Indian journalist, she dwelt wistfully upon the many peaceful avenues along which her life might have run. 'I would have liked,' she said, 'to be a writer. I would have liked to do research in history, or perhaps in anthropology... If I wanted to have an easy life, I could have become an interior decorator... I could even have become a dancer...'[2] The possibilities, apparently, were infinite; but none of them had succeeded in deflecting her from the political mainstream wherein she would find her fulfilment. The world of political action had always been more real to her than any other; and despite her reticence—or perhaps because of it—only in the political arena could she express the fierce emotions and ambitions that smouldered beneath her calm and reserved manner.

In January 1966, however, Indira Gandhi's opportunities for political self-expression did not appear promising. She had ascended to the *gaddi* (throne) from which her father had ruled India as undisputed leader; but her position was in no way comparable to his. With the passing of Nehru, the Prime Ministership had been considerably devalued, while the importance of the organisational and provincial leadership of the Congress had correspondingly increased. Shastri, during his brief tenure of power, had been cautiously reasserting the Prime Ministerial authority when his demise and the second succession struggle had intervened to reverse the process.

Indira Gandhi's inheritance, for a variety of reasons, was even more attenuated than Shastri's had been in 1964. Shastri's election, though dependent on the backing of the party bosses, had had the seal of unanimity. Mrs. Gandhi's, on the other hand, had been contested; and the laurels of her victory were well outweighed by the price implicit in the support of her sponsors. Even more than the organisational leadership of the Party, it was the Congress Chief Ministers who had decided the outcome of the contest, a factor which was bound to have serious repercussions on Centre-State relations. Indira Gandhi's All-India image and Kamaraj's wishes had no doubt influenced the Chief Ministers' choice; but the most decisive consideration was probably their confidence that a Central Government headed by Indira Gandhi would be more amenable to pressure from the States than a government headed by Morarji Desai. There was also the sobering fact that, in spite of the public backing of Mrs. Gandhi by almost the entire Congress leadership at the Centre and in the States, as many as 169 Congress M.P.s—almost a third of the Congress Parliamentary Party—had chosen to defy the Chief Ministers' mandate and vote for Desai. Clearly, Desai had been able to project himself as a rallying point for dissident Congressmen, thereby demonstrating that inner-party factionalism, which had long existed at the State level, could be mobilised and promoted to the Centre as well.

The new Premier's position was also restricted by more subjective factors. When Shastri became Prime Minister, he had behind him a long record as a senior Cabinet minister and was also a respected member of the elderly and exclusive fraternity that prided itself on winning India's independence. Indira Gandhi, however, was relatively young and lacking in governmental experience; and in a country where age is traditionally invested with authority, her elders would naturally expect her to bow to their superior wisdom. This would be especially the case in party affairs. Like her father, Mrs. Gandhi had preferred not to soil her hands with the manipulatory techniques of political 'bossism,' and she lacked in consequence a grip on the party machinery. This was clearly indicated by the fact that in U.P., her home-state, the Congress leadership had backed her rival in the succession contest. But while Nehru, greater than the Party and secure in his exalted status, could stand without such props, the same could not be said of his daughter. Her lack of a firm organisational base was bound to be a source of weakness, curtailing severely her role in party affairs.

Finally, there were the peculiar implications of the new Prime Minister's sex. A leading political journal commented in August 1966:

'A woman ruler is under a special handicap until she has been able to consolidate her position. In the beginning every group leader wants to advise and control her and so faction fights start among them. Either the ruler is able to satisfy everyone that she is not too close to anyone in particular, as Queen Elizabeth I did, and enjoy a long tenure of office, or fail to survive the initial period of uncertainty, as was Sultana Raziya's* sad fate.'3

Ever since the active participation of Indian women in the Civil Disobedience movements of 1930–32, women had become a familiar sight on Congress platforms and in decision-making bodies. It was not so surprising then, despite the astonishment it caused abroad, that the sex of India's third Prime Minister aroused little comment in the Indian press. Such notice as it received was favourable, the idea of a woman Prime Minister being welcomed as a sign of modernism and progress. Indira Gandhi herself impatiently brushed aside the questions of sceptical foreign journalists and declared that her sex was irrelevant and immaterial. But for all her protestations, the fact that she was a woman undoubtedly had political significance.

Indira Gandhi was by no means the only woman politician in the country. Women, though in proportionately small numbers, were represented in Congress Committees, in legislatures and in the Central and State Governments. At the time of Mrs. Gandhi's election as Prime Minister, a woman, Sucheta Kripalani, was Chief Minister of U.P., India's largest and most populous State. The role of a woman politician, nonetheless, was closely circumscribed in practice, though not in law or theory, by the fact that she functioned within an essentially male-dominated social structure and value system. While women were permitted and even welcomed in high positions, few Indians would have expected or desired such women, however great their abilities, to provide strong and independent leadership. Their function, by and large, was to act as obedient and ornamental figure-heads, filling in for the male patrons or relatives from whom they took their cue.

Seen in this context, the elevation of a supposedly malleable woman to the Prime Ministership indicated the desire of her sponsors to neutralise the independent powers of that office and manipulate it to their own advantage. That they had underestimated the woman in question would in time become apparent, leading Nijalingappa to recall belatedly the ancient Sanskrit proverb: 'One cannot know a woman's heart.'4 For the moment, however, Indira Gandhi was expected to conform to the

---

*Sultan Raziya is the only Queen Regnant in Indian history. She succeeded her brother on the throne of Delhi in 1236 A.D. According to the chronicles, she was a learned and able ruler who cast aside the traditional restraints of the harem, holding court and transacting public business like a male sovereign. After a reign of three and a half years, she was deposed by her factious nobles who resented her partiality to her Abyssinian Master of Horse. She attempted to recover her throne by marrying one of the rebel nobles. But she and her husband were defeated in battle, captured and put to death.

example set by Sucheta Kripalani in U.P.; namely, to act as a non-controversial and unifying figure-head for a badly divided party until a suitable replacement emerged after the general election a year later.

Political observers may therefore be forgiven for referring to Indira Gandhi as a 'lame-duck' Prime Minister who was merely keeping the seat warm, or as an ornamental election mascot who would be replaced on the shelf once she had served her purpose. They had not yet discovered the two most remarkable features of Indira Gandhi's personality—her determination to rise to a challenge and her shrewd instinct for survival. While confessing to an interviewer that she had accepted the Prime Ministership with 'a shade of reluctance', she added: 'I am always reluctant when I enter into something, but then I give it my best.'[5] Now that she was on the tiger, she would not easily be persuaded to dismount. The odds against her staying on were heavy; but she had three important assets—the Nehru name, a national Pan-Indian image and a mass appeal that could be expanded and used to by-pass the official party machine. And in the turbulent times ahead, she would learn to use these assets with increasing confidence and skill.

*          *          *

It was Indira Gandhi's misfortune to succeed to the Prime Ministership at a moment when India's problems—serious and multifarious at the best of times—had converged into an economic crisis of unprecedented magnitude. This was the product of an unhappy and unforeseen conjuction of disasters. 1965 had been a year of unparalleled drought, resulting in an acute food shortage, and the drought had coincided with the Indo-Pakistan War. The cost of the China War of 1962 had already made a serious dent in India's Third Five-Year Plan; and the Pakistan War, less than three years later, involved another sharp rise in military expenditure, depleting still further the country's scarce resources for development. To make matters worse, the United States, India's largest aid-giver, had halted all economic assistance on the outbreak of the recent hostilities, thereby seriously jeopardising the future of the Fourth Plan. Meanwhile, the food scarcity and the war combined to creat a state of galloping inflation: prices were spiralling, famine appeared imminent, and simmering economic discontent threatened at any moment to erupt into violence.

Feeding indirectly on this economic discontent were the forces of regionalism and linguism, which were acquiring a cutting edge that threatened to disrupt the national solidarity achieved during the recent war. The North-South cleavage over Hindi had by no means healed, and the Official Language controversy had yet to be settled on an enduring basis. For the moment, however, the most pressing political issue was the demand for *Punjabi Suba* or a Punjabi-speaking State. Ever since

Independence the Sikh community had been pressing for a linguistic partition of the existing bi-lingual Punjab and the creation of a Punjabi-speaking State in which the Sikhs would predominate. Nehru had firmly opposed the idea; but by 1966 the demand had grown so strong that a weakened Centre was in no position to resist it, especially when Sant Fateh Singh—the politico-religious leader of the Akali Dal*—served notice of his intention to fast to death unless *Punjabi Suba* was conceded. The Congress found itself on the horns of a dilemma: to concede the Akali demand would mean abandoning a position to which it was firmly committed and letting down its Hindu supporters in the projected *Punjabi Suba*; not to do so would precipitate a Sikh agitation which would certainly turn violent and might even acquire the dimensions of a revolt.

Equally thorny, though not so urgent, was the problem of Naga** secessionism. Since the late 1950s, massive and brutal military repression in Nagaland had tarnished India's international image, without breaking Naga resistance. Despite an uneasy cease-fire between the Indian Government and the Naga rebel government, there seemed little hope of a peaceful settlement within the framework of the Indian Union.

Finally, there were the problems of foreign relations, and especially those with Pakistan. The implementation of the Tashkent Agreement was bound to meet with obstacles. Hindu chauvinists in the Jana Sangh and their fellow-travellers in the Congress were strongly opposed to the promised Indian withdrawal from the strategic Haji Pir Pass in Kashmir, which had been won after much hard fighting. There was also a fundamental difference in the interpretation of the Tashkent Agreement by the two countries. While Pakistan stressed the importance of an early settlement of the Kashmir dispute, the Indian Government remained firmly committed to the position that Kashmir was not negotiable. Given the rigidity of both sides on this point, an early normalisation of relations seemed unlikely. There remained, also, the Sino-Indian dispute, which, though settled on the ground in China's favour, had yet to be terminated by a diplomatic settlement. Here, too, the new Government would be greatly handicapped by the inflexible stand taken by its predecessors which had, for all practical purposes, shut the door on a negotiated settlement. Meanwhile, the Peking-Rawalpindi axis would continue to pose a serious threat to India's security and divert the country's meagre resources from the urgent tasks of economic development.

In its relations with other powers, the prestige and respect which India had enjoyed in the hey-day of Nehruvian non-alignment had been drastically eroded since 1962, until by 1966 she seemed in danger of

---

*The party of militant Sikh nationalism.
**The Nagas, a colourful and fiercely independent tribal people in the hill regions of the north-east, had been resisting integration into the Indian Union ever since 1947.

almost total diplomatic isolation. The Soviet Union, once the most loyal supporter of India's stand on Kashmir, was moving slowly but noticeably towards a new role in the sub-continent, which, like that of the United States, involved the maintenance of a balance of power between India and Pakistan. Indo-American relations, never intimate, had recently touched a new low with the suspension of American aid, while Britain's Labour Government had tilted even more openly towards Pakistan during the recent war. Even India's pre-eminence in the Third World of the non-aligned had greatly diminished. The Cairo-Belgrade-Delhi axis, which Nehru had cultivated so assiduously, had been allowed to wither under the neglect of his more parochial successors, a fact which was brought home by the pro-Pakistan sympathies of the Arab world.

Only a strong and united government, firmly committed to radical and imaginative action, could hope to mobilise the country's internal resources and manpower, cope with the economic crisis, de-fuse inter-necine political disputes and rebuild India's international standing. But the Congress Party in 1966 was clearly in no position to provide such government. Concerned more with factional rivalries than with the necessity for organising the masses and recruiting cadres capable of implementing its programmes, the Congress leadership presented the spectacle of a house divided against itself and was fast losing its public credibility. And while the proximity of the next general election ensured that the Party would soon be judged by the electorate, it was also a disincentive to the bold and drastic remedies that the county's predicament required.

It was over this scene of decline, confusion and incipient collapse that Indira Gandhi had been called upon to preside. And while she lacked the powers that the situation required, she as the country's chief executive would have to bear the greatest responsibility. It was not an enviable position. Ram Manohar Lohia, the most irreverent and irrepressible of India's Opposition leaders, was not being entirely facetious when he expressed the hope that the Congress Government would soon be dismissed, so that 'this pretty woman does not have to suffer pain and trouble beyond her endurance.'[6] 'We will have a pretty face for a time', he cynically observed, 'and she will be burdened with the weight of her father's and Mr. Shastri's misdeeds. To that we can safely add the burden of her own misdeeds.'[7]

If Indira Gandhi was, indeed, staggering beneath the weight of her dismal inheritance, she gave no sign of it at her first press conference as Prime Minister-Designate on 19 January. 'I feel neither excited nor nervous', she assured newsmen. 'This is just another job I have to do. I have done a number of jobs in the past and, yes, I feel up to it.'[8] In reply to the doubts expressed by Vijayalakshmi Pandit regarding her health, Mrs. Gandhi asserted: 'Those who have watched me grow know that I am frail and hardy at the same time.'9 She dismissed with some petulance the suggestion that her sex might prove a handicap. 'It is only foreigners,' she complained, 'who doubt the capabilities of a woman, just because they do not have so many women rising in the political field in their own countries. Indians, I am sure, harbour less doubts in that way.'10

When questioned about the country's problems, her replies tended to be vague and non-committal. 'India will honour the pledge given by the late Prime Minister,' she said with reference to the Tashkent Agreement. 'I have already welcomed it. It is the first step. Any step towards peace is a good step.' 'The Chinese threat to our frontier still remains,' she continued. 'If conditions are created in which we can talk of peace, certainly we will do so. But certain things will have to happen before that.' She was eagerly questioned about the composition of her Cabinet, but refused, very sensibly, to show her hand. 'Wait and see,' she quipped. 'I did not begin forming the Cabinet before I was elected.'11

Indira Gandhi's election had been welcomed optimistically as a victory for youth, which would achieve at last the transfer of power from the elders who had won Independence to a younger and more forward-looking generation. It was natural, then, that her Cabinet should be expected to include a generous infusion of new blood. What emerged, however, from the web of Cabinet-making was more or less a reflection of the status quo. Kamaraj is reported to have opposed any major changes in the existing Cabinet, arguing that these could be made later, if and when the Prime Minister encountered resistance from any of her colleagues in the implementation of the Government's programme. Mrs. Gandhi does not seem to have taken the same view and was particularly keen to remove Nanda from the crucial Home Ministry, where he might function as a de facto Deputy Prime Minister. She intended instead to give the Home portfolio to Swaran Singh, a docile and uncontroversial Sikh, while herself taking over the latter's portfolio of External Affairs. Although she stuck to her own plans till the eleventh hour, Nanda was adamant in his desire to retain Home. Failing that, he threatened to opt out altogether from the Cabinet, and he was able to canvass support from Kamaraj and even from President Radhakrishnan. Mrs. Gandhi had planned to submit her list to the President on the 22nd evening, but the wrangle with Nanda created an unexpected delay. Eventually, at midnight on the 23rd, Mrs. Gandhi gave way and told Nanda that he could retain Home. It was 3 a.m. on the 24th morning when she arrived at the presidential palace and presented her finalised list to a doubtless bleary-eyed President.

Indira Gandhi's exercise in Cabinet-making, the first of many, must have brought home to her the strong pressures to which she was subject and her own impotence in resisting them. All the major portfolios—Home, Defence, Finance, Food and External Affairs—had to be left undisturbed. Her only consolation was that three of her nominees—Asoka Mehta, Fakhruddin Ali Ahmed and G.S. Pathak—had been included in the Cabinet, while Dinesh Singh, a close confidant, became a junior minister in the External Affairs Department and was also officially designated by the President to 'assist the Prime Minister in such functions as may be assigned by her.'[12]

On 24 January, at a formal ceremony in the Asoka Hall of Rashtrapati Bhavan, Indira Gandhi and her colleagues were sworn in by President Radhakrishnan. The new Prime Minister revealed her agnosticism when she chose to 'solemnly affirm' her allegiance to the Constitution, rather than 'swear in the name of God.' Among the spectators were Kamaraj, Krishna Menon, and the Nehru aunts—Vijayalakshmi Pandit and Krishna Hutheesing. Almost at once the new government was plunged into a series of crises which, according to the *Socialist Congressman*, were to make Mrs. Gandhi's first two months in office an 'ordeal by fire.'

The most urgent problem was that of food supplies, the mismanagement of which had been creating a law and order problem of alarming dimensions. The Centre's hesitant approach to the question of food distribution and the retention of the discriminatory and obstructive system of regional food zones had resulted in a violent agitation in Kerala, where rice—the staple food—was in short supply. Addressing a public meeting in Delhi on 31 January, Mrs. Gandhi appealed to the people of Kerala to change their food habits and eat what was available. A few days later, she signed a public pledge not to eat or serve rice—one of her favourite foods—until the Kerala rice situation returned to normal. Such appeals and gestures, however, could only have rhetorical value so long as the Government failed to adopt a firm and coherent strategy for the procurement and distribution of foodgrains. The shortage had reached such proportions that it could have been met by nothing short of a drastic reorganisation of the distribution system to eliminate hoarding, profiteering and other artificial impediments to food supplies. Such a reorganisation would have required nationalisation of the foodgrain trade, compulsory procurement, full-scale rationing and abolition of food zones. But these were measures for which the Government did not have the political will, the mass organisation, or the administrative capacity.

When the Congress met at Jaipur in early February for its annual session, the food problem, predictably, was the dominant issue. The leadership came under heavy fire, and the stormy proceedings demonstrated dramatically the new Prime Minister's helplessness to bridge the gap between the Government she headed and the Party's angry rank and file. On the eve of the session, a Convention of Socialist Congressmen, spurred on by the participation of G.L. Nanda, met and presented the Congress President with a memorandum criticising the Government for its failure to implement the Bhubaneshwar Congress resolution on Socialism. The meeting of the Congress Working Committee at the start of the session saw a sharp clash between Kamaraj and C. Subramaniam, the Union Food Minister, over the latter's plans for American collaboration in fertiliser production. There was also criticism from both Left and Right of Planning Minister Asoka Mehta's rather vague note on the economic situation.

Matters came to a head in the All India Congress Committee when Left and Right united behind an amendment to the official resolution on the food situation moved by Subramaniam. The amendment called for the immediate abolition of food zones. Amid general pandemonium, Mrs. Gandhi, who appeared visibly shaken, was pushed to the microphone to defend her colleague. She appealed to the angry delegates to withdraw the amendment, promising that the Government would examine the question of abolition. She was unable, however, to control the meeting and had to retire in some embarrassment. The amendment would probably have been carried, thereby administering a serious rebuff to the Congress High Command, had it not been for the forceful intervention of Kamaraj, who announced abruptly amid scenes of confusion that the amendment had been withdrawn following the Prime Minister's assurance.

Mrs. Gandhi's intervention in the debate on the Tashkent Agreement had a better reception. While reiterating India's stand on Kashmir, she said amid applause: 'If the Tashkent Agreement establishes peace between India and Pakistan, the surrender of Haji Pir Pass is a small price to pay for it.' Despite some criticism from chauvinistic elements, the official resolution approving the Agreement was unanimously adopted.

On 1 March, in her reply to the debate on the President's opening Address, the new Prime Minister made her debut in the Indian Parliament. Her performance does not appear to have enhanced her stature. As Minister for Information and Broadcasting she had rarely appeared in Parliament, and she was as yet unaccustomed to the complexities of Parliamentary procedure and the skills of political repartee. Nor was she proficient yet in the art of public speaking; she read out her speech with a somewhat monotonous and school-girlish sing-song intonation, rarely departing from her written text. Unchivalrous Opposition members made the most of her inexperience; her speech was constantly interrupted, and the Speaker had to come to her rescue. 'This obstruction cannot be allowed,' he scolded unruly members. 'You must let others hear the Prime Minister.'[13]

In the course of her speech, Indira Gandhi informed the House that the Government would soon review its food policy. She also promised to examine the question of lifting the National Emergency which had been in force since 1962. The Government's emergency powers were wide and had acted as a serious curb on normal political freedom. She was, therefore, warmly cheered by the Opposition when she assured the House: 'I myself feel strongly about the matter. I do not want to prolong it a day longer than necessary. I am anxious that fundamental rights which are enjoined in our Constitution should be restored.' In reply to Communist accusations of an imminent sell-out to the United States, she protested: 'Much as we want aid, we are not going to debase ourselves to get it. Foreign aid if it comes will help us; but if it does not, we can and shall manage without it.'[14]

Events were to show, however, that Indira Gandhi, for all her good intentions, was in no position to make good her promises. Under pressure from conservative Congress Chief Ministers, both food zones and the Emergency continued, despite the Prime Minister's known views on these matters. When the United Left Front of Opposition parties in West Bengal threatened to hold a general strike on 10 March to protest against the Government's food policy and to demand the release of arrested Opposition leaders, Mrs. Gandhi visited Calcutta and advised the Congress Chief Minister of West Bengal to release the arrested leaders and adopt a conciliatory approach. Her advice was sensible, but it was rudely brushed aside by the local Congress leadership. The result was violent rioting in Calcutta on a scale that necessitated army intervention. When at last the conciliatory policy initially suggested by her was adopted, the political climate was too bitter to permit of success.

In the two instances where the Prime Minister was able to have her way, the results were salutary. As with the old Bombay province in 1959, Mrs. Gandhi had now reached the conclusion that only a linguistic reorganisation could solve the Punjab problem, and she was fortunate in having the support of Kamaraj in this view. In response to a personal appeal from her, Sant Fateh Singh, the Sikh leader, had agreed to postpone his fast for a month. Meanwhile, on 9 March, the Congress Working Committee passed a unanimous resolution in favour of the creation of *Punjabi Suba*. The decision, a startling reversal of Congress policy, was totally unexpected, and even the Punjab Congress was taken unawares. While a Sikh agitation had been averted, the Hindu minority in the projected *Punjabi Suba* inevitably felt let down. Communal rioting, instigated by the Hindu-revivalist Jana Sangh, erupted in several areas of the Punjab and even spread to Delhi. In reply, Mrs. Gandhi declared: 'I have been accused of many things, but never of lack of courage.'[15] This time the party leadership was united behind her, and the Govern-

ment acted vigorously to restore law and order. Mob violence reached
its peak when three Congressmen were burnt alive in the town of Panipat
near Delhi, an atrocity which provoked a truly Nehruvian outburst
from the Prime Minister. Addressing a civic reception at the Red Fort for
the visiting Yugoslav Premier, she stormed:

'There are no tears in my eyes; there is anger in my heart... Is it for
all this that so many freedom-fighters and martyrs have sacrificed their
lives? How would I hold my head high and say India is a great country
and meet foreign dignitaries when violence and discord have fouled
the atmosphere?... I have a great deal of patience and tolerance,
but not beyond a limit. All necessary force will be used to put down
internecine fighting. The political parties who are indulging in violence
are doing the country great harm. They are not true Indians. Those
among them who profess to understand Hinduism know nothing about
Hinduism.'[16]

Indira Gandhi's bold decision on the Punjab paid off in the next few
months. While the Sikhs were delighted with the unexpected concession
of their demand, the Hindi-speaking population of the Punjab were
happy with the creation for them of a new State of Haryana. A dispute
over which of the two new States would get Chandigarh, the capital of
the united province, was shrewdly side-stepped by Mrs. Gandhi's quick
decision to make the city a Union Territory.

Amid the many preoccupations of these troubled months, Mrs. Gandhi
also found time to open negotiations with the leaders of the Naga rebel
government, despite criticism from chauvinistic elements in the Congress
and in Opposition. Her objective was, through a combination of firmness
and persuasion, to get the Nagas to accept a solution within the Indian
Constitution. The first round of talks in February was cordial, with the
Prime Minister and the Naga leaders agreeing on joint efforts to prevent
violations of the cease-fire by Naga splinter groups. A fortnight later,
the Mizo tribes of Assam, whose legitimate grievances had been long
neglected, were also in armed revolt, demanding like the Nagas a separate
nation. The Government responded with massive military force, and in
three weeks the revolt had been effectively crushed.

Despite charges that she had encouraged Mizo secessionism by her
negotiations with the Naga rebels, Mrs. Gandhi refused to abandon the
Naga peace talks, which were resumed as scheduled in April. Nor did
she hesitate to make minor concessions to facilitate the negotiations.
Though the Government had stated that political talks with the Naga
leaders would be conducted by Indian officials, when the 'Prime Minister'
of the Naga underground insisted that he would talk only to his equal, the
Prime Minister of India, Mrs. Gandhi agreed to conduct all the talks

herself. Again, while the Government had stated that there would be no further negotiations unless the rebel leaders agreed in principle to accept the Indian Constitution, Mrs. Gandhi agreed to continue the talks without preconditions. Even the controversial Michael Scott, whose attempts to internationalise the dispute had been strongly castigated in Parliament, was allowed for the moment to continue as a member of the Nagaland Peace Mission. The talks went on, and while no agreed formula emerged, the policy of coercion plus conciliation undoubtedly paid dividends in the long run. The process of negotiation itself succeeded in reducing tension and breaking Naga unity. The Indian army, meanwhile, proceeded with its 'pacification' of Nagaland and, over the years, was able through a combination of bribery and intimidation to extend its control of the Naga tribes.

*     *     *

Any attempt to tackle the country's economic crisis at its roots would have called for drastic social and economic reorganisation. But radical measures and 'hard' decisions could scarcely be taken by a government which lacked committed administrative cadres or by a political party which, though committed to socialism, was dominated by the landed and trading classes. Any attempt to impose socialism from the top would not only have disrupted the fragile unity of the Congress, but would almost certainly have led to Indira Gandhi's removal from the Prime Ministership. Mrs. Gandhi, in any case, was fitted neither ideologically nor temperamentally for the role of a revolutionary leader. She was, above all, a pragmatist and a gradualist. And while she had always described herself as a socialist, socialism was a term she preferred not to define, except to say that her concept of it was not dogmatic. 'I suppose you could call me a Socialist,' she told an American journalist, 'but you have to understand what we mean by that term. Socialism, like democracy, has such a wide range. It covers what is happening in Sweden, the Soviet Union and China. We used the word because it came closest to what we wanted to do here—which is to eradicate poverty. But we always meant an Indian product, suited to Indian conditions. You can call it Socialism; but if by using that word we arouse controversy, I don't see why we should use it. I don't believe in words at all. If some of the people in this country who care so much about words devoted half the time they devote to words to actually doing something, then we would be much better off.'[17]

Asked during the succession contest whether she was a representative of the Left, Mrs. Gandhi had replied: 'I am a representative of all India, which includes all shades of opinion.'[18] Three weeks later, in an interview with *Link*, the Left-wing weekly, her pragmatism expressed itself in an apologia for the right-ward trends in government which she herself had been criticising only a few months back. When reminded of her statement on the eve of the Durgapur Congress criticising the gulf between the socialist promises of the Congress and their implementation, she replied that, while there had been some retrograde deviations from accepted policies, this had been due to 'the compulsions of the need to meet some urgent deficiencies' and that she had no doubt about 'the good faith of those responsible for these departures.' She added, significantly, that she was now 'in a better position' to appreciate the complexities which had led to decisions of which she had formerly been critical.[19]

Indira Gandhi's swift transition from the role of critic to that of apologist followed naturally from her new position as the official head of a government in which she was by no means supreme. Nevertheless, whatever the limitations on her freedom of action, she was anxious that her government should not appear as a mere caretaker administration. She was enough of a political realist to see that if she, or indeed the Congress Party, was to survive the general election due in February 1967, her government must at least appear to be dynamic and purposeful. The limits of such dynamism were clearly defined by the essentially middle class composition of the Congress and by the tenacious grip of its conservative bosses on the party machinery. While her options were few, the economic situation demanded urgent action. If the Congress was to go to the polls with any confidence, economic distress must be alleviated or, at the very least, a full-scale famine averted.

'How can anybody who is the head of a nation afford not to be a pragmatist?' Indira Gandhi exclaimed in an interview. 'You have to be pragmatic, you have to be practical, every day. But you have to marry your pragmatism to some sort of idealism, or you'll never get people excited about what you want to do. For that reason, I believe we must set our goals high, even if we fail to attain them.'[20]

It was in this spirit of adventurous pragmatism that the new economic strategy associated with Indira Gandhi's first term of office was planned and executed. She herself was no economist. According to an unconfirmed report, when asked at a press briefing what were India's two greatest problems, she replied vaguely: 'Inflation and rising prices', a tautology which newsmen gallantly censored from their reports. Mrs. Gandhi appears to have been aware of her own limitations and was content to follow the advice of her economic experts. Three of them she had inherited from her predecessor—Finance Minister Sachindra Chaudhuri, Food Minister Subramaniam and L.K. Jha, head of the powerful Prime Minister's Secretariat—while the fourth, and most influential, Asoka Mehta, had been Vice-Chairman of the Planning Commission under Shastri and was now elevated by her to the newly created post of Minister for Planning. Working as a team and generally in agreement, they represented an essentially technocratic and apolitical approach to economic problems. None of them had a significant political base in the Congress Party, and they shared a strong antipathy to ideology, whether of the Right or the Left. Together they formulated what they considered a modern and progressive blue-print for action on the economic front. As described by Asoka Mehta, the new economic programme embodied four main points: a) Devaluation of the rupee as a means of promoting exports and securing massive foreign aid; b) the promotion of a 'green revolution' through State assistance to scientific, capitalist farming; c) the liberalisation of controls on private industry; and d) a vigorous family planning campaign.

Pragmatic this programme may have been; but non-controversial it certainly was not. While it owed much to the promptings of American and World Bank economists, it bore little relation to the socialism to which the Congress stood committed. While the new agricultural strategy was bound to enrich the big farmer and increase rural inequalities, the liberalisation of industrial licensing would appear as a surrender to Big Business. Politically, the most controversial item would be devaluation, which was bound to be seen as a humiliating surrender to American pressure. These implications were to become increasingly clear in the next few months.

Indira Gandhi seems to have accepted the advice of her economic team without reservations, though with her political experience she should, perhaps, have known better. Her job was to sell this economic package to the Party and the country; and she certainly did her best. On the advice of her new Press Secretary, George Verghese—one of India's leading journalists—she overcame her shyness of the mass media, holding frequent press conferences and making a monthly 'person to person' broadcast on All India Radio. Projecting herself as a symbol of modernism and progress, Mrs. Gandhi expressed her contempt for dogma, whether socialist or capitalist, and called for the co-operation and participation of youth and intellectuals. Initially, she was successful enough to be hailed in many quarters as an Indian Kennedy.*

The Prime Minister's new image took clear shape in her inaugural address to the annual session of the Federation of Indian Chambers of Commerce and Industry on 12 March. Here she announced her intention of convening 'Round Tables' of younger industrialists, technicians and managers from both public and private sectors to discuss economic problems. While she defended the Fourth Plan against the Federation

*Asked about this time to name the three non-Indians whom she most admired, Mrs. Gandhi mentioned Kennedy, along with Roosevelt and Einstein.

President's call for reduced investment in the public sector, her tone was conciliatory and even apologetic. 'Mr. President,' she said, 'you spoke of rigidity in planning and urged Government to move with the times. I do wholeheartedly agree with this sentiment. We have no desire to be rigid. But sometimes rigidity creeps in almost unconsciously. However, we are reviewing many things, the structure of controls, for instance.'[21]

On 2 March, in an interview with a British newspaper, Indira Gandhi had confidently asserted: 'There will be no famine. We have scarcity, but there is no question of starvation. It has been highly exaggerated. If we get help it is welcome. But if we don't get help, we shall manage... A lot of people, even quite poor people, come to me and say: "We don't like this attitude of begging".'[22] Less than a month later, however, she would find herself in the invidious position of visiting Washington in the supplicant role that she had thus derided. Given the inability of her government to take 'hard' decisions on food distribution, it was clear by then that the only alternative to famine was a massive inflow of American foodgrains. In the long run, too, an Indo-American entente was the logical cornerstone of the Government's economic strategy. Only massive American aid on a long-term basis could rescue the sinking Fourth Plan, while American collaboration in fertiliser production was expected to provide the basis of the projected 'green revolution'. Aid, however, would inevitably carry strings, and these would involve controversial re-adjustments in India's policies both at home and abroad.

Before her departure for Washington on 25 March, Mrs. Gandhi was at great pains to emphasise that the purpose of her visit was not to beg for aid; hers, she maintained, was primarily a goodwill visit in response to a long-standing invitation, originally extended to Shastri and subsequently renewed to his successor. Nonetheless, few political observers doubted that economic aid would figure prominently in her talks with President Johnson, and some were apprehensive of the outcome. 'It would be unwise on her own and the Government of India's part,' warned *Link*, 'to give the impression to the people of this country that her visit is not extremely significant. It is, because it is being made at a time when Indian capacity to resist America's extortionate diplomacy has been weakened by double-mindedness in the Indian Cabinet.'[23]

The American visit was Indira Gandhi's first foreign tour as Prime Minister; and judged by its aims, both real and ostensible, it was undoubtedly successful. The American mass media gave generous courage to her visit, and the American public was greatly excited by its glimpse of this exotic, Oriental leader with her so-called 'feminine mystique'. Praise was lavished upon her aristocratic and gracious bearing, her elegant clothes and her immaculate hair-dos. Mrs. Gandhi, for her part, responded warmly. In her reply to President Johnson's welcome address, she called India and the United States 'friends committed to common ideals' and added that the two countries 'cannot and should not take each other for granted or allow their relations to drift'.[24] A recurrent theme in her speeches and interviews was India's importance as a democratic alternative to Chinese Communism.

Mrs. Gandhi's talks with the American President were cordial, and they are reported to have had long private conversations while the Prime Minister's aides were closeted with American and World Bank officials. The President is believed to have been greatly impressed by the candour and informality of his guest, and he announced paternally at a party that he would see to it that 'no harm comes to this girl'.[25] Indeed, he was so charmed by her that he waived protocol and invited himself to dinner at the Indian Embassy after a cocktail party in his honour. There followed a game of musical chairs, as place-cards were hastily shifted, and P.N. Haksar*, the odd one out, was dropped from the table. Johnson is reported to have spent a total of three and a half hours at the Indian Embassy that evening, and his gesture was interpreted as the ultimate mark of favour.

The warmth of Johnson's hospitality was not merely a spontaneous Texan response to Indira Gandhi's personal charm and tact; it must certainly have been strengthened by the trend of Indo-American talks. Soon after her arrival, Mrs. Gandhi accepted the American proposal for an Indo-American Education Foundation—an Indian equivalent of the Ford Foundation, which would be endowed with 300 million dollars from American PL–480 rupee funds in India. The proposal was an old one and, though pressed hard by the United States, had been rejected by both Nehru and Shastri as giving the United States undue influence over higher education and research in India. While the other negotiations remained secret, Johnson and his advisers are believed to have extracted from the Indian Prime Minister a promise to devalue the rupee in the near future. She is also understood to have indicated her willingness to encourage American collaboration in Indian industry, especially in fertiliser production, and to reduce State controls on the Indian economy. Addressing a gathering of American businessmen in New York, she promised that India would treat foreign investors 'completely on a par with national investors'.[26] In the sphere of foreign policy, she is said to have agreed to tone down Indian criticism of the American role in Vietnam.

In return for these concessions, Mrs. Gandhi received an American undertaking for 3.5 million tons of foodgrains and 900 million dollars in non-project aid and a World Bank assurance to consider additional

*Later head of the Prime Minister's Secretariat and one of Mrs. Gandhi's chief advisers, Haksar was well known for his pro-Soviet and Marxist views.

project loans. Apparently, the only hitch that arose during her visit was her refusal to join President Johnson on the dance floor at a White House banquet in her honour. While assuring him that she had enjoyed ball-room dancing as a student, Indira Gandhi politely explained: 'My countrymen would not approve if they heard I had been dancing.'[27] She does not appear to have foreseen that her countrymen would approve still less of the political and economic implications of her visit.

'Is there a country today which needs nothing from others?' Indira Gandhi queried in a broadcast to the nation on 25 April. 'The fear that we have "sold out" under Western pressure or that we are going to be dominated by foreign capital is absurd.' In reply to attacks on the Government's fertiliser policy and the proposed Indo-American Education Foundation, she asserted that her government was 'not wedded to any dogma.' 'Our socialism,' she said, 'is one that is related to India's needs and aspirations and the reality of the Indian situation.'[28]

The Congress Left, nonetheless, was by now attacking her far more fiercely than it had Shastri. 'They no doubt regard her as a heretic,' wrote one political commentator, 'and throughout history heretics have been despised more than the infidel.'[29] Mrs. Gandhi's close advisers, and by implication she herself, were accused of surrendering to the United States and of going back on everything for which Nehru had stood. In Parliament Krishna Menon led the assault. Referring to India's foreign policy as 'flotsam', he demanded an explanation for the Government's silence on the Vietnam War. He went on to condemn the Indo-American Foundation as 'an intrusion into the cultural and intellectual life of the Indian people' and expressed the fear that India might soon become another Brazil.[30] Mrs. Gandhi, however, stuck to her guns. On 30 April she hit back at the critics of American aid, dismissing as 'rank misrepresentation and distortion of facts' charges that the country was being sold out. 'History,' she said, 'is replete with instances of developing countries having accepted aid from developed ones. Lenin took American aid after the Russian Revolution.'[31] Addressing a meeting of the Congress Parliamentary Party a fortnight later, she pointed out that Congressmen by their strident criticism of the Government were playing into the hands of the Opposition, and she told opponents of Government policies that they should leave the Congress.

Her critics, however, could not so easily be silenced. In the first week of May, dissident factions from both Left and Right had combined during elections to the executive of the Congress Parliamentary Party to administer a rebuff to the Government, and in particular to block the election of all those known to have the Prime Minister's backing. Mrs. Gandhi's growing isolation in the Party was made even clearer at the Bombay session of the All India Congress Committee later in the month, when many members of the Congress Right opportunistically joined the Left in attacking her for deviating from her father's progressive policies. Stung by this charge, she replied caustically: 'Today his (Nehru's) erstwhile critics have to tell me what his policies were.' After denying any deviation from accepted policies, she raised her voice and announced: 'If it is necessary to deviate from the past policies, I would not hesitate to do so. I must pursue the policies which are in the best interests of the country as a whole. If you do not agree with these policies, you have every right to remove me and have your own leader.' 'Congress is big, but India is bigger,' she warned her opponents, appealing from them to public opinion. The conservative *Indian Express* commented approvingly on her speech: 'Mrs. Gandhi has more than a flash of her father's spirit. With his combativeness, she combines a directness of thought and speech which tries to meet and answer the challenge of her critics logically and, more often than not, convincingly... The Congress would do well to remember that in the country as a whole Mrs. Gandhi ranks as its greatest talisman.'[32]

The Congress, however, was by no means unanimous on this point; and the Government's decision on 6 June to devalue the rupee by 35.5 per cent further weakened the Prime Minister's position. Rumours of devaluation had been in the air for some time, though consistently denied by the Government. Mrs. Gandhi and her advisers are believed to have taken the decision during their American visit, when told by the World Bank that devaluation was an essential pre-condition for further economic aid. Following the Prime Minister's return from abroad, preparations for devaluation had begun in secrecy. The Congress President had only been consulted at the eleventh hour and had objected vehemently to the proposal, on the ground that it would be a humiliating surrender to American pressure and would adversely affect Congress fortunes in the general election. His views, however, were ignored, as were those of dissidents in the Cabinet. The Emergency Committee of the Cabinet was not consulted till the 5th June, by which time a commitment had already been made to the World Bank. The opposition and reservations of some of her senior colleagues failed to move Mrs. Gandhi and she is reported to have remained silent at the meeting, except to repeat every now and then that foreign aid would not be forthcoming without devaluation.

When a formal meeting of the full Cabinet was called on the 6th, most members thought that they were being summoned to discuss the re-organisation of the Punjab. They were confronted instead with the more or less accomplished fact of devaluation, and their consent was no more than a formality. The Prime Minister's mind was made up. According to Asoka Mehta, she was even prepared, in the event of opposition from her colleagues, to reshuffle the Cabinet and had already seen the President in this connection. Taken unawares and unable to formulate any coherent alternative, Mrs. Gandhi's colleagues bowed to her wishes and to the persuasive arguments of her economic advisers. A few hours later, when Kamaraj was informed by the Prime Minister of the Government's decision, he reiterated his opposition and called for a meeting of the Congress Working Committee to discuss the decision before its official announcement. This proposal was firmly turned down.

'Let me be frank with you', Indira Gandhi told the nation in a broadcast on 13 June. 'The decision to devalue the rupee was not an easy one. It was taken after the most anxious and searching consideration. How much easier it would have been to have evaded a decision, to have drifted along—waiting, hoping! There are times in the history of every nation when its will is tested and its future depends on its capacity for resolute action and bold decision. This is such a time in India.'[33]

By deciding on devaluation, Indira Gandhi had revealed that she could, when necessary, take an unpopular decision. By swiftly imposing that decision on her reluctant colleagues, she had also demonstrated her political sagacity and skill. She appears, however, to have underestimated both the widespread opposition that would enable her opponents to undermine her position and the inertia that would negate the economic benefits of devaluation. The decision was condemned by the entire Opposition, and especially by the Communists who called it an 'economic coup' and demanded the Government's resignation. Within the Congress, devaluation created a hitherto unparalleled cleavage between the governmental and organisational leadership. It was predictable that Morarji Desai and his followers would attack the decision and make political capital of it. More alarming was the anger of the Congress President, whose support had been so vital for Mrs. Gandhi. He had felt for some time that he was not being consulted sufficiently, and devaluation was the last straw. 'A big man's daughter, little man's big mistake,' Kamaraj is said to have exclaimed with reference to his role in making Mrs. Gandhi Prime Minister.

Had it not been for the proximity of the general election and their continuing desire to keep out Morarji Desai, there is little doubt that the party leadership would have seized this opportunity to oust Indira Gandhi from the Prime Ministership. As it was, Kamaraj was determined that she and her advisers should not escape unpunished and that devaluation should be debated openly in party forums. When the Congress Parliamentary Party met on 6 July, criticism of devaluation had become synonymous with criticism of the Prime Minister, who was openly attacked for not consulting the organisational leadership. When the Congress Working Committee met a fortnight later, criticism of devaluation was almost unanimous and the Government was clearly on the defensive. Mrs. Gandhi herself sat in silence, leaving it to Chaudhuri and Mehta to explain the decision. Not a single Cabinet colleague or Chief Minister came to their defence. Among others, T.T. Krishnamachari, acting as Kamaraj's spokesman, condemned devaluation and pointed out that he, as Shastri's Finance Minister, had successfully resisted similar American pressure. According to *Link*, 'The Working Committee discussion reflected popular feeling on devaluation in clearer terms than any opposition rally of protest could have done.'[35]

Amid this political furore, little attention could be paid to the economic measures that were essential if devaluation was to succeed in its objectives. While Indira Gandhi and her advisers managed to survive the political storm, they were unable without the backing of the Party to surmount the governmental confusion and inertia that paralysed vital follow-up action.

Devaluation had been seen as a solution to the problem of India's balance of payments deficit. The United States and the World Bank, India's major creditors, had refused to underwrite the country's debts unless the depreciation in real terms of the rupee was officially recognised and its parity with the dollar accordingly re-adjusted. In theory devaluation might have stimulated economic growth by promoting Indian exports on a more competitive basis and by discouraging imports. This would depend, however, on two further factors—firstly, the ability of the Government to retrench private consumption and Government expenditure, thereby preventing further inflation; and secondly, the capacity of the Indian economy to reduce its dependence on imports. In practice, neither of these conditions was met. The failure of the monsoon in 1966 for the second year in succession and the continuing food shortage inevitably had inflationary effects on the economy, and the Government was unable to hold the price-line. At the same time, the Government lacked the political will and discipline to retrench its own expenditure. Mrs. Gandhi is reported to have written to all Chief Ministers suggesting a cut in public spending; but no one was willing to pay the political price of retrenchment, especially in an election year. The United States, meanwhile, insisted on the liberalisation of controls on industry and, as most domestic industries continued to depend on imports, prices of manufactured goods rose.

The best that can be said of devaluation is that it was a formal recognition of an existing economic reality and that it brought in the foreign aid necessary for the Fourth Plan. But as a solution to the balance of payments problem and a stimulant to greater productivity it failed miserably. Dependence on imports continued and the profitability of exports failed to increase significantly. For the Indian people, prices continued to spiral and economic hardship increased.

\*     \*     \*

By July 1966 it had become only too clear that the Indira Gandhi Government would have to refurbish its image and seek fresh support if it was to survive the post-devaluation storm. The open rift between the Prime Minister and the Congress President, and the alienation of the Congress Left, had isolated Mrs. Gandhi and her advisers. The chief beneficiary had been Morarji Desai, who remained outside the Government waiting for a suitable moment to take over the Prime Ministership. During her first six months in office, Mrs. Gandhi had paid scant attention to political manoeuvres, relying instead on the dubious panaceas of her economic advisers to maintain the prestige of her government. The devaluation crisis must have brought home to her the weakness of this strategy. While the economic dividends promised by her advisers failed to materialise, her political standing was being steadily eroded. With her acute sensitivity to political currents, she took heed of the danger signals and responded with characteristic resilience. While Asoka Mehta was deputed to try and woo Morarji Desai from his intransigent opposition, Mrs. Gandhi herself attempted to placate the Congress Left.

The Prime Minister's new orientation first became apparent in the sphere of foreign policy. India's international relations had received a marked fillip from Mrs. Gandhi's assumption of office. In contrast to her predecessor, she shared her father's keen interest in world affairs and was as much at home with foreign statesmen as with Indian politicians. Her Prime Ministership had been marked from the outset by a flurry of diplomatic activity in the Foreign Office.

In regard to Pakistan, Mrs. Gandhi, though refusing firmly to re-open the Kashmir question, had proceeded with the troop withdrawals and exchange of prisoners stipulated in the Tashkent Agreement. In an interview with *Le Monde* in February, she had stated that the door was also open for talks with China. Later in the same month, when President Nkrumah of Ghana visited Delhi on his way to Peking and Hanoi, she had seized the opportunity to discuss the prospects of an improvement in Sino-Indian relations. A month later, en route to Washington, she had found time to visit President de Gaulle in Paris and is reported to have charmed the General and his aides with her elegant French. Marie Seton, an eye-witness, wrote of that occasion: 'Never since the first day I met her had Indira projected her personality with such confidence and sparkle. She suggested the skill of a seasoned politician whose natural candour had not been submerged by the magnitude of the problems besetting her.'[36] On her way back from the United States, Mrs. Gandhi had also stopped over in London for a talk with Prime Minister Wilson, whose pro-Pakistan statements had strained Indo-British relations, and in Moscow, where she discussed the implementation of the Tashkent Agreement with the Soviet leadership.

During these early months, Indian foreign policy had been greatly inhibited by the compulsions and implications of American aid. Nevertheless, personal, political and economic factors soon combined to ensure that the Indo-American honeymoon would be no more than a brief marriage of convenience. Despite criticism from the Indian Left, Indira Gandhi might well have persisted in her initial friendliness to the West had it not been for the somewhat crude and heavy-handed diplomacy of the American Administration, expecially in the delicate matter of food aid. Food supplies from the United States proved to be irregular and dilatory, with each shipment having to await the President's personal sanction. For a country on the brink of famine, this 'ship-to-mouth' existence was a bitter lesson in the disadvantages of living on foreign charity, with all the economic uncertainties and political pressures that it involved. Mrs. Gandhi, in particular, is reported to have felt this humiliation keenly, and it appears to have left a permanent scar on her view of Indo-American relations. 'It was not a position she liked being in,' says L.K. Jha,* 'and she was determined never to be in it again.'[37]

The impact of the Indo-American entente had been most noticeable in India's approach to the Vietnam War, and it was here that the cracks first appeared. In deference to American requests, the Indian Government had remained conspicuously silent on Vietnam. On 1 July, however, Mrs. Gandhi, under the pressure of public opinion, broke this silence with a statement 'deploring' American bombing of Hanoi and Haiphong. She is believed to have been advised by Krishna Menon—she still consulted him unofficially—that it was time for an Indian peace initiative, and a peace appeal was drafted by the Foreign Office, reportedly with Krishna Menon's assistance. It was significant that the Indian peace proposals were incorporated in the Prime Minister's broadcast to the nation on the eve of her departure on an official visit to the Soviet Union via Egypt and Yugoslavia. While the proposals marked a definite advance on the Government's hitherto non-committal attitude, they were still vague enough not to offend the United States. Whereas Tito and Nasser called for a halt in American bombing as the necessary pre-condition for peace talks, Indira Gandhi had called for a Geneva-type peace conference and a cessation of bombing and other hostilities, without spelling out which must come first. It was not surprising then that her peace plan was greeted with some suspicion in the Kremlin.

*Then head of the Prime Minister's Secretariat and one of her chief economic advisers; later India's Ambassador in Washington.

In the months that preceded Indira Gandhi's Russian visit, the Soviet leadership had been greatly displeased by the right-ward trend of Indian policies at home and abroad. Ever since Mrs. Gandhi's trip to Washington there had been a pronounced coolness in the Soviet attitude to her personally; Kamaraj, by contrast, was hailed by pro-Soviet elements in India as the only consistent radical in the Congress leadership. Devaluation had been openly criticised in the Soviet press, especially when it was followed by indications that the Government of India was having second thoughts about the profitability of Indian trade with Russia and Eastern Europe. The Soviet Union, for its part, had caused some alarm in New Delhi by its ambiguity on the Kashmir question and its expanding relations with Pakistan, and by the efforts of the Soviet Communist Party to heal the rift between the Left and Right Communists in India.

Seen in this context, Mrs. Gandhi's visit to Moscow on 12 July was undoubtedly an attempt on her part to reassure the Soviet leaders of her continuing friendship and good intentions. As a token of her goodwill, she agreed in Moscow to sign a communiqué which marked a significant advance on her recent Vietnam peace proposals. To the surprise and anger of the United States, India joined the Soviet Union in demanding an immediate and unconditional halt in American bombing of North Vietnam, condemned 'imperialist aggression' in Vietnam and stressed that the Vietnam problem could only be settled within the framework of the 1954 Geneva Agreements. Indira Gandhi's negotiations with the Soviet leaders appear to have been somewhat strenuous. 'Madam, you need a holiday!' Kosygin is reported to have advised her at the end of her visit when he noticed her obvious fatigue.[38]

When asked at a press reception on 12 March whether she favoured the suggestions of Presidents Tito and Nasser for a non-aligned conference, Mrs. Gandhi had replied: 'Not immediately.'[39] During her foreign tour later that month, she had conspicuously omitted Cairo from her itinerary, thereby breaking a long standing Nehru tradition at a time when Nasser stood alone in opposing the Pakistani move, backed by several Arab countries, for an Islamic Bloc in West Asia. Mrs. Gandhi's visits to Cairo and Brioni in July were therefore significant, indicating her intention of reviving her father's close contacts with Egypt and Yugoslavia. Her desire to restore the anti-colonial content of Indian non-alignment was further demonstrated when in October she hosted a tripartite non-aligned summit conference in Delhi, attended by Presidents Tito and Nasser. While there were natural differences in emphasis between the three participants, they were able to achieve a wide measure of agreement, expecially on the dangers of Western neo-colonialism and the need to combat it through closer consultation and economic co-operation with each other. 'A brutal and tragic conflict is raging in Vietnam', Mrs. Gandhi reminded the conference in her inaugural address. 'It must be ended before it destroys the entire country and spreads and engulfs the world.'[40] Vietnam figured prominently in the talks, and the final communiqué revealed a near unanimity among the three countries about how the war should be ended.

In domestic politics, too, there was a noticeable change in the Prime Minister's position. Though refusing to sacrifice the architects of devaluation, she made a series of conciliatory gestures to the Indian Left. The much-condemned proposal for an Indo-American Education Foundation was abandoned. Subsequently, in an interview with *Blitz*, the Left-wing weekly, Mrs. Gandhi expressed her disapproval of some recent collaboration agreements with Western private investors and promised a thorough investigation. At the same time, she refused to give in to Right-wing criticism of the size of the Fourth Five-Year Plan, with its large investment in heavy industry and the public sector. She is also believed to have partially mended her fences with Kamaraj. Owing largely to their combined efforts, the Congress Election Manifesto issued in September reflected a new Left-of-Centre consensus and was welcomed by the Congress Left as a step in the right direction. While omitting any reference to the role of private industry, the manifesto stressed the need to keep the 'commanding heights' of the economy in public hands and to bring the banking system under 'social control'.

Towards the Communists, too, Mrs. Gandhi adopted a conciliatory tone, and they were not unresponsive. When a large Communist procession marched to Parliament House to demand the Government's resignation, their attack was directed not at Mrs. Gandhi, but at her unpopular advisers—Chaudhuri, Subramaniam and Mehta—and at leaders of the Congress Right such as S.K. Patil and Morarji Desai. The Prime Minister herself escaped criticism and was urged to rid herself of her unpopular colleagues and form a new and more progressive government.

A prominent Opposition leader is reported to have likened Indira Gandhi to 'a fickle pilgrim who travels one year to the Ganges and the next to the Jumna, acting like a capitalist in Washington and a socialist in Moscow.'[41] The swinging of the pendulum, however, was by no means the result of fickle feminine caprice. Mrs. Gandhi's new Left-of-Centre orientation was as natural and logical in political terms as her earlier Right-of-Centre stance. Both were flexible and well-considered responses conditioned by her instinct for self-preservation in an unstable and rapidly developing political situation.

*        *        *

Addressing the All India Congress Committee at Ernakulam (Kerala) in September 1966, Indira Gandhi had given the Congress the election slogan, 'One Country, One Team.' emphasising thereby that the party must go to the polls united and with a single programme for the whole country. While the AICC session did succeed in securing a consensus for the Congress Election Manifesto, the next four months before the general election were to demonstrate that the Prime Minister's slogan could be no more than a pious hope, given the strength of divisive forces in the Congress and the country. Though Mrs. Gandhi herself had been trying since the devaluation crisis to regain the political initiative and rebuild her waning popularity, such success as she had achieved had been at the cost of appeasing her critics by retracing many of her earlier steps. Her position remained insecure and her powers as Prime Minister continued to be restricted.

Kamaraj, meanwhile, had emerged as the favourite of the Moscow-oriented Indian Left. The Congress President's successful ten-day visit to the Soviet Union, following closely on Mrs. Gandhi's, had done much to boost his prestige. The Kremlin had received him with the honours due to a visiting Head of State. According to the Indian press the Soviet leadership had been greatly impressed by the fact that Kamaraj was 'a man of the masses and has no airs about him' and as such 'truly represents the Indian people.'[42] Implicit in such remarks was a comparison unfavourable to the Prime Minister; but whatever her feelings, she could not afford yet to dispense with Kamaraj's support. At a reception to welcome him back from his foreign tour, she felicitated him: 'We are indeed fortunate that at this critical time we have a captain like you to guide our ship.'[43] Kamaraj, we are told, did not return the compliment. The extent of the Prime Minister's continuing dependence on the Congress President and other organisational bosses was to be dramatically revealed during the Cabinet crisis that followed on the anti-cow-slaughter agitation.

The demand by Hindu chauvinists for a national ban on cow-slaughter dated back to pre-Independence days. Enlightened, secular opinion had consistently opposed it as being obscurantist and patently unjust to low caste groups, Muslims and other minorities, for whom beef was a staple food. In November 1966, however, the Jana Sangh and other reactionary Hindu elements had launched a nation-wide campaign for the banning of cow-slaughter. Their aim was to make political capital of a religious issue on the eve of the general election. The agitation culminated in an orgy of violent rioting and arson in New Delhi by a mob of 100,000 naked *sadhus* who attempted to march on Parliament House.

When legislation to prohibit cow-slaughter had been suggested in 1956, Nehru had described the proposal as 'futile, silly and ridiculous' and had threatened to resign on the issue. His daughter though less categorical in her opposition, made it clear during the 1966 riots that she would not, as she put it, be 'cowed down by the cow-savers.'[44] 'This is not an attack on the Government,' she told Parliament. 'It is an attack on our way of life, our values and the traditions which we cherished.'[45] She went on to suggest, tongue in cheek, that the funds being spent by those who were behind the agitation would be better employed in saving cattle in the drought-stricken areas of U.P. and Bihar.

One of the by-products of the anti-cow-slaughter riots was the resignation of Home Minister Gulzarilal Nanda. It was common knowledge that Mrs. Gandhi would have liked to dispense with Nanda when she assumed office and that he had been forced upon her by Kamaraj. It was not surprising, then, that she refrained from coming to his defence when he was attacked for his weak handling of the *sadhus'* demonstration in the capital. Stung by the Prime Minister's attitude, Nanda offered his resignation in a long letter which criticised the functioning of the Government as a whole and attributed the short-comings of the Home Ministry to Mrs. Gandhi's lack of confidence in him personally. 'I had hoped,' he wrote, 'for a sense of personal fulfilment in working as a member of your team. I was soon to experience the pain of unreciprocated confidence. Slowly but surely the political image of the Home Minister, on which alone depends the success of his diffiult assignment, was undermined by methods which cannot be retold without causing pain and hurt. Throughout these eight or nine months, I have pleaded time and again that I may be allowed to strengthen the political wing of the Ministry. On a number of occasions, I brought to your notice that I was not getting adequate secretarial assistance... All these appeals were ignored... I was made to feel that I had no say in the making of decisions at the policy-making level. Have you ever thought to yourself how I was expected to function with the kind of tools you gave me to work with?' 'I continued to work,' he concluded in a more conciliatory vein, 'because the thought uppermost in my mind always was not to do anything which would embarrass you and the Party when you were face to face with some of the most difficult problems this country has ever faced. There was this sense of personal attachment to you born out of long years of association with Jawaharlal.'[46]

Indira Gandhi, however, had by now grown impatient of the patronising attachment of her father's colleagues. She and what was often labelled her 'Kitchen Cabinet'—Subramaniam, Mehta and Defence Minister Chavan—are believed to have considered that the time was ripe for a major Cabinet reshuffle which would assert the Prime Minister's independence of the party bosses and give the Government a new look. Nanda's resignation was accordingly accepted, and Mrs. Gandhi herself temporarily took over the Home portfolio on 9 November. Late the same night, Finance Minister Chaudhuri and Commerce Minister Manubhai Shah were summoned to her residence and told to their astonishment that she had decided to drop them from her Cabinet. The next morning news of the Prime Minister's intentions appeared in the press. But Kamaraj and the Syndicate, though taken unawares, were determined not to be out-manoeuvred. President Radhakrishnan, too, is reported to have advised Mrs. Gandhi to consult the party leaders before making such drastic Cabinet changes on the eve of a general election. While she succeeded, despite opposition, in appointing Chavan to the Home Ministry in place of Nanda, Mrs. Gandhi, after a forty-five minute interview with Kamaraj, had to surrender to pressure and abandon the idea of dropping Shah and Chaudhuri. Far from refurbishing the Government's image and demonstrating the Prime Minister's independence, the attempted reshuffle had ended in a humiliating public set-back for Mrs. Gandhi.

Given the keen rivalry within the Central Congress leadership, the selection of Congress candidates for the coming general election was bound to assume crucial importance. Indira Gandhi's strength, and even her survival, after the elections would depend largely on how many of her supporters were elected to Parliament. It was not surprising then that the rival factions used all their leverage to influence the decisions of the Congress Central Election Committee on party nominations. Mrs. Gandhi's lack of control over the party machine proved a serious handicap to her influence on the choice of candidates, and this was amply demonstrated by the affair of Krishna Menon's nomination.

Though Menon was the sitting M.P. for the North Bombay constituency and had won by an overwhelming majority in the 1962 general election, he was now denied the party nomination owing to the hostility of S.K. Patil, the Bombay Congress boss, and Morarji Desai. Both Mrs. Gandhi and Kamaraj were known to favour Menon's candidature; but neither was willing to make an issue of it, and each sought to shift the onus onto the other. Mrs. Gandhi had publicly voiced her support for Menon's re-nomination, and his rejection was seen as a direct challenge to her from the Syndicate. The Prime Minister, it was rumoured, was tired of being obstructed and was even thinking of resigning in disgust; but as it happened, she did nothing of the sort. When the matter was referred back to the Central Election Committee at Kamaraj's instance, Mrs. Gandhi remained silent at the meeting in order to avoid clashing swords with the Syndicate. The result was Menon's secession from the Congress—he decided to contest his old seat as an Independent—and yet another public demonstration of the Prime Minister's impotence in party affairs.

\*      \*      \*

'The choice of a Prime Minister is never a vocal issue at election time in a parliamentary democracy,' Krishna Menon warned the Congress leadership in a public statement.[47] It was sound advice; but the Congress did not heed it. The verdict of the electorate was taken for granted; and the leadership contest, which would normally have followed the general election, had already begun well in advance. Morarji Desai was generally known to be planning yet another bid for the Prime Ministership, especially now that Mrs. Gandhi appeared to have alienated her erstwhile sponsors, Kamaraj and the Syndicate. Kamaraj himself and Y.B. Chavan were also considered possible contenders. Asked on 25 December about her differences with the Congress President, Indira Gandhi confidently declared: 'Here is a question of whom the party wants and whom the people want. My position among the people is uncontested.'[48]

This appeal from the party to the country was to be characteristic of Mrs. Gandhi's strategy in the factional struggles within the Congress leadership. Her mass appeal was her strongest weapon, making her a valuable election symbol for Congress candidates, and she was learning how to use it. Her arduous and extensive election tours, which took her to virtually every State in the Union, were carefully organised with an eye on the post-election leadership contest. In the first two months of 1967, Mrs. Gandhi toured 15,200 miles and addressed 160 public meetings. Wherever she went, she solicited the support, not only of the crowds she addressed, but of the various Congress candidates, State leaders and Chief Ministers.

Indira Gandhi was no stranger to the art of electioneering; but this was the first time that she was heading the Congress election campaign. While her election tours afforded her a unique opportunity to project her image in the country at large, she would experience also the occupational hazards of leading an increasingly unpopular and divided party to the polls. Like her father, she was not an inspiring orator, and the tone of her public speeches was quiet and conversational. But unlike Nehru, she did not allow herself to indulge in abstract, philosophical digressions. Though she was often vague and unconvincing in her defence of the Congress Party's obvious failings, her arguments were always practical and simple—sometimes to the point of being facile—and illustrated by metaphors and analogies that were immediately intelligible to the common man in terms of his own experience. Her obvious aristocratic refinement, which made her an object of awe and veneration for large numbers of the Indian masses, was blended with an earthy, maternal common sense with which the average housewife could identify. This subtle synthesis of aristocracy and populism was to be the secret of her political charisma. In a typical speech at Rai Bareilly (U.P.)—formerly her husband's constituency and now her own—she told her audience:

'My family is not confined to a few individuals. It consists of crores of people. Your burdens are comparatively light, because your families are limited and viable. But my burden is manifold, because crores of my family members are poverty-stricken and I have to look after them. Since they belong to different castes and creeds, they sometimes fight among themselves, and I have to intervene, especially to look after the weaker members of my family, so that the stronger ones do not take advantage of them.'[49]

It was no easy task to apologise to an angry electorate for the Government's glaring failures on the economic front. Indira Gandhi sought to do so by analogies which, whatever their literary and rhetorical merit, bore little relation to socio-economic realities. 'The nearer you get to the peak, the more difficult it is to climb,' she reminded a Bombay audience. 'It is more difficult, not only because the mountainside becomes very much steeper, but the air is more rarefied, the wind is stronger and it needs all your physical strength and stamina just to stay on and not be blown off. And not only to stay on but to advance is something which really strains a person's fullest physical capacity.'[50] The metaphor seemed better suited to Mrs. Gandhi's own predicament than to that of the nation, which appeared to be descending a slippery, downward slope.

The general election found the Opposition mounting a militant offensive against the Congress, spurred on by signs that the monolithic party which had ruled India uninterruptedly for twenty years was at last tottering to its grave. Widespread economic distress, supplemented by emotive issues like language and cow-slaughter, had created an unprecedented popular groundswell of anti-Congress feeling. The Opposition parties, however negative, obscurantist or parochial their programmes, were the obvious beneficiaries, and they made the most of their opportunity. Congress election meetings were frequently disturbed and Congress leaders persistently heckled. Indira Gandhi did not escape her share of public abuse; but far from intimidating her, it sparked off some of her most spirited public speeches. When adherents of the Swatantra leader, the Maharani of Jaipur, attempted to break up Mrs. Gandhi's public meeting in Jaipur City, she refused to withdraw, though advised to do so by local Congress leaders anxious about her safety. Instead she lost her temper and raged at her audience:

'I am not going to be cowed down. I know who is behind these demonstrations, and I know how to make myself heard. I am going to do some plain speaking today. Go and ask the Maharajas how many wells they dug for the people in their States when they ruled them, how many roads they constructed, what they did to fight the slavery of the British? If you look at the account of their achievements before Independence, you will find a big zero there.'[51]

Conflict, even when it turned violent, seems to have brought out the best in her. When she insisted on addressing a stormy public meeting in the State of Orissa, another Swatantra stronghold, a stone from the audience hit her squarely on the nose, fracturing the bone. Though the pain was excruciating, Mrs. Gandhi refused to retire. Facing the turbulent crowd with a blood-stained handkerchief, she stormed: 'This is an insult not to me but to the country, because as Prime Minister of India I represent the country!'[52] Public opinion in general was outraged by the incident; and Indira Gandhi's physical courage undoubtedly paid political dividends, especially when she continued to tour the country and address election rallies with her nose and head swathed in bandages. She herself, once her initial anger and humiliation had subsided, appears to have taken a humorous view of the episode. 'I am most upset,' she complained to her aunt Krishna after the fracture had been set. 'As soon as I came out of the anaesthesia, I asked the doctor if he had done any plastic surgery and given me a beautiful nose. You know it is too long, and here was a chance to give me a beautiful nose.'[53] The doctor, however, had not seized the opportunity, and Indira Gandhi's nose, like her political prestige, survived the Opposition's onslaught undiminished.

\*          \*          \*

'When you go to battle, you must go with the point of view of winning,' Mrs. Gandhi had said in December 1966. 'Nobody can win a battle if he goes thinking that he cannot perhaps win. If you have that thought, then already half the battle is lost.'[54] She herself had followed this maxim and campaigned vigorously for the Congress in the general election. But no amount of self-confidence could restore the ruling party's popularity on the eve of polling. Corruption, factionalism and inertia in the Congress had undermined the party's moral authority and political credibility at a time of grave economic hardship. Long accustomed to a monopoly of power, the Congress leadership had turned a blind eye to the signs of public disaffection, and the results of India's fourth general election in February 1967 came as a bolt from the blue. The Congress lost 83 seats in the Union Parliament, though retaining a slender majority of 25, and was swept from power in eight States, its place being taken by various Opposition coalitions. Except in Kerala and West Bengal, where the Communists gained, the Congress debacle benefited feudal, communal and regionalist parties, such as the Swatantra, the Jana Sangh and the D.M.K. While the Congress remained the largest single party in the country, it had lost its dominant position. India had moved from a state

of one-party dominance to an embryonic multi-party system, a develop-
ment which was bound to affect seriously both the balance of Centre-
State relations and the stability of a greatly weakened and demoralised
Central Government.

In a broadcast to the nation on the election results, Indira Gandhi
commented optimistically: 'Democracy implies choice. Choice involves
alternatives. It is a healthy sign that alternatives are emerging and
competing.'[55] She herself could afford to be cheerful. She had been
returned to Parliament by a vast majority from her own constituency,
while many of her rivals in the Congress had been ignominiously routed
at the polls, the most notable instances being Kamaraj and S.K. Patil.
Though the party she led had been badly mauled, Mrs. Gandhi's position,
paradoxically, had never been stronger. For one thing, the Congress
President and the Syndicate, following their electoral reverses, were in no
position to play the role of king-makers at the Centre and force a change of
leadership on the new Congress Parliamentary Party. For another, the
slender majority of the Congress at the Centre and its defeat in several
States was a powerful argument in favour of maintaining the status quo in
leadership so as not to splinter further such strength as the party retained.
It could also be argued that in the changed context of non-Congress
Governments in several States, the Prime Minister must be a pragmatic
and unifying All-India figure who would be acceptable to Opposition
parties, a notion which seemed to rule out Morarji Desai and strengthen
the case for Mrs. Gandhi's continuation.

Initially, however, an acrimonious leadership contest—the first
involving an incumbent Prime Minister—appeared inevitable. Desai,
having stood aloof in the past three years from the governmental and
organisational leadership of the Congress, had emerged from the general
election with his prestige intact. He seemed determined to contest the
leadership, and New Delhi again became a market-place for pre-succession
canvassing and horse-trading. The apportioning of responsibility for the
Congress election reverses was a hotly-debated issue, with the rival
factions attempting to lay the blame at each other's door. On the one
hand, Mrs. Gandhi's supporters asserted that the elections had demonstrated her popularity with the masses and that she could not be held
responsible for the defeat of colleagues whom she had wanted to drop
in any case. The Congress reverses, they argued, were the result of the
party's organisational weakness, for which the Prime Minister was not
to blame. On the other hand, Desai's followers declared that the party
bosses who had made Mrs. Gandhi Prime Minister had been rejected by the
electorate, that her government's policies had been the cause of the
party's unpopularity, and that the Congress in this moment of adversity
needed the strong leadership which Desai alone could provide.

In the context of the leadership struggle, much importance was attached to the question of whether or not a lame-duck session of the pre-election Parliament should be held as scheduled to deal with the business left over from the previous session. The holding of such a session was vigorously opposed by Mrs. Gandhi and her supporters for a variety of reasons—it would mean postponing the leadership election, thereby allowing Desai more time to canvass M.P.s and giving the party bosses an opportunity to recover from the electoral blow they had suffered; and by exposing the Prime Minister to the jibes of the triumphant Opposition, it would damage her prestige on the eve of the leadership election. Mrs. Gandhi had her way, and the lame-duck session was scrapped.

As the date for the meeting of the new Congress Parliamentary Party approached, sentiment in favour of a unanimous choice of leader was growing overwhelming in the Parliamentary Party itself and at the level of State leadership. A contest, it was feared, would bring to a head the divisions in the ruling party and might even split the Congress at the Centre and in those States where it retained power. At a moment such as this, the Congress, it was felt, must close its ranks. Thus it was that the two rivals found themselves under mounting pressure to accept a compromise.

The Congress President, despite his diminished stature, was now able to assume a mediatory role. Also active in the cause of unanimity was D.P. Mishra, Chief Minister of Madhya Pradesh, who was generally regarded as a supporter of Mrs. Gandhi's. Mishra is believed to have advised Mrs. Gandhi to offer Desai the Deputy Prime Ministership, thereby clipping the latter's wings and averting a contest. The proposal, however, was not well received in the Prime Minister's camp. Indira Gandhi had long been impatient of the checks and balances imposed upon her by the party elders, and she had no intention of exchanging the tutelage of Kamaraj for that of Morarji Desai. Her younger advisers asserted vehemently that she had a majority in the Congress Parliamentary Party and that her prerogative of forming her Cabinet must be unfettered. While rejecting, therefore, the creation for Desai of the post of Deputy Prime Minister, Mrs. Gandhi indicated her willingness to accommodate him in the Cabinet with No. 2 rank and a senior portfolio other than Home. Desai, for his part, would accept no less a price for his withdrawal than the Deputy Prime Ministership with the crucial Home portfolio.

Both sides seemed set for a public trial of strength, when the collective intervention of four powerful State leaders—Mishra of Madhya Pradesh, C.B. Gupta of U.P., Brahmananda Reddy of Andhra and Nijalingappa of Mysore—who controlled between them 178 of the 435 members of the

Congress Parliamentary Party, strengthened Kamaraj's hand and enabled him to impose a compromise formula. Indira Gandhi and Morarji Desai were both told bluntly by the four Chief Ministers that unless they agreed to a compromise neither could expect their support in a contest. While Desai reluctantly abandoned his insistence on the Home portfolio, Mrs. Gandhi is reported to have resisted for two hours his appointment as her Deputy. Even after she gave in and agreed to the proposal, her more ambitious supporters—Chavan, Jagjivan Ram, Asoka Mehta and Dinesh Singh—would not let matters rest. At their prompting, she summoned Desai the next morning and warned him that the Deputy Prime Ministership would be no more than a formal designation and that his powers would be no greater than Nanda's had been as No. 2 in the Cabinet. Desai was furious, and the agreement reached the night before appeared to have broken down, when Kamaraj, Mishra, Gupta and Reddy intervened again, this time decisively. They are reported to have sternly reprimanded Indira Gandhi for what they considered her recalcitrant behaviour, and they succeeded in making her announce to the press her decision to make Desai Deputy Prime Minister. The leadership struggle appeared to be over; and Mrs. Gandhi was unanimously elected leader of the Congress Parliamentary Party on the following morning.

'How could I have defeated her when God was on her side?' Morarji Desai exclaimed fatalistically to an Indian journalist. There is little doubt that in the event of a contest Indira Gandhi would have defeated Desai with an even larger majority than in the previous year. It was not surprising then that she felt somewhat cheated of her due by the compromise that had been forced upon her. Though she had to accept Desai as Deputy Prime Minister for the sake of unanimity, she was determined not to allow the Congress President or the new Deputy Prime Minister to interfere with the formation of her Cabinet. One of her supporters in the Cabinet is reported to have observed: 'To have a weakened Morarji in the Cabinet is one thing; to have two conflicting groups is another.'[56]

In marked contrast to the formation of her first Cabinet in January 1966, this time Indira Gandhi kept her own counsel. The organisational leadership of the Congress was not consulted, and even Kamaraj was shown the list only a short while before it was due to be submitted to the President. When he queried some of the changes, he was told abruptly that they were intended to avoid 'complications.' The only leader whom Mrs. Gandhi is believed to have taken into confidence was Y.B. Chavan.

The composition of the new Cabinet reflected the Prime Minister's increased independence and the post-election weakness of the Syndicate. Mrs. Gandhi's close confidants—Asoka Mehta, Dinesh Singh and

Fakhruddin Ali Ahmed—were given control of the key economic portfolios, notwithstanding the advice of D.P. Mishra and others that Mehta
had become a political liability owing to devaluation and should be
dropped. Jagjivan Ram, who had staunchly opposed Desai's appointment as Deputy Prime Minister, was rewarded for his loyalty with a
senior portfolio. Also included in the Cabinet were Maharaja Karan
Singh of Kashmir and K.K. Shah, both believed to be loyal supporters
of the Prime Minister. The remainder of the team was made up of
nominees of the Chief Ministers of Maharashtra, Mysore, Andhra and
Madhya Pradesh, who had backed Mrs. Gandhi in the leadership
struggle. Morarji Desai's followers were not admitted to the Cabinet,
while Sanjiva Reddy, a member of the Syndicate, was dropped, despite
Kamaraj's intervention on his behalf. At the level of junior ministerships,
too, the younger elements who had been active in Mrs. Gandhi's
leadership campaign were suitably rewarded.

With the announcement of the new Cabinet, the power struggle
within the Congress leadership appeared to have been resolved. But
the unanimity achieved could not have been expected to endure. Morarji
Desai's presence in the Cabinet as Deputy Prime Minister, and the
long-standing rivalry between him and the Prime Minister, provided a potential rival centre of power in the Government around which dissident
factions might rally. At the same time, the role of some Chief Ministers in
the formation of the Cabinet implied that factional conflicts between 'ins'
and 'outs' at the State level would be projected at the Centre. The organisational leadership of the party, moreover, had been completely by-passed
in the formation of the Government; and this hiatus between the
organisational and legislative wings of the Congress did not augur well
for party unity or consolidation. The political fortunes of the
organisational bosses were, for the moment, at a low ebb; but it would
not be long before they would attempt to reassert their authority. Given
these factors, the new power balance represented at best a sullen and
negative unity which had been forced upon the Congress by the threat
from the Opposition.

\*       \*       \*

Indira Gandhi's re-election as Prime Minister in March 1967 marked
the end of the first phase of her leadership. Till then she had been a
Prime Minister on approval, and few political observers would have
predicted with any degree of confidence the continuation of her leadership.
1966 had been economically and politically the most troubled year since
Independence, and the Government had had to face a blow by blow
succession of crises. While the general election had shown dramatically
that the public standing of the Congress was at its lowest ever, in-fighting

within the party had never been so open and bitter. That Mrs. Gandhi had weathered these difficult times and emerged with her personal prestige enhanced was a testament both to her perseverance and her growing political skill. She had survived the initial period of uncertainty, and there could be little doubt, barring any major catastrophe, that she would continue to lead the country so long as the Congress retained its parliamentary majority. She had also served notice on the Congress leadership that she would be no figure-head and that she intended to rule as well as reign. Though new to the art of political management, she had learned quickly from her mistakes and had indicated that she intended to make the maximum strategic use of the Prime Ministership and the vast governmental patronage it commanded.

Paradoxically, though, Indira Gandhi's growing political stature, instead of making for strong and stable leadership, would make her increasingly the target of attack for envious and disgruntled elements in the party leadership who resented her independence and were determined to oust her at an opportune moment. It was, perhaps, with some irony that Morarji Desai commented on Mrs. Gandhi's re-election as leader on 12 March 1967: 'We are placing on her head a crown of thorns.'[57]

Shortly after she assumed office in 1966, Indira Gandhi had told an interviewer: 'Just because I'm Prime Minister I don't intend to give up all the things that make life worth living. I don't believe any of us can live in compartments.'[58] But however jealously she guarded the privacy and informality of her home, her public responsibilities and pre-occupations could not fail to overflow into her personal life. Her duties as Prime Minister left her with little time for personal friends, domestic pursuits or her favourite forms of recreation—reading, music, films and mountain-climbing. Clothes, jewellery, flower-arrangement, interior decoration and other aesthetic interests, which she had cultivated enthusiastically during the Teen Murti days, must now have appeared trivial and frivolous beside the national undertakings for which she bore chief responsibility. Despite her long involvement in politics, she cannot at first have found it easy to adjust to the all-consuming demands on her time and energies of her role as Prime Minister.

She appears also to have chaffed under the protocol and security arrangements which severely curtailed her personal freedom and spontaneity. When a friend strongly recommended the film *Becket*, then showing in Delhi, she exclaimed with girlish enthusiasm: 'Oh, I'd love to see it; but I suppose a Prime Minister can't just walk up to the box-office and buy a ticket.'[59] She arranged, however, for a private showing. Though impatient of restraints on her freedom of movement, Mrs. Gandhi appears, nonetheless, to have been acutely conscious of the dignity of her office and was keen to preserve its privileges, however minor. When Ram Manohar Lohia brought a privilege motion in Parliament, complaining that his taxi had been halted outside Parliament House to allow the Prime Minister's car to pass, Mrs. Gandhi, while conceding that other ministers should not have special privileges above ordinary M.Ps., maintained that the Prime Ministership was 'something special.'[60]

'Man does not live by beauty alone,' an Opposition member had warned Mrs. Gandhi in Parliament. 'History shows that a little less than two hundred years ago beauty did not save a queen from the guillotine.'[61] Though she must have been growing accustomed to such jibes, political anxiety does seem to have told upon her, frequently clouding the brief periods of leisure that she could snatch from her public duties. She is reported to have complained to a colleague: 'Previously, whatever happened my sleep was hardly ever disturbed. But now at times I can't sleep well.'[62]

The initial, transitional period must have been the most difficult. In time she would learn to insulate herself from the pressures and worries of her office, maintaining a calm and often complacent equilibrium amid the most trying and disturbing circumstances. 'I do remove myself from a place if I need to or if I am tired,' Indira Gandhi confided to a foreign interviewer. 'I do have the feeling sometimes if I am addressing a meeting that I am watching the whole procedure from the outside. And I sort of say: "Now I wonder what she is going to say or what she is going to do".'[63] This capacity for detachment and withdrawal would be useful in the years ahead, shielding her more vulnerable emotions from the barbs and irritants to which her office exposed her and enabling her to cope with the uncertainties of political life.

CHAPTER IX

# STRUGGLE FOR SUPREMACY

ALTHOUGH THE formation of Indira Gandhi's second ministry appeared
to have decided the leadership question, the unity of the Congress was
to be strained severely by a series of inner-party conflicts of increasing
magnitude, which culminated in November 1969 in the Great Split.
Mrs. Gandhi as Prime Minister naturally played a leading role in the
Congress drama, and her opponents and supporters alike have tended to
credit her with the chief responsibility for the split. Seen in its historical
context, however, the split was the result of a complex of factors, of
which Indira Gandhi's personality was by no means the most central.
The clash of personalities in the party leadership was symptomatic of a
deeper malaise which had its roots in the objective conditions of Indian
politics. The Congress at this juncture was the arena for serious factional,
organisational and ideological conflicts which overlapped, interacted and
reinforced each other, and in the midst of which the preferences of
individual leaders could have only marginal importance.

Factions, or personal groupings based on the ties of kinship, caste,
region and economic dependence, were probably inherent in the
application of a competitive political system to a traditional and semi-
feudal society. Factions had existed in the Congress virtually since its
inception, competing among themselves for Congress offices and
patronage. Such competition had intensified since the advent of Independence and the Congress Party's virtual monopoly of governmental
patronage. Though long active at the State and local levels, factionalism
in the Congress had been largely excluded from the Centre by the
dominant leadership of Nehru. But the passing of Nehru and the
succession struggles that followed had opened up Central politics to the
same group rivalries that had plagued the States. Factionalism at the
Centre fed upon factionalism in the States: while Nehru's insecure
successors sought to bolster their position through the support of State
leaders, the latter used their increased leverage at the Centre against
their own rivals at the State level. The result was a continuous power-
struggle at all levels of Congress leadership and the rapid erosion of such
party discipline, confidence and comradeship as the Congress had built

up during the Independence movement, and without which it could not hope to remain united.

The Opposition's spectacular gains in the 1967 general election had led to a temporary closing of ranks within the Congress. The factional rot, however, was too deeply embedded in the political consciousness of most Congressmen to permit of genuine unity and reorganisation. On the contrary, the fact that the Congress share of the national cake had greatly diminished would in the long run act as a spur to keener inner-party competition, while the party's slender majority at the Centre and in those States where it retained power would provide a powerful lever to dissident factions who now held the balance of power between Govern-ment and Opposition. In the course of the next four years, factionalism, and the political fragmentation, competitiveness and insecurity it re-flected, were to affect the Indian political system on an unparalleled scale, raising serious doubts about the survival of parliamentary government. It was to be a period of acute political cynicism and instability: Ministries would rise and fall in quick succession in several States as opportunist factions and parties manoeuvred for power and corrupt legislators sold themselves to the highest bidder. It would have been surprising indeed if the Congress and the Central Government had remained uninfected by this virus.

The Congress Party had long ceased to have any semblance of genuine party democracy. Party committees and offices were controlled for the most part by a self-perpetuating hierarchy of bosses, headed by the Congress President and the Syndicate, who were able to control and manipulate a passive and often bogus primary membership. The election debacle, however, had failed to bring home the necessity for democratising and reactivating the Congress organisation at its roots. Instead, it had merely brought to the fore a sterile controversy about the respective responsibility of the governmental and organisational leadership of the party for its electoral reverses and about the future role of the two wings in relation to each other. In 1951 Nehru had decisively broken the in-dependence of the party organisation and asserted his supremacy over Government and Party alike. But in the changed situation of 1967, Kamaraj and the organisational leadership were asserting their claim to formulate Congress policies and supervise their implementation by the Government. This claim could not fail to be resisted by the Prime Minister and her colleagues, on the ground that the Government, which had a wider responsibility to Parliament and the nation, could not accept such limits on its independence and that the proper role of the party organis-ation was to assist in the implementation of Government policies.

For four decades the Congress, while airing its commitment to social justice, had upheld the interests of the propertied élite goups who do-

1. Indira Gandhi, a profile

2a. Indira in Congress uniform with her parents, circa 1930

2b. Indira with Nehru in Prague, 1938

3a. Indira and Feroze Gandhi during their wedding ceremony, 1942

3b. Indira with Mahatma Gandhi, circa 1942

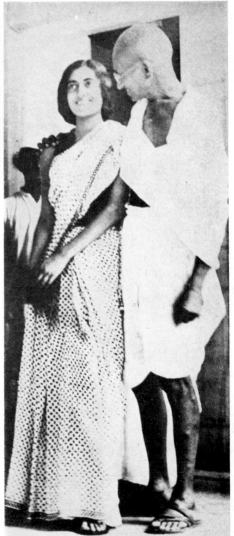

4a. Mrs Gandhi with her son Sanjay
and her father at Feroze Gandhi's
funeral, 1960

4b. Indira Gandhi celebrating Christmas
with her sons, Sanjay (*left*) and
Rajiv (*right*), and her daughter-in-
law, Sonia, 1970

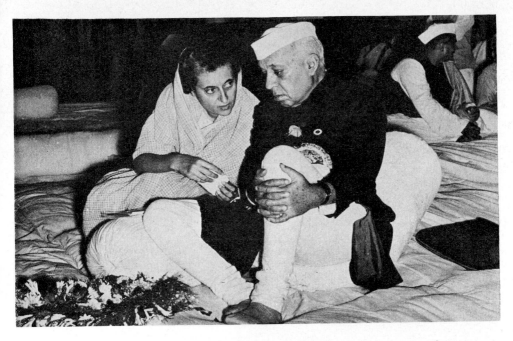

5a. Indira Gandhi with Nehru at the Bhubaneshwar Congress session, 1964, shortly before his death

5b. Indira Gandhi seated beside her rival, Morarji Desai, at a Congress meeting, 1969

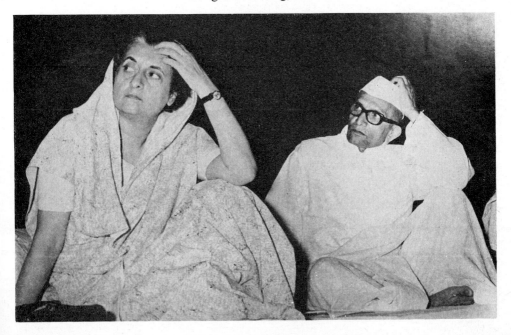

6a. Indira Gandhi crowned with flowers after her election victory in March 1971

6b. Mrs Gandhi at a military post near the Kashmir border, December 1971

7a.  Mrs Gandhi chatting with Premier Kosygin of the Soviet Union,
circa 1969

7b.  Mrs Gandhi being received by
President Nixon at a White House
banquet in her honour,
November 1971

8a. Mrs Gandhi receiving Sheikh Mujibur Rahman, Prime Minister
of Bangladesh, at Delhi airport, September 1972

8b. Mrs Gandhi with President Bhutto of Pakistan and his
daughter at the Simla Summit Conference, June 1972

minated its leadership. Attempts at ideological clarification and advance had been fiercely resisted as undermining party unity, which had to be based on the widest possible consensus. The 1967 election, however, had brought to a close the era of 'broad-bottom' government. By dramatically strengthening parties both to the Left and the Right of the Congress, the electorate had served notice that it would no longer tolerate vague, Centreist postures, especially at a time of intense economic hardship. The result was a growing realisation in the Congress that it could no longer survive by sitting on the ideological fence. Large numbers of Congressmen, prompted by the instinct of self-preservation, were coming round to the view that the party must project itself to the masses with a programme of radical reform if it wished to avoid extinction at the next general election in 1972.

Ideological differences in the party often coincided with factional rivalries, giving the latter a wider mass appeal. This polarisation was reflected in the attitude of rival Congress factions to the various Opposition parties in the new situation of non-Congress Governments in the States and demands for a National Government at the Centre. While the 'Young Turks', as the younger leaders of the Congress Left were called, favoured co-operation with the Communists and other Left parties, the Syndicate leaned towards an understanding with the Right-wing Swatantra and Jana Sangh. Both sides saw 'like-minded' Opposition parties as potential allies in a coalition government at the Centre in the event of the Congress splitting. The Opposition, for its part, was anxious to share power at the Centre, and would do its utmost to drive a wedge between rival groups in the ruling party and to profit from their internecine warfare.

Given the strength of these divisive pressures, it is highly unlikely that the Congress under any leadership could have survived intact for the next five years. Certainly, had the party been led by Morarji Desai, the split would have come much earlier than it did. As it was, Indira Gandhi did her best during the next two years to avert, or at least postpone, the parting of ways towards which the Congress was being thrust by political currents that were beyond the control of individuals. Mrs. Gandhi had been careful throughout her political career to avoid being identified with any faction and to project herself as a unifying national figure. She was experienced in the politics of consensus that characterised Congress decision-making, and so far she had functioned within its limits. During her tenure as Congress President, and again during her first term as Prime Minister, she had demonstrated her ideological flexibility. Neither by temperament nor by political training and conviction was she cut out for the role of polarising the Congress. It was ironical, then, that by the summer of 1969 political developments and her own responses to them would cast her in that very role.

As matters stood at the beginning of her second term in 1967, Indira Gandhi had nothing to gain, and possibly much to lose, by precipitating a split in the Congress. Her unanimous re-election as Prime Minister had established her claim to lead the country in her own right, rather than by the grace of the party bosses. Given time and political stability, the strategic advantages of her office and the patronage it controlled would enable her to consolidate her position in the Party and reassert the supremacy of the Prime Ministership. A split, on the other hand, would deprive her party of its narrow majority and, even if it did not lead to the fall of her govenment, would plunge her into turbulent and uncharted seas. Only in the last resort, when a direct challenge had emerged within the party both to her leadership and to the Left-of-Centre consensus that she considered essential to the party's survival, would she risk this leap in the dark. In the meanwhile, she steered clear of the hazardous politics of polarisation and relied instead on the tactics of political management and persuasion to maintain her position in inner-party disputes.

*          *          *

Scarcely a month had passed since the formation of Indira Gandhi's second government when internal differences in the Congress leadership were brought to the fore by the question of the party's nomination for the Union Presidency and Vice-Presidency, for which fresh elections were due to be held. The presidential office had assumed new importance in the changed political situation. A substantial body of opinion in the Opposition and in the country at large was propounding the view that the President should no longer be an ornamental figure-head, but an active Head of State who would hold the scales impartially between the Congress and other parties, especially in Centre-State relations, and exercise his own discretion, if necessary, to prevent abuses of the Constitution by the Central Government. Though the Constitution in theory provided the President with extensive discretionary and emergency powers, under Nehru's Prime Ministership the convention had been firmly established that these powers could only be exercised on the advice of the Prime Minister. This continued to be the position of the Congress Party.

The Opposition Parties, anxious to follow up their success in the general election, had persuaded K. Subba Rao, then Chief Justice of India, to resign his office and accept their joint nomination for the presidential election. Subba Rao was known to be a man of forceful and independent views who would be no rubber-stamp in the hands of the Central Government. The President would be elected by an electoral college of

Central and State legislators, in which the Congress had a narrow majority of 2 per cent. In the fluid state of Indian politics at the time, the victory of the Congress candidate could not be guaranteed; and defeat, coming so soon after the general election, would have a shattering impact on the party's prestige.

The Congress leadership had two alternatives. It could either put up President Radhakrishnan for another term, or it could allow him to retire and, in accordance with previous practice, put up Vice-President Zakir Husain for the presidency. Radhakrishnan, whose national eminence was undisputed, was almost certain to win in a contest. Zakir Husain, on the other hand, was a Muslim, and his nomination against Subba Rao, a Hindu, might polarise the electors, including Congressmen, on Hindu-Muslim lines. The issues involved in the choice found the Congress leadership seriously divided, with the Prime Minister and the Congress President on opposite sides.

Kamaraj was of the view that Radhakrishnan—a Hindu, a South Indian and a certain winner—should be given another term and that it would be folly for the Congress to risk defeat so soon after its election reverses. Indira Gandhi was equally firm in her view that Zakir Husain must be the Congress candidate. Her conviction was the result as much of strategic considerations as of principles. With non-Congress governments in several States and inner-party rivalry in the Congress, it was imperative that she should have a President whom she could trust to act according to her advice. Radhakrishnan, owing to his outspoken public criticism of her government's performance in the previous year and his close contacts with Kamaraj, did not inspire such confidence. Husain, on the other hand, though an eminent scholar and educationist, was not noted for the independence of his views; and his position as a member of the minority community and the Prime Minister's nominee would effectively bar him from playing an independent political role. At the same time, the elevation of a Muslim to the country's highest office would emphasise at home and abroad India's commitment to secularism at a time when the implementation of the Tashkent Agreement with Pakistan had come to a standstill, thereby strengthening Indian relations with the Islamic world and the Congress Party's appeal for India's 60 million Muslims.

Despite the rationale behind Mrs. Gandhi's strategy, the risk involved was considerable. There was a distinct possibility that a substantial number of Hindu Congressmen might vote for Subba Rao, and in the event of Husain's defeat the Prime Minister, as his chief sponsor, would probably have to resign. Mrs. Gandhi's mind, however, was made up, and she refused to succumb to pressure from Kamaraj, Morarji Desai and other Congress leaders. When C.B. Gupta, D.P. Mishra and others advised her not to disturb the status quo, she replied firmly that she had already made a commitment to Husain and that she would resign unless the party adopted him as its candidate. In the tussle that ensued, she skilfully countered Kamaraj's opposition by negotiating with the Opposition in a bid to secure their support for her presidential candidate, in return for Subba Rao's adoption as the Congress candidate for the Vice-Presidency. The Opposition seemed amenable to this compromise, and it looked as though Mrs. Gandhi might be able to present her opponents in the Congress with a *fait accompli*. But Kamaraj, anxious not to be out-manoeuvred, re-adjusted his tactics. While withdrawing his opposition to Husain's candidature, he insisted that there must be no deal with the Opposition and that the Congress must put up its own candidate for the Vice-Presidency. When the Congress Parliamentary Board met, Husain was accordingly adopted as the party's candidate. At the same time, Mrs. Gandhi was denied permission to carry on negotiations with the Opposition over the Vice-Presidency, and V.V. Giri, a veteran South Indian trade unionist was adopted as the Congress candidate for that post.

Kamaraj had thus succeeded in placing the responsibility for Husain's election on Mrs. Gandhi's shoulders, while ruling out any possibility of her securing the Opposition's support for his candidature. If Husain won, the whole Congress High Command would share the credit for defeating the Opposition; if he lost, they could blame the Prime Minister's obstinacy for his nomination. Indira Gandhi's position was not an enviable one in the tense period of canvassing that followed. The combined Opposition had turned the presidential election into a campaign to bring down the Congress Government at the Centre. The Jana Sangh, in particular, was playing on Hindu sentiment to wean Congress electors away from their party's Muslim candidate. Mrs. Gandhi, however, appears to have been confident that a frontal assault by the Opposition would strengthen, rather than splinter, Congress solidarity, threatening as it did the very survival of the ruling party. She also expected that secular and radical elements in some Opposition parties would vote for Zakir Husain, thereby counteracting any cross-voting from Congress ranks. Her calculations proved correct, and the presidential election on 7 May vindicated her strategy. Zakir Husain defeated Subba Rao by an unexpectedly large margin of about 7 per cent of the votes.

*        *        *

Zakir Husain's impressive victory marked the end of the Opposition's short-lived unity and acted as a much-needed shot in the arm for the Congress, boosting the prestige of the party and especially that of the Prime Minister. Now that her stand on the presidential nomination had been vindicated, Indira Gandhi, had she so desired, might have followed up her advantage with a major drive against her opponents in the party leadership. The more ambitious of her advisers are believed to have advocated such a course. The Congress Working Committee was scheduled to meet shortly after the presidential poll for a marathon one-week session, the purpose of which was to debate the party's organisation and programme in the light of the recent general election. Two rival viewpoints had emerged on the eve of the Working Committee session. Kamaraj, on the one hand, held the Government's poor performance responsible for the election debacle and was convinced that the Government must be made accountable to the Working Committee for its future policies. His view was reputed to have the support of Morarji Desai, Jagjivan Ram and G.L. Nanda. The 'Indira Gandhi Plan', as the press dubbed the opposite view, blamed the election reverses on the inertia of the party organisation and its lack of support for Government policies. Its aim was to establish the supremacy of the Prime Minister and the Government over the party and to restructure the Congress organisation along the lines of a British parliamentary party. The Working Committee session was widely expected to be the scene of a major confrontation between these rival plans and their exponents. Several political observers confidently predicted that the Congress President would be ousted and sent packing to Madras.

The anticipated show-down failed to materialise, owing largely to the Prime Minister's caution and her overriding desire to preserve unity. By the time the Working Committee met, Mrs. Gandhi appears to have decided that it would be impolitic and foolhardy to bring matters to a head. The party bosses, though weakened lately, were by no means a negligible force and continued to control the Congress organisation. A direct attempt to subordinate them to her will would have precipitated a major conflict, which she was anxious to avoid. Thus it was that the Working Committee witnessed a general rapprochement between the rival groups. Mrs. Gandhi herself rarely intervened in the long discussions, though she listened attentively. When she spoke, she avoided controversy and was unexpectedly conciliatory and accommodating. Far from attempting to assert her supremacy, she conceded in principle the accountability of the Government to the party organisation and even agreed to the formation of a liaison committee for this purpose.

When the A.I.C.C. met a month later, the entire leadership came under heavy fire from angry delegates who were anxious for their own and the party's survival. Mrs. Gandhi, however, showed no inclination to use this sentiment against her rivals in the Old Guard, and she rejected suggestions that there was any conflict between younger and older elements in the party. While thanking Kamaraj for his offer to take 'on his broad shoulders' the responsibility for the general election, she maintained generously that this responsibility had to be shared by the Congress as a whole.

In the sphere of ideology, too, Indira Gandhi gave ample evidence of her desire to avoid polarisation. Though mildly favourable to the Left view she preserved a non-partisan attitude and revealed considerable flexibility in her efforts for a generally acceptable Left-of-Centre consensus. This consensus had found expression in the Ten-Point Programme adopted by the Working Committee in May 1967 and later ratified by the A.I.C.C. The Ten Points included measures such as social control of banking, nationalisation of general insurance, the expansion of State trading in imports, exports and foodgrains, restriction of industrial monopolies, land reforms and abolition of princely privileges. It was a programme of moderate reform designed to retrieve the Congress Party's popularity with the masses, and it represented the very minimum that the Congress Left would accept. Even so, Desai and other conservatives were by no means reconciled to this programme and made no secret of their intention to stall its implementation. Mrs. Gandhi and her advisers, for their part, lent no support to attempts from the Left to secure the implementation of the programme or to radicalise it further.

The Prime Minister's pragmatism was particularly evident on the question of bank nationalisation, which figured prominently at the Jabalpur session of the A.I.C.C. in October 1967. Desai had made it clear that banks would not be nationalised so long as he was Finance Minister. Kamaraj is believed to have advised Mrs. Gandhi to ignore Desai's opposition and proceed with the implementation of the party's directives. But the Prime Minister, though personally inclined towards nationalisation, was not willing to provoke a trial of strength with Desai on the issue. Asoka Mehta, then the leading advocate of bank nationalisation and one of Mrs. Gandhi's closest advisers, later complained: 'She was not particularly interested in the Ten-Point programme or in bank nationalisation until it became politically useful. Although she had a big majority in the Cabinet, she allowed Morarji to squash the proposal when it came up in 1967.'[1] The result was a temporary victory for Desai's ineffectual token scheme for social control of banking and a public demonstration of Indira Gandhi's readiness to compromise with the Congress Right. She proved equally tolerant of attempts by the Right to shelve the rest of the Ten Points and refused to make an issue of their implementation, despite the party's clear mandate for these measures.

However conciliatory the Prime Minister's attitude, it was obvious that she could not hope to play a decisive role in party affairs so long as she lacked a grip on the party machinery. The key post of Congress President was due to fall vacant at the end of 1967, when Kamaraj's term expired. Mrs. Gandhi naturally wanted to fill it with a person of her own choice, who would include her nominees in the Working Committee and the A.I.C.C. Secretariat, thereby giving her a foothold in the party organisation. But this was not to be; and she had to acquiesce in the choice of a new party president by the usual process of Congress consensus-making. Kamaraj himself was keen to continue for another term; but Mrs. Gandhi was adamant that he must retire, and in this, at least, she had her way. Her own preference for his successor was G.L. Nanda, who shared her Left-of-Centre politics and whose stature had diminished sufficiently for him not to pose any threat to her own position. Though she did her best to canvass support for Nanda, the response was lukewarm. The Congress Right, meanwhile, sponsored S.K. Patil as a rival contender for the post.

When it became clear that a consensus could only be achieved for a candidate other than Patil and Nanda, Indira Gandhi announced that she herself was willing to assume the post. By combining the offices of Prime Minister and Congress President, as her father had done in 1951, Mrs. Gandhi would have made her position unassailable. But for that very reason the move was strongly and successfully resisted by other Congress leaders. Though she succeeded in ousting Kamaraj, Mrs. Gandhi had to accept Nijalingappa, a somewhat slow-witted conservative and one of the original members of the Syndicate, as the choice of a party consensus. She gave in gracefully and told the press: 'I think the Congress President (Nijalingappa) is his own man. He has been a great friend of Mr. Kamaraj. He also knows me since my early childhood. There is no need for any controversy—nor do I think there is any.'[2] The new Congress President reciprocated with a flattering if clumsy compliment to the Prime Minister in his address to the Hyderabad session of the A.I.C.C. in January 1968. 'Since Mrs. Gandhi has become Prime Minister,' he observed, 'husbands are handicapped in their quarrels with their wives. It is the duty of all of us to make of her era as Prime Minister the best that India has ever had.'[3]

Despite such professions of loyalty, Nijalingappa soon made it clear that the Prime Minister could not expect to meddle in party affairs. Mrs. Gandhi had hoped to influence the composition of the Congress Working Committee, for which fresh elections were held at the Hyderabad session. She discovered, however, that a cabal of party bosses—including Chavan, hitherto her staunch supporter—had combined to by-pass her completely in the preparation of the official list for election to the Working Committee. Nijalingappa, emboldened by this formidable line-up against the Prime Minister, flatly refused her request to include Dinesh Singh one of her close confidants, in the new Working Committee. An important factor contributing to Mrs. Gandhi's isolation and discomfiture at

Hyderabad was the bitter and implacable hostility of Kamaraj, who had been infuriated by the ignominious manner in which he had been made to step down and been ignored in the choice of his successor. Henceforth, he would apply himself systematically to the task of securing agreement among other leaders on an alternative leadership at the Centre, even if it meant a mid-term general election.

A significant development at Hyderabad was the manner in which the Central Congress leadership capitulated to the demand of power-hungry State leaders for a free hand in toppling non-Congress governments, even in States like West Bengal where such governments were implementing progressive reforms. It soon became clear at the session that only those Central leaders who backed this opportunist line could expect the support of State bosses in Central politics. Indira Gandhi, despite her own reservations, had to accept this *quid pro quo* and fall in line with the Hyderabad call for toppling non-Congress governments. She must, therefore, have been doubly incensed to find that her support for the State bosses did not prevent the latter from joining hands with her rivals to out-manoeuvre her in the party's organisational elections.

The Hyderabad session marked a watershed in the evolution of Indira Gandhi's political strategy. It indicated that so long as Congress politics turned on narrow factional and regional alignments, the Prime Minister, lacking a provincial or an organisational base in the party, was bound to come off badly. It also demonstrated in action that State bosses could unite to impose their will on the national leadership by playing on factionalism at the top, a precedent which did not augur well for the unity or authority of the Central Congress leadership. So far Mrs. Gandhi had sought to maintain her authority and the stability of her government by eschewing ideological controversy. At Jabalpur and again at Hyderabad she had avoided raising economic issues for fear of polarising the party. But in so doing she had surrendered the political initiative that she had acquired during the presidential election and had left the field open for factional manoeuvres by those who wished to contain and undermine her power. In the course of the following year, her opponents would make increasingly overt attempts to discredit and challenge her leadership, compelling her to reconsider her position and seek new sources of political support.

*          *          *

It was in the sphere of foreign affairs, traditionally the Prime Minister's special responsibility, that the first signs of ideological polarisation appeared in the Congress. Following her brief flirtation with the United States in the early months of her Prime Ministership, Indira Gandhi had adhered by and large to a moderately anti-colonial foreign policy based upon close relations with the Soviet Union, the United Arab Republic and Yugoslavia. During the Arab-Israel War of June 1967, she had come out firmly and unequivocally against Israel. In a strongly-worded statement in Parliament, she had branded Israel as the aggressor and condemned the 'wanton' Israeli attack on the Indian U.N. contingent in Gaza. In the peace manoeuvres that followed the war, she had thrown India's full diplomatic weight behind the Arab demand for an Israeli withdrawal from the occupied territories.

Mrs. Gandhi's position as Head of Government, her cosmopolitan background and her long diplomatic experience had given her considerable advantages over other Congress leaders and had enabled her to set the dominant tone of Indian foreign policy. In September 1967, she had taken direct charge of the External Affairs portfolio. Even so, it had become clear at an early stage that her views were by no means unanimously endorsed by her colleagues. Morarji Desai, in particular, had made no secret of his aversion to Soviet Russia and his desire for a pro-West foreign policy. This cleavage between the Prime Minister and the Deputy Prime Minister had become obvious during the latter's visits to various non-Communist countries in mid-1967. On a visit to Japan, Desai referred to the idea of regional co-operation in South-East Asia in such a manner as to raise suspicions of a U.S.-sponsored Indian initiative to contain China. Mrs. Gandhi, on the contrary, had sought to leave the door open for negotiations with China and had been at great pains to stress that the regional co-operation India envisaged would be economic and would pose no threat to China. On a visit to the United States, Desai deviated from the official Indian demand for an immediate halt in American bombing of Vietnam. He also spoke of 'Two Chinas', referring to Taiwan as an independent State, although Mrs. Gandhi had explicitly ruled out Indian recognition of Taiwan. While in West Germany, Desai indirectly supported the Hallstein doctrine, as against the Prime Minister's attempts to expand relations with East Germany. The efforts of the Indian Foreign Ministry, with Mrs. Gandhi's backing, to clarify the Government's policies and dispel the confusion created by Desai's statement had provoked an angry reaction from Desai and his supporters, marking the first open clash between the Prime Minister and her Deputy.

These differences had been patched up and a ministerial crisis averted. But matters came to a head in the summer of 1968, when the announcement of Soviet arms supplies to Pakistan, followed closely by the invasion of Czechoslovakia, provided Mrs. Gandhi's opponents with a promising opportunity to discredit and embarrass her. In July 1968 India was officially informed about the supply of Soviet arms to Pakistan, rumours of which had been current for the last two years. There was an immediate outcry from the Indian Right, both in Opposition and in the Congress.

Mrs. Gandhi responded with a letter to Kosygin in which she stressed the danger to India's security arising from Russia's decision and appealed to the Soviet Premier to reconsider the matter. The Kremlin, however, was unmoved by her arguments. Kosygin replied that good relations between Moscow and Pakistan would work in the interests of peace in the sub-continent and assured Mrs. Gandhi that Soviet arms would not be used against India. In the context of similar American assurances in the 1950s having proved worthless, this was small comfort for the Indian Government. Mrs. Gandhi, nonetheless, was determined not to allow Indo-Soviet relations to be damaged by this development, and she succeeded in bringing her colleagues round to her view.

Hardly had the Prime Minister ridden the storm created by the arms question when the problem of Indo-Soviet relations was dramatically re-opened by the Soviet invasion of Czechoslovakia. Educated opinion in the country had reacted sharply against the suppression of Czech sovereignty and democracy, and the Government could not afford to remain silent on the issue. Mrs. Gandhi's personal sympathies probably lay with Czechoslovakia; but as Prime Minister she was anxious to prevent the issue from becoming a lever for plunging India into the Cold War.

Parliament was sitting when news of the invasion was received, and the non-Communist Opposition was vociferous in demanding that the House be adjourned on the issue. Though passions were running high, Mrs. Gandhi firmly refused an adjournment, while promising to make a statement to Parliament after studying the facts. Her statement, which was made later the same day, was tactfully worded. While she went much further than her father had done in criticising Russian repression in Hungary, she stopped short of actually condemning the Soviet invasion. 'Our relations with the Soviet Union, Poland, Hungary and Bulgaria are close and many-sided,' she reiterated. 'We value these friendships and wish to preserve and extend them. However, we cannot but give expression to our anguish at the events in Czechoslovakia. This House will no doubt wish to convey to them our view that they should carefully consider all aspects of the situation which has arisen as a result of the action of their armed forces and its possible consequences... I am sure I reflect the opinion of the House when I express the hope that the forces which have entered Czechoslovakia will be withdrawn at the earliest possible moment and the Czech people will be able to determine their future according to their own wishes and interests... The right of nations to live peacefully and without outside interference should not be denied in the name of religion or ideology.'[4]

The Prime Minister's statement was the culmination of a day of hectic lobbying and canvassing. The draft statement had been hotly debated in the External Affairs Committee of the Cabinet, with Morarji Desai arguing for stronger criticism of the Soviet Union. Mrs. Gandhi had pointed out that this would only alienate Moscow and jeopardise India's supply of arms without any positive benefits to the Czech cause. Most of her colleagues had supported her stand, and Desai had acquiesced in the majority opinion. The conflict, however, did not end with the Cabinet decision. Mrs. Sucheta Kripalani*, egged on by some party bosses hostile to Mrs. Gandhi, decided to defy the Congress Whip and move an amendment in Parliament accusing the Soviet Union of violating the U.N. Charter. She was supported by Asoka Mehta, who had for some time been drifting away from the Prime Minister and chose to resign from the Cabinet on this issue. In the event, the amendment was rejected by an overwhelming majority. Though it had the backing of the non-Communist Opposition, Desai refrained from giving it his support, and few Congress M.Ps. voted for it.

Two days later, the Government was again under fire for its decision not to vote for the West-sponsored U.N. resolution on Czechoslovakia. Explaining the decision in Parliament, Mrs. Gandhi affirmed support for the entire resolution with the sole exception of the word 'condemn.' In a spirited defence of her position, she asked the House:

'What is our objective? Is our objective to gain some kind of a propaganda point? Is it just to condemn or use words like that, or is it to state our positive support for the people of Czechoslovakia?... I think that we should not take any stand which would make it more difficult for us to help the Czechoslovak people... Perhaps there is nobody in this House who has had such close contacts with Czechoslovakia for so many years as I have had personally, not as a member of the Government, but ever since I was a small girl. I have known the people of the country fairly well and I have known large sections of people in the universities and in other spheres of activity... It is easy enough to condemn, but to condemn or not to condemn is not the point. What is more important and, indeed, what is vital for Czechoslovakia is the withdrawal of all foreign troops, the restoration of the legitimate government to power and restoration of their sovereignty to the people of Czechoslovakia. We are all in favour of these objectives and we do not think that these objectives can be furthered by beginning with condemnation... We are second to none in our sympathy for the people of Czechoslovakia... We also feel deeply moved at what has happened. But a Government cannot be swept away by emotions... Would it not have been easier for me today to vote with the majority of nations? Is it not easier for me to

*Mrs. Kripalani was by this time one of the Prime Minister's leading critics.

say that since so many people are shouting, let me say, all right, I agree with you? It would certainly be easier for me to say this. But I have taken a particular decision. I have not taken it because I am afraid of the Soviet Union. I have not taken it because I am afraid of being called the stooge ... of the U.S.A.. I have taken it because I consider it to be the only path along which we can work towards helping Czechoslovakia in the longer run.'[6]

Indira Gandhi's firm stand in favour of moderation during the Czech crisis did much to revive her flagging popularity with the pro-Soviet Left, which had been growing impatient of her compromises on economic issues. Congress Leftists, and especially the 'Young Turks', now rallied round her, while she in turn appears to have condoned increasingly their attacks on Old Guard leaders like Desai and the Syndicate. Thus, although the Government had emerged intact, the Czech issue had shaken up inner-party alignments and set in motion the much dreaded process of ideological polarisation in the Congress. While the Prime Minister began to rely increasingly on Left-wing support, the Old Guard was closing its ranks and had already begun to plot in deadly earnest her removal from office.

On 24 August 1968, Nijalingappa, the Congress President, noted in his diary: 'Morarjibhai (Morarji Desai) is extremely unhappy about the Prime Minister's approach to many problems, especially the methods and men she employs to bring down the prestige of leaders. Discussions are going on everywhere. I am afraid if a vote is taken what would happen to her. But I am also afraid that such a step would break the party and the whole country would be in chaos. I am convinced that this lady should remove herself from the baneful influence of fellows like Dinesh. I have to carefully watch the situation.'[6]

The lady, however, was not willing to sacrifice Dinesh Singh, a radical young princeling from U.P., even though he had become a red rag to older Congress leaders. His rapid elevation to the role of her most trusted lieutenant and his arrogant manners had made him even more unpopular with the Congress leadership than Krishna Menon had been under Nehru. No efforts were spared to discredit the Prime Minister's favourite, and scurrilous rumours were circulated about his relationship with her. What Nijalingappa appears to have found particularly galling was Dinesh Singh's refusal to account to him for the political funds he was collecting. A few months later, on 12 January 1969, the Congress President would complain in his diary: 'I telephoned the Prime Minister for money. She denies having received anything. I am not inclined to believe her.'[7]

According to a prominent Indian journalist, Mrs. Gandhi was informed in the midst of the Czechoslovakia controversy of a conspiracy to oust her.[8] Some senior Congress leaders were to tell her to her face that she must resign and, if she refused, to bring a vote of no-confidence against her in the parliamentary party. But this offensive had to be postponed because Kamaraj had second thoughts, owing presumably to his reluctance to precipitate a Left-Right split. When Asoka Mehta, Sucheta Kripalani and other dissidents persisted in requisitioning a special meeting of the Congress Parliamentary Party on 27 August to debate the Government's policy on Czechoslovakia, the occasion only served to demonstrate that the Prime Minister was firmly in the saddle. Her critics were shouted down and, if thumping of desks was any indication, Indira Gandhi had the confidence of most Congress M.P.s.

*  *  *

In the months that followed the Czech crisis, factional warfare in the Congress escalated rapidly and began to assume an increasingly ideological complexion. The offensive came largely from the younger and more radical groups in the party who had long been chaffing under its Old Guard leadership. Morarji Desai was the favourite target of their attacks, representing as he did the interests of Big Business. In December 1968, Chandrashekhar, a young Congress radical, joined with the Communists in Parliament to accuse the Deputy Prime Minister of partiality to the Birlas, India's largest business house, and to question the business dealings of his son and private secretary, Kanti Desai. Mrs. Gandhi refused to come to the defence of her beleaguered colleague and remained neutral amid the storm of accusations and counter-accusations. As a result, she was widely suspected of condoning and even instigating these attacks to further her own factional aims.

At the Prime Minister's New Year's Day press conference on 1 January 1969, a hostile reporter asked her: 'What are your views about the activities of the "Young Turks" who attack the Ministers and sometimes even the whole Government and who, at the same time, swear their loyalty to you?' Her reply was noncommittal. 'We have always given considerable latitude to our party,' she said. 'This is not something that is happening for the first time. If you look into the parliamentary records you will find that this has happened in the last twenty years several times.' The newsman was not satisfied. 'I would like to know when it happened, except when you came to power,' he demanded. 'It did not happen when Shastriji was here, much less when your father was in power.' When he insisted that she cite a precedent, Mrs. Gandhi lost her temper and snapped back: 'This is not a cross-examination... I resent the tone of the question. I am not going to be spoken to like that.' Her interrogator apologised, and the question was allowed to drop.[9]

Chandrashekhar, as later years were to show, was very much his own man, and it is unlikely that his charges against Desai were the result of Mrs. Gandhi's prompting. This is not to deny that his exposures served the Prime Minister's interests. She was aware of the Syndicate's desire to oust her at the first opportune moment. The Syndicate had by now overcome their former antipathy to Desai, and he would be their most likely choice as her successor. She cannot, therefore, have felt any grief for the damage done to the Deputy Prime Minister's public image. Though careful not to identify herself openly with his critics, she refused to support disciplinary action against Chandrashekhar. Desai and the Syndicate were furious. The Congress President noted ominously in his diary on 12 March 1969: 'I am not sure if she deserves to continue as Prime Minister. Possibly soon there may be a show-down.' He added on 25 April that Desai had 'discussed the necessity of the Prime Minister being removed.'[10]

The Prime Minister, meanwhile, was veering further to the Left. This was the result, not merely of factional compulsions, but also of her growing awareness that the Congress, with its existing leadership and programme, was a sinking ship. The anti-Congress trend reflected in the 1967 general election, far from being reversed, had been gathering momentum during the last two years. Mrs. Gandhi's tours in the States had given her ample opportunity to observe this at close quarters, and she could not fail to notice that her own image was being tarnished by the general unpopularity of the Congress leadership.

On a visit to West Bengal in October 1968, Mrs. Gandhi had found herself besieged in a bungalow at Jalpaiguri by a crowd of stone-throwing demonstrators. When a *lathi*-charge by the police had failed to disperse the crowd, the Prime Minister with her usual *sang-froid* had come out, climbed a wooden fence and addressed the demonstrators. But she had been unable to pacify them and had to make an unceremonious exit under police escort. Two months later, on a visit to Jamshedpur in Bihar, she was two hours late for a public meeting owing to a sudden change of programme. Instead of welcoming her arrival, the assembled crowd had mobbed her car, jeered at her and shouted: 'Why are you late?' Once again the police had to use their *lathis* to clear her way.[11]

To a politician sensitive to popular currents, incidents such as these appeared, not as isolated outbursts, but as an unmistakable warning of the doom that would overtake the Congress if it did not dramatically improve its image before the next general election in 1972. Her impressions were confirmed by the party's debacle in the 'mini general election' of February 1969, when four States went to the polls. The Congress was routed in West Bengal and Punjab; and while it marginally improved its position in U.P., it fell short of an absolute majority.

When the Congress assembled at Faridabad in April 1969 for its annual session, the hall in which it was to meet was burned down by a sudden fire, an accident which many Congressmen interpreted as an omen of the fate awaiting their party. In the course of the session, two rival viewpoints emerged on virtually every issue—political, economic and organisational—cutting across the usual regional and personal affiliations. The tone was set by Nijalingappa's controversial presidential address and Mrs. Gandhi's reply. The Congress President strongly criticised the poor performance of the public sector, called for greater encouragement of private enterprise and castigated the Young Turks for their lack of party discipline. The Prime Minister, who spoke immediately after him, staunchly defended the role of the public sector, stressed the need for State controls, especially where foreign collaboration was involved, and made a sharp attack on the weakness of the Congress organisation and its failure to support Government policies. Though Mrs. Gandhi was more outspoken than ever before, she still held back from taking the final plunge. She remained equivocal on the thorny question of bank nationalisation and, while calling for re-thinking on economic issues, she agreed to defer such decisions till the A.I.C.C. session due to be held at Bangalore in July. She also agreed to the post-ponement of fresh party elections for a year, thus allowing the Syndicate to retain its hold on the Congress organisation.

The Faridabad session had ended on an inconclusive note, and the Congress, though in a state of deadlock, remained united. But it was clear by now to most political observers that this stalemate could not continue for long. The pressure of political developments in the country, the steady decline of the Congress and rival views of how to arrest it, had made some sort of ideological polarisation in the party inevitable. This had coincided with the escalation of the power struggle within the Congress leadership. Indira Gandhi was aware of the plots being hatched to dislodge her from office. She was also aware of the urgent need to resuscitate the Congress Party's public credibility. She was as anxious as other Congress leaders to avoid a polarisation that might split the party. Till Faridabad she had been moving cautiously, feeling the ground and testing reactions. The favourable response of the party's rank and file to her Left-of-Centre stance had been encouraging and appears to have convinced her that only by identifying herself with a radical, socialist programme could she assert her leadership over the Congress and rehabilitate the party in the eyes of the masses. In the following months she would cast aside her initial hesitation and pursue this strategy with a political sagacity that was as ruthless as it was unexpected.

*          *          *

The *cassus belli* for the battle that had been brewing between Indira Gandhi and Syndicate was provided by the election of a new Union President. Zakir Husain's death a few days after the Faridabad session had reopened a question which had been settled to Mrs. Gandhi's satisfaction in 1967. If control of the presidency had been important to her then, it was even more crucial in the conditions of 1969. As opposed to her opponents' control of the Congress organisation, the Prime Minister's strength lay in her hold on the Congress Parliamentary Party and in the weapon of dissolution, which she could use to appeal to the country against the party. A hostile President, however, might tip the scales against her by using his discretionary powers to deny her a dissolution and by dismissing her government if it lost its majority after a split. The Syndicate were quick to grasp the point and were equally determined to install a President who would work in their interests.

In the prevailing atmosphere of mutual suspicion and hostility, both sides played their cards carefully. This time Mrs. Gandhi was reluctant to express her preferences openly, lest they be shot down at once. Her first preference for the presidency appears to have been Vice-President Giri. From her point of view, he had all the necessary ingredients for a suitable President. He was personally friendly to her; he could be relied upon not to meddle in Congress politics; his promotion from the Vice-Presidency to the Presidency would be in accordance with precedent; his record as a labour leader would make him acceptable to the Left Opposition and to the Communist-dominated Governments of West Bengal and Kerala; and as a South Indian he would also be acceptable to the ruling D.M.K.* in Madras. The Syndicate, however, ruled him out at an early stage, on the grounds that he was too old for the post and that in the unstable situation that might emerge from the 1972 general election the President should be a politically experienced senior Congressman. Mrs. Gandhi did not press Giri's name. Instead she suggested Jagjivan Ram, a loyal Cabinet colleague, to whom the same objections could not apply. Jagjivan Ram shared her Left orientation, and his origins as an Untouchable would make him an appropriate choice in the Gandhi Centenary Year. Jagjivan Ram, however, was too closely identified with the Prime Minister's group to be acceptable to the Syndicate. The latter had made up their minds to sponsor one of their own number, Sanjiva Reddy,** for the post.

An attempt was made to secure a consensus in the party for Reddy's

*The Dravida Munetra Khazagam, the party of Tamil regional and linguistic nationalism, had swept to power in the state of Madras in 1967.

**Mrs. Gandhi had dropped Reddy from her Cabinet in 1967, making him Speaker of the Lok Sabha, the Lower House of Parliament. He is believed to have been disgruntled ever since and to have nursed a sense of grievance against her.

candidature; but his affiliations with the Syndicate and his hostility to Mrs. Gandhi made it impossible for her to accept his nomination. When talks between the Prime Minister and the Congress President ended in a stalemate, Nijalingappa derided in his diary what he considered her arrogance and obstinacy. 'During the course of our talks,' he wrote in exasperation, 'for the second time she asserted, "I am the Prime Minister of India".'[12]

The odds, however, were heavily against the Prime Minister getting her way. About this time, the Syndicate is believed to have secured the support of Chavan for its plans to oust Mrs. Gandhi. Chavan, who had the undivided backing of the powerful Maharashtra State Congress, had been growing disgruntled with his position in the Cabinet and is said to have been particularly incensed by the Prime Minister's reliance on Dinesh Singh. He is believed to have entered into a secret compact with the Syndicate, under which he was to become Deputy Prime Minister in a new government led by Morarji Desai, with a promise of the Prime Ministership after the 1972 general election. In return, he was to throw the full weight of the Maharashtra Congress behind Reddy's candidature, which would be the first step towards Mrs. Gandhi's removal.

In the face of this formidable alliance, Indira Gandhi's prospects looked bleak on the eve of the Bangalore A.I.C.C. session. Reddy's nomination would pose a direct threat to her security; but she was powerless to prevent it. The decision would be taken at Bangalore by the eight-member Congress Parliamentary Board, in which her opponents, with Chavan's backing, would have a clear majority. There was now only one way in which she could break loose from the net that was closing in on her, divide her opponents and rally the party round herself. She would have to play the card of ideological polarisation.

The Bangalore A.I.C.C. session was being held primarily to pass a resolution on economic policy, which had been shelved at Faridabad. The session was preceded by strenuous canvassing by the Young Turks on behalf of their own note on economic affairs, which called for radical changes in government policy. They had met Mrs. Gandhi, Kamaraj, Chavan, Jagjivan Ram and Fakhruddin Ahmed to seek their support and had served notice of their intention to oppose the official resolution unless their suggestions were incorporated in it. Left to themselves, they would have had little chance of securing a majority in the A.I.C.C., but their demands were to receive support from a powerful quarter.

On the eve of the Congress Working Committee meeting in Bangalore, Indira Gandhi drafted a comprehensive note on economic policy for the Committee's consideration. The main points of this controversial document were: 1) a ceiling on unproductive expenditure; 2) nationalisation of banks; 3) special efforts to develop backward areas; 4) the appointment of a Monopolies Commission; 5) greater autonomy for public sector enterprises; 6) the building of a committed cadre to manage public enterprises; 7) the reservation of most consumer industries for the small-scale sector; 8) the exclusion of foreign capital from fields in which indigenous technological know-how was available; 9) special assistance to rural co-operatives; 10) a ceiling on incomes and on urban property; 11) nationalisation of the import of raw materials; 12) special rural programmes; 13) agrarian land reforms; and 14) a minimum wage for agricultural labour.

'These are just some stray thoughts rather hurriedly dictated,' Indira Gandhi wrote at the end of her economic blueprint.[13] Chavan subsequently observed that the note was not 'a scientific document', but 'an expression of a restless mind trying to tackle complex problems.'[14] Taken as a whole, Mrs. Gandhi's 'stray thoughts' were too ambitious, discursive and, in some respects, radical to be capable of practical application by the existing governmental apparatus and party organisation. Its significance, however, lay, not in its potential for immediate implementation, but in its political impact. Based as it was on the Ten-Point Programme of June 1967, it could not be opposed by Left-oriented Congress bosses like Kamaraj and Chavan. At the same time, it was radical enough to satisfy the Young Turks and to make its author the rallying point of the Congress Left. By the shrewd timing of her note, Indira Gandhi hoped to detach Kamaraj and Chavan from their conservative allies in the Syndicate, thereby breaking the cabal that had formed to thwart her on the presidential nomination.

On 10 July Mrs. Gandhi's 'Stray Thoughts' were placed before the Congress Working Committee by Fakhruddin Ali Ahmed, a loyal Cabinet colleague. She herself arrived in Bangalore a day late, pleading a sudden indisposition. The obvious purpose of her delayed arrival was to gauge the reaction to her missile and to avoid pressures to withdraw it. Her indisposition, however, may well have been a genuine result of the anxiety and tension accompanying the decision she had taken. For three long years she had steered clear of any open alignment with the party's competing groups and factions. Now the dye was cast, and she had announced to the country and the party that she stood with the Congress Left against the party's conservative leadership. For the first time in her career she had staked her political future on an ideological issue.

As expected, Morarji Desai and the Syndicate reacted strongly to Mrs. Gandhi's note. Nevertheless, they were quick to see its immediate political aim and were shrewd enough not to fall into the trap. A compromise resolution drafted by Chavan included most of the Prime Minister's suggestions and was unanimously adopted by the Working Committee. Mrs. Gandhi's opponents hoped thus to take the wind out of her sails and to reserve their energies for the presidential nomination. When the Congress Parliamentary Board met on 12 July, Mrs. Gandhi proposed Jagjivan Ram's candidature; but when a vote was taken Reddy was adopted by a majority of five to two, with Jagjivan Ram himself abstaining. In 1957 Nehru had been similarly out-voted on the presidential nomination. But while Nehru's position was secure and he could afford to accept the majority decision gracefully, the situation was very different in 1969. The Board's decision was not only a personal affront to Mrs. Gandhi but a serious challenge to her leadership. For the moment, however, she had no option but to acquiesce in the majority verdict, even to the extent of filing Reddy's nomination papers herself.

This public humiliation cannot have been easily palatable, and it was obvious to those who knew her that Indira Gandhi would not surrender meekly. On 15 July an apprehensive Congress President recorded in his clumsy and pompous style:

'In view of the temper of the Prime Minister she may do any odd thing. She is keenly feeling that she being the "Prime Minister of India" her opinion regarding the President's selection ought to have been accepted. She seems to be taking too much for granted and is overbearing and haughty. She has been taught a lesson now. Being wilful and brought up by a father who was always grooming her for the Prime Ministership obviously and patently, I feel she will do something nasty in a huff. She is so very much angry and upset about Chavan and then Morarji; she expected that being her Cabinet colleagues they should go with her in whatever she does. Wrong approach. Let us see what she may do. It is a pity that accepting Kamaraj's strong desire we made her Prime Minister.'[16]

Twenty-four hours later, Nijalingappa's fears were confirmed when the Prime Minister hit back hard and with lightning speed. On 16 July, in a polite but firm communication, she wrote to Morarji Desai: 'I know that, in regard to some of the basic issues that arise, you entertain strong reservations and have your own views about the direction as well as the pace of change... I have given deep thought to this matter and I feel that, in all fairness, I should not burden you with this responsibility in your capacity as Finance Minister, but should take it directly upon myself... I am advising the President* accordingly.'[16] Without awaiting Desai's reply, Mrs. Gandhi announced her decision to the press. In an angry rejoinder, Desai accused her of lack of courtesy, rejected her request to continue as Deputy Prime Minister and resigned from the Cabinet. 'I regard it as a matter of ordinary courtesy', he wrote, 'that

*Vice-President Giri had been sworn in as acting President after Husain's death.

you should have discussed your precise misgivings with me before taking the decision that you say you have taken... There is bound to be speculation whether your decision stems from misgivings about the implementation of the Bangalore resolution or something else.'[17]

To demonstrate that by ousting Desai she had not merely done 'something nasty in a huff,' Indira Gandhi announced on 19 July, within three days of assuming the Finance portfolio, the nationalisation by presidential ordinance of India's fourteen major banks. Few economists or political commentators doubted that the motive for bank nationalisation was political. Mrs. Gandhi is believed to have rushed the decision through against the advice of T.P. Singh, the Finance Secretary, and L.K. Jha, Governor of the Reserve Bank of India, who pointed out that the Government lacked the necessary managerial cadre and had not prepared a coherent new investment policy. Gadgil, the head of the Planning Commission, was not even consulted, and the Cabinet is reported to have hastily approved the draft ordinance within a few minutes. Although Parliament was due to meet the next day, the Prime Minister had decided on a presidential ordinance in order to pre-empt resistance from within the party. The parliamentary legislation that followed also bore the signs of inadequate preparation and contained legal flaws which later enabled the Right-wing Opposition to challenge it successfully in the Supreme Court.

Nevertheless, the decision was so popular in the country at large that the Syndicate had to abandon its plans to bring a vote of censure against the Prime Minister in the Congress Parliamentary Party on the issue of Desai's dismissal. Bank nationalisation was represented by the Prime Minister's supporters as a transfer of the country's financial resources from monopoly capitalists to the masses. At a more realistic level, the Government assured the farmers' lobby, small traders and businessmen and the urban petty bourgoisie of expanding credit on easy terms, and bank nationalisation received enthusiastic support from these sections. The Communists and other Left parties also welcomed the measure as a step in the right direction.

According to Kuldip Nayar, Dinesh Singh later admitted to him that bank nationalisation had been planned well before the Bangalore session as a means of boosting Mrs. Gandhi's popularity if the Syndicate proved recalcitrant on the presidential nomination.[18] In this respect, at any rate, the measure yielded handsome dividends. For days afterwards, large crowds gathered at 1, Safdarjang Road to felicitate the Prime Minister on her bold decision. Indira Gandhi's personal popularity in the country had never stood so high. Where others had passed resolutions and prevaricated, she alone had had the courage to act, and to act swiftly and decisively. Amid the political instability and demoralisation prevalent at the time, she had emerged as the hope of the masses and a potentially dynamic agent of change. In a society where the traditional and the modern are inseparable, some mystics saw Indira Gandhi as an incarnation of *Shakti,* the female cosmic energy, breathing new life and vigour into the decaying corpse of Indian politics.

*           *           *

On 13 July, the day after Reddy's nomination, Vice-President Giri had announced his intention of contesting the presidency with the backing of some Left Opposition parties. Mrs. Gandhi was at once suspected of having instigated his decision, though there was no concrete evidence to suggest this. She certainly had no reason to desire Reddy's success, and she must have welcomed the fact that he would have to face stiff competition. For the moment, however, there was nothing she could do to help Giri against the official Congress candidate without exposing herself to disciplinary action, a risk which she was not yet ready to take. Hence her docile agreement to file Reddy's nomination herself.

The popular acclaim that greeted bank nationalisation appears, however, to have greatly boosted her confidence and spurred her on to greater boldness. The country was clearly behind her, and her acute sense of political timing soon convinced her that she could not afford to let the grass grow under her feet. This was the moment to press home her advantage and score another resounding victory over the Syndicate by securing the defeat of their presidential nominee. As the presidential election approached, her public attitude to the contest became increasingly ambivalent. Her strategy was to build up strong pressure for a free vote, which would enable her supporters to throw their weight behind Giri.

At a meeting of the Congress Parliamentary Party Executive on 29 July, the Prime Minister agreed to join the Congress President in a verbal appeal to the party to vote for Reddy, but ruled out a written appeal on the ground that it might be legally challenged as interference with free voting. The Syndicate had reason to be alarmed by Mrs. Gandhi's equivocations. They began to negotiate seriously with the Right-wing Opposition, and secured the latter's assurance that their second preference votes would go to Reddy*. At the same time, the Syndicate sought to appease Mrs. Gandhi by accepting her nominees for the posts of Vice-President and Speaker of the Lok Sabha** when the Congress Parlia-

---

*The Swatantra, Jana Sangh and B.K.D. had sponsored C.D. Deshmukh as a third candidate. This, however, was only a token gesture, and it was understood that when Deshmukh was eliminated in the first count their second preference votes would go to Reddy.

**'House of the People,' the directly elected Lower House Parliament.

mentary Board met on 5 August. These concessions, however, failed to reassure the Prime Minister. When the Congress Parliamentary Party met on the next day, she merely reiterated her previous statement that the controversy over the presidential nomination should be regarded as closed, while carefully avoiding a personal endorsement of Reddy's candidature. The meeting ended in pandemonium when Mrs. Gandhi's supporters castigated Mrs. Tarkeshwari Sinha* for writing a newspaper article slandering the Prime Minister. Mrs. Gandhi herself condemned the article as a serious breach of party discipline. When its author rose to reply, she was shouted down so vociferously that the uproar could be heard by pressmen a hundred yards away from the hall.

Chandrashekhar, one of the Prime Minister's most active supporters, later commented:

> 'If the Syndicate had worked in a more gradual and restrained way, they would probably have succeeded in containing Mrs. Gandhi. She would not have split the Congress unless her survival was at stake. Even after Sanjiva Reddy's nomination, she was reluctant to bring things to a head. It was only after Tarkeshwari and others said openly that Reddy's election was only the first step and that afterwards Mrs. Gandhi would have to be ousted that she decided to back Giri. Reports had also come in from the States that Giri had a good deal of support.'[19]

During the next ten days, the situation developed with startling rapidity. Mrs. Gandhi's supporters began to canvass actively for Giri, while her opponents accused her of aspiring to be a dictator and of joining hands with the Communists to disrupt the Congress. On 10 August, Nijalingappa entered in his diary:

> 'I have written to the Prime Minister that in view of the developments in the party and outside it is necessary that she should issue a statement. I am not sure what she will do. She is riding a very high horse and her pride and presumptuousness do not seem to have any limits. Pride goeth before a fall. During the last one week there have been demonstrations of taxi-drivers, rickshaw-walas, students, etc. before her house and she has been addressing them as if she is the only one who works for the poor, and complaining against a few individuals. Even the name of the Congress is not mentioned.'[20]

On 11 August the Prime Minister's group launched a signature

---

*Mrs. Sinha, a Congress M.P. and former Deputy Minister, was known chiefly for her glamorous appearance, her bold and risqué humour and her love of controversy. An old friend of Feroze Gandhi's, she was one of the Prime Minister's most victriolic critics and an ardent supporter of Morarji Desai.

campaign among Congress M.P.s in favour of a free vote according to conscience. Giri was represented as the candidate of a broad national consensus, as opposed to the nominee of a clique of Congress bosses, and Reddy's sponsors were accused of conspiring with the Right-wing Opposition to oust the Prime Minister and instal a coalition government at the Centre. On 13 August, Jagjivan Ram and Fakhruddin Ali Ahmed, both members of the Cabinet and the Congress Working Committee and loyal to Mrs. Gandhi, wrote to Nijalingappa demanding a free vote in view of the conscientious objections of many Congressmen to Reddy, following the deal that had been struck with reactionary parties like the Swatantra and Jana Sangh. Their letter was widely believed to have been drafted at the Prime Minister's residence with her concurrence. On the following day, Mrs. Gandhi indirectly supported their arguments in a letter to Nijalingappa:

'(It is) a matter of deep anguish to me that our colleagues and leading members should have been convinced that attempts are now being made at the highest level in the party to compromise with political parties totally opposed to our principles and accepted programmes... Elections are a medium to fight for our values and voting is a process of association with these values. I cannot think of winning elections by clouding principles. I do not think therefore that in these circumstances and for constitutional reasons, it would be right for me to have a whip issued.'[21]

The 'Conscience Theory' proved to be a brilliant stratagem. While it avoided open opposition to Reddy's candidature, it effectively undermined his appeal for Congress legislators. Meanwhile, the situation remained fluid, and the Syndicate were unable to take retaliatory action in the absence of any tangible breach of party discipline. So long as the Prime Minister refused to issue a party whip, her supporters were free to canvass for Giri behind the scenes. Mrs. Gandhi herself is believed to have personally telephoned all the Chief Ministers to seek their support for Giri.

On 14 August, when the Congress Parliamentary Party Executive issued an appeal in favour of Reddy, it was strongly opposed by the Prime Minister, who refused to allow her name to be associated with it. The drama reached its climax on 15 August, the day before polling. In a statement timed to make the next morning's headlines, Mrs. Gandhi at last came out in the open and advised the electors: 'Vote according to conscience.' In a letter to Nijalingappa, she warned of serious divisions in the party if a free vote was not allowed. She wrote with some irony:

'Instead of ... enlightening us about your talks with the leaders of the other parties and any understandings which you might have reached with them to get their support, you have sought to assure me that you were not going to topple my Government, but would allow me to continue as Prime Minister until 1972. I must record a strong protest at this attempt to inject power politics into a discussion involving fundamental issues. I need no personal assurances, nor do I seek to retain my office at all cost. But we should like to have answers to the basic questions which have been posed.'[22]

'Your demand for a free vote,' the Congress President replied indignantly, 'is in fact a demand for the right to vote for Mr. V.V. Giri—a candidate nominated by the Communists and communalists. History does not record an instance where a Prime Minister, after proposing her party's candidate, not only works against him, but proclaims her support for the candidate of the Opposition. If this tragic fact was not staring us, I would have thought of it to be a tale from *Alice in Wonderland*.'[23]

The result of the presidential poll was to be announced on the night of 20 August. The hours of counting must have been among the most anxious periods of Indira Gandhi's political life. Giri's victory was by no means in the bag. After all, Reddy remained the official Congress candidate and could also count on the votes of the Right-wing Opposition. Now that the Prime Minister was openly identified with Giri's candidature, his defeat would restore the Syndicate's dwindling political fortunes and leave them free to take disciplinary action against her. She had taken a calculated risk. Fortunately for her it paid off, though only just, when Giri was declared elected by a narrow margin. Mrs. Gandhi's supporters were jubilant; yet, even amid the victory garlands and felicitations, she must have realised that the struggle was not over. The Syndicate would never forgive the humiliation they had suffered, and it could only be a matter of time before the Congress split.

*        *        *

Following the news of Sanjiva Reddy's defeat, the Congress President announced his intention of taking disciplinary action against those who had led the free vote campaign and served formal notices on Mrs. Gandhi, Jagjivan Ram and Fakhruddin Ali Ahmed, requiring them to show cause why disciplinary action should not be taken against them. At the same time, a group of about 60 Congress M.Ps. demanded disciplinary action against the Prime Minister and warned that, following her example, they too would in future vote according to their conscience in Parliament. Mrs. Gandhi's group countered this offensive by announcing their intention of bringing formal charges against the Congress President for his secret negotiations with the Jana Sangh and Swatantra.

Both sides began to prepare for a show-down at the meeting of the Congress Working Committee on 25 August. The atmosphere in the capital was electric, and the air bristled with exaggerated rumours. Reports circulated that Mrs. Gandhi's supporters would forcibly occupy the Congress headquarters before the Working Committee could meet and that there would be rioting in Delhi if disciplinary action was taken against her. On 22 August the situation was further inflamed by the statement of the C.P.I.(M)*, followed by that of the C.P.I., that they would support a progressive government led by Indira Gandhi. On the day of the Working Committee meeting, 22 of the 40 Independents in the Lok Sabha promised similar support, while a large number of Congress M.P.s, spurred on by fear of a dissolution, met and pledged their loyalty to the Prime Minister.

Owing largely to Chavan's role as a peace-maker, the anticipated trial of strength failed to materialise. Chavan, who held the balance of power in the Working Committee, was anxious to avoid further polarisation. Although his Maharashtra contingent had voted loyally for Reddy in the presidential contest, his desire to preserve a Leftist image had made him reluctant, especially after bank nationalisation, to be identified with the Syndicate. He appears to have recognised that he had backed the losing side and that he must mend his fences with Mrs. Gandhi if he wished to remain in her Cabinet.

When the Working Committee met, the Syndicate without Chavan's backing could not muster a majority for disciplinary action and was forced to accept a compromise. While the Prime Minister's group formally withdrew its charges against the Congress President, the Syndicate accepted a unity resolution and allowed the show-cause notices to Mrs. Gandhi and her colleagues to lapse. The truce was sealed by a dinner invitation from Mrs. Gandhi to the entire Working Committee. The dinner had to be cancelled because Nijalingappa took to his bed after the unaccustomed exertions of the preceding weeks; but Mrs. Gandhi, to the astonishment of Nijalingappa's followers, demonstrated her good-will by visiting the ailing Congress President at his residence.

The spirit of forgiveness and reconciliation did not, however, survive the end of the month. The Syndicate's reluctant agreement to drop disciplinary action had amounted to a virtual surrender, and it was clear that unless they hit back soon they would be unable to sustain the morale and loyalty of their supporters. Indira Gandhi, having carried off two impressive coups at her opponents' expense, might have been

*The Communist Party of India (Marxist), which had broken away from the Communist Party of India (C.P.I.), accusing the latter of bourgeois reformism and subservience to Moscow, was the largest single party in the States of Kerala and West Bengal.

expected to rest on her laurels. Success, however, appears to have encouraged her to consolidate her position still further. D.P. Mishra and other advisers are believed to have convinced her that she must press on to capture the party organisation before the Syndicate recovered from its wounds. In a personal letter to Lord Fenner Brockway, an old friend, Mrs. Gandhi indicated that the struggle was by no means over when she wrote on 27 August:

'During the last few weeks, the question was whether India should be a modern nation responding to the challenges of the age or a country where a handful could impose their will on the people. The three issues at stake were whether 1) the Congress should be a mass-based organisation as envisaged by Mr. Gandhi and my father or one ordered by a handful of party bosses; 2) it should adhere firmly to its declared policies of secularism and socialism; and 3) in a democracy the elected head of Government can be overruled by the party organisation which is not responsible to Parliament. The forces which are arraigned against us are entrenched and powerful and now very angry, so the road ahead will be far from smooth.'[24]

On 28 August, Nijalingappa opened the next round of hostilities by announcing that the question of Morarji Desai's return to the Cabinet was still open. The next day, in a speech to the Congress Parliamentary Party, Mrs. Gandhi replied that the Prime Minister must be free from interference by the organisational leadership and cited the British precedent of the conflict between Prime Minister Attlee and Harold Laski, Chairman of the Labour Party. In the same speech, she called upon progressive ex-Congressmen and other socialists to join the Congress. Her appeal was interpreted as an invitation to Krishna Menon and other Leftists to strengthen her ranks.

On 23 September, Mrs. Gandhi launched her offensive for control of the Congress organisation when her supporters began to collect signatures for a requisitioned meeting of the A.I.C.C., the purpose of which would be to elect a new party president and Working Committee. When the Syndicate tried to oust some of her supporters from key organisational posts in the States, she retaliated by dismissing four of their followers from the Government. The requisitionists had soon collected well over the number of signatures required by the party constitution, though according to an Indian journalist H.N. Bahuguna* later confessed that there were some forgeries among them.[25] The Working Committee was to meet on 1 November to consider the requisition, and there was little

*One of Mrs. Gandhi's leading supporters from the Congress Left; at present Chief Minister of U.P.

doubt that the demand would have to be conceded. The Syndicate, reeling under a succession of blows, was growing desperate. On 28 October, in a long open letter to Mrs. Gandhi, Nijalingappa gave full vent to his spleen. He wrote in a bitter tirade:

'I do not know who, in your opinion, constitutes the Syndicate. But I know that the Press often uses the term to refer to those who worked for the election of Shri Lal Bahadur Shastri, and later on for your election in 1966 and 1967... At that time, you did not find the... Syndicate reactionary. You did not think that their position in the organisation was based on the bogus primary membership that they controlled. Nor did you think they were a handful of people who were arrogating to themselves the right to choose the party's nominee for the highest office. You knew very well that it was their efforts that led to your election as the leader of the Parliamentary Party... You seem to have made personal loyalty to you the test of loyalty to the Congress and the country. All those who glorify you are progressives ...The baits and threats that the Government can use are being used freely and openly to secure regimentation and personal loyalty. All these create the impression that, in your scheme of things, there is no place in the party or Government for anyone who differs even slightly from your personal views and likes and dislikes. It appears that everything is permissible and pardonable to those who are recognised supporters of the personality cult that is threatening democracy in the organisation.'[26]

The Working Committee was evenly divided between the two factions, Chavan having thrown in his lot with the Prime Minister. But on 31 October, the day before the Committee was to meet, Nijalingappa dismissed Fakhruddin Ahmed and Subramaniam, both supporters of Mrs. Gandhi, from the Working Committee. It was a clumsy and desperate last-minute bid to reduce Mrs. Gandhi's group to a minority, and he could hardly have expected her to submit. The next morning, the Prime Minister and her group boycotted the official Working Committee and held a rival session at Mrs. Gandhi's residence. Each group had ten of the twenty-one members of the united Working Committee, with one uncommitted member attending both meetings and being warmly received by both sides. The atmosphere in the capital was explosive, and there were large demonstrations in support of Mrs. Gandhi. When the Congress President and other members of the Syndicate arrived at party headquarters for the meeting of the official Working Committee, they were mobbed and manhandled by supporters of the Prime Minister. Mrs. Gandhi promptly dissociated herself from the incident and telephoned Nijalingappa to apologise personally.

Even now, after they had literally come to blows, both sides were hesitant to take the final step and split the party. The Prime Minister's group accused Nijalingappa of violating the party constitution by arbitrarily expelling two members of the Working Committee and called upon him to convene a meeting of the full Working Committee, followed by a requisitioned session of the A.I.C.C. Meanwhile, the official Working Committee censured Mrs. Gandhi for holding a rival meeting, but decided to defer disciplinary action against her. In a letter to the Prime Minister on 3 November, Nijalingappa charged her with committing 'an unpardonable act of gross indiscipline' and asked her to 'return back [sic] from the brink to which you had led yourself and renounce the ways of intrigue and disruption.'[27] Mrs. Gandhi replied coolly the next day:

'I should like to emphasise that we are not dealing with a mere technical or legal problem... It has to be frankly recognised that there is a sharp cleavage in our approach to the economic and social problems which confront the country today. There is no doubt that our people and the vast majority of the rank and file of our organisation solidly support the steps I have recently taken... The only forum to test this, if it is so desired, is to take the matter to the AICC or the plenary session of the Congress and to have a democratic decision... It was little expected that the democratic and the constitutional right of the AICC members to have a requisition meeting would be set at nought by you and your supporters in the Working Committee on absolutely untenable, flimsy and tactical grounds. May I then humbly ask who has violated the constitution of our party?'[28]

For several days the correspondence war raged late into the night, as the two protagonists vied with each other in releasing their long accusations and counter-accusations just in time to capture the next morning's headlines. Meanwhile, attempts at a compromise continued behind the scenes, largely at the instance of some Congress Chief Ministers who were anxious to avoid a split. On 7 November, Mrs. Gandhi invited Nijalingappa to lunch to discuss a settlement. The talks were to have continued over dinner; but the Prime Minister suddenly cancelled the engagement. The quarrel had clearly gone too far for the protagonists to kiss and make it up. While Mrs. Gandhi was unwilling to make peace except on terms that left her supremacy unchallenged, the Syndicate could not have accepted her terms without a total loss of face. In any case, with the complete breakdown of mutual trust between the two sides, no assurances could have carried conviction. Morarji Desai expressed the Syndicate's feelings when he exclaimed: 'We have been hoodwinked by this lady before. Never again.'[29]

Both sides now made strenuous efforts to project the split to the party and the country as a conflict of principles. While Indira Gandhi took her stand on democratic socialism, the Syndicate made the fanciful claim that it was defending Indian democracy from her attempts to establish a Communist dictatorship. In view of the ideological background and composition of the rival factions, neither claim could have borne close scrutiny; but Mrs. Gandhi's undoubtedly carried greater conviction. By her bold and decisive leadership during the last few months, she had succeeded in winning over the Indian Left and in convincing large sections of the country's youth and intelligentsia that she was fighting their battle. On 8 November, in an open letter to all Congressmen, she emphasised:

'What we witness today is not a mere clash of personalities and certainly not a fight for power. It is a conflict between two outlooks and attitudes in regard to the objectives of the Congress and the methods in which the Congress itself should function. It is a conflict between those who are for socialism, for change and for the fullest internal democracy and debate in the organisation . . . and those who are for the status quo, for conformism and for less than full discussion inside the Congress. . . The Congress stands for democracy, secularism, socialism and non-alignment in international relations. . . But within the Congress there has been a group which did not have total faith in these objectives. People of this group paid only lip service to these ideals. . . I know that this group constantly tried to check and frustrate my father's attempts to bring about far-reaching economic and social changes.'[30]

Nijalingappa sought to counter these arguments when he wrote to Mrs. Gandhi on 11 November:

'The persistence with which you are attempting to paint your bid for one-man rule in the organisation and the Government as a conflict between the so-called progressive and radical section of the Congress and the so-called reactionary section . . . cannot mislead anyone except the storm-troopers. No aspirants for dictatorial powers in the 20th century have omitted to put on the garb of socialism. . . You have referred to bogus membership and bossism in the organisation. . . But I am not aware of any action that you initiated when you were the President of the Congress, and had the primary responsibility for the functioning of the organisation, to deal with the problems of bogus membership and bossism.'[31]

On 12 November the split at last became final when the Syndicate formally expelled Indira Gandhi from the Indian National Congress, on the ground that she had rebelled against the official Working Committee by sponsoring a rival Working Committee and A.I.C.C. 'This stand of the Prime Minister,' the charge-sheet read, 'is in keeping with her conduct at the time of the Presidential election, the tenor of her public pronouncements on her position as the Prime Minister of India, her constant denigration of the Congress organisation, her tendency to divide Congressmen among those who are her supporters and those who are not..., her peculiar attitude to questions of discipline, her basic and over-riding desire to concentrate all power in her hands so that her colleagues are her nominees in any offices they might occupy.'[32]

Mrs. Gandhi was informed of her expulsion as she arrived at the Presidential palace for an official luncheon in honour of the President of Hungary. She is reported to have received the news calmly, without betraying any emotion. The official Working Committee, known henceforth as the Congress (O)*, had called upon the Congress Parliamentary Party to elect a new leader forthwith. But Mrs. Gandhi was confident of a majority in the parliamentary party and in Parliament as a whole, and her calculations proved correct. About 310 of the 429 members of the Congress Parliamentary Party met in the Central Hall of Parliament with the Prime Minister in the chair to reject the official Working Committee's directive to elect a new leader. A rump of pro-Syndicate M.P.s, claiming to represent the real Congress, boycotted the meeting and crossed over to the Opposition benches in Parliament. Their defection deprived the Government of its majority in both Houses of Parliament. But with the promised support of Opposition parties such as the Communists, the Socialists and the D.M.K. and of a large number of Independents, the Government faced no immediate threat to its position.

In a circular letter to all A.I.C.C. members, Nijalingappa pleaded in vain: 'The conflict in the Congress is not a conflict between those who believe in Socialism and those who do not. It is not a conflict between haves and have-nots. A look at the ranks behind the Prime Minister will be sufficient to expose the hollowness of such claims. It is a conflict that has been forced on the organisation by her obsessive desire for absolute power in the organisation and in the Government.'[33]

If the Syndicate had hoped that their expulsion order would bring Indira Gandhi, chastened and repentant, back to heel, they must have been disappointed. She may well have suffered considerable strain and anxiety during these tense weeks; but such fears and misgivings as she experienced were soon dispelled amid the exhilarating glow of popular acclaim. However factional the origins of the conflict, ideological issues had been raised in the course of the power struggle, and Indira Gandhi

---

*The Congress (Organisation), as opposed to the ruling party led by Mrs. Gandhi, which was known as the Congress (R)—Requisitioned or Ruling.

had managed to convince the common man that she stood for his interests against those of the corrupt and cynical élite that had ruled India for the last two decades. Every day large crowds gathered at her residence to congratulate her on her courage and resolution, and she handled them skilfully with a shrewd understanding of mass psychology. After acknowledging their eulogistic compliments with becoming modesty, she would assert in ringing tones her passionate concern for the exploited and under-privileged. Often, in the midst of her most ardent rhetoric, her voice would quiver and break with emotion; and the militant champion of the masses would be transformed in that instant into a fragile woman who needed the protection of her people from the tough politicians pitted against her.

The meeting of the requisitioned A.I.C.C. in Delhi on 22 November vindicated Mrs. Gandhi's claim that a majority of the party was behind her. 446 of the 705 A.I.C.C. members attended the session, which marked the grand finale of the Congress split. Mrs. Gandhi, on the whole, maintained a dignified silence about her opponents and left it to her supporters to abuse and castigate them. Even so, her address to the A.I.C.C. was notable for its uncharacteristic emotionalism. After tracing her family's and her own long involvement with the Congress, she spoke of her expulsion from the party. Her voice broke and the tears rolled down her cheeks. For a moment it seemed as though she would be unable to continue her speech. But she recovered quickly and asserted amid much applause: 'Nobody can throw me out of the Congress. It is not a legal question, nor one of passing a resolution to pronounce an expulsion order. It is a question of the very fibre of one's heart and being.' Then, turning to less sentimental issues, she told the delegates:

'I want to assure you quite categorically that we shall not take a single step backward in implementing the economic programme. We want to go forward more speedily, and I hope with your help and the cooperation of the people and our organisation we shall be able to fight the battle against poverty more effectively... The main question is how to translate these slogans into reality.'[34]

\*　　　\*　　　\*

Perhaps the most dramatic feature of the Congress split was its startling revelation of Indira Gandhi's unsuspected personal potential. *The New York Times* commented in August 1969: '...she has proved herself a courageous, tough-minded politician as well as an exceedingly skilful tactician—a Prime Minister in her own right and not a transitional figure, trading on her legacy as the daughter of Nehru.'[35] The shy and retiring woman who had nervously addressed the Jaipur Congress in February 1966 and suffered in silence the jibes of the Opposition in

Parliament had been transformed in the course of three years into a confident and charismatic leader, who was as skilful, and even ruthless, in dealing with seasoned colleagues and rivals as she was adept at handling large crowds.

To many observers, the metamorphosis appeared sudden and miraculous; but those who had watched Indira Gandhi closely were not surprised. The qualities of leadership that she now displayed had long been present, though veiled by the natural public shyness of a woman who had till recent years chosen to exercise her influence behind the scenes. Her initial diffidence had slowly but surely receded as she grew accustomed to public office. Though she was cautious and pragmatic by temperament, the pressure of circumstances had impelled her to take an increasingly committed position on controversial issues. As the political struggle escalated, her doubts and hesitations were progressively discarded. Each victory that she scored had released new sources of energy and self-confidence, and the exhilaration of success had emboldened her to assert herself with increasing vigour.

Mrs. Gandhi's long apprenticeship in Congress politics had left her with few illusions about her party colleagues, and she was as well-versed as they in the cynical and devious ways of political management. As the power struggle developed, she had demonstrated with ruthless efficiency that she could turn against her opponents their own weapons of factional intrigue and manipulation. And these weapons were all the more devastating when allied to the Nehru name and a wider ideological appeal to the nation.

In her administrative duties, too, Indira Gandhi had developed a style of her own that was both efficient and informal. Chalapathi Rau, an old friend, commented: 'Visitors are rarely asked to wait. Appointments are kept almost to the minute—thanks to a gift for combining listening with economy of speech. "Do away with the introductions, plunge into the subject", is Indira Gandhi's instruction to aides. She is a believer in putting in preparatory work, whether it is a meeting, a public speech or a press conference. She works on her speeches almost to the last minute.'[36]

Mrs. Gandhi had soon learned how to deal with the influx of self-seeking aspirants who flocked to her for jobs and promotions—an essential skill for a Prime Minister. Though she was always courteous and often sympathetic, she had her own way of tactfully warding off tiresome supplicants, even when they happened to be influential. When the Secretary of a key ministry was due to retire and called on her to seek an extension of his term, she diverted him with questions about his recent visit abroad. The verbose official was greatly flattered by the Prime Minister's attentive interest, until he was suddenly informed that his time was up and politely dismissed before he could make his request.

Though she continued to be shy of Parliamentary debates and her attendance in Parliament was perfunctory, Mrs. Gandhi was growing less sensitive to criticism and was learning to hit back at her assailants. The attacks on her were often personal. In August 1966 she had been accused in Parliament of accepting a mink coat as a gift from Dharma Teja, a notorious shipping magnate who had been found guilty of massive fraud. In December 1968 it was alleged in Parliament that P.N. Haksar* had been specially flown to New York to write the Prime Minister's much-applauded speech to the U.N. General Assembly. Mrs. Gandhi snapped back in a temper that the charge was 'absolutely ridiculous.'[37] About this time, an Opposition M.P. alleged that twenty-four items of baggage belonging to Rajiv Gandhi's bride-to-be had been flown out from Italy before the wedding and passed unchecked through Customs. Mrs. Gandhi denied the accusation and maintained that her Italian daughter-in-law had received only one item of unaccompanied baggage which had been cleared after due inspection by Customs. Attacks such as these may well have annoyed and upset her, but they had failed conspicuously to tarnish her public image. Of all the Congress leaders, she alone continued to be regarded as incorruptible.

Indira Gandhi's growing political stature at home had been paralleled by her expanding role on the world stage. Her domestic preoccupations had not deflected her from the task of building her image and that of the country abroad. Between September and November 1967 she had paid State visits to Ceylon, the Soviet Union, Poland, Yugoslavia, Bulgaria, Rumania and the United Arab Republic. In May 1968 a tour of South-East Asia had taken her to Singapore, Malaysia, Australia and New Zealand. In September 1968 she had toured Latin America, visiting Brazil, Argentina, Chile, Venezuela, Uruguay, Columbia, Trinidad and Guyana. In January 1969 she had attended the Commonwealth Prime Ministers' Conference in London; and later in the year, she paid official visits to Burma, Afghanistan, Japan and Indonesia. She was the first Indian Prime Minister to visit many of these countries, and her travels soon made her one of the best-known leaders in the world. Frank Moraes, a critical Indian journalist, has recorded an episode which indicates that Indira Gandhi's name was becoming familiar even in some of the more remote corners of the globe. He wrote in November 1968:

'One Sunday morning two months ago I happened to be in the mountains in Bulgaria... An old peasant asked me where I came from. "India", I told him. His eyes lighted. "Ah", he exclaimed,

---

*As Secretary to the Prime Minister, Haksar was one of her most influential advisers in both administrative and political matters. He was known for his intellectual brilliance and his Marxist leanings.

"Gandhi". Thinking he meant the Mahatma, I nodded. But the peasant meant somebody else. "Irina Gandhi", he went on. He meant Indira. That's fame.'[38]

Mrs. Gandhi's international fame was due in no small measure to her unique position as the woman Prime Minister of a country where women are traditionally exploited and under-privileged. This alone was sufficient to win her considerable press coverage all over the world. Her sex had other advantages too. When she visited London in January 1969, a British journalist commented on her appeal for women: 'One great advantage is that wherever she goes, about half the population is automatically on her side.'[39] At the same time, her femininity appealed to the chivalrous instincts of the other half. During her London visit, she arrived an hour late for a press luncheon because the morning session of the Commonwealth Prime Minister's Conference had lasted longer than expected. Though the assembled pressmen were furious by the time she arrived, they were instantly disarmed when she rose and apologised in her most charming manner.

Qualities other than her sex and its curiosity value also helped her to project a favourable image abroad. Her modern and rational outlook usually made a good impression on journalists and intellectuals; her tact and social graces went down well with her foreign counterparts; and she was spontaneous enough to break through security cordons and establish a rapport with crowds of spectators. When asked to cite the most memorable moment of her South American tour, she recalled with a smile that as she had emerged from the residence of the Governor-General of Trinidad, an urchin in rags had suddenly sprinted across the street, marched up to her, saluted smartly and marched away.

While she savoured the spontaneity of such encounters, Mrs. Gandhi was meticulous in her attention to the formal details of her foreign tours. Her official speeches were carefully prepared and tactfully worded with the assistance of her aides. The Prime Minister's appearance received equal attention. The austere Indian politician with tousled hair and a simple *khaddar* sari who boarded her aircraft in New Delhi would disembark a glamorous and elegant cosmopolitan, clad in rich silks, brocades and fur coats, her face carefully made up and her hair immaculately styled.

Indira Gandhi had not confined her role in foreign affairs to that of a decorative roving ambassador. Between September 1967 and January 1969, she had held personal charge of the External Affairs portfolio, and her role in the making of Indian foreign policy had revealed her growing practical grasp of the problems involved. Though committed to India's traditional non-alignment, she had shown a pragmatism and independence that indicated her capacity to think afresh. The Soviet Premier's visit to India in February 1968, the first such visit since Krushchev's fall, was widely seen as a feather in her cap, providing her with a certificate of good conduct from the Soviet leadership and deflating the opposition of Indian Communists to her government. While it was one of her chief aims to maintain Indo-Soviet friendship, Mrs. Gandhi was firm in her resistance to Soviet pressures that ran counter to Indian interests. While promising that India would not go nuclear, she refused to sign the nuclear non-proliferation treaty sponsored by the Soviet Union and United States, on the ground that it would close the options of non-nuclear countries while leaving nuclear powers free to go on proliferating their armaments. She also avoided committing India to the Brezhnev plan for collective security in Asia, a Russian attempt to counter American and Chinese influence. Though she released Sheikh Abdullah, the imprisoned Kashmiri leader, in January 1968 as a token of her intention to liberalise Indian rule in Kashmir, she rejected Soviet advice to settle with Pakistan on Kashmir.

Mrs. Gandhi had staunchly resisted attempts to castigate the Soviet Union for its arms supplies to Pakistan. But she was not averse to offsetting Russian friendship with Pakistan by improving Sino-Indian relations, and she had initiated some tentative moves in this direction. At a press reception in September 1968, she had expressed her willingness to re-open talks with China. At her New Year's Day press conference in January 1969, she reiterated: 'We are today stuck in a particular position. That does not help solve our problem with China. We should try and find a way of solving it. What that way is, at the moment I do not know.' When asked whether such a solution would involve compromising India's old position on the border dispute, she answered diplomatically: 'You do not solve the question by saying, "Here I stand and here I shall remain".' When her questioner demanded 'a straight answer', she refused to commit herself and replied: 'Unfortunately straight answers are not possible.'[40] Her caution was necessitated by the strength of anti-Chinese sentiment in a country which had not yet forgotten or forgiven its humiliating defeat in 1962. Even her vague feelers to China provoked such a hostile reaction from Indian chauvinists that they had to be abandoned, and the Sino-Indian Cold War continued.

Political power, and the responsibilities and controversies in which it involved her, had added new dimensions to Indira Gandhi's personality, developing latent faculties and talents and revealing to the public gaze facets which had formerly been clouded by her reticence. The most remarkabale feature of her years in office had been her ability to stretch her capacities in proportion to the demands made upon her. The strain, however, must have been considerable; and in personal terms, the price of political success was high. The greater her involvement in political conflict, the less time she had for other more personal interests and for her family and friends. Her sons, who had returned from England, were both living with her, and she was soon to become a grandmother. But however much she tried to maintain the normal rhythms of domestic life, and especially the ritual of eating with her family, her public engagements and political preoccupations constantly intervened. Even her birthdays had become public occasions, with crowds of well-wishers converging at 1, Safdarjang Road. In November 1967, she wrote regretfully to a friend: 'I wish my birthday could remain private and personal. As it is, there is never time for one's friends and relatives. The 19th was even more hectic than usual ... so it was far from being a holiday.'[41]

Nevertheless, she had found her vocation, and it was too late to turn back. As far as one knows, the thought of retirement never crossed Mrs. Gandhi's mind, or if it did was instantly banished. She had rejected the role of a figure-head Prime Minister and had fought vigorously to assert her supremacy. Following the Congress split, she had emerged in the eyes of her countrymen and of the world as the dominant figure on the Indian political scene. But there were still bridges to cross and mountains to climb. For all her popularity, she was as yet only the leader of a minority government, dependent on the shifting support of other parties and exposed to the bitter attacks of her opponents. For the moment she was the heroine of the crowd; but the crowd, she knew only too well, could be fickle.

Indira Gandhi had yet to show that she could rally the country round her on an enduring basis and that she could provide it with better government than the tired old men she had ousted. In the years ahead, she would have to bear in mind the advice she had once tendered to a conference of Indian students: 'The world is not interested in excuses for failure... The world is interested in who wins. Very few care to find out why one has lost. It is success and victory which matter.'[42] And her victory would be measured, not only by her capacity to mobilise votes, but by her success in making good her promises of radical economic and social change.

## CHAPTER X

# UNDISPUTED LEADER

REFLECTING ON the prospect of an ideological split in the Congress, Nehru had written in his autobiography:

'...was the Congress, constituted as it was, ever likely to adopt a really radical social solution? If such an issue was placed before it, the result was bound to be to split it into two or more parts, or at least to drive away large sections from it. That in itself was not undesirable or unwelcome if the issues became clearer and a strongly-knit group, either a majority or minority in the Congress, stood for a radical social programme.'[1]

Nehru himself had never taken the plunge and split the party. And the Congress, while paying lip-service to his socialist views, had continued to function as a party of the status quo. Such thrust as the party's socialistic policies acquired had been directed at the urban rich and the old, feudal aristocracy. The economic interests of the rich, high-caste peasant farmer, traditionally the social backbone of the Congress, had been carefully protected, and he had been left secure in his domination over the small peasants, share-croppers, landless labourers and Un-touchables who made up the vast majority of India's population. The green revolution had merely reinforced this domination, with its massive governmental assistance to the rich capitalist farmer. So long as this agricultural élite retained its stranglehold over the rural economy, the Congress party and the State apparatus, radicalism would remain a slogan.

In 1969 Indira Gandhi had a unique opportunity to break the traditional Congress pattern of socialist promise and capitalist performance. She had emerged from the split with her popularity unrivalled and with a widespread public belief in her sincerity of purpose. She had won the support, not only of Congress radicals, but of the entire Indian Left. She might now have pressed ahead to purge her band-wagon of opportunist elements and reorganise the Congress as a genuine mass movement with new cadres committed to socialist programmes. Such a course would naturally have cost her the support of influential senior Congressmen and deprived her party of its traditional social base among the rich farmers. But these losses might have been compensated by a close alliance or coalition with other Left-wing parties and by the mass support that radical measures would have generated.

That this opportunity was allowed to pass was inherent in the nature of the Congress split and the personalities involved. 'Strong language and a capacity to criticise and attack the old Congress leadership is not a test of Leftism in politics,' Nehru had warned Subhas Bose in 1939.[2] Judged by this dictum, the Congress split thirty years later had, for all its ideological overtones, been largely factional in origin, and so it would remain. Had the Syndicate not challenged her leadership, there is little doubt that Mrs. Gandhi, like her father, would have placed Congress unity before socialism. Though she had emerged from the split as the leader of the Indian Left, Indira Gandhi was neither a Lenin nor a Mao Tse-tung but a cautious and pragmatic Congresswoman. She had shown a capacity to take risks when the immediate situation demanded it; but this did not mean that she would stake her political future on a comprehensive and sweeping programme of social change. Such a programme would have required a drastic change both in the social composition of the Congress and in its methods of political organisation. Though more sensitive than other Congress leaders to popular aspirations, Mrs. Gandhi in the last analysis remained a product of the traditional Congress mould, and it was unrealistic to expect her to revolutionise the Congress. Nevertheless, this was what large sections of the country's poor, its youth and intelligentsia confidently expected of her. While encouraging such expectations and the mass support they brought her, Mrs. Gandhi would also take care to reassure the propertied classes, on whom her party remained financially and politically dependent, that she would protect their essential interests from 'Left adventurism.' It was a strategy which involved riding two horses at once, a feat which she would perform with remarkable acumen and success during the next two years.

\*     \*     \*

By March 1971 Indira Gandhi was to find herself in a position of supremacy that appeared—outwardly, at any rate—to rival that of her father at the zenith of his political career. For the moment, however, her future was by no means secure. She had emerged from the split as the most popular, dynamic and promising figure on the political scene. What was doubtful was the extent to which her personal charisma could be politically effective in consolidating and expanding the strength of the Congress (R) at the Centre and in the States.

Mrs. Gandhi was now the leader of a minority government, dependent on the parliamentary support of various Leftist and regional parties.

Such support, it was obvious, would not be extended without some quid pro quo; and the bargaining and concessions that this implied would hardly be conducive to strong government and long-range decision-making. The balance of Centre-State relations, already shaken by the 1967 elections, had been further altered by the allegiance of three important State Governments—those of U.P., Mysore and Gujarat—to the Congress (O).

Nor was the Congress (R) leadership free from internal pressures and differences. The Congress split had involved the amputation of one limb of the party; but it had not cured the Congress of the factional and regional rivalries that arose from the general malaise of India's parliamentary system. Barring its radical slogans, there was little to distinguish the new Congress from the old, either in its composition or in its methods of functioning. To the annoyance of some sections of the Congress (R), after the exodus of the Syndicate control of the party organisation was taken over by a new caucus of bosses, sometimes called the 'Indicate.' It included, apart from Indira Gandhi, two senior Cabinet Ministers—Chavan and Jagjivan Ram—and four State leaders—D.P. Mishra of Madhya Pradesh, Sukhadia of Rajasthan, Brahmananda Reddy of Andhra and Naik of Maharashtra. Together they ran the party in a manner that was hardly more democratic than that of the Syndicate, filling its key committees and offices with their nominees.

Indira Gandhi was ostensibly the undisputed leader of the Congress (R), both in party and governmental affairs. Her colleagues vied with each other in expressing their personal loyalty to her and their commitment to her socialism. Nijalingappa complained to an Indian journalist: 'The Congress Party President would never stand up when the Prime Minister came to attend the party's meeting. I never did, but Jagjivan Ram* has degraded the office by standing up whenever Mrs. Gandhi enters.'[3] Notwithstanding such outward manifestations of loyalty, Mrs. Gandhi must have known that many of her supporters during the split had backed her because they wished to exploit her popularity for their own factional ends. Their commitment to her policies was dubious, and given the chance they would be as ready as the Syndicate to confine her to the role of a popular figure-head.

Some of the Prime Minister's advisers are believed to have felt that her best course would be an immediate general election, which would end her dependence on other parties and on unreliable elements within the Congress (R). But she was wise enough to reject such hasty action. She knew from long experience that charismatic leadership and radical slogans were not sufficient to win a general election. Votes, especially

*Elected President of the Congress (R) at the party's plenary session in December, 1969.

in the politically backward rural areas which accounted for most of the electorate, depended on the local ties of caste and economic dependence. And the mobilisation of local support required an organisational machinery that would link local bases of support with Central leadership and programmes. The Congress organisation, once an invincible monolith, had long been decaying and the split had administered the final blow. The process of reorganisation would require time and large financial resources. Meanwhile, a snap election could prove disastrous.

Brushing aside suggestions for a mid-term poll or for a coalition government, Mrs. Gandhi applied herself to the task of consolidating her party, while dividing and discrediting her opponents. She relied mostly on the usual Congress techniques of political management to achieve her ends, making the most of the patronage and strategic advantages of her position as Prime Minister. The overwhelming majority with which Parliament rejected a no-confidence motion soon after the split made it clear that there was no immediate threat to her government's continuance. Now the chief endeavour of the Congress (R) leadership was to make up the numerical losses resulting from the split by securing large-scale defections from other parties. The result was an intensification of the political horse-trading and legislative floor-crossing that had become characteristic of Indian politics. The doors of the Congress (R) were thrown open to all who chose to enter, even if they happened to be defectors from the Right-wing Swatantra and Jana Sangh. It was not surprising that along with the younger and more committed elements who joined the party came large numbers of opportunists, hoarders, black-marketeers and corrupt fixers and middle-men.

Its ranks swollen by these new recruits, the Congress (R) made strenuous attempts to topple the Congress (O) governments in Gujerat, Mysore and particularly U.P., the Hindi heartland, control of which had been vital to the stability of central governments since ancient times. Mrs. Gandhi herself hotly denied charges of trying to dislodge State governments opposed to her. 'I have neither the intention nor the time to do such things,' she assured a public meeting in Gujerat. 'It is for the people and the legislators to decide which Government they want in office.'⁴

Nevertheless, the Prime Minister's tours of the States were widely regarded as part of a campaign to undermine hostile State governments. In January 1970, C.B. Gupta, the Congress (O) Chief Minister of U.P., accused her of trying to bring down his government and alleged that her official visits to U.P. during the last two years had cost the State exchequer Rs. 4,000,000. *The Statesman*, a leading conservative newspaper, commented sardonically: 'A socialistic pattern should at the least prescribe that the Prime Minister does not cost too much; and that where she is more often a faction leader than a Prime Minister, the privileges which rightly belong to the latter are not conferred on the other.'[5] Though she was unable to wrest U.P. from her opponents, Mrs. Gandhi drew huge crowds wherever she went and succeeded in winning over many members of the Congress (O) and other parties. Her success provoked a suggestion from a hysterical Opposition leader that Chief Minister Gupta should arrest the Prime Minister in U.P. for disturbing law and order. Gupta, however, is reported to have confessed: 'I can't fight her, because I am too old now and she is using money which is coming from all sources.'[6]

The Congress (O) and its allies, convinced that Mrs. Gandhi's personality was the Congress (R)'s most potent asset, had launched a personal smear campaign against her. The subject of their vendetta, however, was undaunted. 'I do not mind being attacked at all,' she had told an interviewer. 'I consider it a challenge. If I think I am doing right, I do not care what other people say, and I cannot be influenced by criticism when I am convinced... I have been like this ever since I was a child.'[7] Unlike her detractors, she avoided personal abuse; and her dignified refusal to reply in kind made a favourable impression on the Indian public, who saw it as an example of feminine modesty and decorum. Referring to the campaign against her, Indira Gandhi told a cheering audience in U.P.: 'Who am I—a frail, little woman—when the people are sovereign.'[8] At other times she dismissed the sniping of the Opposition in a lighter vein. On a visit to Gujerat in January 1970, she remarked that the multiple identity attributed to her by her opponents puzzled her and suggested they hold a seminar to decide once and for all whether she was Hitler, Stalin, Mussolini or George III.

Instead of attacking personalities, Mrs. Gandhi spoke to her audiences of her passionate concern for their rights and of the obstacles that her opponents were placing in the way of change. The Right-wing played into her hands with their vehement opposition to popular measures like bank nationalisation and the abolition of princely privileges. Some Opposition leaders had appealed to the Supreme Court against the legislation nationalising banks. In February 1970 the court struck down the Act, on the ground that it was discriminatory and offered inadequate compensation. Though she accepted the verdict, Mrs. Gandhi pointed out at a public meeting on 10 February: 'Surely it shows that obstacles are placed in the way of those who want to bring about any change and do something new.'[9] Four days later, she re-nationalised banks by a presidential ordinance which circumvented the Supreme Court's objections to the original legislation. In the eyes of the nation, this confirmed her determination to implement the Congress programme, despite the attempts of the Right-wing, aided by the judiciary, to thwart her. In March 1970, a prominent political commentator observed:

'In the capital the impression is now widespread that Indira Gandhi is powerfully entrenched. She has out-manoeuvred all her competitors and detractors, befuddled those who were seeking to topple her minority Government, made herself the subject of debate and controversy within the opposition parties, and emerged as the only national leader commanding relevance and respect.'[10]

By June 1970, Mrs. Gandhi's position was strong enough for her to undertake a major Cabinet reshuffle, the most sweeping since the Kamaraj Plan of 1963. The Cabinet changes demonstrated her supremacy in the Government, bringing under her personal control its most crucial departments. To the astonishment of most observers, Chavan meekly submitted to being transferred from Home to Finance. At the same time, Dinesh Singh, who had considered himself indispensable, was summarily moved from External Affairs, where he had become a serious political liability, to a minor ministry. The Prime Minister herself assumed the key portfolio of Home which, together with the expansion of the Cabinet Secretariat, gave her complete control of all internal security and government intelligence. A leading political weekly commented on the effect of these changes:

'The new position of power enjoyed by the Prime Minister has apparently created a strange paralysis in the ministries of the Government of India. It is maintained that Indira Gandhi's colleagues, fearful of taking positions contrary to the Prime Minister, have gradually and almost gratefully fallen into the habit of referring matters to the boss... all manner of decisions, major and minor, consequential and inconsequential, comic and serious, are being taken in the Prime Minister's Secretariat... The Prime Minister's Secretariat, structured as it is at present, will find it impossible to cope with the increasing burdens of decision-making which are being foisted upon it by irresponsible ministries. Under such overwhelming pressures, delays and snap decisions are inevitable. Questions are being asked whether this method of functioning is at all healthy and whether it doesn't lead to a *durbari\** atmosphere.'[11]

The Opposition was quick to seize upon this point and to accuse Mrs. Gandhi of dictatorial ambitions. In July 1970, replying to such charges in a no-confidence motion, she protested:

'It is obvious that the entire motion is designed as a personal attack on me and on the supposed concentration of power in my hands...

*Courtly or feudal.

I did not create the Cabinet Secretariat... I did not invent the Prime Minister's Secretariat either... As is well known, in England, as well as in many other countries, Intelligence is directly with the Prime Minister, and I am sure that these countries did not take inspiration from the reshuffle in this country.'[12]

On 7 January 1970, Indira Gandhi had written to the Maharaja of Dhrangadhra, the spokesman of the Concord of Princes*: 'I can assure you that on Government's part there has never been any question of offending the self-respect of the former Rulers (princes), much less of humiliating them in any way.'[13] Nevertheless, in the following months negotiations between the Government and the princes failed to produce an agreed compromise on the abolition of princely privileges and privy purses, one of the Ten Points in the Congress programme. The princes had been playing an increasingly active political role, and in several States their support for the Right-wing Opposition had secured the defeat of the Congress in the 1967 general election. It was hardly surprising then that most Congressmen saw the abolition of privy purses as an act of just retribution. In August 1970, Mrs. Gandhi introduced in Parliament a bill to amend the Constitution and abolish the large public pensions and other perquisites guaranteed to the Indian princes. Though the measure was attacked as a breach of faith with the 250-odd princes who had merged their states with the Indian Union in 1947, Mrs. Gandhi justified it on egalitarian grounds, and public opinion was firmly behind her.

The constitutional amendment received the necessary two-thirds majority in the Lok Sabha, but was defeated by one vote in the Upper House. The President, on the Prime Minister's advice, now issued a proclamation withdrawing his recognition of the princes and thereby depriving them of their privileges. Once again Mrs. Gandhi had succeeded in demonstrating her radical bonafides at the expense of her opponents. The Congress (O), which had joined the Jana Sangh and Swatantra in opposing the bill in Parliament, had been caught on the wrong foot and publicly exposed as a party of the status quo, unwilling to implement the Ten-Point Programme of the undivided Congress.

Indira Gandhi had also been waging a subtle campaign against those sections of the business community who were subsidising her opponents. In January 1970, she had told a gathering of Gujerati mill-owners: 'I may not be a financial wizard. In fact, I know very little about finance. But I do have enough intelligence and I do have the eyes to see what is happening in my country, and I do have the ears to hear the voices of my people.'[14] In effect, her message to the business community was that if they backed her and made the small concessions that her mild dose of

*An organisation formed by the princes to negotiate with the Government.

socialism required, she would protect them from the far Left. In December 1970, she spelled this out at the annual meeting of the Associated Chambers of Commerce and Industry:

'You have spoken, as many business people speak, about not bringing politics into economics. But you have no hesitation in trying to influence politics in every way you can to serve your own interests... In other countries whole classes have been wiped out. We are trying to prevent it. We are trying to have a kind of change which will prevent it, which will be peaceful, which will give a place to all in our country without thinking of wiping them out. It is for the business community to decide whether they will agree to have this sort of change or they will, by not agreeing at this stage, invite something which will be far more drastic, and certainly for which people like us will not be responsible.'[15]

This carrot-and-stick strategy was to be typical of Indira Gandhi's approach to the propertied élite. While socialist slogans were freely used to win mass support, Mrs. Gandhi was quick to reassure the rich that she stood for peaceful and gradual change. She confided to an Indian journalist: 'If I don't do anything to take the wind out of the sails of the Communists, the entire country will go Red.'[16] In her Independence Day address from the ramparts of the Red Fort, Delhi, in August 1969, she had said:

'When banks were nationalised, some rumours were set afloat that this step was directed against a particular section of our society... But I want to assure the rich and the capitalists that the step that we have taken is not directed against them. It is only in the interest of the people, and a measure which is in the interest of the masses is in their interest also.'[17]

Thus it was that the Government confined its radicalism to largely symbolic populist gestures like bank nationalisation and abolition of princely privileges, while avoiding any interference with the essential interests of the country's commercial and landed classes. Measures such as the imposition of ceilings on urban property, nationalisation of general insurance and State take-over of the wholesale trade in foodgrains were discreetly shelved, even though they were part of the Ten-Point Programme. Although a Monopolies Commission had been established, the House of Birla, the largest monopoly in the country, was given a licence to set up a new fertiliser plant with American collaboration. 'You are no Leftist; you are just pragmatic,' D.P. Mishra is reported to have twitted Mrs. Gandhi about this decision. 'Of course I am pragmatic,' she replied. 'Is there anything wrong in being that?'[18] The Government's budget for 1970, the first prepared and presented by Mrs. Gandhi as Finance Minister, made no more than some token gestures towards social justice and was received with relief by most businessmen.

The most crucial point in the Congress programme was the implementation of land reforms. On this point, too, Indira Gandhi surrendered against her better judgement to the strong conservatism of State leaders. At a conference of Chief Ministers in September 1970, she warned: 'Statesmanship lies, not only in heeding danger signals, but heeding them in time; not only in agreeing to act, but acting in time.'[19] In her address to the conference, she made a forceful plea both for the implementation of existing land legislation and for further land reforms, pointing out that the green revolution was widening the gap between the rural rich and poor, with dangerous implications for political stability. She failed, however, to convince even those Chief Ministers who belonged to her own party, and the conference decided to shelve the issue by referring it to a committee for further consideration. Though she appears to have been sincere in her desire for land reforms, Mrs. Gandhi refused to condone mass agitation for this purpose. When the Communists and Socialists launched a peaceful 'Land Grab' movement to occupy and re-distribute surplus land, one of their targets was the Prime Minister's four-acre farm near Delhi. Speaking in Parliament, Mrs. Gandhi strongly condemned the movement as being based on class hatred, envy and acquisitiveness—strange words coming from a socialist.

\*          \*          \*

Indira Gandhi's international role during these turbulent months confirmed and enhanced her prestige at home. Free from the interference of the former Deputy Prime Minister, she had been able since the split to shape Indian foreign policy according to her own lights. Indo-Soviet relations had shown a marked improvement, coinciding with the new Congress (R)—C.P.I. entente at home; and in October 1970 Russia terminated its arms aid to Pakistan. The humiliation of the Rabat fiasco\* in September 1969 had since been erased by the Prime Minister's impressive performance in world forums. In September 1970, she had addressed the third Conference of Non-Aligned Countries at Lusaka. In a strong speech against neo-colonialism, she reminded the delegates:

'We have all been subjected to domination, exploitation and the humiliation of racial discrimination... The big powers have never accepted the validity of non-alignment. Neither colonialism nor

\*At Pakistan's instance, India's invitation to the World Islamic Conference at Rabat (Morocco) was cancelled at the last minute after the Indian delegation had arrived in Rabat. It was a diplomatic debacle which discredited Dinesh Singh, then Minister for External Affairs, and encouraged domestic criticism of the Government's pro-Arab foreign policy.

racialism has vanished. The old comes back in new guise. There are subtle intrigues to undermine our self-confidence and to sow dissension and mutual distrust amongst us. Powerful vested interests, domestic and foreign, are combining to erect new structures of neo-colonialism. These dangers can be combated by our being united in our adherence to the basic tenets of non-alignment.'[20]

On 23 October, Mrs. Gandhi attended the silver jubilee celebrations of the United Nations and addressed the General Assembly for the second time. While avoiding direct criticism of the United States, she referred to the role of imperialism in the Middle East and Vietnam conflicts and complained: '...the U.N. has been afflicted by the same malady as the League of Nations; that is, the attempt to direct and control its activities and to use it as an instrument for national ends. To the extent it could be so used, it was applauded and when it did not serve such purpose it was ignored.'[21] What was implicit in her speech was made clear when she pointedly declined a dinner invitation from President Nixon who had recently renewed American arms aid to Pakistan. Her speeches at Lusaka and the U.N. were well received both in the world press and at home.

*       *       *

As 1970 drew to a close, the political tide was clearly running in Indira Gandhi's favour. The Congress (R) had emerged victorious from various parliamentary by-elections since the split. A mid-term election in the problem-State of Kerala had vindicated the party's alignment with the C.P.I., returning a Congress (R)—C.P.I. coalition to power and isolating the C.P.I. (M). In West Bengal, another C.P.I. (M) stronghold, the imposition of President's rule had given the Congress (R) an opportunity to consolidate its position, while the Central Government cracked down hard on Maoist guerillas. The effects of the green revolution and a good monsoon had resulted in a bumper harvest and relieved the food shortage. After three years of industrial recession and inflation, the economy was showing signs of recovery. The Fourth Five-Year Plan, postponed for two years owing to the scarcity of resources, had at last been launched with an impressive investment outlay twice that of the Third Plan.

It was impossible, however, to predict how long this favourable trend would last. 'Mrs. Gandhi naturally holds the trumps,' a political weekly commented in October 1970. 'Her prestige in the country, despite the uneasy heartland*, is unchallenged... To carry on until 1972 with the present limited political leverage at the Centre and in the States may well

---

*Uttar Pradesh or U.P., where the Congress (O) retained control of the State Government.

be disastrous—and certainly so if the 1971 monsoon decides to be moody.'[22]

Indira Gandhi herself appears to have arrived at the same conclusion. Ever since the Congress split, her opponents had been daring her to face the electorate in a general election. Few had expected her to take up the challenge; but by the end of 1970, her accurate sense of political timing had convinced her that this was the moment to put her popularity to the test. All she needed now was a dramatic and popular issue on which to appeal to the country; and the Right-wing Opposition unwittingly provided her with it.

In response to an appeal from some princes and Opposition leaders against the abolition of privy purses by presidential action, the Supreme Court struck down the presidential order as being ultra vires of the Fundamental Rights laid down in the Constitution. It was a direct challenge from the judiciary to both the executive and the legislative powers. After an emergency meeting of the Cabinet on 27 December 1970, Mrs. Gandhi drove to the presidential palace and advised President Giri to dissolve Parliament and hold a fresh general election. A presidential proclamation to this effect was issued at once. It was the first time since Independence that Parliament had been dissolved before the end of its normal five-year term.

In a broadcast to the nation on the night of the dissolution, Indira Gandhi sounded what were to be the main themes of her election campaign. Explaining her decision to seek a fresh mandate, she declared: '...we are concerned, not merely with remaining in power, but with using that power to ensure a better life to the vast majority of our people and to satisfy their aspirations for a just social order. In the present situation, we feel we cannot go ahead with our proclaimed programme and keep our pledges to our people.' She went on to trace her government's attempts during the last year to implement its programme, stressing in particular bank nationalisation and the abolition of privy purses, and citing the obstruction of 'vested interests' and 'reactionary forces'. She referred also to the break-down of law and order resulting from the 'violent activities' of 'extremists' and the divisive tactics of communalists. She concluded: 'Time will not wait for us. The millions who demand food shelter and jobs are pressing for action. Power in a democracy resides with the people. That is why we have decided to go to our people and to seek a fresh mandate from them'.[23]

*          *          *

The Congress (R)'s election manifesto reflected the peculiar mixture of radicalism and pragmatism, populism and elitism, that made up the ruling party's political strategy. It was a vague and low-key appeal which made few ambitious promises to the masses or threats to the pro-pertied classes. The Congress (R) asked for a mandate to 'continue the advance to socialism through democratic process', abolish princely privileges, 'reduce *glaring**\* disparities in income and opportunity', protect and promote the interests of minorities and Untouchables, expand the role of the public sector, control prices and amend the Consti-tution where necessary. At the same time, the manifesto emphasised the need for stable government, promising to 'put down the forces of violence and disorder' and to 'give scope to the private sector to play its proper role in the economy'. It was a largely non-controversial programme which could alarm no one except the princes.

The manifesto, however, was of minor importance. The central issue on which the election was being fought was Indira Gandhi's right to govern the country. 'The whole battle will be fought around her,' a political journal predicted. 'This is not at all healthy, but every political party has played a part in giving her this extraordinary position—a position which also gives her the power to achieve the speedy transforma-tion in her party which the election demands. This is no time to falter.'24

Mrs. Gandhi's ability to implement her egalitarian programme would depend as much on the actual personnel of the future Lok Sabha as on the size of her majority. It was reasonable to expect, therefore, that the choice of party candidates would be dictated, not by the old criteria of factional influence, caste and finance, but by commitment to socialism. Neverthe-less, the manner in which the Congress (R) had evolved since the split allowed little scope for change in the selection process. In the absence of any radical transformation of the structure or composition of the party, candidates were bound to be chosen in much the same manner and for much the same reasons as they had been by the old Congress.

There was little that Indira Gandhi could do single-handed to alter this. While she had an important say in the choice of party candidates, it was impossible for her personally to scrutinise and judge the claims of every applicant for party nomination. Nor could she afford, on the eve of a general election, to alienate State leaders who were anxious to nominate their own protégés. All that she could do was to intervene in specific cases and areas, and her influence on party nominations could at most be marginal. In these circumstances, the choice of most party candidates remained in the hands of the essentially conservative State bosses, who handed out party tickets to their own relatives, friends and financers. While the Congress (R)'s list did contain some new and young blood, most of its candidates belonged to the same élite groups which had dominated the undivided Congress, and commitment to socialism was the least important factor in their selection.

*Author's emphasis.

The obvious inadequacy and opportunism of most of the party's candidates were responsible for general scepticism in the press on the party's election prospects. Few political analysts denied that Mrs. Gandhi would continue as Prime Minister after the election; but many doubted that she would secure an absolute majority and predicted a coalition government at the Centre. Even the most generous estimates did not expect the Congress (R) to improve on the performance of the undivided Congress in 1967. What these analyses failed to take into account was the extent to which the electorate might be swayed by Indira Gandhi's soaring popularity and credibility, by the soundness of her election strategy and by the folly of her opponents.

Shortly after the dissolution, the Congress (O), Swatantra, Jana Sangh and S.S.P.* had formed an electoral pact, generally known as the Grand Alliance. The alliance was manifestly a marriage of convenience, with its constituents unable to agree on a common programme other than the slogan of '*Indira Hatao*' (Remove Indira). To this Mrs. Gandhi promptly replied with the far more effective and popular slogan of '*Garibi Hatao*' (Remove Poverty). As opposed to the motley grouping of disparate parties to oust her, she ruled out an alliance with other parties at the national level and made it clear that her party aimed at an absolute majority and at giving the country the strong and stable government that ramshackle coalitions had conspicuously failed to provide.

This line did not, however, prevent the Congress (R) from reaching State-level electoral understandings with the ruling D.M.K. in Tamil Nad (Madras), where the Congress (R) was virtually non-existent, and with the C.P.I. and Muslim parties in several other States. The pro-Moscow Communists were a relatively minor political force by this time, having lost both their revolutionary fervour and most of their mass following to the C.P.I. (M). Even so, the C.P.I. was still in a position to tilt the balance in a large number of constituencies, and its active support for Congress (R) candidates provided them with what they lacked most, trained and committed political workers. Mrs. Gandhi was wise enough to see these advantages and to overrule the objections of anti-Communist elements in her party to an alliance with the C.P.I.

By far the most decisive feature of the Congress (R)'s election campaign was the impact of Indira Gandhi's personality. The Grand Alliance had turned the election into a referendum on Mrs. Gandhi's leadership, and she had taken up the challenge. Nehru, during his Prime Ministership, had been the star performer in his party's election campaigns. But never before had attention been focused so exclusively on an individual leader as it was in the 1971 general election. While the Opposition spoke of

*Samyukta Socialist Party, a right-wing populist group.

little else but Mrs. Gandhi and her misdeeds, the ruling party's candidates spared no efforts to project themselves to the voter as her personal nominees. There was scarcely a Congress (R) poster to be seen which did not carry a portrait of the Prime Minister. Her smile sparkled at the electorate from thousands of Indira badges, the production of which is said to have rivalled that of Mao badges during the Chinese Cultural Revolution.

The Opposition naturally cited such facts as evidence of the personality cult that was threatening Indian democracy. But Mrs. Gandhi herself had little choice in the matter. She was the Congress (R)'s most valuable electoral asset, and it was inevitable that the party would make the most of her appeal. Significantly, this appeal no longer derived from the Nehru legend, but from the independent image that she had been building for herself since 1967. The customary references to Nehru and Gandhi, which had been so much a part of Congress electioneering, were now few and far between. Instead, the main theme of Congress (R) election speeches was Indira Gandhi's heroic struggle against the forces of reaction represented by the Syndicate and her selfless commitment to the war on poverty and social injustice.

The 'Indira Wave', which had been gathering strength since the nationalisation of banks, reached its peak during Mrs. Gandhi's marathon election tour, a feat of energy and endurance which surpassed the most strenuous exertions of her father. From mid-January 1971 till polling began on 5 March, Mrs. Gandhi was almost continuously on the move. According to the record kept by her staff, she covered 30,000 miles by air and 3,000 by road and rail, addressing altogether 409 election meetings with a total attendance of 20 million people. While on tour, she maintained a daily average of addressing 15 election meetings, attending personally to 30 official files and 30 telephone calls, giving 20 interviews and receiving 5 deputations. Throughout these weeks, she is reported to have kept up an eighteen-hour working day, with four or five hours for sleep and rest. Not a single meeting, we are told, was cancelled because of illness or fatigue. Even if one allows for the usual official exaggeration, it was a performance unparalleled in India's parliamentary history, and it could not fail to yield political dividends.

In 1967, too, Mrs. Gandhi had canvassed strenuously for the Congress. But this time there were no brick-bats, and the only hazards she had to face were mechanical. On 1 March, while touring the State of Orissa, she had a narrow escape from a plane crash. The Air Force plane in which she was travelling was flying over a town where she was to have addressed a public meeting. At the last minute the local landing strip had been found unfit for use; but Mrs. Nandini Satpathy, the Orissa Congress leader who was accompanying Mrs. Gandhi, suggested that the plane should circle the airfield so that the crowd could get a glimpse of the Prime Minister.

The pilot was doing this when he noticed that one engine was on fire and immediately made a forced landing. Had Mrs. Gandhi overflown the town as intended, the fire would have been noticed further from the airstrip, and a landing would have been difficult. It had been a close shave; but she emerged unruffled from the aircraft, greeting the crowds who had surrounded it, and took advantage of the halt to address another election meeting in a neighbouring town.

*     *     *

Wherever she went, Mrs. Gandhi drew huge crowds and her presence overshadowed the short-comings of the candidates for whom she spoke. Her speeches were simple and direct, often achieving the intimacy of private conversation, with occasional flashes of homespun wit which appealed to the common man. When she indulged in political rhetoric, her voice carried conviction. 'She has improved her public speaking,' a prominent journalist observed. 'Instead of the hesitant, shrill-voiced jumble of irrelevancies, we have forthright, impassioned oratory. She fires her audience.'[25]

Indira Gandhi's electoral strategy was double-edged. To the propertied middle classes, she promised the political stability and conditions for economic growth which only a strong Central Government could guarantee. At the same time, she kindled new hope among the Harijans, the Muslims and other exploited and under-privileged sections of the masses, who had so far been politically apathetic. While warning her audiences that poverty could not be abolished overnight, she asserted that she had at least made a beginning in the face of strong opposition and that she intended to continue the good work. Despite the scepticism of political commentators, she was able to ride both horses, convincing the rich and the poor that she would protect each from the other.

In 1967 the electorate had rebuffed the Congress and decided to give the Opposition a chance. But most non-Congress governments in the States had proved no better, and in some cases worse, than their Congress predecessors. Such credibility as the Right Opposition parties retained had been shattered by their unprincipled electoral alliance, by their scurrillous personal vendetta against Mrs. Gandhi and by their lack of any positive programme. The electorate, encouraged by the confidence that Mrs. Gandhi inspired, was now inclined to give an apparently rejuvenated Congress another chance. The 'Indira Wave' had reversed the anti-Congress trend of 1967, and it now proceeded to sweep aside the cautious calculations of election analysts. To the astonishment of the electorate, the Opposition and most Congress (R) candidates themselves, Mrs. Gandhi's party swept the polls, winning a two-thirds majority in the Lok Sabha and about 70 seats more than the undivided Congress had secured in 1967. The Grand Alliance was all but annihilated, with most of its leaders routed at the polls. The only non-Congress parties to improve their position were the C.P.I. and the D.M.K., which had been allied with Mrs. Gandhi, and the C.P.I. (M), which had opposed her.

For many politicians and journalists, Indira Gandhi's landslide victory was nothing short of a political miracle. Some bewildered Opposition leaders, unable to believe that the country had rejected them, indulged in fanciful allegations that the polls had been rigged by the use of invisible ink and chemically-treated ballot-papers supplied by Soviet Russia. Others were more reasonable and conceded that the elections had been as fair as they could be in prevailing circumstances.

This is not to suggest that the electoral process had been free from abuse and malpractice. As in previous elections, there had been a good deal of bribery, intimidation and abuse of governmental power, factors for which the Grand Alliance partners, who controlled several State Governments, were no less to blame than the Congress (R). The role of money was far larger in 1971 than in any previous general election, with a single candidate's election expenses ranging anywhere from Rs. 100,000 to Rs. 10,000,000. Elections were bound to be expensive in a country where candidates had to canvass a vast and mostly illiterate electorate, spread out over large rural constituencies, and where the best-approved method of collecting votes was to buy the support of local faction-leaders. The expanding role of money was also a reflection of the mushroom growth of the black-market economy in recent years. The business community, anxious to keep a foot in every camp, had poured enormous sums of 'black' money into the coffers of most political parties. The Congress (R) had been accused of using the Central machinery of industrial licensing to extort election funds from businessmen; but the Grand Alliance, most observers agreed, had not suffered from any shortage of funds.

However much the financial resources and governmental influence of the Congress (R) may have aided its election prospects, they could not of themselves have won the party a mandate which the undivided Congress had failed to secure in 1967. Nor was it sufficient to say, as some of the Prime Minister's admirers did, that the victory had been a personal vote for her. Mrs. Gandhi, after all, had campaigned for the Congress in 1967, and the results had been very different. The key to Indira Gandhi's popularity and her party's success in 1971 lay in the fact that she had convinced the electorate that she could provide both stability and social change.

The contradictions inherent in a political strategy which capitalised both on the insecurity of the propertied classes and the discontent of the masses would become clear in the near future. Meanwhile, the Congress

(R)'s promises had been taken at face value, and this was largely due to Indira Gandhi's leadership and the public confidence she was able to command. It was in this sense that the general election had been a personal triumph for the Prime Minister, vindicating her strategy, destroying her critics and detractors and humbling those within her party who had doubted the soundness of her judgement.

Radiant in her hour of triumph, Mrs. Gandhi showed no signs of the fatigue that might have been expected to follow upon her exertions during the preceding weeks. Her shoulders heaped high with victory garlands, she received the huge crowds who came to congratulate her with an air of quiet satisfaction. Addressing a press conference, she twitted newsmen on their sceptical forecasts and declared that she herself had never been in any doubt about the outcome of the contest. 'I have never gambled', she said, 'and I do not intend to gamble in the future.'[26] 'It was not really much of a surprise,' she later assured the author, explaining that the pre-election estimates supplied by various State leaders had indicated that her party would win at least 300 seats.[27]

In a letter of congratulation, Mrs. Martin Luther King wrote euphorically to Indira Gandhi: 'Your victory is one more giant step for womanhood. You epitomise, without rancour and bitterness to males, what a free woman has the capacity to become.'[28] Mrs. Gandhi herself saw it somewhat differently, and in a letter to John Grigg, a friendly British journalist, she gave her own interpretation of her victory:

'Newspapers here and abroad have, as usual, missed the essential point about these elections... The question is not one of the majority. What has been extraordinary and exhilarating is that the elections became a sort of movement—a people's movement... The peasant, the worker and, above all, the youth cut across all caste, religious and other barriers to make this their own campaign with tremendous enthusiasm... All sections were repelled by the campaign of hate and vilification concentrated against me.'[29]

\*        \*        \*

On 17 March 1971, Indira Gandhi was elected leader of the Congress Parliamentary Party for the third time in succession. On this occasion there had been not so much as a hint of rivalry, let alone a leadership contest, and her election was unanimous in the fullest sense. In this moment of undisputed leadership, Mrs. Gandhi's mood was sober, even humble, reflecting her awareness that her massive electoral mandate carried with it a heavy responsibility. The electorate had been generous in giving her its overwhelming confidence and unfettered parliamentary power. Henceforth there could be no alibis or excuses for failure. If

Indira Gandhi failed to meet the high expectations that she had raised, the country would lose faith, not only in her, but in the parliamentary system. It was not surprising, then, that Mrs. Gandhi's triumph was mixed with some embarrassment, and even apprehension, at the size of her electoral majority. Sounding a note of warning, she told Congress M.P.s after her re-election as leader:

> 'In your generosity you have said that the victory is mine. This is not correct. This is the victory of all of us working together... Removing poverty is a very big task. I do not know whether we can do it. We are human. We may make mistakes. We may falter. But we have to show that whatever happens we shall put all our energy into the task of removing poverty... This election is a key which has opened the door, but the journey ahead remains. It will be a long and difficult journey. We have a big majority. *The big majority makes some things easier. Some things may be more difficult\**.'[30]

The Congress split, its aftermath of competitive radicalism and the election campaign and its results had all combined to politicise the country to an unprecedented degree and to raise hopes which any government or party would have been hard pressed to satisfy. Apart from Indira Gandhi's charisma, the new Congress had little to recommend it or to distinguish it from the old. Though its programme was more radical, its composition and structure were no better, and in some instances worse, than those of the undivided party, and it would have to govern through the same decadent administrative apparatus. Sooner or later public disappointment was bound to set in, and there was little that Indira Gandhi and a few other individuals could do to prevent this. In these circumstances, it was fortunate for the ruling party that public attention was diverted almost immediately from domestic issues by an external crisis, the successful handling of which would carry the Indira Wave to new heights, leading to the virtual deification of the Prime Minister and winning her laurels which even her father had failed to attain.

*       *       *

In December 1970 Sheikh Mujibur Rahman and his Awami League had secured an absolute majority in elections for the Pakistan National Assembly, capturing virtually every seat from East Pakistan on a Six-Point Programme of maximum provincial autonomy which verged on secession. Though the Bengalis of East Pakistan formed a majority of the country's total population, Pakistani politics had been dominated since Independence by a small élite of politicians, bureaucrats and generals from the

---

*Author's italics.

western wing, and particularly from the Punjab province. Unwilling to
come to terms with Bengali nationalism and transfer power to the Awami
League, Pakistan's military rulers, backed by Z.A. Bhutto, the leading
politician in West Pakistan, had refused to convene the newly-elected
assembly. Events now moved rapidly. The Awami League launched a civil
disobedience movement, there were violent outbreaks, and on 25 March
the Pakistan army began military repression on a scale that approached
genocide. Thousands of refugees, bearing tales of hair-raising atrocities,
began to stream across the Indian border. Though Mujibur Rahman had
been arrested by the Pakistan army, his lieutenants in the Awami League
proclaimed the independence of Bangladesh and launched an underground resistance movement.

Indian public opinion had been too preoccupied with domestic politics
to take serious note of the crisis brewing in Pakistan, and news of the
Bangladesh revolt burst upon the Indian scene with explosive suddenness.
To those who had opposed from the outset the creation of Pakistan,
the uprising came as a final indictment of Jinnah's Two-Nation Theory
and as a heaven-sent opportunity for India to step in and smash Pakistan
once and for all. Indira Gandhi, however, refused to allow her better
judgement to be swayed by chauvinistic public opinion. She was convinced
that military intervention by India at this stage would not only amount
to a flagrant breach of international law, but would also be self-defeating,
lending weight to Pakistani propaganda that the revolt was a conspiracy
by Hindu India and undermining the solidarity of Muslim Bengali
nationalism. On 27 March she told the Lok Sabha: '. . . in a serious
moment like this, the less we as a Government say, I think the better
it is.'[31] On the same day she warned the Rajya Sabha: '. . .it is not possible
for the Government to speak in the same words as Honourable Members
can do. . . a wrong step, a wrong word, can have an effect entirely different
from the one which we all intend. The House is aware that we have to act
within international norms.'[32]

During the next few days, Mrs. Gandhi worked hard to secure the widest
possible national consensus for her cautious policy on Bangladesh; and
in the immediate aftermath of her election triumph, she had her way, not
only in her own party, but with the Opposition as well. On 31 March she
was able to move a resolution in Parliament which had the support of the
entire Opposition. The motion was carefully worded and used the neutral
term 'East Bengal', instead of Bangladesh or East Pakistan. It expressed
'grave concern' at the Pakistan Government's repression in East Bengal,
called upon other governments to persuade Pakistan to halt the genocide
at once and assured the people of East Bengal of the full 'sympathy and
support' of the Indian people.[33]

In the Cabinet itself there were conflicting views on the issue. Swaran

Singh, the Minister for External Affairs, is believed to have favoured non-involvement and the sealing of the border to stop the refugee influx. The rival view was for immediate diplomatic recognition of the independence of Bangladesh backed by military intervention. The Prime Minister steered a middle course. The heads of the armed forces are believed to have advised against any military action until they had had time to make adequate preparations. They also pointed out that the impending monsoon would make large-scale operations in Bangladesh difficult and that the right moment for a military strike would be in the winter, when Chinese intervention across the Himalayas would be difficult. In the light of this advice, Mrs. Gandhi refused to force a military confrontation, and a naval blockade to prevent the transfer of troops from West Pakistan to Bangladesh was abandoned for fear that it might escalate into war.

At the same time, Mrs. Gandhi rejected suggestions about sealing the border to refugees on the ground that it would be both inhuman and geographically impossible. And while she continued officially to treat the Bangladesh revolt as Pakistan's internal problem, she was determined that it would not be crushed for want of Indian assistance. Though she had ruled out direct intervention, she resorted to the tactics of slow erosion, subsidising guerrilla warfare as China and Pakistan had done during the Naga and Mizo revolts in India. The *Mukti Bahini*, the Awami League's guerrilla arm, was provided with a base in Indian border areas, large numbers of young refugees were given military training by the Indian army, and the Indian Border Security Force provided the guerrillas with full assistance in money and arms.

Though the guerrilla war undermined the morale of Pakistani troops in Bangladesh, it could not of itself break the iron grip of the powerful Pakistani military machine. Waves of refugees continued to pour across the border, reaching an average of 30,000 per day and a total of ten million in the course of the next eight months. The daily cost of maintaining the refugee camps rose to the astronomical figure of Rs. 27,500,000 and, despite international assistance, the main burden had to be borne by the Indian exchequer. The refugee problem represented a colossal drain on India's meagre resources and a heavy strain on her administrative system, especially in the border States where the camps were situated. As time went by, the Government's attitude began to appear as a timid, do-nothing policy that would take the country to economic ruin. Public pressure mounted for military intervention, and it was argued that a war would be less expensive than keeping the refugees indefinitely.

On 24 May Mrs. Gandhi, speaking in Parliament, referred for the first time to East Bengal as Bangladesh, called for a political settlement of the Bangladesh crisis and stated that Pakistan's internal problem had now become an internal problem for India. Even so, she refused to be hustled into precipitate action and chided her critics in the Lok Sabha:

'If it gives some solace to Honourable Members to abuse the Government and blame them for lack of courage, for lack of direction and even of understanding, I certainly do not want to deprive them of this comfort. To some Members, guts are equated with voice-power and the use of passionate words. I wish life-were so simple. Now, this Government may have many faults; but it does not lack courage, nor is it afraid of taking a risk if it is a necessary risk... we are not merely concerned with the legal aspect of this situation... We are concerned with one thing and one thing only—our own national interest and security and naturally that of the heroic people of Bangladesh. That is why it is important to act calmly.'[34]

Speaking at a public meeting in August 1971, Mrs. Gandhi refused to concede the demand for recognition of the Bangladesh Government-in-exile. 'There are some in this country who are attempting to make political capital out of the Bangladesh issue,' she warned. '...This is no occasion for such irresponsible action. We have full sympathy with the demand for the recognition of Bangladesh. We have never said that we shall not recognise Bangladesh. But the Government will take any such step only after careful consideration of all aspects of the question.'[35]

With her massive majority in Parliament, Mrs. Gandhi could afford to ignore public pressure and tackle the problem in a cool and level-headed way. Though some critics attacked her for pursuing a policy of drift and attributed this to the Soviet Union's restraining influence, later events were to show that such charges were unfair. Preparations for a military solution had begun at an early stage and, what was unusual in a government so prone to leakages, had been shrouded in total secrecy. Mrs. Gandhi later told the author:

'It was pretty obvious to us that if other countries did not take a hand in trying to stop the atrocities and the holocaust in Bangladesh, there would be a war. We did not know when it would come, but we were sure it would come, and therefore it was our duty to the country to prepare for a defensive war... A large section of opinion in this country was that we should have marched in our troops straight away, and it was a very few of us who were strongly against anything like this. We thought we should give full opportunity for international opinion, and even the better sense of the Pakistani Government, to prevail.'[36]

*         *

Indian diplomacy during these months aimed at securing a peaceful political settlement in Bangladesh through international pressure and, failing that, at preparing the ground for a military solution. The Prime Minister played a key role in formulating and implementing the Government's international strategy. T.N. Kaul, then Foreign Secretary, told the author at the height of the Bangladesh crisis: 'Mrs. Gandhi talks less, but she is as actively interested in foreign affairs as her father. Decisions on foreign policy are definitely hers, though matters are of course discussed in the Political Affairs Committee (the inner circle) of the Cabinet. The existence of a separate Minister for External Affairs relieves her of the burden of administrative details, but the initiative in foreign policy rests with her.'[37]

The recent and unexpected détente between the United States and China, Pakistan's traditional allies, had left India in a vulnerable and isolated position. Despite Indian protests, American shipments of arms to Pakistan continued unabated. The State Department is also believed to have made it clear to the Indian Ambassador that India could not expect American assistance, even if she were involved in a war on two fronts with China and Pakistan. While the Soviet Union was sympathetic to India, it was by no means certain that Russia would support India in the event of war. It was against this alarming international background that Mrs. Gandhi decided in August 1971 to sign a twenty-year 'Treaty of Peace, Friendship and Co-operation' with the Soviet Union.

The treaty had first been suggested by Moscow in 1969; but Mrs. Gandhi had declined the proposal for fear that it would be unpopular at home, while jeopardising the future of India's relations with the United States and China. These objections no longer applied. Mrs. Gandhi's domestic position was unassailable, China had not responded to the feelers she had sent out, and the United States was tilting towards Pakistan. The treaty was bound to be seen as a deviation from India's traditional non-alignment; but Mrs. Gandhi had decided that this was a small price to pay for Soviet backing in the current crisis.

The treaty in its final form is believed to have differed from the original Soviet draft both in its inclusion of a statement of the Soviet Union's respect for India's non-alignment and in its vagueness on the question of military aid. Its operative clauses ruled out any assistance, direct or indirect, by the two countries to any third party which engaged in armed conflict with either of the two signatories and provided for immediate 'mutual consultations' and 'appropriate effective measures' to counter any military threat to either country.

The manner in which the Indo-Soviet Treaty was negotiated and presented to the country was characteristic of Mrs. Gandhi's political style. The negotiations were conducted in Moscow in complete secrecy by D.P. Dhar, Mrs. Gandhi's personal emissary and close confidant. The Political Affairs Committee of the Cabinet was not taken into confidence until the draft had been finalised, and the Cabinet as a whole was not informed till the morning of the day on which the documents were signed. With her usual dramatic sense of timing, Mrs. Gandhi publicly announced the treaty in her speech at a mass rally to commemorate the August Revolt of 1942. Though condemned in some quarters as a surrender to Russian blackmail, the announcement was welcomed by public opinion in general and did much to boost Indian morale.

Referring to criticism of the treaty, Mrs. Gandhi told an interviewer: 'I would make it clear that it does not preclude us from signing similar treaties with other countries. It truly supports our policy of non-alignment. By signing it, we have not joined the Soviet Bloc.'[38] Although its wording was ambiguous enough not to conflict directly with non-alignment, the treaty undoubtedly marked a departure from India's traditional foreign policy. It was also a major turning point in the development of the Bangladesh crisis. The Kremlin now opened up its arsenals to supply all India's military needs and began increasingly to endorse the Indian position on Bangladesh.

When Mrs. Gandhi visited Moscow in September, she was warmly received by the Soviet leadership. In the course of her visit she worked hard to convince the Kremlin that the Bangladesh crisis and the refugee problem presented a threat to India's very existence. 'One cannot but be perturbed when fire breaks out in a neighbour's house,' was how she put it in a speech at a luncheon hosted by Kosygin.[39] The Soviet Premier, for his part, openly criticised the Pakistan Government for its policy of repression. The joint communiqué issued by the two Prime Ministers called for urgent measures for a political solution of the East Bengal crisis in accordance with 'the wishes, rights and interests of the people as well as the need for the speediest and safe return of refugees.'[40]

In the meanwhile, India had launched a major diplomatic offensive to secure the support of a large number of second-rank powers. On 10 August Mrs. Gandhi had written personally to twenty-four Heads of Government, drawing their attention to the secret military trial of the captive Mujibur Rahman and appealing to them to use their influence to restrain the Pakistan Government. On 24 October she set out on a three-week official tour which would take her to Belgium, Austria, Britain, France, West Germany and the United States, enabling her to appeal to Western public opinion and to use her diplomatic skills at the summit level.

By this time, tension on the eastern border was escalating rapidly with frequent skirmishes as Pakistani troops pursued guerrillas across the Indian border. On the eve of the Prime Minister's departure, the press reported a large build up of Pakistani troops near the border and there was speculation about an imminent Pakistani attack. 'One cannot leave with a light heart at such a moment,' said Mrs. Gandhi in a broadcast to the nation on 23 August. 'Our country is facing danger. Yet, after much thought, I decided to undertake the journey. The invitations were of long standing and it seemed important in the present situation to meet leaders of other countries for an exchange of views and to put to them the reality of our situation.'[41]

By adhering to her foreign schedule despite the danger of war, Mrs. Gandhi sought to show the world that, while she was prepared for a war, she had no intention of starting it. In her public speeches and private talks in the countries she visited, she made a subtle distinction between the internal and international aspects of the Bangladesh crisis. She stressed, on the one hand, that it was not a dispute between India and Pakistan, but between the Pakistan Government and its own people. As a corollary to this, she rejected categorically suggestions that the problem could be solved by negotiations between her and President Yahya Khan of Pakistan and maintained that a political settlement could only be effected through negotiations between the Pakistani military junta and the democratically elected leadership of the Awami League. On the other hand, she asserted that the massive refugee burden foisted on India had internationalised the problem, that the refugees could only be repatriated after a democratic political settlement and that it was the duty of the world community to put pressure on the Pakistan Government for such a settlement, pending which India would be free to take such defensive measures as she chose. In an address to the India League in London, Mrs. Gandhi declared:

> 'Everybody today is busy telling us that we must show restraint. I do not think that any people or any Government could have shown greater restraint than we have in the face of such tremendous provocation and threat to our safety and to our stability. But where has the restraint taken us? With all our restraint we are not getting any nearer to a solution... People have asked me how long India can manage. Actually that date has long since been passed. I feel that I am sitting on the top of a volcano and I honestly do not know when it is going to erupt.'[42]

In an interview on B.B.C., Mrs. Gandhi made it clear that she would not be satisfied with assurances of sympathy and admiration for her handling of the refugee problem. 'It's a little bit of an irritant,' she complained, 'because, well, it's nice to be admired; but if people think you say a few flattering words and that is enough, well it is not—because we are getting the verbal admiration and it seems to us the others are getting the more material help.'[43] At a Foreign Press Association luncheon in London, she warned newsmen: 'Nothing... will work if people continue to equate India with Pakistan. We are tired of this equation which the

Western world is always making... We are *not* equal and we are not going to stand for this kind of treatment.'[44]

In contrast to the mild and non-controversial note she had struck on previous foreign visits, this time her tone was sharp and uncompromising. She spoke, not as a supplicant, but from a position of strength which reflected both her increased self-assurance and her confidence in the political stability and military preparedness of her government. In her speeches, interviews and press conferences, she made it plain that she was weary of international equivocation and that she had no patience with legalistic hair-splitting.

In her appearance on the B.B.C. programme 'Panorama', Indira Gandhi's firmness bordered on truculence. 'We are not dependent upon what other countries think or want us to do,' she asserted. 'We know what we want for ourselves and we are going to do it, whatever it costs... we welcome help from any country; but if it doesn't come, well, it's all right by us.' Putting her interviewer on the defensive, she demanded: 'When Hitler was on the rampage, why didn't you say, "Let's keep quiet and let's have peace with Germany and let the Jews die, or let Belgium die, let France die"?' Asked why she refused to have talks with Pakistan, she snapped back: 'Talks with whom—and about what? Up to now, President Yahya Khan is telling everybody... that the situation in Bangladesh is absolutely normal. Now, either he doesn't know what is happening, or he is telling a deliberate untruth. Either way, where is the foundation for a talk?'[45]

Despite differences in emphasis, the governments of Western Europe, and of Britain and France in particular, had already been favourably disposed towards India, and Mrs. Gandhi's visits merely confirmed this trend. Her visit to Washington, however, was of a different order in view of President Nixon's well-known partiality to Pakistan's military rulers. The visit proved a timely and shrewd tactic, carrying the Indo-American diplomatic struggle into Nixon's own territory and enabling Mrs. Gandhi to appeal, within the limits of diplomatic propriety, to American public opinion against the Administration's unco-operative attitude. Although Nixon avoided any references to Bangladesh in his public speeches during the Indian Premier's visit, she herself lost no time in taking the bull by the horns. In her reply to Nixon's welcome address on her arrival, she said: 'I am haunted by the tormented faces in our overcrowded refugee camps reflecting the grim events which have compelled the exodus of these millions from East Bengal. I have come here looking for a deeper understanding of the situation in our part of the world...'[46]

The talks that followed lacked the warmth that had marked Mrs. Gandhi's meetings with President Johnson during her last official visit in 1966. Partly, this was the result of a personal coolness between the two leaders, and partly of the wide cleavage between their views on Bangladesh. Nixon is believed to have given a vague assurance to exert pressure on Pakistan for a political solution, while Mrs. Gandhi made an equally vague undertaking to abstain from military action in the meanwhile. As an earnest of his good intentions, Nixon had announced a halt in American arms supplies to Pakistan on the eve of Mrs. Gandhi's visit; but in the following weeks American arms continued to reach Pakistan through secret shipments and via other friendly countries.

The Indo-American summit was widely regarded as having ended in serious disagreement. When asked if this was so at the National Press Club in Washington, Mrs. Gandhi replied tactfully: 'I think this report was largely based on the fact that we met for longer than was expected or scheduled. But that is only because we had so much to talk about.' To a suggestion that she should meet the Pakistani President, she replied firmly, but with a touch of humour:

'You can only meet a person if there is a two-way trust. I said in London that I may want to shake hands with everybody. But if there is a clenched fist, well, you just can't shake hands with it. And this is the situation. If you have been noticing the sort of remarks which the President of Pakistan is making, either about me or in general, it is not an attitude which shows that there could be a very friendly conversation. From my side, I am always friendly. I have never said a rude word about anybody... that happens to be not only because I find life more pleasant that way and that I was brought up in that way, but in the last elections I found that it paid very great political dividends!'[47]

Her reply, received with much amusement and applause by American pressmen, referred to Yahya Khan's drunken outburst at a recent dinner for a visiting Chinese delegation. 'If that woman thinks that she is going to cow me down, I refuse to take it,' he had blustered.[48] Indira Gandhi, very sensibly, did not reply in kind. In an interview with *Newsweek*, she observed calmly: 'I am not concerned with the remark, but it shows the mentality of the person.'[49] Her own dignity and decorum undoubtedly helped to win her a sympathetic hearing from Western politicians and journalists and to strengthen the credibility of India's case, so much so that on her return to India an Opposition M.P. criticised her for having 'projected a personal image' abroad.[50]

As on previous foreign tours, Indira Gandhi's personal charm and so-called 'feminine mystique' figured prominently in the press coverage she received, especially after the interest aroused by her dramatic success in recent Indian politics. Nor did she neglect, even at this critical juncture, the importance of being elegant and well-groomed whenever she appeared in public. Her immaculate appearance owed as much to her personal taste as to the demands of Western camera-men. According to one reporter, when she arrived in London she made 'a dashing appearance out of the plane in a most unusual ankle-length yellow cape'. 'I designed it myself,' she confided. '...Actually I had some material given to me and I though it would be nice to make a cape out of it... If I had the time, what I really would love to do is to design saris and jewellery.'51 In between her duels with the press and her talks with politicians, Mrs. Gandhi had found time for more relaxing pursuits. She had met a number of artists, intellectuals and old friends, among them Iris Murdoch in London, the painter Miro in Paris and Ginsberg, the American poet. She had watched Nureyev perform at the Royal Ballet in London and attended a Beethoven concert in Vienna. In New York she had fitted in some shopping for her family.

In an optimistic report to the Indian Parliament on the results of her foreign tour, the Prime Minister claimed:

'I think that these countries as well as others realise that it will not help to deal with peripheral problems without finding a political solution in Bangladesh through negotiations with the already elected leaders of the people of Bangladesh and in accordance with their legitimate wishes. Most countries also realise that the release of Sheikh Mujibur Rahman is essential and intend to impress this upon the military regime of Pakistan. After a long period of tragic indifference and sheltering behind the thinly disguised legalistic formulation that it was merely an internal affair of Pakistan, there is now a growing sense of urgency in seeking a solution... During my visit to the United States, I was informed that a decision had been taken to stop further shipments of arms to Pakistan. A formal announcement has since been made. I was given to understand that no arms are being supplied from the United Kingdom, France and the Federal Republic of Germany.'52

In the parliamentary debate that ensued, one member referred to the Indo-Soviet Treaty as 'a handicap in the Prime Minister's baggage'. 'I do not know who was handicapped,' Mrs. Gandhi promptly replied. 'It certainly did not handicap me. No foreign official or Head of State or Head of Government whom I met even mentioned the Treaty... I think they all understood the situation.'53

Even China, despite her declared support for Pakistan, had not been excluded from Mrs. Gandhi's diplomatic campaign, and every attempt had been made to neutralise the Chinese in the event of an Indo-Pakistan war. India had supported China's candidature for U.N. membership, even though this would give Peking permanent membership of the Security Council with the right of veto. Mrs. Gandhi had written

personally to Chou En-Lai to congratulate China on her admission to
the U.N. Subsequently, the Indian Government had decided to ignore
anti-Indian tirades in the Chinese press and a hostile speech by the
Chinese delegate at the U.N.. During her Western tour, Mrs. Gandhi
had made it a point to say that India would continue her efforts to norma-
lise relations with China and that Peking would be judged by its actions,
not by its words.

By the end of November 1971 all the avenues of personal and governmental diplomacy had been tried, short of direct negotiations with
Pakistan's military regime which would have compromised India's
basic position on Bangladesh. Indira Gandhi could say with an easy
conscience that she had done everything in her power to secure the
independence of Bangladesh without a war. If that had proved insuffi-
cient, she was now ready for a more drastic solution, although she was
still unwilling to fire the first shot.

*         *         *

On the afternoon of 3 December 1971, Indira Gandhi was telling a
public meeting in Calcutta: 'I want to reiterate that I do not want war.
I earnestly desire peace. I know what war means in terms of human
suffering. I will be the last person to start a war. But if a war is thrust
upon us, we are prepared to fight in defence of our freedom and our
ideals.'[54] The next morning found her in New Delhi announcing to
Parliament: 'A war has been forced upon us, a war we did not seek and
did our utmost to prevent... We should be prepared for a long struggle.'[55]

The third full-scale Indo-Pakistan war had begun in the late afternoon
of 3 December when the Pakistan Air Force launched a surprise attack
on eight Indian military airfields in the western sector. The Pakistani
air raids marked the culmination of India's skilful policy of defensive
provocation. Guerrilla activities in Bangladesh, strongly supported by
Indian forces across the border, had been slowly but surely undermining
Pakistan's position in East Bengal, weakening the morale of her troops
and greatly increasing the cost in men and money of holding Bangladesh
by force. During the last fortnight, Indian and Pakistani troops had been
clashing directly in border areas, and on 23 November the Indian Government had announced that its troops would cross the border in self-
defence to stop Pakistani shelling of Indian border towns.

Rather than face a slow erosion of his position, and confident that the
United States and China would come to his aid in the event of war,
President Yahya Khan had taken the desperate decision to escalate the
conflict with an attack on the western front. As a pre-emptive strike,
unlike that launched by Israel in 1967, the Pakistani air raids proved a
miserable failure, and the damage inflicted was negligible. The real

purpose of the attack appears to have been political rather than military. It was calculated to internationalise the situation on the eastern front, and secure immediate intervention by the Super Powers and the U.N. to freeze the eastern border and halt guerrilla activities. The next two weeks were to show that Yahya Khan had made a disastrous miscalculation.

Following her public meeting in Calcutta, Mrs. Gandhi had been attending a conference at the West Bengal Governor's residence when she received a message from Delhi informing her of the Pakistani attack. A short while later, she was flying back to the capital on an Air Force plane escorted by a group of fighter aircraft. Later the same night, she presided over an emergency meeting of the Cabinet, followed by a conference with Opposition leaders who assured her of their full support. The President declared a national emergency, and the Indian war machine went smoothly into action. Two days later, Mrs. Gandhi announced at last to a tense but jubilant Parliament her government's recognition of Bangladesh. The Mukti Bahini was fighting alongside of the Indian army in Bangladesh and, in theory at any rate, the war in the east was waged under a joint Indo-Bangladesh command.

India's military strategy had been prepared well in advance. Its aim was to secure a quick surrender of Pakistani forces in Bangladesh before the United States, China or the U.N. had time to intervene. A fifteen-day plan for the conquest of East Bengal was now put into operation. On the western front, Pakistan had followed up her air strike with a massive attack along the western border which aimed at a break-through in Kashmir. India, however, confined herself to fighting an essentially defensive action in the west, giving full priority to the eastern campaign. The soundness of this strategy was vindicated by its dramatic and rapid results.

In marked contrast to the Sino-Indian war of 1962 and the 1965 war with Pakistan, this time there was perfect harmony and co-ordination between the political and military leadership and between the three Services themselves. The Indian army, air force and navy were put under the supreme command of General Manekshaw, the Army Chief of Staff. The army received full and efficient air support at every step, while the navy imposed a complete blockade of the East Bengal coast and was able to carry off a surprise attack on Karachi, West Pakistan's main port and naval base. Indian forces stood up well to the Pakistani thrust in the west, relieving pressure on Kashmir by pushing forward into West Pakistan. Within the first twenty-four hours the Pakistan air force had been virtually put out of action in the east, and India had full command of the air. The Indian blitzkrieg now moved rapidly towards Dacca, the capital of East Bengal, by-passing and isolating Pakistani troop concentrations on the way.

After the first few days, it was clear that India was poised for a decisive victory. The only danger now was of international intervention on Pakistan's behalf. Although the Chinese were confining themselves to verbal attacks, there was a distinct possibility of the United States coming to Pakistan's help. Nixon had accused Mrs. Gandhi of having failed to keep faith with him and the State Department had issued a statement branding India as the aggressor. The U.N. Security Council would probably have followed suit, had it not been for the Soviet veto. All American economic aid to India had been cut off, though military and economic aid to Pakistan continued. To the argument that this open bias might throw Mrs. Gandhi into Moscow's arms, Kissinger, according to the Anderson Papers, replied: 'The Lady is cold-blooded and tough and will not turn into a Soviet satellite merely because of pique. We should not ease her mind.' On 9 December the U.S. Seventh Fleet, led by a nuclear aircraft-carrier, set out for the Bay of Bengal, with the ostensible aim of evacuating American nationals from Bangladesh. According to the Anderson Papers, the real purpose of this naval exercise was to act as a decoy, alarming India and diverting her air and naval forces from their operations against Pakistan. Had the Indian Government reacted as expected, the effect would have been to delay the fall of Dacca, giving the United States time to lobby the U.N. and Pakistan an opportunity to register some gains in Kashmir.

Mrs. Gandhi, however, refused to be intimidated or deflected from her objective. At a midnight conference attended by the Prime Minister, D.P. Dhar* and the Service Chiefs, it was decided to ignore the approach of the Seventh Fleet and Mrs. Gandhi urged Manekshaw to try and complete the Bangladesh operation as soon as possible. At the same time, she did not neglect to take precautions against the possibility, however remote, of American intervention. In accordance with the Indo-Soviet Treaty, Dhar visited Moscow for consultations and is believed to have returned with an assurance of full Soviet support, including a promise to attack Sinkiang if China came into the war. On 12 December, Kuznetsov, the Soviet Deputy Premier, arrived in Delhi, where he remained till the end of the war. To counter the American threat, a Soviet fleet sailed from Vladivastock, following on the heels of the U.S. Seventh Fleet. At the Security Council, too, Russia gave full diplomatic support to India, vetoing two American resolutions for a cease-fire, with Britain and France abstaining. Mrs. Gandhi had done her preparatory work well, and her pre-war diplomacy was now paying off.

The Indian plan went according to schedule, and by the middle of

*Then Chairman of the Indian Government's Foreign Policy Planning Committee.

December the fall of Dacca was imminent. Unable to get round the Soviet veto in the Security Council, the United States sponsored a resolution in the U.N. General Assembly calling for an immediate cease-fire and withdrawal of troops. The resolution was carried by an overwhelming majority, reflecting the obsessive fear with which secessionism was viewed by most governments, and especially those of the Third World. On 15 December Mrs. Gandhi appealed to American and world opinion in an open letter to President Nixon where she countered the charge that she had not given him a chance to bring about a political settlement.

Taking her stand on fundamental human rights and appealing to the principles of the American Declaration of Independence, she traced the causes of the Bangladesh uprising, pointed to the failure of the international community to effect a just political settlement and reminded the world that it was Pakistan which had begun the war:

'War...could have been avoided if the power, influence and authority of all the states, and above all of the United States, had got Sheikh Mujibur Rahman released... Lip-service was paid to the need for a political solution, but not a single worthwhile step was taken to bring this about... We are asked what we want. We seek nothing for ourselves. We do not want any territory of what was East Pakistan and now constitutes Bangladesh. We do not want any territory of West Pakistan. We do want lasting peace with Pakistan... We are deeply hurt by the innuendoes and insinuations that it was we who have precipitated the crisis and have in any way thwarted the emergence of solutions... When Dr. Kissinger came in August 1971, I had emphasised to him the importance of seeking an early political settlement. But we have not received, even to this day, the barest framework of a settlement which would take into account the facts as they are. ...it is my sincere and earnest hope that...you...will at least let me know where precisely we have gone wrong before your representatives or spokesmen deal with us with such harshness of language.'[56]

On 13 December the beleaguered Pakistani military headquarters in Dacca had been given an ultimatum to surrender peacefully by the morning of the 16th. There was little doubt that they would have to comply; but the timing remained uncertain. On the afternoon of the 16th, New Delhi had not yet received confirmation of the surrender. According to one account, Mrs. Gandhi was closeted in her office at Parliament House with a Swedish television team when she received the news on her secraphone. 'Good!' she exclaimed tersely. Then, turning to the Swedes, she said: 'Gentlemen, will you excuse me for a few minutes? I have an announcement to make in Parliament.'[57] Minutes later, she was in the Lok Sabha informing a wildly cheering House of the unconditional surrender of the Pakistan army in Bangladesh. Dacca, she said, was now 'the free capital of a free country' and added that Indian troops would not stay in Bangladesh a day longer than necessary.[58]

The surrender had not come a moment too soon. The Seventh Fleet was now within thirty hours sailing distance of the Bengal coast. More serious, perhaps, was the likelihood of a U.N. General Assembly resolution condemning India and calling for sanctions against her. The day after the surrender in the east, Mrs. Gandhi forestalled any such move by announcing a unilateral cease-fire on the western front. Though unpopular with Indian chauvinists, it was a statesmanlike gesture which aimed at reassuring the Pakistani people and the world in general that India had no aggressive designs on West Pakistan.

Indian forces had been more than holding their own in the west and, after the surrender in the east, India might conceivably have turned all her forces to an invasion of West Pakistan. In practice, however, such a venture would have been hazardous and impractical. Pakistan's military machine in the west was still intact and would have been a hard nut to crack. Russia would not have supported the continuation of the war, while the United States and China would probably have felt compelled to intervene. Virtue and expediency thus combined to rule out an invasion of West Pakistan, and Mrs. Gandhi saw this clearly.

The decision to declare a unilateral cease-fire after the liberation of Bangladesh had formed part of India's original strategy, and the actual announcement is believed to have been prepared and typed four days before the fall of Dacca. Even so, it was rumoured that the cease-fire had been the result of Super Power pressure. Mrs. Gandhi reacted sharply to this suggestion in an interview with *Time* magazine: 'There have been suggestions that we were pressured into cease-fire by the Russians who in turn were being pressured by the Americans! The decision was made right here, at the moment of surrender in Dacca. We were able to inform the Soviet Union right away only because Mr. Kuznetsov happened to be here. I am not a person to be pressured—by anybody or any nations.'[59]

*        *        *

The war had left India in a commanding position on the sub-continent. Pakistan had lost not only her entire eastern wing but 5,619 square miles of territory in the west and over 90,000 prisoners of war. Indira Gandhi was generous in her praise for the armed forces and their leadership. To Manekshaw, rewarded for his services with the rank of Field-Marshal\*, she wrote: 'The co-ordination between the three Services, so impressi-

*The first in the history of the Indian Army.

vely demonstrated during the campaign, owes much to your brilliant leadership. I particularly valued your co-operation, your clear-headed counsel and unfailing good cheer throughout this crisis.'[60] The Prime Minister herself received from President Giri the decoration of *Bharat Ratna*, the country's highest civilian award. She had given India what neither Nehru nor Shastri had been able to deliver, a decisive military victory. National honour, which suffered so greatly in 1962, had been vindicated and national pride had never stood so high.

Asked about her role in the conduct of the war, Indira Gandhi later said: 'The decisions were really taken by those who were actually running the war; but I was obviously in very close touch, in twice-a-day touch. On the day of Dacca's fall, I think we got a message every few minutes.'[61] While she had been wise enough not to interfere with military operations and to allow the armed forces a free hand in their own sphere, she had kept close control over all decisions with political implications. Mutual trust and respect had resulted in perfect co-ordination of the political and military conduct of the war and avoided the conflict and confusion which had paralysed the Indian war effort in 1962.

This cooperation owed much to the good personal rapport which Indira Gandhi had been able to establish with the armed forces, from the officer corps down to the ranks. Her sex, contrary to some expectations, was no obstacle in this relationship. During the tense months that preceded the war, she had paid frequent visits to refugee camps and remote military outposts in forward areas, even under hard weather conditions. Her political stature, physical stamina, efficiency and dignified bearing had won her the respect and deference of the armed forces. This did not prevent her from chatting to the *jawans** with an informal and maternal ease that presented a marked contrast with the severity of their élitist officers. Her visits, especially to the sick and wounded, brought a welcome feminine warmth and grace into the grim and regimented routine of military life. While in some respects she was a symbol of Indian womanhood, appealing to the protective instincts of the average solider, she could when necessary command respect as a figure of authority, reviewing troops and taking the salute.

Although the independence of Bangladesh was the outcome of a complex of factors, it was widely seen as a personal victory for Indira Gandhi, who had played the role of mid-wife to the infant republic. She herself occasionally deprecated this tendency. 'The credit for winning the war is being attributed to me, which is not right,' she told a mass rally in Delhi. 'This work has been accomplished not by me but by the people—men, women, old and young—of Bangladesh. We only rendered

*Ordinary soldiers.

them the help that we were capable of.'[62]

Nevertheless, without Indian intervention, Bangladesh could not have achieved Independence in the near future; and no single person had done more to shape Indian policy than Indira Gandhi. After his release by Pakistan's new President, Z.A. Bhutto, Sheikh Mujibur Rahman stopped over in Delhi on 10 January en route to Dacca and expressed in generous terms his gratitude to India and to Mrs. Gandhi in particular. At a mass rally in his honour, she took the opportunity to remind her own people: 'I made three promises to the people... I said: we shall see that the refugees return to their motherland; we shall help the Mukti Bahini and the people of Bangladesh in every way; and we shall certainly see that the Sheikh is free. All three promises have been fulfilled.'[63]

The creation of Bangladesh had taken Mrs. Gandhi's domestic popularity to heights which her role in the Congress split and her socialist promises had not achieved. In a country where the cult of personality is deeply rooted and where mysticism mingles with politics, Indira Gandhi appeared as an ominipotent Mother Goddess who had protected her own people and liberated another from the forces of evil. The idea that a woman should lead her people to victory did not appear incongruous in a country where Durga, the Goddess of War, is widely worshipped. Hindu mythology has it that Durga was created by the gods after their expulsion from the heavenly heights by the demons. Armed with various divine weapons, Durga, according to the legend, had fought alone against the demon hordes, vanquishing them and restoring the gods to their rightful place. Many Indians saw Indira Gandhi as an incarnation of the same *Shakti* or female energy.

\*        \*        \*

In an interview on American television, Indira Gandhi was asked about the price in human terms of the recent war. She replied with the following lines from a poem by Ralph Chaplin which had been one of her childhood favourites:

'Mourn not the dead
But rather mourn the pathetic throng
Who see the world's great anguish and its wrong,
But dare not speak.'[64]

She had not only spoken but acted decisively, and she had good reason to be satisfied with the results. The immediate refugee problem had been solved, and the return of the ten million refugees was being organized with a speed and efficiency that astounded those who had doubted its feasability. More significant was the fact that the emergence of Bangladesh had drastically and irrevocably altered the power balance on the sub-continent. India was now generally acknowledged as the leading power in South Asia, facing no real challenge from Iran to Indonesia. Though Pakistan made a remarkably rapid recovery under Bhutto, she could never again hope to rival India's supremacy. While opinions differed on the merits of India's actions, Indira Gandhi's personal prestige as a leading world statesman was unquestioned. In a Gallup poll of seventy non-Communist countries in May 1971, she emerged as 'the most admired person in the world.'

The real test of statesmanship, however, would lie in the making of a just and durable peace. Fortunately, military victory had not gone to Mrs. Gandhi's head, and she was firm in her view that there could be no lasting stability on the sub-continent without an Indo-Pakistan peace settlement. Pakistan had suffered a shattering blow; but with American and Chinese assistance a truncated but more cohesive Pakistan might soon regain her pre-war level of military strength. Though Pakistan would never again present a major threat to India, her hostility could continue to be a source of tension in the sub-continent, requiring vast military expenditure, and an irritant in India's relations with the Super Powers. It was also impossible to ignore the fact that large sections of India's 65 million Muslims had reacted unfavourably to the break-up of Pakistan; and if their fears of Hindu domination were to be stilled, peace with Pakistan was essential.

While insisting that negotiations between India and Pakistan must be strictly bilateral, Mrs. Gandhi responded readily to Bhutto's call for a summit conference. India, with a crushing military victory to her credit, 90,000 prisoners of war and large chunks of Pakistani territory in the west, held the trump cards and could afford to be generous for the sake of a lasting and comprehensive settlement. Mrs. Gandhi's diplomacy was now concentrated on persuading Pakistan to accept a package deal which would include recognition of the status quo in Kashmir. To prepare the way for a Kashmir settlement, she shrewdly lifted all political restrictions on Sheikh Abdullah, the champion of Kashmiri self-deter-mination, and began direct negotiations with him. Abdullah is believed to have reciprocated with a personal assurance to Mrs. Gandhi that he would not re-open the question of a plebiscite in Kashmir and would confine himself to a demand for greater autonomy within the Indian Union.

Shortly before the Indo-Pakistan summit, an Italian journal published an interview with the Pakistan President in which he described Indira Gandhi as 'a mediocre woman with mediocre intelligence', pointing contemptuously to her poor academic record at Oxford. 'There is nothing great in her,' he was quoted as saying. '. . . It is the throne that makes her look great and also the name she carries.' He went on to say that 'the most disturbing thing' about his forthcoming visit to India was his 'misfortune in coming into contact with Madame' and added reassuringly: 'Let me tell you that with all her saris, smiles, rosy face and red *tilak\**, she is not going to make any impression on me.'[65] Bhutto later announced that he had been misreported; but if the report was even partially accurate, it was an astonishing display of male chauvinism and diplomatic indiscretion. Although the Pakistani leader's abusive outburst caused a furore in India, Mrs. Gandhi herself did not allow it to deflect her from her diplomatic objectives. With her usual dispassionate single-mindedness, she maintained a dignified silence on Bhutto's comments, and plans for the summit continued unaltered.

Nevertheless, the past died hard, and when President Bhutto arrived in Simla\*\* by helicopter on 28 June the two leaders greeted each other coldly, though the crowd of press photographers prevailed upon them to stage a formal handshake. As the conference proceeded, their personal rapport showed some improvement, and in the end it was their joint intervention that saved the talks from failure.

While Pakistan was determined not to compromise her stand on Kashmir and to confine the talks to the return of occupied territory and prisoners of war, India hoped for an overall settlement, knowing that her position would never be so favourable. On the question of returning prisoners of war, the Indian side maintained that the prisoners had been taken under the joint command of India and Bangladesh and could not be discussed without the latter's participation. Owing to these differences, the talks dragged on without any sign of a breakthrough. The draft treaty presented by the Indian delegation shuttled back and forth between the two sides, as each amended and counter-amended it. Press reports had announced the failure of the summit, when a sudden, last-minute intervention by the two leaders saved the situation.

In a private meeting with Mrs. Gandhi, Bhutto is believed to have assured her of his sincere desire for peace, pointed to his domestic insecurity and pleaded that, whereas she could afford to be generous, he could not return home empty-handed or with a humiliating peace in his baggage. He is also reported to have given her a verbal assurance that he would recognise Bangladesh in the near future. Mrs. Gandhi, despite Bhutto's past record of chauvinism, appears to have been convinced that he was India's best hope for a peaceful Pakistan and that he should be trusted, if only because his own interest lay in reducing the power of the Pakistan army. Though willing to make concessions, on two points she remained

*Religious or ornamental mark worn on the forehead by Hindus.
\*\*A town in the foot-hills of the Himalayas, formerly the Viceregal summer capital, now the capital of India's Himachal State.

adamant—a renunciation by Pakistan of the use of force to settle the Kashmir dispute and recognition of the principle of bilateralism between the two countries, excluding mediation by the U.N. or other powers. Those were her minimum aims, and she adhered to them firmly.

Whether Pakistan would accept these terms remained uncertain till the very last. On 2 July, the last day of the summit, the talks appeared to have failed, and Bhutto hosted a dinner for Mrs. Gandhi on the eve of his departure. Towards the end of the meal, she suggested to him that they put their heads together and make a final effort to break the stalemate. After some hectic negotiation, during which the two leaders rushed back and forth between each other and their respective advisers, a compromise formula emerged, and an agreement was signed shortly after midnight. Though it fell short of the no-war pact desired by India, 'he agreement was based on the Indian draft. In return for an Indian withdrawal from occupied territory in West Pakistan, Pakistan accepted the existing line of control in Kashmir and undertook not to alter it by force, thus enabling India to retain her territorial gains in the Kashmir sector and to eliminate the U.N. presence on the old Kashmir cease-fire line. As a corollary to this, Pakistan committed herself to a bilateral and peaceful settlement of remaining disputes.

The Simla meeting appears to have altered President Bhutto's opinion of Mrs. Gandhi. In an interview with an Indian journalist, he described her as 'a lady with a great sense of discipline in her approach to matters.' He continued: 'She makes up her mind and tenaciously pursues her objectives... I found her to be really her father's daughter in every sense of the word; and when I say that I wish to add that I have always held Mr. Nehru in the highest admiration...'[66]

                    *          *          *

During the last two years, the Simla spirit has seen many fluctuations. The implementation of each step in the agreement, starting with the withdrawal of troops and leading up to the return of prisoners, has been accompanied by much wrangling and procedural bickering. India and Pakistan have yet to establish normal diplomatic, commercial and cultural relations, and the Kashmir dispute, though decided de facto still awaits a formal settlement. Mrs. Gandhi, meanwhile, has been wise enough to take internal steps to de-fuse the Kashmir controversy. Indian rule in Kashmir has been progressively liberalised, while a modus vivendi has been reached with Sheikh Abdullah who has gradually been assimilated into the mainstream of Indian politics.

On 17 March 1971, after the last Indian troops had left Bangladesh, Mrs. Gandhi had arrived in Dacca on a State visit to the new republic. She was given a hero's welcome, and the diplomatic result of her visit was a twenty-five-year Treaty of Friendship modelled on the Indo-Soviet Treaty of the previous year. Since then, the early euphoria of Indo-Bangladesh amity has cooled into a more realistic approach. The unhealthy diplomatic and economic dependence of the infant State on India has inevitably generated some resentment among its people, as their initial gratitude wears thin. In this context, Pakistan's recognition of Bangladesh in February 1974 and Sheikh Mujibur Rahman's affection-ate reconciliation with Bhutto at the World Islamic Summit has alarmed some observers in New Delhi, who fear a revival of Islamic solidarity. While it is true that Mrs. Gandhi has met her match in Bhutto and that India has lost her mediatory role between Pakistan and Bangladesh, in the long run détente between the latter countries can be expected to create a healthier atmosphere in the sub-continent, removing yet another obstacle in the way of Indo-Pakistan relations.

India's relations with the Super Powers have shown little change since the December War. Indo-Soviet co-operation has continued to develop, involving closer economic links between the two countries and greater co-ordination of their foreign policies. This has naturally raised fears, both at home and abroad, that India is becoming too dependent on Russia and too subservient to Moscow's international aims. Mrs. Gandhi, however, continues to reject such criticism, asserting that she is quite capable of preserving India's independence.

Despite America's stand during the war, Mrs. Gandhi has stated more than once that she would like to restore friendly relations with the United States, provided the latter comes to terms with the new situation on the sub-continent. In an interview with *Time* magazine in December 1971, she warned: 'If . . . the United States refuses to recognise what sort of person I am and what sort of country India is, then I cannot say what will happen and what sort of relationship we will have.'[67] She added that India was quite prepared to do without American aid.

India's decision in January 1972 to exchange ambassadors with Hanoi was not merely a retaliatory gesture against the United States, but an indication of her desire to play a more active role in South and South-East Asia. A few months later, Mrs. Gandhi did not mince her words when she told an American interviewer: 'When we hear America's leaders talk about how they have gone into Vietnam to defend and develop the Vietnamese, it just sounds like an old version of "the white man's burden" to us. Therefore, what we in India say is that it would be better for American troops to get out of Asia altogether. On the other hand, if America genuinely wants to help us and be friends with us—we welcome it.'[68] Indo-American relations, despite some marginal improvement, remain for the most part cool and distant. While the Americans continue to supply arms to the Iran-Pakistan axis, India is busy trying to mobilise other countries against the American plan for a naval base in the Indian Ocean.

The most conspicuous gap in Indian foreign policy continues to be the absence of normal relations with China, a potential ally against Russian and American pressure. China's success in tackling social and economic problems very similar to India's could also make her a valuable source of information, technical skills and economic co-operation. Questioned about the prospects of a Sino-Indian rapprochement, Mrs. Gandhi told the author:

'It takes two to shake hands really... We have never made difficulties ...It has always been clear to us that the policy of the West, imagining an Asia without China, was very unrealistic, as I think that today their veering round to considering China withouth Asia is equally unrealistic. So we think that you cannot ignore a country like China, or any country for that matter, and if there are differences—and there are bound to be differences between almost any two countries—one has to try and resolve them by talking. There is nothing that cannot be solved if one really wants to.'[69]

Despite discreet overtures from New Delhi, Peking has made it clear that Sino-Indian relations cannot be expected to improve until India arrives at a just peace with Pakistan, including a settlement of the Kashmir dispute. Underlying this stipulation is a genuine fear on China's part that India is tied to the Soviet Union. If Mrs. Gandhi desires Chinese friendship, she will first have to convince Peking that she will not be party to any Soviet plans for encircling China.

A constant feature of Mrs. Gandhi's foreign policy has been her energetic effort to build closer ties with a large number of smaller powers, both in the West and in the Third World, as a means of countering Super Power pressure. 'I do not want to fall into the trap of the pundits of tripolarity,' she has explained. 'These are as alien to the true interests of India as the theories of bipolarity. The fact is that the world does not consist merely of one or two or even three Big Powers, however big they may be. There are also a very large number of nations which are sensitive, assertive and proud of their individual personalities. We certainly want to be friends, but let us not be too exercised about where we stand with Russia, China and America. What is important is that we stand for ourselves.'[70]

Comparing Indira Gandhi with her father, a well-known analyst of Indian foreign policy has observed: '...she has completely re-shaped the whole of India's foreign policy, even though it is still couched in anachronistic terminology and dangerously precarious in its administration. The most crucial aspect of Mrs. Gandhi's new foreign policy is that it has established a link between India's security and other foreign policy objectives. This link Mr. Nehru was never able to establish.'[71] It was this sense of realism that led her to revise non-alignment, abandoning Nehru's concept of equidistance from the Super Powers when the situation demanded closer relations with the Soviet Union.

For all its short-comings, India's foreign policy remains the sphere in which Indira Gandhi's leadership has achieved the most concrete and enduring results, far surpassing the achievements of both her predecessors. To the extent that Indian foreign policy is a reflection of Mrs. Gandhi's personality, the secret of its success lies in the fact that she is always practical, level-headed and flexible. While she may lack her father's intellectual perspectives, she is also free from the abstraction and emotionalism of his responses. If India has not so far attained the status of a Great Power, the fault lies, not with Indira Gandhi's handling of foreign affairs, but with the relative weakness of the country's economic base and its consequent dependence on external aid.

# CHAPTER XI

# IMAGE AND REALITY

IN MARCH 1971, in a letter to a foreign friend, Indira Gandhi complained bitterly: 'Our own press has done everything possible to mislead the public about me personally and about my aims and objectives. Even though everything they had said about my father much earlier and then about me is being proved wrong all the time, the columnists continue with their supercilious analyses. The real trouble is that they have no depth or values themselves and do not care to have contact with the people. Their judgement is circumscribed by their own limited experience, so they try to fit people into preconceived and prejudiced forms. Neither my father nor I can fit into any of these.'[1]

She was referring, of course, to the cynicism of the Indian press about her political motives and her electoral prospects. Since then the press has had to eat humble pie, and Indian journalists have accepted the fact that Indira Gandhi, whatever their opinion of her, has come to stay. In recent years the press has continued to point out the more obvious weaknesses, contradictions and failures of the Congress Party and its Ministries at the Centre and in the States; but Mrs. Gandhi herself remains, for the most part, above criticism and suspicion. Although the eulogistic flattery and adulation that followed upon the 1971 general election, and later the creation of Bangladesh, have subsided, Indira Gandhi's personal integrity and political bona fides are rarely questioned, even in the more critical sections of the press. The attack is on her advisers, on her government's policies and, occasionally, on her own tendency to turn a blind eye to maladiministration and corruption in her party and government. In the triple crisis — economic, political and moral—which India faces, Indira Gandhi is the only leader who retains public credibility. And the press, like the rest of the country's élite, continues to regard her as India's best hope of political stability.

In the course of the last eight years more has been written about Indira Gandhi than about any other Indian leader, living or dead. Her every action and comment, every available detail of her life, public or private, is noted, published and read with avid interest by the educated public. Where fact is not available, fiction and rumour suffice, and no imaginative effort has been spared to divine her intentions and desires.

No other individual or subject receives as constant and detailed coverage from the mass media, whether from the press or the State-owned All India Radio—dubbed All Indira Radio by the Opposition. Newspapers and weekly journals, including those in India's various regional languages, continue to churn out 'profiles' of the Prime Minister, and almost every major publishing house in the country has at least one 'definitive' biography of her to its credit. Like moths round a flame, journalists and hagiographers circle constantly round their subject, hoping ultimately to capture 'the essential Indira' and commit her to paper.

Indira Gandhi, however, remains as elusive and enigmatic as ever. The temperamental reticence of her childhood and early life has in recent years been reinforced by considerations of political tact and secrecy. Mrs. Gandhi's political style requires that she play her cards close to her chest, only revealing them when the moment is ripe for a grand slam. Describing her attitude to the press, B.G. Verghese* told the author: 'She is very shy of the press. At the beginning, I persuaded her to hold a press conference every month. But she gave up this practice after I left. She treats press conferences as a necessary evil. Instead of using the press as a forum, she is very evasive in her answers and tries to disclose as little as possible.'[2]

In this game of journalistic hide-and-seek, Indira Gandhi is usually the winner. Over the years, she has perfected a technique which enables her to ward off inquisitive newsmen and interviewers. She is always on her guard with the press and, unlike her father, she rarely allows herself to be provoked into emotional outbursts. In the early years of her Prime Ministership, she was wont to lose her temper and lash out at pressmen who persisted in asking her awkward questions. Since then her style has matured, and she fields questions with calm and good-humoured self-confidence, silencing interrogators with humorous and cryptic retorts and sometimes turning inconvenient questions back at them.

In private interviews Mrs. Gandhi is more forthcoming. She is usually gracious and charming to interviewers, and her style is chatty, informal and jocular. 'Hardly the right time to take a picture,' she admonished an eager British photographer. 'I have a pimple coming up on my nose. Whatever you do, hurry up!' She enjoys recounting anecdotes from her past and sometimes talks about herself with a narcissism that is considered characteristic of the Nehrus. As Welles Hangen noted, 'She has her father's knack for appearing to be modest while saying consistently immodest things about herself.'[3] But unlike her father, she never really lets her defences fall, and there are large areas of feeling and experience

*Once her Press Secretary, now editor of the Hindustan Times, a leading newspaper.

which she refuses to discuss or glosses over with generalisations. If her
interviewer insists on cross-examining her, her replies become curt and
monosyllabic and a nerve near her eyebrow begins to twitch ominously.
She is never directly rude; but she has her own quiet way of withdrawing
from a tiresome or unpleasant conversation. Her high-pitched, girlish
voice becomes glacial; her large, hooded eyes lose their expressive
sparkle and take on a far-away look; and her jaw sets in a stubborn
line. She fidgets impatiently; and if a sheet of paper is handy, she doodles
abstractedly on it. After an interview with Lord Chalfont for the B.B.C.,
she wrote to a friend: 'It began quite well, but I am afraid at the end
my mind wandered off and I did not take trouble over the answers,
especially as they were rather personal—personal philosophy and so on—
which I am wary of discussing with others.'[4]

'Frankly, I find it quite impossible to think of myself as a leader,'
Indira Gandhi said in August 1972. 'I have seen no change in me since
I have been the Prime Minister or since I have been in the Government
from what I was before. It is a very genuine feeling, not just a slogan or
a cliché.'[5] It is not a statement which can be taken literally; like most
people, she has changed and matured with the years. Her political skills
and talents, like her poise and self-confidence, have naturally developed
with the experience of her years in office. Nevertheless, in several respects
the Prime Minister of today has much in common with the lonely school-
girl of Anand Bhawan and the retiring hostess of Teen Murti; and perhaps
the most important is the fact that she remains a very private person.

Those to whom Indira Gandhi opens her heart are few and their
discretion is absolute. To the world in general she reveals very little of
herself. That she has succeeded in preserving her privacy in the midst
of such overwhelming publicity is no mean achievement. Whether such
reticence is desirable in a national leader is questionable; certainly,
Indira Gandhi is a much misunderstood person in journalistic circles.
She herself complains about her biographers: 'Most of the books to which
my attention has been drawn are very, very superficial. Nobody has
bothered to find out what the facts were.'[6] Facts, however, are hardly
adequate. Indira Gandhi's personality has to be pieced together from
many sources; and as in a jigsaw puzzle, the stray remark, the slight
inflexion and the occasional laugh or frown are often more revealing
than a full-length interview.

\*          \*          \*

Asked whether her political activities allow her to lead a personal
life, Indira Gandhi has said: 'I think that political life, personal life, or
outdoor life, or life of any other kind, is all one and the same thing.
Life is one and not a number of things cut up into several parts. Therefore,

one can have a personal life even when one engages in politics. And even when one is at home with the family, one can nevertheless be engaged in politics, because one discusses politics and everyone is interested in it.'[7]

Elsewhere she has stated that she 'views life as an integrated process, where activities and interests are different facets of the whole, rather than being separated into compartments or labelled under different heads,' that she 'considers recreation and relaxation to be attitudes of mind' and that she 'finds recreation in whatever she is doing.'[8] It is a view of life which owes much to the mystical unity of being postulated by the philosophy of *Vedanta*. With Indira Gandhi, though, it is not merely a metaphysical ideal, but a practical and convenient way of living.

While her working hours are long and she is never free from her political preoccupations, there is no artificial dichotomy between her public and private life. Her official and domestic activities are not structured into separate roles, but mingle freely. This means that she feels free to express her personal and spontaneous impulses while acting in her official capacity—chatting informally about personal matters to a visiting Head of State; taking her little grandson to office with her and dandling him on her knee while she discusses complex affairs of state with a colleague; or withdrawing into her own thoughts at an official conference or public meeting. Conversely, it means that she may apply the most exacting standards of efficiency to minor household affairs, such as the planning of a menu, the laying of a table or the selection of her wardrobe.

Indira Gandhi's day begins early. She has accustomed herself to making do with little sleep, and however late she retires at night, she is up at six the next morning. Like her father, she starts the day with Yogic and other exercises. She spends little time preening herself before a mirror, and claims that she 'can have a bath and get dressed in five minutes—which very few men can do.'[9] After breakfast, during which she scans the daily newspapers and marks relevant items, she is ready for her private secretary who arrives with urgent correspondence and files.

At 8.30 every morning Indira Gandhi, sometimes trailing her grandson behind her, walks the fifty yards from 1, Safdarjang Road to 1, Akbar Road, the neighbouring house, where she holds her morning durbar*. For an hour she is accessible to most people who wish to see her. Her visitors include Cabinet Colleagues and State leaders, deputations of party workers, peasants, students and others, donors to the Prime Minister's National Relief Fund, foreign tourists and newly-wed couples. Their purposes are manifold. Some wish to lobby her, some to petition

---

*Court.

her and others to be photographed with her or to receive her *darshan* (blessing). For many victims of official injustice, this morning audience is an informal court of appeal. Their petitions are handed over to the Prime Minister's secretaries for investigation, and in many cases action is taken.

The Prime Minister's *durbar* draws a varied cross-section of Indian society, and the apparent ease with which she steers her way through it is the result of much social and political experience. According to their status and their purpose, visitors are either received indoors for a private audience or greet her on the lawns outside. In either case, interviews are brief, owing to Mrs. Gandhi's gift for combining economy of language with a capacity for instantly putting people at ease and grasping the essentials of their problems. Though she moves rapidly from one group or individual to another, few people feel neglected. With a quick but expressive smile, the querulous raising of an eyebrow or a look of quiet sympathy, she circumvents the usual long-drawn courtesies and plunges to the heart of the matter. Explaining her technique, she has said:

'...I am always direct... I never spend my time in preliminaries ... in India the first half-hour is spent in how-are-you, how-are-your-children, how-are-your-grandchildren; this kind of flowery thing. And I have no time for flowery things. Not that I don't believe in them, but I think that first I should get the job done, *then* sit and talk. So I say: Hurry up, get to the point.'[10]

By ten o'clock, Mrs. Gandhi is at her office in South Block* or in Parliament House when Parliament is in session. Here she deals with official files and correspondence and receives ministers, officials and diplomats. She is back home for lunch at one o'clock, rests for an hour and then returns to office. Apart from the usual administrative routine, there is often a Cabinet meeting to preside over or a foreign dignitary to be received at the airport. When the Houses are sitting, the Prime Minister's work-load is particularly heavy. She has to attend important debates and often has to rush to the rescue of a beleaguered colleague during question-hour. Her evenings are spent at her residence dealing with party affairs—discussing tactics with her senior lieutenants and adjudicating in factional disputes. Unless her presence is required at an official banquet, she dines quietly with her family and then settles down again with her official files, retiring to bed around midnight.

It is a long working day—never less than twelve hours, and often sixteen; but it does not exclude her family and friends. According to Usha Bhagat, the Prime Minister's Social Secretary, 'She doesn't have

*An enormous Lutyens building where the main departments of government are located.

separate times for doing different things. She is one of the few people who can do several things at the same time without being distracted. She may be chatting with relatives or friends while important notes are being brought in to her. Or she may be telling her grandson a story when she is interrupted by a very important telephone call; she will attend to it and then continue with her story. So she has no fixed hours set aside for work, relaxation or being with her family. All these aspects are integrated.'[11]

In 1972 it was estimated that Mrs. Gandhi had spent an annual total of 120 days—or one in every three—away from the capital. Frequent and strenuous tours of the States are an essential part of the Prime Minister's job. Though these trips may be irksome and tiring, especially in the heat of the summer, Mrs. Gandhi enjoys the opportunity they give her to experience the kaleidoscopic variety of the sub-continent and to make herself known to its diverse communities. Her travels are organised with the same efficiency as her normal schedule. Most of her journeys are by special aircraft, and her entourage usually includes her security chief, a physician, a secretary, a personal servant and sometimes one of her social secretaries. Her intinerary is always crowded, and she has little time for sight-seeing or relaxation. She carries a streamlined travel kit, with her clothes for each day packed in separate cases. Though she projects herself as an All-India figure when she is in the States, she does not ignore regional sentiment. She wears the traditional saris of the area, samples the local food and prefaces her Hindi or English speeches with a few words in the regional language.

'There are never holidays for me,' Indira Gandhi has complained. 'They are what are called "busman's holidays".'[12] During the scorching Delhi summer, she snatches the occasional break in Simla, the nearest hill-station. She also tries, as far as possible, to keep her Sundays to herself. In recent years she has taken to disappearing from the capital on her birthday to avoid the crowds of visitors who collect at her residence. Her whereabouts are kept a close secret, and she usually spends the day with her family at some quiet country retreat.

'...I get much more done than before,' Mrs. Gandhi claims. 'When one works at greater speed, one must organise one's time more efficiently, and when one's faculties are exercised to the full, one has a greater sense of fulfilment.'[13] Nevertheless, many people find it surprising that a woman of fifty-six, with a history of poor health, is able to cope with so many demands on her physical and mental resources. Some attribute her physical endurance and stamina to Yoga, others to the tonic effects of power. Indira Gandhi's enthusiasm for her work undoubtedly does much to sustain her. Equally important is the care she takes of her health. Unlike most Indian politicians, she avoids rich food, aims at a balanced diet and tries to keep regular hours and to snatch some rest every after-noon. She is particularly conscious of the need for physical exercise. In reply to some anxious enquiries about her health, she complained: 'My real trouble is not getting enough exercise in the fresh air.'[14]

Recently, the physical strain of her occupation seems to have been telling on her, and she is more frequently 'indisposed,' as the Indian press euphemistically puts it. In the unhealthy, rumour-ridden atmosphere of New Delhi, the Prime Minister's health has become a subject for morbid curiosity, and the odd ailment or sign of fatigue excites as much attention as China-watchers devote to the health of Chairman Mao. When Mrs. Gandhi paid an official visit to Canada in June 1973, stopping over in London on her way, there was speculation that the real purpose of her visit was medical. In January 1974, when she was confined to bed with 'flu on the eve of an official visit by Mrs. Bandaranaike, the Ceylonese Premier, the *Statesman* complained:

> 'It would have been out of character had the Prime Minister's advisers allowed the news about her illness to be publicised. Mrs. Gandhi's health, they would have one believe, is her personal problem with which the media should not be concerned... One wishes that some of these advisers had persuaded her not to set such a crushing pace for herself during the first phase of her poll campaign in U.P.*...'[15]

Mrs. Gandhi herself does not welcome such solicitude. When a con-cerned official suggested at the end of a tiring day of electioneering that she should transfer from her jeep to a closed car, she snapped: 'How dare you! I have travelled in open jeeps for years.'[16] Meanwhile, there are wildly exaggerated rumours about her health, and the diagnosis ranges from cancer and tuberculosis to failing kidneys. The truth probably is that Indira Gandhi, like most people, has the occasional bout of influenza and other minor complaints. Certainly, no one with any serious ailment could function at the pace she does and continue to look as well. Like many other people with an early record of ill health, she appears in middle age to have developed a tough and resilient constitution. As far as one can see, she is physically in better shape than most of her political contemporaries, and her health is unlikely to fail for many years to come. The rest is gossip and, in the case of her opponents, wish-ful thinking.

*     *     *

'I have always been a doer,' Indira Gandhi recently told an Indian journalist. 'I am far less lonely than many people. For one thing, I like

---

*The elections in February 1974 for the state legislature of U.P. were seen as a crucial trial of strength between the Congress and the Opposition.

being by myself. I am not lonely like a lot of people who have to kill time. I have never had enough time to do everything I wanted to even when I was small.'[17] While she may not experience the loneliness and boredom that are the product of idleness, Mrs. Gandhi has had to live with the emotional isolation that has dogged her since her childhood. Partly, this has been temperamental, partly it has been inherent in her position. Like other celebrities, she cannot fail to notice that she is surrounded by people who court her friendship and favour for ulterior motives. While she likes praise and may not be averse to moderate flattery, as Nehru's daughter she has learned from an early age to beware of those from whom it emanates. And even with those whose affection she can trust, the nature of her office sets her apart and implies that there are large areas of her life which she cannot share. She herself has explained it thus:

> 'You feel lonely not because you are in power, in authority, but because according to what you do or are doing certain people are with you. As your capacities draw you, you may leave some people behind. It's one section of you they can understand, but they can't understand the whole of you. So the loneliness comes, because there are so few people who have been through all the experiences which you have been through and which you can therefore share with any one person.'[18]

Mrs. Gandhi's critics say she is cold-blooded, calculating and fickle in her relationships, turning on her charm when it is expedient and shedding her erstwhile favourites without any qualms when they cease be useful. The instances most often cited are those of Asoka Mehta and Dinesh Singh. Her behaviour has been compared unfavourably with the trust and loyalty that Nehru placed in his colleagues and associates. Mrs. Gandhi herself has been quoted as saying that her father was 'a saint strayed into politics; since he never had to struggle in his life, he lacked the necessary ruthlessness.'[19] Elsewhere she has said: 'I am less romantic and emotional than he was. Women are more down to earth than men.'[20] There is no doubt that she has fewer illusions than her father about the nature of political loyalties. She is aware that many of her most ardent supporters follow her because she is powerful and that their devotion will not survive their self-interest. But she can hardly be blamed for using those who are bent on using her and for discarding them when they have served their purpose.

Political survival in contemporary India necessarily requires a large measure of cynicism, ruthlessness and artifice. Indira Gandhi cannot afford to be as sentimental as her father. Nevertheless, while she is careful to avoid being exploited or duped, she can be kind, generous, affectionate and loyal when she is convinced of a person's sincerity.

Owing to old antagonisms, she has little contact with her aunt Vijayalakshmi Pandit and her branch of the family; but she takes a benevolent interest in the welfare of other more distant relatives, especially those on her mother's side. She may be slow to form friendships; but when she does, they are close and enduring. According to those who know her intimately, she is a considerate and entertaining companion, has a lively sense of humour and is an excellent mimic. Despite the many demands on her time, her friends can always count on her sympathy and assistance when they are ill or in trouble. She has been known to interrupt a heavy schedule to comfort and console someone in distress. On such occasions, she is capable of great tenderness and self-effacement, listening attentively and sympathetically to other people's personal problems.

Indira Gandhi's compassion is not confined to her own intimate coterie. In her position, she receives innumerable requests for assistance, and naturally she has to be selective. But she has a strong philanthropic instinct, and wherever she is convinced that there is genuine suffering, she is ready to help. Where governmental assistance is not possible, she has been known to make donations from her personal funds.

Referring to criticism that she is artificial and unemotional, Indira Gandhi has protested: '...they react by saying that I am tough, cold, frosty. I am not, I am a very normal human being... I never put on an act; I am always what I am. If I'm cross, then I show myself cross. If I am happy, then I show myself happy.'[21] Her friends confirm that, while she can be moody and bad-tempered, she is always natural and spontaneous; and these are qualities she respects in others. In October 1971 she wrote to Mary Shelvankar*, who had been her hostess in Moscow: 'I do want to say "thank you" for your thoughtfulness, your gifts and for being yourself. But naturalness and spontaneity worry a lot of people who are not used to them. So many people waste a lot of energy putting on an act. Although, perhaps, it is just as well that they hide their real nature!'[22]

In November 1970, Mrs. Gandhi donated Anand Bhawan, the family home in Allahabad which she had inherited from her father, to the Nehru Memorial Trust for conversion into a museum. At a formal function on the occasion, she wept and spoke of 'the flood of memories' that had overwhelmed her. For the last twenty-five years she has lived in Delhi; but according to Yashpal Kapur, a close associate, she continues to regard Allahabad and Anand Bhawan as her real home, and often refers nostalgically to her life there.[23] Perhaps this is why some of her closest friends are those who have known her and the family since the

*Wife of the Indian Ambassador in the Soviet Union.

Allahabad days—people like Padmaja Naidu, Phupul Jayakar, Mohammed Yunus and Chalapathi Rau. With her old and intimate friends, she is completely relaxed: they are free to drop in on her un-invited and she chats with them on the telephone. She also maintains friendly contacts with a wider circle which includes politicians, social workers, intellectuals and artists. Some of them are people she met through her father, and many are foreigners—among them the Mount-battens, Iris Murdoch, Jenny Lee, Yehudi and Hepzibah Menuhin, Benjamin Britten, Peter Pears, Frida Laski, Sybil Thorndike and Margaret Mead. She corresponds with them occasionally and arranges to meet them when she is abroad; and when they visit Delhi they usually stay with her.

1, Safdarjand Road is an essentially functional home, and there is little trace of the *salon* atmosphere of Teen Murti House, still less of the lavish hospitality of Motilal Nehru's Anand Bhawan. Explaining the contrast, Mrs. Gandhi's social secretary says: 'She has intense relation-ships with her friends, but she doesn't need to be surrounded by them. In that respect, she is more self-sufficient than her father. Also, living as she does in a smaller house and without a hostess, she can't keep the kind of open house her father did.'[24] Security problems make it difficult for her to drop in on friends or to dine at their homes. Her social outings are largely confined to brief appearances at wedding receptions held by friends and relations, Cabinet colleagues and senior officials.

Although Mrs. Gandhi does not entertain much, she does give the occasional dinner party. These are usually small buffet suppers, and she rarely invites more than twenty people. On such occasions, she is no longer the Prime Minister, but the informal and attentive hostess of the Teen Murti days. There is no ceremony or ostentation. She waits perso-nally upon her guests, passing them their plates and helping them to food and sees that they are not neglected or left out.

'She is a far more fulfilled person,' says Usha Bhagat of the Prime Minister as she is today. 'She is much less irritable and more confident than she was in the early days.'[25] For all the social and other constraints that public life imposes on her, Indira Gandhi is emotionally more balanced and secure than ever before. Political success has no doubt played a large part in giving her this sense of fulfilment. Equally important is the intimacy and stability of her family life, which presents a marked contrast to the strains and uncertainties of her childhood and marriage. Living with her permanently are both her sons, her daughter-in-law, a grandson and, recently, a granddaughter. She is close to her sons, devoted to her grand-children and, as far as one knows, her relations with her daughter-in-law are smooth and harmonious. Sonia Gandhi, who comes from a middle class Italian background, met Rajiv Gandhi at Cambridge. His mother is believed to have had initial misgivings about their proposed marriage and advised them to postpone the decision. Later she yielded as graciously as Nehru had done in her own case, presiding over the wedding in New Delhi and welcoming her foreign daughter-in-law into the family circle.

Indira Gandhi, by all accounts, has been an understanding and indulgent mother. She has fiercely defended her sons from publicity, and has not permitted political considerations to interfere with the independence and privacy of their lives. When she sent them abroad for their education, there was a certain amount of criticism, in view of the Government's policy of discouraging and restricting Indian students from studying abroad. But Mrs. Gandhi later told one of her biographers: 'I couldn't care less what people say. I though it was necessary for my boys to go to England.'[26] She has always been careful not to allow her own political concerns to overflow into family life. 'Politics generally aren't discussed with the family,' says Usha Bhagat. 'Not that there's any rule about it. Now and then her sons might mention some particular, local grievance or issue and discuss it with her; but there aren't any general political discussions.'[27] Asked by a journalist why her sons were not in politics, Mrs. Gandhi replied: 'I tried my best to keep them away from it.'[28]

Rajiv Gandhi, after a somewhat abortive academic career at Cambridge, has settled down to a well-paid but inconspicuous job as a pilot with Indian Airlines, the State-owned domestic air service. He is believed to be quiet and self-effacing and shuns the public eye. His brother Sanjay, however, figures prominently in the news and in the gossip of Delhi drawing-rooms. During the 1971 general election, his active participation in the Congress campaign aroused suspicions that he was being groomed by his mother for a political career. But his interest in politics appears to have been transitory and his real concerns lie elsewhere. After serving an apprenticeship with Rolls Royce in England, he has been pioneering a project for an indigenously produced small car. Having personally designed and built the prototype, he is now the manager of *Maruti*, the company set up to produce the car.

The Maruti project, referred to by the Opposition as 'India's Watergate,' has been responsible for the most personal and victriolic criticism that Indira Gandhi has yet experienced. The Opposition argues that the project is inconsistent with the Government's planning priorities and that the grant of a licence to Sanjay Gandhi to start the project in the private sector involved favouritism and nepotism. It is alleged that the land for the factory lay in a prohibited area near a military base, that it was released through the intervention of the Congress Chief Minister of Haryana in return for the dropping of corruption charges against him, and that its acquisition has caused great hardship to the peasants who were cultivating it and had to be evicted. Sanjay Gandhi has also been

accused of inducing private businessmen to invest in the venture in
return for government licences and concessions. There is no legal evidence
to sustain any of these charges; but the Government's denials have not
succeeded in dispelling suspicion. The Opposition continues to raise
the matter in Parliament and outside, making the most of it to tarnish
Mrs. Gandhi's otherwise clean public record. In a recent parliamentary
debate, a Left Communist leader described the Prime Minister as 'the
fountainhead of all corruption in the country,'[29] while Madhu Limaye,
a veteran Socialist leader, wrote an open letter to the President in May
1973, urging him to dismiss Mrs. Gandhi and set up a special tribunal to
try her for 'gross abuse of power and propriety in granting a baby-car
licence to her own jobless son.'[30]

It is a measure of the extent to which Indira Gandhi values her family
life that she has refused to allow repeated public attacks of this kind to
disrupt it. Asked by a journalist about rumours that she had been having
problems with Sanjay and that he had walked out of her home, she replied
firmly: 'He has not. He is staying exactly where he is. He is a very straightforward person, extremely hardworking.'[31] In reply to the suggestion
that Sanjay's advantages as her son have assisted his project, she says:
'It might have helped him in some ways. But I think it might have helped
him more had he not been my son. Because now what he is doing, he is
doing in spite of constant anti-propaganda, questioning and so on, whereas had he been able to implement the proposal on his own, none of these
difficulties would have arisen.'[32]

Mrs. Gandhi has made it clear that she has no intention of being
pressurised into revoking the Government's licence for *Maruti*. She
raises the issue herself at public meetings and asks her audiences how
she can be expected to encourage the initiative and enterprise of India's
youth while suppressing the talents of her own son. In September 1973,
she told an interviewer:

> 'It is obvious that some people are opposing my son's project and
> attributing all kinds of irregularities to it merely to malign me... In
> fact nothing irregular has been done and no favour shown to the
> project. I would not countenance any violation of rules and procedures.
> There is nothing wrong in a young man proving his capacity... Here
> a young man has been working with singleness of purpose for a number
> of years in the most difficult circumstances and with no encouragement
> or help. Whatever he built up was done with his own hands.... I
> admire his spirit and endeavour.'[33]

According to Usha Bhagat, 'Mrs. Gandhi is very tolerant of her sons'
friends, who are a very mixed crowd indeed. They are often present at
table; and even if she doesn't participate in their talk, she listens and

isn't bored because she is so interested in her sons and their lives.'[34] Nevertheless, sharing a house with two independent young men, both of whom have their own careers and friends, is bound to cause some embarrassment to a person in her position, bringing to mind the anomalous situation created by Feroze Gandhi's presence at Teen Murti in the early fifties. Mrs. Gandhi may be tolerant and understanding; but Delhi gossip is not. When the Jagota brothers and their sister were arrested for trespassing in the Prime Minister's house and charged with espionage, there were rumours that the charge was trumped up and that the alleged trespassers had an unsavoury connection with Sanjay Gandhi. Denying an allegation in Parliament that she and members of her family had met the arrested persons, Mrs. Gandhi protested angrily: 'This has no foundation, is absolutely malicious, mischievous and a downright falsehood.'[35] Rumour, however, is not so easily silenced. Though her critics have been quick to capitalise on the situation, she has refused to countenance suggestions that her sons should live separately. In effect, Mrs. Gandhi has made it clear that, where a choice is involved, she prizes her family life more than her public image.

*          *          *

'I don't enjoy what most people mean by politics—maneouvring and things like that, I simply can't stand it,' says Indira Gandhi. 'I don't think it's a nice thing to be at all, what the world thinks of as an "adroit politician".'[36] Although practical politics is the field in which she has excelled, she is also what might be called a civilised and cultivated woman. Her cosmopolitan education and background have left her with a wide range of non-political tastes and interests. Unlike most Indian politicians, she can talk intelligently on most subjects, and she is sensitive to their subtleties. In recent years, her life has been almost entirely politicised. But while she has little time to indulge her various hobbies, she retains her interest in them.

She has always been a compulsive reader, and she still finds time to read when she is travelling, or in brief snatches during her busy daily schedule. Her tastes and interests are remarkably heterodox. She reads women's magazines, scientific journals, the National Geographical, biographies and modern fiction and verse. Her bookshelves include works by T.S. Eliot, Jean Paul Sartre, Albert Camus, André Malraux, Erich Fromm, Kingsley Amis, Eugene Ionesco, Han Suyin, J. Krishnamurti and J.K. Galbraith. The lives of other successful people appear to hold a special interest for her, and her library contains biographies or autobiographies of Helen Keller, Albert Schweitzer, Paul Robeson (an old family friend), Dylan Thomas, Stephen Spender, Charlie Chaplin, Yehudi Menuhin, Pearl Buck, Simone de Beauvoir,

Leonardo da Vinci, Bernard Shaw, Beatrice Webb, Harold Laski, Jennie Lee, Franklin Roosevelt, Aneurin Bevan, the Dalai Lama, Mao Tse-Tung and Marshal Tito. There are also several works of anthropology, a subject which is believed to have interested her immensely.

She keeps herself informed of world trends, and the issues which interest her most at present are youth unrest and ecology. She wrote to Chester Bowles* in August 1972: 'The involvement of the young people in trying to build a new image of America is exciting. I am not surprised that you should be with them. But the path of change is strewn with many obstacles.'37 Charles Reich's book, *The Greening of America*, greatly impressed her, and she arranged to meet him when she was last in the United States.

Mrs. Gandhi is a good linguist. Like the rest of India's Westernised elite, she was brought up to be bi-lingual, speaking English and Hindustani with equal fluency. Since her entry into active politics, she has mastered Hindi**, speaking it with such profficiency that her speeches in Hindi are generally rated higher than those in English, and has also picked up a smattering of some regional languages. During her schooling in Switzerland, she acquired a sound grasp of French and still speaks it fluently. When she visited Canada in June 1973, Prime Minister Trudeau was reported to have been greatly impressed by her 'impeccable' French and remarked: 'She speaks the language even better than us.'38

Words generally—their structure and resonance and the images they evoke—continue to fascinate her as much as they did during her prison term in 1942, when she diverted herself by coining whimsical names for the drab objects in her barracks. Crossword puzzles are one of her favourite pass-times. She does the *Times of India* crossword every day and is reputed to be good at it. Having discovered her solving a crossword puzzle when he called on her at her office in South Block, Karan Singh, a Cabinet colleague, decided to present her with the latest Crossword Puzzle Dictionary, in the hope that 'it helps on those irritating occasions when the right word simple refuses to surface.'39 Thanking him for the gift, the Prime Minister added, possibly with a hint of irritation, that she was in the habit of finishing most of the day's crossword at breakfast and had no time to refer to dictionaries.40

Indira Gandhi is known to have a strong aesthetic sense which expresses itself in her appreciation of the arts and also in her own style of living. Apart from some ballet classes in Switzerland, some violin lessons, and her brief training in Manipuri dance at Shantiniketan, she has had no formal education in the fine arts. Her response to art is im-

*A former American Ambassador in India.
**The national language, a Sanskritised variant of Hindustani, the language of northern India.

pressionistic and intuitive; but her appreciation is genuine and spontaneous and her judgement shows taste and discernment. The works of art in her home include antique Indian bronzes and miniatures, tribal curios and some paintings by contemporary Indian artists. She is fond of music—classical and folk, Indian and Western. Her choice depends on her mood: when she is tired, she likes gentle piano and violin music. Her favourite Western composers are Bach and Beethoven, but she also enjoys Joan Baez. She is interested in dance—Indian classical, Western ballet and modern and experimental forms; but she seems to be most at home with the lively and rhythmic folk and tribal dances of India's various regions, and she often joins in herself for a quick turn when troupes of folk dancers call upon her and perform in her garden. She always goes to the theatre when she is abroad and has done much to encourage the productions of the National School of Drama in Delhi. She enjoys good films, especially those of Ingmar Bergman, Jacques Cousteau and Roberto Rosselini, a personal friend. Private screenings are often arranged for her on Sundays in the auditorium of the presidential palace.

Her aesthetic sensibilities are not confined to the arts, and she is sensitive to beauty wherever she finds it. 'In every country and in every town,' she has noted, 'one suddenly comes across an aspect which is beautiful. I love the autumn colouring of trees in Europe or on our mountains. I love the rain and walking out in it. One of my favourite cities is Florence and another is Taormina. I love old cities or old parts of cities. But I also like some of the very new architecture.'[41]

Asked on one occasion what she would like to do if she retired from office, Indira Gandhi speculated: 'In theory, I'd like to lead a lazy life, but I'm not that kind of person. I would like to design, just for fun... clothes, houses, interiors... Even now I sketch things sometimes, and when I was in college in England, I designed my own clothes.'[42] Functional and decorative arts seem to hold a greater attraction for her than the fine arts, appealing both to the aesthetic and practical aspects of her personality, and she has integrated them into her domestic life.

1, Safdarjang Road has undergone many improvements since she first moved in in 1964; and it is an elegant and comfortable, though unostentatious, residence. Structural changes and additions have been made to improve its appearance and to provide more space for Mrs. Gandhi's growing family. The interior is tastefully furnished with handloom upholstery in soothing shades of rust and green. The furniture and pictures are neatly arranged with a geometrical precision that reflects the Prime Minister's meticulous eye for detail. According to Yashpal Kapur, she hates untidiness of any sort and is forever straightening furniture and other objects at home and in her office.[43] Her garden, too, is carefully tended and has been laid out with imagination and an eye for colour.

Although she has two very capable social secretaries to keep house for her, Mrs. Gandhi continues to supervise the household. 'She takes a great deal of interest in such things as menus, furnishing and the garden,' says Usha Bhagat. 'She doesn't have time to plan it all herself. But if we make a particular arrangement of pictures, or choose a particular colour, or decided to plant some seeds in a particular flower-bed, we have to ask her before going ahead, because she is very particular about these things.'[44]

Indira Gandhi has confided to an interviewer: 'I can't really cook, except eggs and some things like that. But I like good food, and I can tell what's wrong with it when it's badly cooked as the household knows to its cost... I love decorating rooms and doing flowers. Like all women, I like changing the furniture around.'[45] Though she can do without it when necessary, she has a taste for good living and is free from the puritanical Gandhian ethic of self-denial as an end in itself. At the same time, she dislikes vulgar ostentation of any kind, and the emphasis is always on quiet and simple good taste.

Her clothes and personal appearance receive the same fastidious attention as her home. As she has no time to shop, saris are usually sent to her residence on approval, and she makes her own selection. Her clothes are never garish, and they are chosen with a shrewd eye for the colours that suit her. She is fond of pastel shades, especially lemon yellow; but she also likes darker colours—brown, black and purple—for the evening. Unlike most Indian women, she rarely wears jewels and, as though to emphasise that she is a working woman, she sports a large, man's wristwatch. She rarely uses make-up, and her hair is close-cropped and easily manageable; but she is always neat, clean and well-dressed, her eyebrows carefully shaped and her delicate hands freshly manicured. Age has been kind to her, giving her a dignified and austere beauty that is far more striking than the prettiness of her youth. Her face is remarkably unwrinkled, though its angles have softened and matured with the years. Her features are severe and solemn in repose; but her smile is dazzling —her large, expressive eyes sparkle warmly and she reveals a row of perfect white teeth. Her build remains slender and youthful, and as a British journalist puts it, she has the 'knack of wearing grey hair as if it is a jewel.'[46]

Though she has never been good at games, Mrs. Gandhi loved skiing when she was at school in Switzerland, and she still enjoys swimming, riding and long walks. She is fond of outdoor life and says that she finds 'equal relaxation in being close to nature and in different forms of art; also in activity—physical, such as hiking in the mountains, or mental, such as reading about an unfamiliar subject.'[47] 'Very early I became a

conservationist,' she has written, 'with a strong feeling of companionship
and kinship with all living beings—animals, birds and insects as well as
trees and plants.'[48] She used to be a keen bird-watcher in the Teen Murti
days. Though she no longer has time for such hobbies, she retains a genuine
concern for the preservation of wild life, and the present 'Save the Tiger'
campaign owes much to her encouragement. She loves animals; and
although there is no room for a menagerie of Teen Murti proportions,
her household includes dogs—a dachshund and an Afghan hound—and
a Siamese cat.

Her interest in the problems of ecology and conservation does not
involve any rejection of science and technology. Like her father, she
sees technology as an essential of modern development, and through
her sons she has had direct experience of the world of machines and
industry. The Government's departments of Space and Atomic Energy
are under her personal charge, and she keeps in touch with the latest
developments, following scientific discoveries and the exploits of astro-
nauts with youthful excitement and optimism.

In the course of the last eight years, Indira Gandhi's life has been
increasingly politicised, leaving her with little time or opportunity for
her various non-political interests. 'She has had to make certain sacrifices
and give up certain things,' says Usha Bhagat. 'She can't move around
incognito anymore. She used to love going to films or browsing in book-
shops or shopping at Cottage Industries*. Now she can't for security
reasons and because she'd be recognised everywhere. Except for very
brief periods when she is abroad and her schedule permits it, she can't
really do these things.'[49]

Asked to state her own opinion of 'Indira Gandhi the woman,'
Mrs. Gandhi has said: 'In spite of always living in the public glare,
she has remained a very private person. Her life has been hard. This
has made her self-reliant, but has not hardened her. On the contrary,
she has learnt to find interest in ordinary things, beauty in any
surroundings and lighter moments in the harshest situations. She feels
that only deep sensitivity, minute observation and a feeling of involvement
can help one to perceive the subtle and changing nuances in people and
situations.'[50]

Self-appraisal is seldom accurate, but it would be true to say that
Indira Gandhi, though immersed in politics, is far from being an exclusively political person. Hers is a many-sided personality, which could sustain
itself in other walks of life, and there are few Indian politicians of whom
the same could be said. Politics, nonetheless, is the life she has chosen
for herself and in which she has excelled; and one must assume, therefore,

*The Cottage Industries Emporium, a State-owned shopping centre.

that it is the career which affords her the largest measure of personal satisfaction and fulfilment. Speculation as to what she would do if she retired from office is purely academic, for there is no reason to think that she will give up politics while she has a say in the matter.

\*　　　\*　　　\*

Indira Gandhi dislikes having to define her political or personal philosophy. When pressed to do so, her formulations are vague, evasive and often contradictory. It is a measure of the extent to which she differs from her father that Nehru enjoyed nothing better than to dilate expansively on his political and philosophical beliefs. His writings were replete with long dialectical soliloquies in which he analysed and reflected upon the development of his thought. In interviews and conversation, he was only too happy to expound his ideological convictions. Ideas fascinated him, and his mind ranged enthusiastically over different branches of knowledge, analysing, selecting and assimilating. His thought was not merely derivative, it was original and creative to the extent that he was able to integrate such disparate philosophies as Liberalism, Marxism and Gandhism into an internally consistent theoretical model which survived in tact the practical compromises and errors of his political career.

Indira Gandhi's thought, by contrast, is a somewhat pale and confused imitation of her father's. While she takes an interest in ideas and in the intellectuals who produce them, she herself is no intellectual. She has neither the capacity nor the inclination for theoretical speculation and analysis, and her grasp of the social sciences—and of economics particularly—is nebulous and uncertain. Ideology concerns her only in so far as it is immediately applicable to a concrete situation. Her pragmatism and intuition enable her to respond magnificently to political events, making her by any standards a brilliant politician. But these very assets are a handicap when it comes to coherent planning and long-term perspectives.

Unlike her father, she has never attempted to commit to paper her view of the world; and perhaps it is just as well. What emerges from her various speeches, writings and interviews is neither original nor illuminating. Tradition and modernity, rationalism and mysticism, populism and élitism mingle freely in a blend which might be termed complex or confused depending on one's point of view. As with other living statesmen, the task of interpretation is further complicated by the difficulty of sifting ideas that are intended for public consumption from those which are genuine articles of faith. Mrs. Gandhi, it must be remembered, defers far more to popular sentiment in her public pronouncements than her father ever did.

In view of her paradoxical position as a woman leading a male-dominated country, the question that recurs most often in Mrs. Gandhi's interviews concerns her attitude to the emancipation of women. Asked whether she is a feminist, she has answered rather subjectively: 'No. Why should I be? I always felt that I could do anything I wanted. My mother was a very strong feminist, but she always felt that being a woman was a great disadvantage... I was brought up as a boy when I was small. I climbed trees, I ran and I never had any feeling of inferiority or envy towards men.'[51] She maintains that her sex has never been a liability in her own career and attributes this to the high status accorded to women in theory, though not in practice, by Indian tradition and also to Gandhi's emphasis on the participation of women in the nationalist movement.

These factors aside, it is obvious that the advantages of Indira Gandhi's birth, family background and education have given her opportunities not available to most of her sex; and it is unlikely that she herself would deny this. Addressing a women's university in Bombay soon after she became Prime Minister, she warned:

'In few countries do women hold higher position in politics and public life than in India. But this should not lead us to think that the old inequalities and disabilities from which the women of India suffered have all ended. Ours is a country in which oppositions and contradictions thrive, and nowhere is this more so than as regards women. If we have women who are among the most progressive in the world, we also have women who are among the most backward. In law, all discrimination between man and woman has been abolished. Yet, we all know the social and economic hardships which our women suffer in addition to the general hardships ... in a society so poor and still so largely mediaeval as ours. In the countries where women had to fight for their rights, it had been easier for men to finally accept the fact of women's emancipation. In India, in spite of the fact that the emancipation of women has released powerful social forces, non-acceptance of equality of women on the part of men is a great hurdle. Another hurdle is the old ideal of a silently suffering Sita which remains at the back of the mind of even a liberated Indian woman.'[52]

Mrs. Gandhi's recognition of the exploitation of women has not led her to patronise any feminist movement in India. Nor has she attempted to spell out how women can achieve equal rights, except to advise them to do 'something creative for society.'[53] Her explanation of her neutrality between the sexes is simple and straightforward. A Prime Minister, she says, must represent the nation and cannot be identified with any particular group or section. Asked whether her election as Prime Minister had opened the way for greater participation by women in politics, her reply was noncommital: 'The women in the world account for half of mankind. Obviously they have a tremendously important role to play in every field of human endeavour. My position does not add or detract from this fundamental truth.'[34]

Indira Gandhi's sex has proved a valuable asset to her and the Congress in elections, enabling her to secure most of the women's vote. But she has not returned the favour by making any special effort to promote the interests of women in politics; and the percentage of women in Indian legislatures, having reached its peak in 1957, has been declining drastically ever since. Mrs. Gandhi's political success may by example, if not by precept, have provided a stimulus to other educated, middle class women, marginally improving their position with their menfolk. But among the masses of rural India, the Prime Minister's sex has not made any significant impact on the status of women. The cult of the Mother-Goddess has been deeply rooted in Indian culture since pre-historic times; and there are many in the villages who regard Indira Gandhi as a *Devi* or goddess. For them she is a larger-than-life figure, a sacred symbol or totem, who can be placed on a pedestal and worshipped when she appears, but whose image can hardly be incorporated into ordinary community life. Mrs. Gandhi herself is by no means ignorant of this tendency and pointed out in a speech to a women's organisation:

'We have thought—our society has thought—that if you call a woman a goddess, you have done everything necessary, even if she is suppressed and has no rights... I would like our women to be treated as human beings. They do not want to be goddesses, but they must have every opportunity to develop their talent, their capabilities, and to use those talents and capabilities in the service of the community.'[55]

It has been fashionable in the Western press to hail India's woman Prime Minister as 'the supreme example of Women's Liberation.' She herself is not opposed to the Women's Lib movement in the West. 'That movement,' she says, '...is part of a bigger revolt that can only be accepted, because until recently a few people were doing the speaking for everybody; today everybody wants to speak for himself. The black people, the brown people, the women—they are all part of the same revolt. And this is good.'[56] Nor is she averse to the activities of non-conformist female militants like Bernadette Devlin, whom she has described as 'a dynamic, interesting and deeply committed person.'[57] In her own public duties, she has firmly refused to allow her sex to inhibit or restrict her in any way. When she received a letter from an orthodox Indian criticising her for shaking hands with Tunku Abdul Rahman, the Malaysian leader, she replied: 'A Prime Minister, whether man or

woman, must act as Prime Minister... Whatever our customs, in international dealings we have to conform to some extent... One may do
*namaskar** to an ordinary person, but it would certainly not be in the
national interest not to shake hands with an important person.'[58] She
is as business-like and direct in her political and administrative dealings
as any male head of government, and she has always maintained that
her sex is irrelevant to her job.

In many respects, Indira Gandhi is representative of the 'new women'
of India's tiny educated élite, women who go to university, take up jobs,
drive their own cars and mix freely with the opposite sex. All the same,
in her political life she is careful not to offend public sensibilities, even if it
means observing minor conventions of feminine modesty and decorum.
Though she often wore Western trousers and dresses in her
youth, since her entry into public life she only wears saris. When she ad-
dresses public meetings, she covers her head with her sari in the traditional
Indian fashion, and when she is electioneering in the villages, her blouses
have a prim, high collar and long sleeves that button at the wrist.

Both in public and private, she remains a very 'feminine' woman,
not only in her appearance, but in her social manners and behaviour.
She is aware of her feminine appeal and charm and makes no attempt
to suppress it. Asked how she feels about being a woman, she has written
sentimentally: 'Being a woman is to perceive the indignity and inequality
which corrodes the human situation; to act with compassion and involvement to find solutions which are born of a fusion of the mind and heart;
to ensure that, instead of confrontation and conflict, there is understanding and enrichment.'[59]

In view of Nehru's outspoken agnosticism and rejection of religious
ritual and superstition, there has been considerable curiosity about his
daughter's religious attitudes. The general view seems to be that she is
more susceptible than Nehru to religion and its trappings. 'Because of
her mother's influence, perhaps, she is more tolerant of these rituals
than her father,' says Usha Bhagat. 'Though she is not religious in any
orthodox sense, she meets *Swamis*** etc. who come to see her and whom
her father would have turned away. She is close to Anandmai*** because
of her mother's contact; but she is nobody's disciple.'[60] According to
Yashpal Kapur, who has worked under her for many years, Mrs. Gandhi,
like her mother and grandmother, has religious faith, even though she
does not pray or meditate regularly. She reads the *Bhagvad Gita*†
regularly, he says, and has visited all the important shrines of various

*The traditional Hindu greeting with folded hands.
**Hindu priests and mystics.
***A well-known female spiritual Guru.
†The most fundamental and philosophical of the Hindu scriptures.

religions in the country, observing their respective rituals.[61]

*Holi, Dussehra, Diwali,* and other Hindu festivals are celebrated with the traditional rites at 1, Safdarjang Road, though Usha Bhagat maintains that Mrs. Gandhi enjoys them more for their festivity than their religious significance. She often wears a string of holy beads which Anandmai is said to have given her, and on *Basant Panchmi**, she is always dressed in the traditional yellow sari. When the Shankaracharaya of Kanchi, a prominent Hindu religious leader, visited Delhi in June 1973, he told the press that the Prime Minister had called upon him at his local temple, received his blessings and spent some time in prayer and meditation. Mrs. Gandhi is certainly not opposed on principle to ritual. She has told an interviewer:

'...ritual has meaning and value for some people. It depends how it is used. The idea was to induce concentration. Take Zen. The tea ceremony; the purpose is to disengage yourself, you have to concentrate and a ritual helps you to do that. You can do it without ritual too. I can concentrate anywhere and anytime now ... I almost go into a trance ... It's very relaxing. I do believe in this question of being detached. Being passionately interested and still ... detached.'[62]

According to unconfirmed reports, her belief in ritual is not limited to its transcendental value. She is widely believed to be superstitious about colours and stones, to consult astrologers and palmists like most Indian politicians and to arrange for *havans* and other Hindu religious ceremonies. She used to keep in close touch with the Mother** at the Aurobindo Ashram in Pondicherry and was reputed to have received her benediction. Mrs. Nandini Satpathy***, a well-known disciple of the Mother, is said to have carried messages back and forth between Delhi and Pondicherry. During the drought of 1973 one of the other disciples wrote to the Prime Minister suggesting she request the Mother to ask Sri Aurobindo for rain. Far from dismissing such a preposterous idea, she replied politely: 'I am grateful to the Mother for her graciousness towards me. Naturally, in a matter of such importance to the country, any help which the Mother can give will make a great difference... I do not wish to bother the Mother. But if you think it proper, you may speak to her about these matters.'[63]

While Mrs. Gandhi has stated categorically that she does not believe in a personal god, she does seem to have a pantheistic faith in a spiritual or supernatural being of some kind. 'I don't believe in God in that

*The first day of spring according to the Hindu Calendar.
**A French mystic who married the late Aurobindo, the famous spiritual leader, and presided over his ashram till her recent demise.
***The present Congress Chief Minister of Orissa State.

particular way as a person,' she has told a British interviewer. 'I do believe or feel that each person has something within him which, for want of a better word, I suppose I would call "divine". But I certainly don't believe in a bearded gentleman sitting up above.'[64] Making the same distinction to an Indian journalist, she asserted that she believed in *Vedanta\**, while conceding that she did not know much about its finer points.

How far her religious behaviour is the result of her personal beliefs, as distinct from her deference to public sentiment, is a point on which Mrs. Gandhi remains ambivalent. She has often stressed that the political secularism to which she is committed is not anti-religious but stands for the political equality of all faiths. 'I have gone to temples,' she says. 'I have gone to Tirupati and Rameshwaram. If I go to a place where there is a famous temple, church, mosque, synagogue, I go there... These things have a great deal of meaning to large numbers of people. Now I feel that if I am Prime Minister I cannot separate myself from the feelings of these people. I am also interested in knowing what moves them in these places. As far as I am concerned, I don't need a temple. I think basically our religion says that it is something within you.'[65]

At the same time, she knows that religiosity is incompatible with a modern and scientific image, and she has always denied that she is superstitious or mystical. About her relationship with Anandmai, she says: 'I don't believe in her for the spirituality and all that. She's a very good friend. It's as a friend that I meet her. She was a great friend of my mother's. So I feel a bond. She's a very comforting person to be with, but there is nothing religious about it. At least, she's not like that with me.'[66]

Whatever her religious beliefs, she remains true to the Nehru tradition of secularism and is not motivated by sectarian prejudice of any kind. She is a product of the composite Hindu-Muslim culture of U.P., she married a Parsi and there are several Muslims in her intimate circle. At the political level, too, she opposes Hindu chauvinism and revivalism. In September 1972 she wrote to the Congress Chief Minister of Mysore: 'I have heard reports of the decision of the Mysore Government to take out a procession of Mother India during the Dussehra festivities... I wonder whether you should support anything that suggests revivalism. At any rate, when your State is facing such a serious drought situation, any expenditure which might be criticised as wasteful should be avoided.'[67]

Her secularism, it is true, is less uncompromising than her father's. When she inaugurated the Asia 1972 Trade Fair in Delhi, she permitted the chanting of Vedic hymns on the occasion, thereby provoking a strong

*The mystical, philosophical essence of Hinduism, which denies the reality of material existence and postulates that pure consciousness is the only reality.

protest from the Indian Muslim League. Though initially opposed to the anti-cow-slaughter agitation, she has permitted the banning of cow-slaughter in most States of the Union. Apart from involving discrimination against minorities, the ban deprives the country of valuable foreign exchange which exports of processed beef could earn. Mrs. Gandhi, however, remains equivocal on the issue. 'Indian cows, she says, 'whether they are sacred or not, are absolutely necessary for the existence of the nation... Can you imagine me giving orders to destroy one of our most precious gifts?'[68] Although she cites the role of cows as producers of milk and dung and as beasts of burden, it is a well-known fact that the vast majority of Indian cows are too starved to perform any of these functions and are no more than an unproductive and destructive burden on the countryside.

The Congress Party, for all its secular professions, has remained a Hindu-dominated body. In practice, though not in law, Muslims and other minorities continue to suffer from widespread discrimination in education and employment, and when there are communal riots the police generally favour the majority community. Faced by a marked revival of Muslim communal parties and the prospect of losing crucial Muslim votes, Mrs. Gandhi has recently been making more energetic efforts to rectify her party's neglect of the Muslim community and of the Urdu language.

Questions of political ideology find Indira Gandhi's thought at its weakest. Socialism is a word she uses often, along with other slogans such as Democracy, Secularism and Non-Alignment. But she has yet to supply a coherent definition of the theoretical and practical content of her socialism. 'I don't think my socialism is of a very dogmatic kind,' she has told the author. 'I have never thought that we should nationalise everything or do many of the things that go with the ... official view of socialism. But I have always felt very strongly about equality ... economically and also socially, especially because here one could not help but be aware of all the evils of the caste system and social hierarchy.' Asked to clarify whether her socialism was closer to Marxism or to the Social Democracy of the Welfare State, she replied:

'I would not put a label on it at all. I do not like labels. I think that Marxism is now not relevant to present society. I think it played a role, a very important role, at a stage in world history, and I have no doubt it has influenced everybody. Even the capitalist countries have been influenced by it. But now, except for the basic thing about the working class ... having their rights, I don't think it is very relevant today. As for the other kind, it isn't just a question of welfare. A Welfare State also here seems to denote that the Government is doing things for the people. I believe in a sort of deeper kind of involvement of the people, so that they have a voice in it—they are not just a figure or a statistic. I feel that this is threatened...by the present industrialised society ... People today are conscious of their needs. I think that that is a very big advance in itself. Now the logical second step is:... what does an individual do about that? And once he realises that he himself is a part of the people, that he is also responsible, I think that may be the real turning point ... The revolution of expectations is here today. But he cannot get those things unless he takes part of the responsibility, unless he feels that when he is asking for something, he also has to give something.'[69]

As a political theory, Mrs. Gandhi's socialism raises more questions than it answers. How, for instance, can the Congress party, controlled as it is by corrupt factions representing the country's dominant élite be expected to adhere to egalitarian policies and secure the participation of the masses in their implementation? Mrs. Gandhi's answer is optimistic but unconvincing. 'Congress,' she told the author, 'has always been more than a political party, and I do not think we will ever be able to confine it in a very narrow way. One can only try and keep people together on a broad path and broad, general agreement with our policies. There is no doubt that some of them are touched by our implementation of policies and, well, being human beings, they will probably resent it. This is what has happened. This has prevented the Congress from implementing all their resolutions passed with great enthusiasm earlier. But I think that a greater realisation is spreading today that some of these things are essential, even if they hurt, ... in order to save everybody from a different and greater hurt perhaps later on. If there is a sort of violent revolution, for instance, all these people would certainly be wiped out.' She adds: 'I am not advocating a violent revolution. But as I see things, if the people feel that this method is too slow for them and it is not solving things, then what can they do? There are not many choices.'[70]

The experience of recent years does not justify Mrs. Gandhi's confidence in the wisdom of the Congress élite. The party leadership, many of whom are rich landlords and property-owners and receive vast funds from the business community, have not seen fit to make egalitarian concessions today in order to avert a revolution tomorrow. Government programmes with an ostensibly socialistic aim have been grossly exploited and perverted to serve the interests of the élite groups to whom their implementation is entrusted. Mrs. Gandhi herself does not deny this. 'This is an old problem,' she argues, 'starting from the Bible, if not earlier—"To him that hath, more shall be given"! This happens in any programme. Suppose we have a programme for Scheduled Castes and Scheduled Tribes. We find that those who are better off within that very narrow class ... take more advantage ... Because to take advantage of any scheme you have to have a certain initiative, and usually those who are more backward have less initiative. So this does happen, and I am afraid it will continue to happen.'[71]

When the author pointed out that the Green Revolution, far from narrowing disparities, had widened the gap between the rich and the poor in the countryside, she replied frankly: 'I don't think we could have expected anything else, because the urgent need was for grain, and so we had to help those people who could provide it immediately. And the same thing happened in industry. We had to have more Indian industries. The only people who could provide them were the Indian industrialists. We didn't really want to make them richer but in the balance we felt that it was better to have Indian industry, and so they were helped, and even today they are helped. Therefore, we have to balance between various things.'[72]

Mrs. Gandhi is aware that during the last twenty-seven years of Independence the balance has been weighted heavily in favour of the ruling élite. She has admitted in public that the implementation of Plan programmes is 'slanted' and that their benefits are not reaching the poor.[73] She has also conceded that the Congress Party leaves much to be desired. Interviewed in September 1973, she said: 'Violent radicalism can be prevented only by convincing the people through our actions that we are removing glaring economic and social injustice and deprivation... I am afraid our performance is disappointing. The party continues to function in a rather flabby way. It devotes too much attention to elections at the cost of solid fieldwork which alone builds the party's base. It lacks the apparatus which could enable it to do systematic work amongst young and rural people, industrial labour and other workers, women and the intelligentsia.'[74]

Mrs. Gandhi, however, has yet to formulate any viable plan for bridging the alarming hiatus between slogans and performance. She has not so far been receptive to suggestions that the Congress needs to be purged or further polarised. In April 1973, when tackled on this point by the editor of *Blitz*, a Left-wing weekly which had backed her during the Congress split, she said: 'There are two kinds of politics. There can be politics of polarisation or there can be the politics of trying to go together. Both have their advantages and disadvantages. But I think that extreme polarisation has greater disadvantages in a society like ours.'[75]

Explaining her emphasis on gradualism, she says: 'In a country as large as ours, where pluralism is a basic fact of life, a political party has to be not only concerned with ideology but also with effective methods of harmonising smaller and larger loyalties. Therefore, a national party in a country like India has an additional reason to aim at carrying with it as large a number of people as possible in every region. Great ideological purity can perhaps be maintained by excommunicating everyone who differs from you even on the smallest details.'[76] Elsewhere she has said: 'A number of younger and more dynamic people have come in (to politics), but it is not possible just to have a complete change or to push aside people who have worked for freedom and for the country, though they may not be young or committed. So one has to achieve a balance somehow between the two.'[77]

Her constant emphasis on 'balancing' conflicting groups and classes owes more to her political pragmatism and to the traditional Congress tactics of 'broadbottom' government than to any theory of socialism, however gradual or moderate. The most obvious flaw in such a strategy is that it seeks to reconcile the irreconcilable; and in trying to keep everyone happy, it risks satisfying no one. A leading political commentator pointed out in December 1972: 'On many occasions, Mrs. Gandhi herself has talked of identifying the party with the aspirations of the masses but, at the same time, assured the privileged groups that the Congress is their best bet. This Gandhian prescription of co-existence had some point before the 1971 elections: the party could not afford to alienate altogether an influential segment of society. But in today's circumstances, such wooliness only aggravates the danger of the party falling between two stools.'[78]

Though the Congress has been making strenuous efforts to woo the country's small but influential industrial working class and to establish its hegemony over the trade union movement, Mrs. Gandhi has made it clear that her brand of socialism does not envisage a leading role for the urban working class. Strikes and wage demands are frowned upon, and the emphasis is on industrial peace and increased productivity. In May 1971 Indira Gandhi admonished a Conference of Trade Union Organisations: 'In a country where there are millions of unemployed and underemployed, what is needed is a fair distribution of opportunities for gainful employment. In this sense, the employed, particularly in the organised sector, who enjoy a measure of social security, should recognise that in our country to be employed is in itself a privilege. Hence they should not seek unilateral gains for themselves, but have some compassion for those who are willing to work, yet are not able to do so because of the comparatively low rate of capital formation in our country.'[79]

As a general proposition, industrial discipline is unexceptionable in an agricultural country, the bulk of whose poor are small and landless peasants. But it is hardly consistent with socialism for a government to deny wage increases to the working class, while patronising rich farmers, allowing prices to soar and turning a blind eye to massive black-market profiteering.

Although her government has nationalised banking, general insurance and coal mines, Mrs. Gandhi is by no means hostile to private industry. She has often stated her commitment to a mixed economy in which private and public enterprise will co-exist. While attempting to curb the expansion of large business houses, her government has done much to promote the interests of smaller industrialists and businessmen and of the urban petty bourgeoisie in general. In rural areas, Mrs. Gandhi has attempted to balance her government's massive assistance to the rich farmers with some ameliorative schemes for marginal farmers and landless labourers. But in the absence of any agricultural income-tax or implementation of land reforms, her Government's agricultural policies have strengthened the dominance of the kulak class in the countryside.

Mrs. Gandhi's international perspective is based on the same nationalistic anti-imperialism that inspired Nehru's non-alignment. In December 1973, the General Secretary of the C.P.I., her electoral ally, conceded that she held anti-imperialist views, though pointing out that she 'was not a committed Leftist' but a centrist in domestic politics.[80] Mrs. Gandhi often harps on the need for self-reliance and for resistance to foreign economic and political encroachment. Nevertheless, self-sufficiency, even in foodgrains, remains a distant objective, and the Indian economy remains dependent on extensive foreign investment, imports and credits. Mrs. Gandhi herself is entirely pragmatic about foreign aid and the compromises it involves, justifying it as a temporary expedient or as 'aid to end aid.' In recent years, serious internal failures and shortfalls have been making the country increasingly dependent on foreign governmental assistance, especially from Soviet Russia, and on private collaboration with Western corporations.

Indira Gandhi is fond of justifying her government's socialistic legislation with arguments that are closer to Mahatma Gandhi and his theories of class collaboration than to socialism. Speaking of land reforms and a ceiling on ownership of urban property, she told an Indian journalist in August 1972: 'These measures are aimed at reducing disparities. If we do not go ahead with them, the poor will rise in revolt. And I am violently against a violent revolution.' Referring to the abolition of princely privileges, she told the same interviewer: 'it was in their (the princes') own interest ... they had never been given a chance to work and show their mettle ... Because they led abnormal lives, they did not develop as normal people. They lacked self-confidence ... As individuals, they will be better. Their talents and their inner resources will be fully used.

They don't have to depend on what their fathers left them.'[81] Her choice of words, was more appropriate to a school-mistress chastising her pupils than to a socialist Prime Minister abolishing feudalism.

Since the successful conclusion of her struggle with the Syndicate, there has been a marked cooling off in the radicalism of Indira Gandhi's public statements. The slogan of *Garibi Hatao* (Remove Poverty), which was canvassed so vociferously in the 1971 general election and did much to raise mass expectations, has proved an embarrassment in recent years, and Mrs. Gandhi has been trying to moderate its effects. In September 1971, when a Congress M.P. wrote to her implying that there had been some ideological back-sliding in her public statements, she replied firmly: '...in our country wishful thinking and the desire for some immediate and magical cure is so prevalent that it is most essential to make people face the realities of life.'[82] In April 1973, she told *Blitz*: 'If anybody tries to say that poverty can go in my lifetime or during my tenure as Prime Minister, it just cannot. It is something which has very deep roots.'[83]

Despite her obvious pragmatism, Indira Gandhi has often been accused by the Right-wing Opposition of being a secret communist, or at any rate a 'fellow-traveller.' Her alignment with the pro-Moscow C.P.I., and with the Soviet Union at the international level, is cited as evidence for this view. The suggestion is more revealing of the weakness of Indian communism than it is of Mrs. Gandhi's ideological leanings. The Kremlin has certainly shown no desire to encourage revolution in India, and when Brezhnev visited Delhi in December 1973 he is believed to have advised the C.P.I. to moderate its line. The C.P.I. itself, though critical of Congress policies, has long ago lost its revolutionary ardour and is committed to a moderate programme of parliamentary socialism and to 'responsive cooperation' with the Congress.

Mrs. Gandhi herself has stated repeatedly that she is no communist and that her mild attempts at reform are designed to pre-empt a red revolution. 'I dislike the word "contain",' she says, 'but if only people paused to think, I am containing communism in India. The Government cannot afford to move even the slightest bit to the Right, because this will in no time begin a move on the part of the communists to take over, interpreting my actions as anti-people. I am no communist,... but I do believe in trying to achieve a socialistic pattern of society in India.'[84]

For the C.P.I.(M), which is committed to the parliamentary path but continues to oppose the Congress, Mrs. Gandhi has no sympathy. Of the C.P.I.(M.L.),* she says: 'These Naxalites, Guevarists or anarchists have much misdirected idealism but no basic framework to effect social

*The Communist Party of India (Marxist-Leninist), an abortive attempt to creat an insurrectionary and extra-parliamentary mass movement.

transformation. However heroic their individual acts mights appear to them, they cannot succeed.'[85] In the last few years, she has not hesitated to authorise massive governmental repression against the C.P.I.(M) and the Naxalites, especially in West Bengal. All the same, she is not a fanatical anti-communist and concedes that the Indian communists have a role to play within the parliamentary system. In reply to a suggestion that she is playing into the hands of the Communists, she has said:

'I am not a communist. What is more, I don't believe in communism. Playing into their hands—what does it mean? That I sometimes think they are right? What of it? These people exist, don't they? They are hundreds of millions. And even if we were to wipe out all the communists physically, do you think that communism would cease to exist? When you live in great poverty, you are tempted to believe that communism is the ideal short-cut to a better world. I once met Dr. Ho Chi Minh. He was, above, all, an exacerbated nationalist. I even got the impression that communism was secondary for him.'[86]

However well-intentioned, Indira Gandhi's brand of socialism is a mixture of vague populism and pragmatism which can scarcely be called a political ideology. In its radical aspects, it is based on an emotional and maternalistic sympathy for the under-dog which has yet to be allied to a viable theory of social change. Mrs. Gandhi has described rationalism as her greatest fault. 'For an Indian,' she has said, 'that is a fault. It is a leftover from my education in Switzerland.'[87] Others might question her assessment of herself and suggest that her greatest weakness is her attempt to rationalise the inconsistencies and contradictions inherent in the theory and practice of her socialistic pattern.

Contradictions, however, do not appear to worry her, and it is unlikely that she loses much sleep trying to resolve them. 'Of course there are contradictions,' she says. 'But tell me—is there any party in the world which has no contradictions? The human being is complex. No two human beings think exactly alike.' It is a line of argument which goes down well in a highly individualistic and pluralistic society where the most glaring contrasts and contradictions are absorbed and assimilated. To the extent that Indira Gandhi's thought reflects such contradictions, it makes her more representative of her people than Nehru ever was. Whether a leader ought to be quite so representative is open to question.

*          *          *

Hiren Mukherjee, a veteran Communist parliamentarian, has commented on Indira Gandhi's performance in Parliament:

'It is remarkable how she has "grown" as she felt more and more secure of her position. She does not throw out ideas like her father did almost everytime he spoke. She does not sparkle, except in rare patches. She does not quite know what to do or say when sudden gusts of emotion sweep or ... of querulousness sieze the House. She is, generally, a great deal better in Committee than in a seething House. And yet there have been occasions when, suddenly rising to the crest ... of the wave of words, she has silenced a master of eloquence like Atal Bihari Vajpayee, or floored a practised veteran of debate like Frank Anthony.'

The same source, however, laments Mrs. Gandhi's tendency to neglect her duties as Leader of the House. 'Quite often,' he complains, 'it is learnt that the Prime Minister was in Parliament House but otherwise busy when her presence in the Chamber was needed... This is why a feeling has grown that she perhaps prefers to talk to and do business with individuals in her office and shies away from confronting the House...'[89] Parliament, of course, has never been one of Mrs. Gandhi's favourite forums; and it is not surprising that, with her massive majority in the House, she considers her attendance there a dreary and tiresome formality.

In the sphere of government itself, opinions differ sharply as to her effectiveness and capability as an administrator. In June 1966, addressing the Administrative Staff College of India, Indira Gandhi herself somewhat immodestly assured her audience:

'...I am an expert at dealing with people. This is something I think I was either born with or I learnt from my very childhood. I had the good fortune of being part of a household where we used to meet a very varied crowd. Even at the height of the independence movement, we had scientists, writers, artists from all over the world staying with us ... in this manner I developed what may be called a "feel" of the people and I find that this intuition helps me with the ordinary people.'[90]

She certainly has a shrewder instinct than her father for sizing up people. She has fewer illusions and is better able to distinguish genuine loyalty from self-interested sychophancy. The integrity and efficiency of her personal staff and most of her Secretariat are unique in the prevailing atmosphere of administrative slackness, intrigue and corruption. Outside her immediate staff, however, her choice of personnel has been less fortunate. Several of her Cabinet colleagues and State lieutenants are people whose public reputation is far from good. Nehru, too, was surrounded by such men. But unlike her father, Indira Gandhi is not blind to their failings; and if she tolerates them, it is because they are politically convenient, not because she has failed to take their measure.

Those who have worked directly under her have found her an exacting but considerate mistress. While she expects a high standard of efficiency from her subordinates, she is sympathetic to their problems, and there is always the personal touch—a throat pastille for a coughing security officer, an expression of concern for a clerk whose wife or child is ailing. Thoughtful and spontaneous gestures such as these have endeared her to her personal staff, who are fiercely devoted to her. She in turn, can be relied upon to protect them and look after their interests.

Nandini Satpathy has remarked enthusiastically: 'She's simply wonderful to work with ... She's very good in personal relations, but she can become irritable or impatient when she finds you don't understand things quickly ... She says half a sentence like "He didn't come," and expects you to remember this is someone she last mentioned days back.'[91] Though she can be irritable, she does not lose her temper as often or violently as her father did when he came across inefficiency or indiscipline. 'He used to lose his temper very badly and then cool down very quickly,' Usha Bhagat explains. 'She never gets as angry, but her anger lasts longer.'[92] Amid the petty intrigue and back-biting that is as typical of present-day Delhi as it was of the Mughal court, Indira Gandhi tries, as far as possible, to be fair and impartial. 'Unlike her more emotional father, she is not easily influenced for or against people,' T.S. Swaminathan* observes. 'She always checks and counter-checks criticism of people before she believes it.'[93]

During the early years of her Prime Ministership, Indira Gandhi was often accused of being dependent on her advisers. Kamaraj, Asoka Mehta, Dinesh Singh, D.P. Mishra and P.N. Haksar were each in turn identified as the power behind the throne. Such ideas arose more from Indian pre-conceptions about female dependence than from a perceptive appraisal of Mrs. Gandhi's personality. In recent years, she has shown conclusively that she is nobody's puppet and that no adviser, however influential, is indispensable. While she takes advice from those whose judgement she trusts, ultimately she keeps her own counsel and her decisions are very much her own. Her critics now contend that she is too secretive, suspicious and intolerant with her colleagues. 'There is no basic honesty in her dealings with people,' Mrs. Tarkeshwari Sinha, a veteran opponent, has asserted. 'She uses one man to demolish another, then demolishes him.'[94]

In reply to such accusations Mrs. Gandhi protests: 'I am not at all distrustful of colleagues. On the contrary, I would say I am far more trustful than most other people. Neither am I secretive. There is absolutely nothing that I have kept to myself.'[95] While her denial may be exaggerated,

*Formerly Cabinet Secretary to the Union Government, now Chief Election Commissioner.

it must be said in her defence that most of the politicians with whom she has had to deal are hardly the sort to inspire excessive trust or candour.

Another common criticism is that she is slow to make up her mind and that vital measures are delayed as a result. It is true that her approach has always been cautious and that she avoids hasty decisions. 'Those who know her well,' says Marie Seton, 'know there can be a period of passivity between Indira Gandhi's reception of a suggestion and her visible response to an idea. It is as if nothing is going to happen. There simply comes a void of seeming indifference and no decision one way or another. She leaves things alone, as if to let them simmer at the back of her mind. She can equally well shelve decisions about people, but it does not mean that she has discarded them or their problems. The time of decision has simply not ripened.'[96]

Routine official business is handled with greater dispatch by the Prime Minister's Secretariat than by any other department of government. On larger political issues, too, Mrs. Gandhi has demonstrated that once she is convinced of the merits of a particular course, she acts promptly and decisively. On the other hand, the volume of governmental business that has been accumulating within the jurisdiction of the Prime Minister's Secretriat has reached such proportions that no single individual or department can hope to deal quickly and coherently with it, and delays are inevitable.

The Administrative Reforms Commission set up by the Government had recommended that 'the Prime Minister should not ordinarily be in charge of a Ministry,' but should concentrate on the task of co-ordination and general supervision.[97] Mrs. Gandhi, nonetheless, retains the portfolios of Information and Broadcasting, Atomic Energy and Space and is Chairman of the Planning Commission, though she has relinquished the important Home portfolio to Uma Shankar Dikshit, an old and trusted follower. Hers is also the deciding voice in External Affairs, Defence and economic affairs. The result of this concentration of authority is that files on relatively trivial matters shuttle back and forth between a series of officials and departments, all equally reluctant to take responsibility for a decision, until the Prime Minister's Secretariat eventually steps in to resolve the stalemate.

Although hers is the supreme voice in all government decisions and appointments, Mrs. Gandhi denies that she is as powerful as people imagine. 'The Prime Minister really has no power at all,' she says, 'because you are completely bound by the rules, the regulations, Parliament and all these things. I cannot appoint just anybody I like ... Some time ago there was a suggestion that we should have the Presidential system and you would then have more power. But it really does not work that way. When you are... forming the Cabinet, you have a certain amount of choice, but otherwise you have to pay attention to regions, to castes, to various things like that. You are bound by that whether you have the power or not. Possibly a person not conscious of such things might put in his own people... But as I am made, I just cannot do it. I have to work in a certain way, even if I find it is slower.'98

Although political pluralism, regionalism and casteism necessarily set limits on the power of any Indian ruler, political analysts have diagnosed a major change in the Central power structure since the 1971 general election, involving a decline in the independence and initiative of individual ministers and a concentration of decision-making powers in the Prime Minister and her Secretariat. This, of course, is no new phenomenon. Cabinet government in India has never meant an even division of power and responsibility between the various ministries of the Central Government. Nehru, in his time, was often criticised for attempting to run the Government as a one-man show. In recent years, this tendency has revived in proportion to the Prime Minister's soaring political fortunes in the country at large since the Congress split.

Since the 1971 election, instead of the Prime Minister deriving her authority from the parliamentary party, the party manifestly derives its authority from her. Lest anyone should forget this, Mrs. Gandhi stands armed with the weapon of dissolution, which she has already used effectively at the Centre and in several States. Cabinet ministers hold their positions primarily because they enjoy the Prime Minister's confidence, rather than by virtue of their position in the party. The system has been characterised as a quasi-presidential form of government without the usual checks and balances of that system—a separation of powers between Executive and Legislature and fixed election dates.

Paradoxically, though, the Prime Minister's pre-eminence, instead of making it easier for her to co-ordinate government policies and supervise their implementation, has tended to hamper efficient team-work in the absence of any clear demarcation or delegation of authority. An over-concentration of power in some spheres has left a vacuum in others. Individual ministers lack initiative, are reluctant to take responsibility even for minor decisions, and are often by-passed by civil servants in their own departments who have direct access to the Prime Minister's Secretariat. The result has been to encourage a good deal of ministerial confusion, insecurity and paralysis, seriously reducing the coherence and effectiveness of the Government as a whole and increasing the power of the professional bureaucracy.

Although she has abolished the special privileges of the élite administrative cadre inherited from the British Raj, Mrs. Gandhi is by no means critical of the bureaucracy as a whole. 'The younger elements coming into our civil services,' she has said, 'are able, efficient, honest and dedicated.'99 Asked how a corrupt and unmotivated bureaucracy with a weakness for intrigue could be expected to implement her socialistic policies, she replied optimistically: 'On the whole, they have a desire to do a good job, and that is something which helps in implementation.'100 Though she has often stated that the present administrative system is obsolete and stressed the need for a 'committed' bureaucracy, nothing has yet been done to reorganise the bureaucracy on more efficient or egalitarian lines. Clearly, the institution of a committed bureaucracy will have to await the advent of a more committed political leadership.

*      *      *

In the Congress Party, as in the Government, Indira Gandhi's supremacy, in its outward manifestations, is greater than Nehru's. The Congress President since the split has been her nominee and obediently transmits her instructions to the party. Hers is the deciding voice in appointments to all party offices, in the composition of the Congress Working Committee and other party organs and in the selection of Congress candidates for elections. She is the supreme arbiter in all inner-party disputes, whether factional or ideological.

Unlike Nehru's authority, Mrs. Gandhi's is not confined to the Central level but extends to the States as well. In the aftermath of the 1971 general election, she was able to dissolve the existing Congress Committees in several States, replacing them with centrally nominated ad hoc committees, and to induce four well-entrenched Congress Chief Ministers—those of Rajasthan, Andhra, Madhya Pradesh and Assam—to stand down in favour of her own nominees. The latter, lacking a strong political base of their own in their respective states, could be relied upon to accept close Central supervision. They owed their positions, not to the support of the Congress Legislature Parties in their States—this was taken for granted—but to the Prime Minister's choice. In the case of Madhya Pradesh, for instance, the State Legislature Party was summoned to Delhi to meet at Mrs. Gandhi's residence and ratify her selection of P.C. Sethi, a Central Cabinet Minister, as its new leader.

This process of centralisation reached its culmination after the February 1972 elections to eighteen State legislatures. In this 'khaki' election, held soon after the Pakistan war, the Congress swept to power with huge majorities in fourteen States, including, astonishingly, the C.P.I.(M) stronghold of West Bengal. The lists of Congress candidates for the elections had been scrutinised and extensively revised by the Prime Minister and the Central High Command. The usual local issues played a minor role in the elections, and the Congress victory was widely interpreted as a vote for Indira Gandhi and her role in the creation of Bangladesh. Since then, all Congress Chief Ministers have been selected by the

Prime Minister and later elected 'unanimously' by the State Congress Legislature Parties. In the case of Abdul Ghafoor, the present Chief Minister of Bihar, even the formality of ratification by the Legislature Party was overlooked. Following his selection by Mrs. Gandhi, he flew to the State capital, drove straight to the Governor's residence and was invited to form a government. It was only after this that someone remembered that he had not yet been formally elected leader of the Congress Legislature Party.

It is paradoxical that the very factors which vest such unprecedented authority in the Prime Minister bar her from exercising it effectively. The pre-split conflict between the governmental and organisational wings of the Congress has been terminated at the cost of the virtual demise of the party organisation. The Congress organisation today is little more than an election machine. Its functions are to collect funds, distribute party tickets for legislative elections and canvass for the party's candidates. Membership of party committees and offices is valued only in so far as it provides access to the legislatures and ultimately to ministerial office and patronage. In between elections, the organisation virtually ceases to exist, and in many districts its offices literally close down. There is no cadre of trained, full-time workers, and most of the party's workers are hired at election time.

In December 1972 it was claimed that Congress primary membership had reached a record figure of over ten millions; but it was admitted unofficially by the leadership itself that 60 per cent of this number were bogus members enrolled by corrupt bosses who wished to manipulate the party's organisational elections. In the absence of a genuine primary base, the party is inevitably a house of cards, controlled at every level by self-seeking cliques who represent fictitious members and who are accountable to none but themselves and the Central High Command.

This anomalous situation has concentrated unparalleled power in the Congress High Command, while drastically reducing the latter's ability to see that its directives receive more than lip-service. Disciplined and effective party functioning requires the existence of a stable leadership structure, extending from the Central to the local level and commanding the confidence and obedience of the rank and file. A strong chain of command, however, is obviously impossible in a situation where provincial and local leadership is patently unrepresentative and unstable. In these circumstances, authority reverts to the Central leadership; but the latter finds itself functioning in an organisational vacuum.

The result of this strange state of affairs is that Indira Gandhi's supremacy in the party is more absolute than her father's at a time when party discipline is weaker and party organisation more atomised than ever before. All sections of the Congress profess loyalty to the Prime Minister and her word, ostensibly, is law; but although she has the appearance of absolute power, she lacks its substance. While all important decisions are taken by her, she is unable to see that they are enforced.

This curious paradox is, perhaps, best illustrated by the series of ministerial crises during the last two years in Congress-majority States. While the choice of Chief Ministers has been left to Mrs. Gandhi, she has been powerless to ensure that her nominees enjoy security of tenure or that they are allowed to function effectively. Since the 1972 elections, six Chief Ministers selected by her have been rejected by inner-party revolts, and efforts continue to bring down the rest. The pattern has become familiar to the point of being farcical. The warring Congress factions in a particular State formally request the Prime Minister to choose a Chief Minister for them. The choice once made is not directly opposed; but disgruntled factions work behind the scenes to undermine and discredit the Ministry thus formed. In time, the Chief Minister is toppled by a revolt within the Congress Legislature Party, and the Prime Minister is again approached to make a fresh choice. In July 1973, when five Madhya Pradesh ministers resigned in a bid to oust Chief Minister Sethi, her protegé, Mrs. Gandhi snapped irritably: 'I am not going to tolerate this situation any more.'[101] Nevertheless, during the last year she has had to stretch her capacity for tolerating such indiscipline.

Factional maneouvres have been feeding on growing popular disillusionment with Congress rule. In 1972 Congress dissidents in Assam and Andhra linked their factional struggles with violent popular agitations against the Government. Again, in the early months of 1974, the mass uprising which shook the State of Gujerat was openly patronised by the Chief Minister's rivals in the party; and when Mrs. Gandhi resisted the demand for a change of leadership, the dissidents resigned en masse from the State Assembly, compelling her to dismiss the Chief Minister and dissolve the legislature.

Factional in-fighting of these proportions has made a mockery not only of the Prime Minister's authority, but of the entire parliamentary system. When the Congress took power in the States in 1972, its election manifesto had promised stable Ministries which would co-operate closely with the Centre. But large Congress majorities in the legislatures have provided no guarantee of stable government. On the contrary, Congress governments in the States have proved as unstable as the non-Congress coalitions which took office after the 1967 elections. The wheel appears to have turned full circle.

The political fragmentation which has been eroding Congress power in the States has not yet travelled to the Centre. But if the present trend continues, there is a distinct possibility of Indira Gandhi being confronted, as in 1969, with a direct challenge to her leadership. Already there are some who blame the Prime Minister's reluctance to delegate power and responsibility for the political chaos that surrounds her. 'Her intuitive responses to a situation are excellent,' said Chandrasekhar, the Young Turk leader, in June 1973. 'It is when she has to choose a team to work with that she goes wrong, possibly because of a feeling of insecurity since her childhood or because she is a woman. She is surrounded by sychophants and flatterers, but not by real supporters who can share power... She is all-powerful in the party because there is no one to rival her. But if there is ever an effective challenge to her power, there will be no one to defend her, because she does not have friends, only sychophants.'[102]

Though Indira Gandhi is aware of the ills of the Congress and of the Indian political system in general, she does not appear to have read the signs as seriously as might have been expected. In November 1972, she suggested humorously that factious Congressmen might benefit from a term in prison, citing the comradeship inspired by gaol-going during the nationalist movement.[103] Addressing the National Students' Union in July 1973, she dismissed leadership struggles in the States as 'small illnesses in a big country.'[104]

In view of the emphasis she had given during the Congress split to the evils of bossism and bogus membership, there were many who expected Mrs. Gandhi to initiate a major re-organisation of the Congress; but no such attempt has materialised. 'I saw Mrs. Gandhi after the 1971 elections,' says Chandrasekhar, 'and suggested that the party organisation could be activised by giving M.P.s and A.I.C.C. members some specific task or responsibility to make them participate in the implementation of policies. There was no response... The trouble is that ministers don't want to share their power and to have anyone else interfering in their spheres to root out corruption.'[105]

Mrs. Gandhi's re-constitution of Provincial Congress Committees in 1971 and 1972 was initially interpreted as an attempt to purge the party of undesirable elements and to bring in new blood. But the changes proved marginal and the existing factional balance was not seriously disturbed. Again, when Congress candidates for the 1972 elections were being screened, the centralisation of the selection procedure raised hopes that more committed elements would be included. What emerged, however, was not materially different from the lists prepared by the undivided Congress in 1967: the proportion of rich farmers and landlords was unaltered, caste considerations were equally predominant and the promised large increase in the percentage of youth and women failed to materialise.

When Mrs. Gandhi was addressing the Congress Parliamentary Party in December 1972, a member interrupted her to demand: 'How can this party function when there are no genuine workers, but only bogus members?' In her reply she conceded that bogus membership was wide-spread and that drastic changes were required.[106] At the Congress plenary session later that month, she elaborated on this point and asserted that she would not be sorry to see a fall in the party's membership if thereby the organisation could be spring-cleaned and reactivated with trained cadres.[107] But although two years have passed, action on these lines has yet to be taken.

In the absence of any major structural change in the Congress, Indira Gandhi has confined her role as a party leader to the task of maintaining the balance between various factions and keeping them together under her leadership. Every so often, when the clash between rival groups in a State reaches dangerous proportions, she intervenes, knocks their heads together and punishes both sides by appointing a third party chosen by her to the office in dispute. Her position as a neutral referee requires that she herself must remain above faction and avoid close ties with any particular group at the Centre or in the States; and she has adhered by and large to this principle.

Though elections to the Executive of the Congress Parliamentary Party are keenly contested, Mrs. Gandhi has frowned upon attempts to link her name with particular candidates and has refused to allow an official list to be issued on her behalf. In the immediate aftermath of the split, she was closely connected with the Congress Forum for Socialist Action, a grouping of Young Turks and Congress Leftists. After the 1971 elections, however, she was careful to put a safe distance between herself and the Forum, and in September 1972 she refused to inaugurate its proposed national convention. When rivalry between the Socialist Forum and the Nehru Study Forum, a conservative, kulak lobby, erupted in public abuse and recrimination, she refused to take sides and made it known that she was opposed to the continued existence of either forum. In deference to her wishes, both groups were wound up, though the factions they represented continue to operate informally.

Indira Gandhi's flexibility has enabled her to preserve an impartial image, while keeping her options open and allowing her room for mane-ouvre. In December 1972, when elections for the Congress organisation were held for the first time since the split, some political observers pre-dicted an attempt by dissident elements to challenge the Prime Minister's authority by capturing strategic positions in the party; but Mrs. Gandhi shrewdly side-stepped the assault. To avoid charges of stifling party democracy, she allowed the elections to proceed unhindered. By the time they reached their final stages, massive rigging, corruption, intimida-tion and manipulation of bogus votes by the rival factions had reduced the electoral process to a farce, and a head-on collision between the competing groups threatened to shatter party unity. At the last moment, amid appeals from all sides to intervene and redress the balance, the Prime Minister stepped in and imposed a choice by consensus for most of the party's elective offices. Her intervention more or less restored the status quo ante, and the composition of the party leadership remained unaltered; if anything, the hold of the dominant groups was strengthened.

'There has never been as little discussion or criticism within the party as there is today,' Chandrasekhar complained to the author in June 1973.[108] Nevertheless, Chandrasekhar, Krishna Kant, another Young Turk leader, and some other outspoken Congressmen have not hesitated to castigate the leadership in various party forums. Except at the Gandhinagar A.I.C.C. session in October 1972, when Krishna Kant's attacks provoked her into losing her temper, Mrs. Gandhi's reaction to such criticism has been tactful and restrained. She prefers to ignore critics in the party, rather than engage in open controversy with them. When Krishna Kant stood for election to the A.I.C.C. in December 1972, she did not make serious efforts to block his election, and he won with the highest number of votes from the Congress Parliamentary Party. At the Simla A.I.C.C. session early in 1972, Chandrasekhar succeeded in forcing his way into the important Central Election Committee, despite the opposition of the High Command to his election. When he announced his intention of standing for election to the Working Committee in December 1972, Mrs. Gandhi wisely had him included in the agreed official list to avoid a contest in which he might emerge as a nucleus for dissent. Her mature and tactful handling of intelligent and popular critics within the party has so far prevented the rise of any organised opposition to her leadership.

*        *        *

'Wherever I go, I am asked when my promises will be fulfilled,' Mrs. Gandhi lamented in May 1972.[109] Such queries have become increasingly persistent and widespread in the course of the last two years. While her skilled political management has enabled her to keep on top of the Congress Party, the weakness of the party organisation, its conservative composition and factional in-fighting has paralysed the implementation of its programmes. Mrs. Gandhi, meanwhile, continues to discourage ideological polarisation in the party, and her approach to policy issues is as pragmatic and elastic as her handling of organisational and factional disputes.

Though the Congress had solemnly promised radical land reforms and substantial assistance to the landless in its 1972 election manifesto, hardly had the elections been won when most of the Congress Chief Ministers began to plead 'practical difficulties' in implementation. At a conference of Congress leaders in May 1972, Mrs. Gandhi, to the dismay of the Left, called for an end to 'competitive radicalism', expressed sympathy for the 'tremendous difficulties' of the Chief Ministers and ruled out any major lowering of land ceilings.[110] The final package of land reforms which emerged in July 1972 proved a considerably watered down version of the recommendations of the Central Land Reforms Committee; and even this marginal reform has been stalled in implementation. A report published in May 1973 by the Planning Commission's Task Force on Agrarian Relations stated frankly: 'With resolute and unambiguous political will, all other shortcomings and difficulties could have been overcome; in the absence of such will even minor obstacles become formidable road blocks in the path of Indian Land reform. Considering the character of the political power structure obtaining in the country, it was only natural that the required political will was not forthcoming.'[111] It has been estimated that all the land released by ceiling laws in the country so far adds up to a mere one per cent of the total cultivated area.

The Congress has been promising since Independence to establish a system of public distribution which would make essential items of mass consumption, especially food, available at fair prices. But all efforts to this end have floundered on the Government's inability to set up the necessary administrative machinery and the Congress Party's reluctance to injure the interests of the farming and trading classes which dominate it. Mrs. Gandhi's experiment in a State takeover of the wholesale trade in wheat during the severe drought of 1973 ended in ignominious failure. Extensive blackmarketing by farmers and traders and the unwillingness of the Congress to compel rich farmers to sell to Government at the fixed price undermined the take-over from the outset. In April 1974 the Government formally withdrew the scheme as part of its attempt to win back the support of rich farmers and traders.

In the sphere of industrial policy, too, the 1972 elections were soon followed by signs of increasing pragmatism. Despite its previous emphasis on the need to curb industrial monopolies, the Government's note on economic policy for the A.I.C.C. in October 1972 stressed the priority of economic growth over redistributive justice and the elimination of private monopolies. Since then, the Government, torn between its socialist slogans and its dependence on the business community for election funds, has followed a vacillatory and incoherent industrial policy, retaining a corrupt and cumbersome system of controls over private industry, while turning a blind eye to the most blatant black-market profiteering. The Congress strategy of 'Growth-plus-Social Justice'— the name by which this confused system goes—has failed conspicuously to achieve either of its targets.

One of the most glaring inconsistencies of Congress rule has been the ostentatious living, often at public expense, of ministers and Congress leaders; and this in times of acute economic hardship when the Government is busy proclaiming its determination to curb unproductive expenditure and conspicuous consumption. In June 1971, following press reports of a lavish wedding banquet held by a Maharashtra Congressman, Mrs. Gandhi wrote to the Maharashtra Chief Minister:

'It will not do for us to speak of socialism and permit such indefensible waste of resources. Often when I have accepted invitations to attend wedding receptions at colleagues' houses, I have felt uneasy and wanted to leave. I think we should all make it a rule to see that weddings in our own households eschew pomp and show and also persuade our party colleagues to err on the side of modesty. In no affluent country today are feasts so lavish as in ours. This is hardly a matter for rejoicing, for waste and ostentation are signs of lack of culture.'[112]

Such exhortations, unfortunately, have fallen by and large on deaf ears and have failed to lend any credibility to the Government's austerity drive. Mrs. Gandhi's own attempts to set a good example have sometimes had unfortunate results. In November 1973, soon after the international oil crisis hit India, the Prime Minister, amid much publicity, drove to her office in an elegant horse-drawn carriage with a liveried coachman borrowed from the President's Household. Crawling along behind the carriage, however, were two cars carrying security guards. It was estimated that the petrol consumed on the occasion was several times that normally used by the Prime Minister's car. As an economy measure the exercise bordered on the absurd and was ridiculed by the Opposition and the press. The large and unprecedented government expenditure on the elaborate security arrangements which surround Mrs. Gandhi on her political and election tours has also been severely criticised in Parliament.

The ideological compromises, surrenders and backsliding of the Congress leadership have inevitably provoked criticism within the party, especially from those who were Mrs. Gandhi's most ardent supporters during the split. At the Delhi A.I.C.C. session in June 1972, a senior Congressman frankly told the assembled delegates: 'You are not the type that can bring about socialism. Socialism could have been brought about by Gandhiji and presumably by Naxalites. But you live in air-conditioned rooms, shave yourselves with foreign blades; you draw Rs. 2,500 a month and live in luxury. If still you talk of socialism, go ahead and do it, but don't bluff us.'[113] Krishna Kant and Chandrasekhar, among others, have continued to attack the leadership for its various compromises, blaming 'the new tribe of manipulators and courtiers which has installed itself near the centre of power.'[114]

Though the criticism has been directed at policies rather than personalities, the target of attack, by implication, has been Indira Gandhi and her ideological pragmatism. The crisis of the Congress, however, is too deeply rooted in its structure and composition to be blamed upon any single individual. As a leading Indian journalist pointed out in June 1973:

'The party cannot do without a clearly defined hierarchy either at the Centre or in the States or a proper division of responsibility. It is too big a country to be run by a single person, however great his or her charisma, or by a small coterie. Its problems are too difficult and too complex to be resolved by a contrived image—of a party or a leader. The image of a strong leader has its uses in mobilising the people to cope with new challenges. But it can be sustained only by hard decisions and resolute action. It cannot but get blurred if it is used merely to arouse expectations which remain unfulfilled...'[115]

*          *          *

In August 1972, when asked to list India's main achievements since Independence, Indira Gandhi replied: 'I don't like to catalogue our achievements ... there is nothing tangible about such things. I would say our greatest achievement is to have survived as a free and democratic nation.'[116] The virtues of the Indian parliamentary system form a theme which recurs often enough in her statements, and she is fond of quoting Churchill's dictum that democracy is the worst form of government except all the others. 'The type of democracy which we have,' she explains, 'a sort of open society, ... although it creates certain problems and gives a lot of licence for all kinds of voices to be raised, strengthens unity...'[117]

Although Mrs. Gandhi has occasionally stretched the Constitution and democratic norms to serve party ends, she has on the whole functioned within the parliamentary framework. The Indian press, and especially those sections controlled by the Opposition, has been critical and even abusive about her. But while supporting suggestions that the newspaper industry should be separated from Big Business, she has consistently rejected proposals for nationalising the press. 'She believes in a free press, though she is not much influenced by it,' says B.G. Verghese. 'Press criticism may annoy her temporarily; but she soon cools down.'[118] Though the judiciary, too, has thwarted her on more than once occasion, she has never defied its verdict. She has resisted the temptation of packing the Supreme Court and has confined herself to appointing a Chief Justice of her own choice when the post fell vacant in 1973.

'The diversity of the Indian people is no problem,' Mrs. Gandhi has observed. 'In fact, it leads to overall unity. If uniformity is imposed people tend to revolt.'[119] She has learned to live with the pluralism of Indian society and with the constitutional forms of provincial autonomy.

Except in the case of the Telengana agitation, she has conceded popular demands for separate Statehood within the Indian Union. In 1971 she authorised the creation of four new States—Himachal in the north and Manipur, Meghalaya and Tripura in the north-east—and two autonomous Union Territories—Mizoram and Arunachal. In February 1974 she allowed the first free election since Independence to be held in the State of Nagaland and permitted a new party, which has close ties with the Naga underground, to take office. In Kashmir, too, Indian rule has been liberalised, and Mrs. Gandhi and Sheikh Abdullah appear to be moving towards an amicable settlement.

Despite her liberalism in such matters, the charge most often levelled at Indira Gandhi is that she is deliberately undermining the parliamentary system with the intention of establishing a dictatorship. In support of this charge, it is alleged that the electoral machinery is being blatantly manipulated and rigged by the Congress in collusion with the administration, that political corruption has reached unprecedented proportions, that police and military terror and repressive detention laws are being used to suppress popular agitations, and that the Prime Minister is concentrating all power in her own hands and deliberately fostering a cult of personality. Nehru, it is often said, would never have countenanced such a travesty of democracy.

Few political observers would deny that the Indian parliamentary system is rapidly disintegrating. The contradictions inherent in the application of the Westminster model to a semi-feudal country, have been compounded by the deepening economic and moral crisis of Indian society. But it would be facile to attribute this decline to the machinations of any individual, however powerful. Certainly, Indian democracy would fare no better, and probably worse, under any of Mrs. Gandhi's colleagues or rivals.

This is not to deny that the cult of personality exists. Indians have a tendency to deify their leaders, and Indira Gandhi, like Nehru and Gandhi before her, is worshipped and idolised. Wherever she goes, crowds of sychophants shower her with flattery and adulation. In December 1972, D.P. Dhar, the urbane Union Minister for Planning, went so far as to perform the *arti** before a larger-than-life portrait of Mrs. Gandhi while inaugurating a photograph exhibition on the Prime Minister. This is a rite usually reserved for Hindu gods and goddesses; but in rural India there are many who credit Indira Gandhi with magical powers, a fact to which she herself humorously alluded at a White House banquet in November 1971. 'In India,' she said, 'I do have the reputation of bringing the weather the people want. Usually, of course, it is rain . . . and even in the driest

*A form of worship which involves passing an oil-lamp round the image of a deity.

of the drought days, when I went somewhere it always rained, not enough to make any difference to anybody, but just two or three drops to say, "well, I was there".'[120]

A typical manifestation of the personality cult is the attempt to name places and institutions after the Prime Minister. Bombay's Alexandra Dock has been re-named Indira Dock, and a new canal systems in Haryana State has also been named after Mrs. Gandhi. Responsibility for the personality cult seems to lie with her followers and would-be courtiers, rather than with the Prime Minister herself. The proposals certainly do not emanate from her, and in several instances she has insisted on their being dropped.

According to one source, when the Women's Department of the Congress wanted to observe the Prime Minister's birthday as Women's Day, she strongly resisted the idea and succeeded in squashing it. In November 1972, when the Central Government, at the request of the Government of Meghalaya State, introduced a Bill in Parliament to establish a new university for the north-east region named after Indira Gandhi, there was considerable criticism from the opposition. Hiren Mukherjee, the Communist M.P., declared that the proposal 'went against every grain of decency' and condemned it as an instance of 'sychophantic adulation.'[121] A few months later, Mrs. Gandhi herself insisted on a Cabinet decision to drop the proposal on the ground that it smacked of a personality cult, and a new Bill was introduced. She is also believed to have reversed a decision to name the capital of the new Union Territory of Arunachal Pradesh after her. Private institutions and organisations have been firmly refused permission to use her name.

Nevertheless, in a situation where Indira Gandhi holds supreme power, the cult of personality cannot be so easily squashed, nor does it require her personal encouragement in order to prosper. Writing about the Prime Minister has become a thriving and remunerative trade in a country full of Indira-watchers, and a large bibliography of eulogistic literature has sprung up around her. 'Indira Priyadarshini,' a particularly eulogistic book on the Prime Minister which had been introduced as a compulsory text in State schools, touched off a heated political controversy when the Opposition in Kerala demanded its withdrawal.

In a letter to Mrs. Gandhi in March 1972, Hiren Mukherjee twitted her:

'Someone might make a study of the literature on you being produced in different parts of India. It will perhaps amuse you, but it should also make you somewhat happy; few people in public life anywhere get anything like such genuine popular acclaim. But I believe you well remember that bit in your father's autobiography when he reports

his leg being pulled at table by someone or other in the family asking the "Jewel of India" please to pass the salt! I hope you have still in your entourage a few who can act likewise.'[122]

Mrs. Gandhi replied: 'In my father's time we were new to such flowery language and so felt amused. Now superlatives are used so indiscriminately that I doubt if anyone can take them seriously. My family and I certainly do not.'[123] Rejecting the suggestion that she is intolerant of criticism, she has told an interviewer: 'As I have always expressed myself freely even to the tallest in the land, I cannot understand why anyone should be inhibited in doing so, whatever the reason. Courage and conviction do not require anybody else's permission. As Congress President and as Prime Minister, I have given the fullest opportunity to all people to express themselves. I have also made it a point to meet whoever wants to meet me.'[124]

Mrs. Gandhi naturally prefers praise to criticism; but according to her staff, she is wary of transparent adulation and prefers honest and disinterested criticism. Like other politicians, she does not relish the opposition and abuse of her critics; but she is reasonably tolerant of it and is never vindictive when she retaliates. People who are openly critical of her may fall from favour; but they are not persecuted or victimised. On the other hand, she does expect a high degree of personal loyalty from her party colleagues and lieutenants. While dissent on policy issues is permitted within the Congress, direct criticism of the Prime Minister is not. When Dinesh Singh, a Congress M.P. and former protegé of hers, indulged in open attacks on Mrs. Gandhi, disciplinary action was taken against him and he was suspended temporarily from party membership.

Mrs. Gandhi's own deprecation of the personality cult arises, not only from her personal distaste for it, but from her awareness that it raises political expectations that she can never hope to satisfy. 'In India people seem to speak in hyperbole,' she has lamented. 'They use so many superlatives. But so far as I am concerned, they have no meaning at all. The only danger there is that this sort of talk encourages people to imagine that results are achieved by some kind of magic and not by a clear analysis or deep assessment of the situation and also, of course, by sheer hard work.'[125] When a sychophantic interviewer assured her that her leadership would be essential to the country's development for the next two decades, she replied modestly: 'No country should depend on one person. The thing is that the people should understand ... and participate. Any one person may be there or may not be there. And if the country is dependent on that person, it is not a happy situation at all.'[126]

This, nonetheless, is the situation in which India finds itself today.

As established political institutions and organisations crumble, Indira Gandhi remains the only constant factor on the political scene. Some of her followers seem to feel that she should sieze the opportunity to establish a 'limited dictatorship' or a 'guided democracy.' Shashi Bhushan, a Congress M.P. who is believed to be close to the Prime Minister, has openly voiced this view. Mrs. Gandhi, however, has consistently rejected such proposals. In December 1969, soon after the split, she chided a dictator-minded interviewer: 'The people can be rescued from poverty only through hard work and not by any single person setting himself up as a guide and dictator. If you look around you, you will find that dictatorships are not faring too well elsewhere ... I cannot imagine my ever becoming a dictator ... Dictatorship is not necessary to fight poverty. Nor does dictatorship give people strength.'[127] In August 1972, she reiterated:

'Our people recognise that democracy is a slow process, but they also know that it is a sure process, because it involves a much larger number of people in the entire process of making decisions and policies. The people are mature enough to settle for slower results, provided they are convinced that we are moving in the right direction and that we are deadly earnest about our objectives. The country is firmly committed to democracy and I do not think it will swerve from the path—unless our democratic parties show total ineptness in the future.'[128]

# CHAPTER XII

# TRENDS

As THE winter of 1974 approaches, India appears to be heading for her most serious economic crisis since Independence. At the time of writing—September 1974—the winter crop is expected to fall short of last year's level by 15 per cent or ten million tons of grain. Hundreds of deaths from starvation have already been reported, and millions more are believed to be on the brink of starvation. The immediate causes of the famine have been the shortage of fertiliser and power, owing to the oil crisis, and the eccentricities of the monsoon, which have resulted in a coincidence of floods and drought. In its wider aspects, however, the economic crisis has been building up since the Bangladesh War of December 1971.

The high cost of the Bangladesh refugees and later of the war was not met by any serious attempt at financial discipline and retrenchment. On the contrary, large-scale deficit financing, unprecedented administrative corruption and continuing unproductive expenditure by the Government and conspicuous consumption by the rich have stepped up inflationary pressures on the economy. The Government has failed abysmally to control the prices of essential mass consumer goods. Apart from the occasional token gesture, the Congress has turned a blind eye to the most flagrant blackmarketing, hoarding and profiteering by the powerful farming and trading interests to whom it is subservient. These interests have succeeded in reducing the public distribution machinery to a shambles. In 1967, though food production was 30 million tons lower than today, the Government was able to procure twice as much grain for its 'fair price' shops as it is expected to do this year. Meanwhile, various other essential commodities, ranging from cooking-oil, soap and cloth to cement, have gone 'underground' and are only available on the parallel black-market at vastly inflated prices. While the country's growth rate has remained at the low figure of 3.5 per cent, in 1973 alone prices rose by as much as 30 per cent, the highest inflation since Independence, and the increase for 1974 is expected to be higher still.

The Indian economy has been aptly described as a system of shortages which operates in the interest of those who control the means of production and supply. Under the anomalous conditions of today, it is more profitable for the farmer, trader and industrialist to hoard or produce less and sell on the black-market than to increase production and sell at official prices. It is an inflationary cycle which can only be broken by drastic economic reform; but such reform is unlikely within the existing political framework.

Most Indian economists agree that the roots of the present inflation are political, deriving from the Government's heavy deficit financing and its inability to maintain an effective public distribution system. Deficit financing, the argument goes, has made it possible for the Government to pay high prices to surplus farmers, to avoid introducing an agricultural income-tax and to allow black-market speculators to operate freely, while at the same time seeking to ameliorate poverty with inflationary doles and subsidies, much of which finds its way, not to the poor, but into the pockets of corrupt administrators. At a press interview in July 1973, Dr. V.M. Dandekar, one of the country's leading economists, commented:

'The root cause of the present inflation is the attempt to eliminate poverty without touching the rich, without even calling a temporary halt to the extravagance of the government and the affluence of the few. It is the consequence of socialist slogans without socialist discipline. The scapegoats have all been destroyed and there will no more be an alibi. The people are beginning to see . . . who is cheating them.'[1]

It is significant that after twenty-seven years of supposedly 'socialistic' planning, the gap between rich and poor has grown substantially wider. The Planning Commission's statistics show that while the consumption of the top 5 per cent of the population has been steadily expanding, the poverty of the lowest 5 per cent has increased in absolute terms. About 50 per cent of the population continues to live below the poverty line, as defined by the Government in terms of the nutritional minimum, and are either unemployed or under-employed. Most of the poor are landless labourers, small farmers and urban unemployed. Living at or very near subsistence level, they are the classes whose very survival is threatened by the current price-rise. Also hit, though to a lesser extent, are lower middle class and working class fixed income groups. For the upper classes, and especially the new rich, with their access to the black-market, living standards have never been higher. They dance frenetically on the edge of the precipice, squandering their accumulated hoards of black money with the frantic and mindless ostentation of a class whose days are numbered.

To some observers the economic situation might appear classically tailored for a radical explosion, approximating as it does to conditions in Chiang Kai-Shek's China and other pre-revolutionary societies. But the most potent stabilising factor in the Indian system is the political apathy and backwardness of the rural masses, weighed down by centuries of casteism and economic exploitation and totally dependent on their semi-feudal landlords for such employment as they can get. It is therefore not surprising that the chief threat to the establishment comes, not from the country's poor, but from the educated unemployed. As a perceptive Indian journalist pointed out in October 1972: 'It is not yet sufficiently realised by the ruling élite that unemployed university graduates constitute the antithesis in the dialectics of power. The middle class is growing so rapidly that it is bound to destroy its present hold under the pressure of its weight or through its own internal contradictions. The chances of a peasant and worker revolution may be remote; but the danger of a revolt of unemployed educated youth is real.'[2] Since then, almost every major State in the Indian Union has experienced some form of student agitation, often violent, against the Government. Given the middle class background of the youth involved and their lack of ideological clarity, a revolt of this kind, if it assumes national proportions, might well prove fascist rather than socialist.

While the Indian economic system heads for disaster, driven recklessly on by its own inflationary death-wish, established political institutions exhibit similar symptoms of decay. Parliamentary democracy in the Indian context has never been synonymous with its counterpart in advanced industrial societies. In a largely illiterate, agricultural society where traditional caste and economic ties continue to dominate, the electoral process, despite universal suffrage, has never meant the genuine participation of the masses. Legislatures and elections have never been more than an arena for the factional competition of the élite groups that control the rural 'vote banks'. And the Congress Party since Independence has never been more than a broad-based coalition of such élite groups eager to share in the spoils of office. The split of 1969 and Indira Gandhi's massive election victory in 1971, involving a certain amount of ideological polarisation and a higher degree of mass politicisation, raised hopes of reform and regeneration. But this initial optimism has been obliterated by the record of the Congress during the last three years.

Never has the gulf between official policies and their implementation been wider; never has administrative mismanagement and paralysis been greater; never has factional intrigue and in-fighting in the ruling party been more widespread; and never has corruption been more blatant and all-pervasive. The unprecedented role of black money in the electoral process has reduced the legislatures to a naked travesty of representative government, while inner-party factionalism has made Congress majorities in the States irrelevant to the needs of stable and responsible government. The disenchantment and cynicism of the electorate has been demonstrated by the unusually low percentage of votes cast in recent by-elections—36 per cent in the Bombay City parliamentary by-election of January 1974.

As economic hardship passes the limits of endurance and popular discontent takes to the streets, the ruling élite finds itself compelled to resort increasingly to the formidable coercive apparatus of the State and preventive detention laws. According to a report published by Amnesty International in September 1974, between 15,000 and 20,000 political prisoners are being held without trial in the State of West Bengal alone and there is evidence of the widespread use of torture in prisons. Nor does the ruthless repression used to smash the railway strike of May 1974 have a parallel in the annals of any democracy. Almost every State government is spending an increasing part of its revenues on the maintenance and training of armed police forces, equipped with rifles, machine-guns, mortars and grenades, in addition to the civil police. In the State of U.P. alone these para-military forces number 40,000, the equivalent of two full army divisions, and the average for other States is 25,000. If these forces prove inadequate, they are reinforced by the Central Reserve Police, which takes its orders from the Central Government, and when all else fails the army is called out to restore order, an expedient which has been used with alarming frequency in recent years. Also alarming is the apparent attempt to divert popular attention by chauvinistic gestures such as the recent explosion of a nuclear device and the *de facto* annexation of Sikkim.

Since Indira Gandhi heads the Central Government and her power is ostensibly unfettered, there has naturally been a tendency to hold her personally responsible for all the country's ills—economic, political and moral. B.G. Verghese, the well-known journalist, wrote in March 1974:

'If the country is adrift and the Government rudderless, it is because there has been a failure of leadership. The Prime Minister has no programme, no world view, no grand design. Thus, bereft of a frame, she has merely reacted to events and failed to shape them. This has been her tragedy. She lacks economic and administrative expertise. Nevertheless, she has a certain political instinct and charisma which would have been the greater if harnessed to a larger purpose. She has a mandate, but no mission.'[3]

This view is not confined to intellectual and journalistic circles. The 'Indira Wave' is now a thing of the past. Sample surveys carried out by the Indian Institute of Public Opinion suggest that Mrs. Gandhi's popularity, having reached its zenith after the creation of Bangladesh, has been dwindling ever since. On several occasions she has had to face hostile demonstrations similar to those that marked her early years in office. In January 1974, for instance, a public meeting in Maharashtra which she was addressing was disrupted when a large section of her audience hurled shoes and sandals at the dais. *'Bhashan mat do, rashan do!'* (Don't give us a speech, give us our food rations), they chanted when she rose to speak.

It is facile, however, to blame the failure of leadership for a disease which has its roots in the country's social and economic structure. Leadership does not operate in a vacuum, and no leadership, however charismatic, can achieve the necessary transformation unless it is based upon a genuine mass movement with a coherent socio-economic programme. Indira Gandhi is herself a product of Congress politics, and so long as she functions within that framework there is little she can do to bring about change, however good her own intentions. This is especially true when the Congress Party has been exposed as a house of cards, lacking ideology, organisation or discipline. In these circumstances, the Prime Minister may have the trappings of supreme power, but she does not have its substance.

This is not to deny that Indira Gandhi will play a major role in shaping political events in the next few years. Though her popularity has declined, she still remains the most popular leader in the country. Perhaps her greatest asset is the absence of a viable alternative. She towers amongst her own party colleagues, none of whom can hope to rival her national stature. The Opposition parties, both Right and Left, are too fragmented and incoherent to pose any serious threat. The Bhartiya Lok Dal, recently formed by the merger of various Right-wing parties in an attempt to create a two-party system, is no more than an opportunist coalition of discredited and ageing politicians which cannot hope to inspire public confidence any more than the Grand Alliance of 1970. The Left, meanwhile, is rendered ineffective by the continuing cleavage between the pro-Moscow C.P.I., which offers conditional support to Mrs. Gandhi, and the C.P.I.(M), which remains implacably hostile.

For the moment, the only serious political challenge that Mrs. Gandhi has to face is the extra-parliamentary agitation led by Jayaprakash Narayan. A romantic hero of the nationalist movement, J.P., as he is popularly known, might have been Nehru's political successor had he so desired. Instead he chose to retire from party politics and to assume the role of Gandhi's moral heir. He has now re-emerged as the leader of the Bihar student agitation which aims at securing the dissolution of the State Assembly and at purging the administration of corruption. Though concentrated in Bihar, J.P.'s movement aims eventually at achieving a Gandhian revolution in the country as a whole. As the only national leader with a personal charisma that could rival Mrs. Gandhi's, J.P. has been able to mobilise the support not only of the students but of large sections of the general public, and he has received the backing of the entire Opposition with the sole exception of the C.P.I.. Though the

Congress leadership has been visibly shaken by the initial success of J.P.'s *satyagraha*, in the long run the movement's lack of any coherent social and economic programme, other than ousting corrupt Congress ministries, is likely to prevent it from developing into a serious national alternative. Its greatest asset—J.P.'s personal popularity—is also its greatest long-term weakness. J.P. is in his seventies and has a serious heart condition. If he were removed from the scene, it is highly unlikely that his disparate following—it ranges from the Right-wing Jana Sangh and Swatantra to the Left Communists—could hold together in a Gandhian *satyagraha*.

If Indira Gandhi is able to tide over the immediate food shortage with international assistance, there is every reason to suppose that she will continue in office till the 1976 general election and probably after. The Congress has lost several prestigious by-elections since 1972; but in national terms the party retains its grip on the electoral system. In March 1974, when elections were held for the U.P. legislature, the Congress, despite much public discontent, managed to win a narrow majority through a combination of factors such as the Prime Minister's charisma, money power, governmental influence and the absence of a coherent alternative. The same factors might well see the party returned to power at the Centre, though with a reduced majority, in 1976. Even so, in view of the general loss of confidence in the electoral process and parliamentary government, control of devalued legislatures will not enable Mrs. Gandhi to deal with the long-term political and economic challenge. As the credibility gap between parliamentary politics and economic and social reality continues to widen, mass discontent is bound to express itself increasingly in extra-parliamentary forms. And Indira Gandhi's political survival will depend on her capacity to meet this threat outside the parliamentary framework.

It is possible to visualise two alternative lines along which Indira Gandhi's political strategy may develop. One would involve an increasing reliance on repression, culminating in the establishment of a dictatorship with military support, similar to Nkrumah's in Ghana and Sukarno's in Indonesia. It is a prospect which New Delhi political circles are fond of discussing. In support of this prediction, it is argued that Mrs. Gandhi's relations with the armed forces have always been cordial and that hers has been the deciding voice in the choice of the Service Chiefs. She has also taken care to establish a good rapport with the military rank and file. After the last Pakistan war, for instance, she wrote personally to all wounded soldiers that they should communicate directly with her if they encountered any delay or difficulty in securing the benefits to which they were entitled. Against this must be weighed the fact that Indira Gandhi, for all her pragmatism, appears to have a sincere commitment to the

Nehru tradition and the liberal values that go with it and that militarism
has always been temperamentally distasteful to her. While she may use
the army occasionally for political purposes, to preside over a military
dictatorship would in all probability be too great a betrayal for her to
contemplate. Besides, the experience of Nkrumah and Sukarno must be
a constant reminder of the fate that befalls civilian leaders who rely too
much on military support.

The second possibility is that Indira Gandhi might break free from
the dead-wood of her own defunct party and form the nucleus of a new
Left consolidation. This would include the two Communist Parties, the
Socialists and other radical elements committed to genuine reform. At
the time of writing, such a prospect seems distant, especially as
Mrs. Gandhi's recent policies have involved a tactical shift to the Right.
Nevertheless, for all her compromises, Indira Gandhi's basic orientation
has always been Left-of-Centre; and as the situation develops and her
Centreist position becomes untenable, an alliance with the Left may well
appear the most logical solution.

These, of course, are mere possibilities. In a situation which is both
fluid and potentially explosive, predictions about the political future of
any individual would be futile. All that one can say is that in the present
crisis Indira Gandhi, despite some erosion of her popularity, retains the
political initiative. And if she responds to the situation with her usual
political sagacity, she can be expected to play a major role in the critical
years ahead.

# NOTES

Abbreviations: P.M.S., Prime Minister's Secretariat.

CHAPTER I

[1] Krishna Hutheesing, *Dear to Behold* (Macmillan, 1969), P. 18.
[2] ibid., P. 21.
[3] Hutheesing, *We Nehrus,* (Pearl Publications, Bombay, 1967), P. 48.
[4] Jawaharlal Nehru, *An Autobiography* (Bodley Head, London, 1936), P. 5.
[5] ibid., P. 118.
[6] ibid.
[7] Indira Gandhi, *The Story of Swaraj Bhawan,* article in Motilal Nehru Centenary Souvenir, 1961, P.M.S.
[8] Michael Brecher, *Nehru: A Political Biography* (Oxford University Press, London, 1959), P. 39.
[9] Hutheesing, *With No Regrets*, P. 11.
[10] Indira Gandhi, op. cit.
[11] Motilal Nehru to Jawaharlal Nehru, 8. 3. 20., Nehru Papers, Nehru Memorial Museum and Library.
[12] Indira Gandhi, article for magazine of a Montessori School, November 1957, P.M.S.
[13] Arnold Michaelis, Interview with Indira Gandhi for *McCall's,* April 1966, P.M.S.
[14] Nehru, op. cit., P. 561.
[15] ibid., P. 562.
[16] Jawaharlal Nehru, *Discovery of India* (Signet Press, Calcutta, 1946), P. 30.
[17] Quoted in Promilla Kalhan, *Kamala Nehru—An Intimate Biography* (Vikas Publishing House, Delhi, 1973), P. 141.
[18] Hutheesing, op. cit., P. 21.
[19] B.R. Nanda, *The Nehrus: Motilal and Jawaharlal* (Allen & Unwin, London, 1962), P. 341.
[20] Nehru, *An Autobiography,* P. 77.
[21] Indira Gandhi, Speech at a women's seminar in Tanjore, June 1965, P.M.S.
[22] Indira Gandhi, article for a Montessori School.

CHAPTER II

[1] Jawaharlal Nehru, *A Bunch of Old Letters* (Asia Publishing House, 1958), P.I., Sarojini Naidu to Nehru, 17. 12. 17.
[2] Nehru, *An Autobiography*, Ps. 69–70.
[3] Krishna Hutheesing, *Nehru's Letters to his Sister* (Faber & Faber, London, 1963), P. 167. Jawaharlal Nehru to Krishna Hutheesing, 3. 10. 44.
[4] Michaelis, op. cit.
[5] Welles Hangen, *After Nehru Who?* (Hart-Davis, London, 1963), P. 165.
[6] Indira Gandhi, op. cit.
[7] Hangen, op. cit., P. 164.
[8] Indira Gandhi, *My Mother,* Hindi article, P.M.S.
[9] Indira Gandhi interviewed by the author.
[10] Hangen, op. cit., p. 164.
[11] Hutheesing, *Dear to Behold*, P. 44.
[12] Hutheesing, *We Nehrus,* P. 52.
[13] Quoted in the *Hindu Weekly,* Madras, 28. 5. 72.
[14] Nehru, op. cit., P. 96.
[15] Krishna Hutheesing, *Dear to Behold*, P. 41.
[16] Jawaharlal Nehru, *Glimpses of World History* (John Day, New York), P. 7, Nehru to Indira Nehru, 7. 1. 31.

[17]Nehru Papers.
[18]ibid.
[19]Indira Gandhi, *My Reminiscences of Bapu*, article in Gandhi Marg, Vol. 3, July 1957, P.M.S.
[20]Quoted in Anand Mohan, *Indira Gandhi—A Personal & Political Biography* (Meredith Press, New York, 1967), P. 241.
[21]Jawaharlal Nehru to Motilal Nehru, 30. 9. 22., Nehru Papers.
[22]Telegram from Motilal Nehru to M.K. Gandhi, Nehru Papers.
[23]Nehru, *An Autobiography*, P. 562.
[24]ibid., P. 240.
[25]Motilal Nehru to Jawaharlal Nehru, 28. 2. 26., Nehru Papers.
[26]Motilal Nehru to Jawaharlal Nehru, 27. 5. 26., Nehru Papers.
[27]ibid.
[28]Motilal Nehru to Jawaharlal Nehru, 5. 8. 26., Nehru Papers.
[29]Hutheesing, op. cit., P. 47.
[30]Jawaharlal Nehru, *Letters from a Father to his Daughter* (Oxford University Press, 1929), P. 1.
[31]Nehru, *A Bunch of Old Letters*, M.K. Gandhi to Jawaharlal Nehru, 29. 7. 29., P. 72.
[32]Nehru, *Glimpses of World History*, P. 1.
[33]ibid., P. 949, 9. 8. 33.
[34]ibid., P. 3, 1. 1. 31.
[35]ibid.
[36]ibid., P. 949, 9. 8. 33.
[37]Indira Gandhi interviewed by Lord Chalfont, October 1971, P.M.S.
[38]Indira Nehru to Jawaharlal Nehru, 20. 1. 31., Nehru Papers.
[39]Mohan, op. cit., P. 99.
[40]Nehru, op. cit., 21. 1. 31.
[41]ibid., P. 3, 1. 1. 31.
[42]Nehru, *Discovery of India*, P. 30.
[43]Hutheesing, *With No Regrets*, P. 109.
[44]Quoted in Kalhan, op. cit., P. 72.
[45]Nehru, *An Autobiography*, P. 240.
[46]Nehru, *Discovery of India*, P. 30.
[47]Nehru Papers.
[48]ibid.
[49]Nehru, *An Autobiography*, Ps. 601–602.
[50]Nehru, *Glimpses of World History*, P. 1, 26. 10. 30.
[51]Michaelis, op. cit.
[52]ibid.
[53]Motilal Nehru to Indira Nehru, Nehru Papers.
[54]Hutheesing, *Dear to Behold*, P. 38.
[55]Hangen, op. cit., P. 166.
[56]Motilal Nehru to Jawaharlal Nehru, Nehru Papers.
[57]Indira Nehru to Jawaharlal Nehru, 20. 1. 31., Nehru Papers.
[58]Nehru, op. cit., P. 54, 21. 4. 31.

CHAPTER III

[1]Hutheesing, *Nehru's Letters to his Sister*, P. 25, Jawaharlal Nehru to Krishna Hutheesing, 22. 5. 31.
[2]Mohan, op. cit., P. 112.
[3]Nehru, *An Autobiography*, P. 563.
[4]Nayantara Sahgal interviewed by the author, 1971.
[5]ibid.
[6]Nehru, *Glimpses of World History*, P. 327, 15. 9. 32.
[7]Telegram from M.K. Gandhi to Jawaharlal Nehru, Nehru Papers.
[8]Indira Gandhi, *My Sixteenth Year*, article in *Roshni*, 4. 11. 59., P.M.S.
[9]ibid.

[10]Nehru, *An Autobiography*, P. 483.

[11]Quoted by A.K. Chanda, formerly Secretary to Tagore, in *The Red Lady of Shanti-nikeetan*, article in Amrita Bazar Patrika Supplement, 19. 11. 72.

[12]Jawaharlal Nehru to A.K. Chanda, 20. 5. 34., Nehru Papers.

[13]Indira Gandhi, *Reminiscences of Tagore*, article in *Women on the March*, January 1961, P.M.S.

[14]ibid.

[15]Banikanta, *Indira of Shantiniketan*, Hindustan Standard, Calcutta, 20. 1. 66.

[16]Quoted in Kalhan, op. cit., P. 136.

[17]Quoted in K.A. Abbas, *Indira Gandhi* (Hind Pocket Books, 1966), P. 71.

[18]Quoted in *Prime Minister: A Profile*, Socialist Congressman, Vol. 8, 19. 11. 68.

[19]A.K. Chanda, op. cit.

[20]Indira Gandhi, op. cit.

[21]ibid.

[22]ibid.

[23]Quoted in Abbas, op. cit., P. 74.

[24]Nehru, *A Bunch of Old Letters*, R. Tagore to J. Nehru, 20. 4. 35., P. 119.

[25]Quoted in Chanda, op. cit.

[26]Prabhavati Devi interviewed by the author, 1971.

[27]J. Nehru, May 1935, Nehru Papers.

[28]M.K. Gandhi to J. Nehru, 15. 10. 35., Nehru Papers.

[29]Quoted in Marie Seton, *Panditji* (Rupa, India, 1967), P. 79.

[30]Indira Nehru to Agatha Harrison, 3. 9. 35., quoted in Seton, op. cit., P. 79.

[31]Agatha Harrison to M.K. Gandhi, 13. 9. 35., quoted in ibid., P. 80.

[32]ibid.

[33]M.K. Gandhi to J. Nehru, 15. 10. 35., Nehru Papers.

[34]Nehru, *Discovery of India*, P. 30.

[35]Quoted in Kalhan, op. cit., P. 137.

[36]M.K. Gandhi to Indira Nehru, 30. 3. 36., Nehru Papers.

[37]Quoted in Hangen, op. cit., P. 167.

[38]ibid., P. 161.

[39]ibid., P. 166.

[40]Nehru, *A Bunch of Old Letters*, Christiane Toller to J. Nehru, 27. 8. 36.

[41]J. Nehru to Agatha Harrison, 15. 7. 36., Nehru Papers.

[42]J. Nehru to A. Harrison, 6. 8. 36., Nehru Papers.

[43]J. Nehru to A. Harrison, 24. 6. 37., Nehru Papers.

[44]Fr. C.E. George, *My Pupil Indira Gandhi*, Amrita Bazar Patrika Supplement, 19. 11. 72.

[45]Emmeline Garnett, *Madame Prime Minister* (Farrar, Straus & Gironx, New York, 1967), Ps. 92–93..

[46]ibid., P. 95.

[47]J. Nehru to A. Harrison, 9. 5. 38., Nehru Papers.

[48]Mohan, op. cit., P. 129.

[49]ibid., P. 130.

[50]Indira Gandhi, article in Argentinian journal *Sur*, 1. 12. 56., P.M.S.

[51]Chalfont, op. cit.

[52] Edward Thompson to J. Nehru, 1. 7. 38., Nehru Papers.

[53]Shanta Gandhi interviewed by the author, 1971.

[54]A. Harrison to J. Nehru, 8. 8. 39., Nehru Papers.

[55]J. Nehru to A. Harrison, 20. 9. 39., Nehru Papers.

[56]E. Thompson to J. Nehru, 3. 12. 39., Nehru Papers.

[57]Lord Linlithgow to Agatha Harrison, quoted in Seton, op. cit., P. 97.

[58]Nehru, op. cit., P. 411, J. Nehru to E. Thompson, 5. 1. 40.

[59]ibid., P. 428, J. Nehru to E. Thompson, 7. 4. 40.

[60]J. Nehru to A. Harrison, 4. 5. 40., Nehru Papers.

[61]Hutheesing, op. cit., P. 66, J. Nehru to K. Hutheesing, 2. 12. 40.

[62]J. Nehru to Indira Nehru, 18. 11. 40., Nehru Papers.

[63]J. Nehru to A. Harrison, 10. 1. 41., Nehru Papers.
[64]Quoted in Abbas, op. cit., P. 88.

CHAPTER IV

[1]Michaelis, op. cit.
[2]Quoted in Mohan, op. cit., P. 213.
[3]J. Nehru to M.K. Gandhi, 25. 7. 33., Nehru Papers.
[4]Nehru, *A Bunch of Old Letters*, P. 214, R. Tagore to J. Nehru, 21. 12. 36.
[5]Michaelis, op. cit.
[6]Quoted in Seton, op. cit., P. 103.
[7]M.K. Gandhi to J. Nehru, 5. 12. 41., Nehru Papers.
[8]Indira Nehru, *Women in the U.S.S.R.*, Bombay Chronicle, 1. 2. 42.
[9]*The Leader*, Allahabad, 21. 2. 42
[10]Nehru Papers.
[11]Michaelis, op. cit.
[12]M.K. Gandhi to J. Nehru, Nehru Papers.
[13]Nehru Papers.
[14]Quoted in Mohan, op. cit., P. 157.
[15]Eve Curie, *Journey Among Warriors* (Heinemann, 1943), P. 432.
[16]ibid.
[17]M.K. Gandhi to J. Nehru, 4. 3. 42., Nehru Papers.
[18]Printed souvenir of the marriage of Indira Nehru, Nehru Papers.
[19]ibid.
[20]ibid.
[21]Hutheesing, *With No Regrets*, P. 142.
[22]Nehru, *The Unity of India* (Lindsay Drummond, London, 1941), P. 223.
[23]Quoted in Abbas, op. cit., P. 93.
[24]Telegram from J. Nehru to Indira Gandhi, 11. 7. 42., Nehru Papers.
[25]Congress Bulletin, All India Congress Committee, 1945.
[26]Chalfont, op. cit.
[27]Indira Gandhi, *A Page From the Book of Memory*, Women on the March, September 1963, P.M.S.
[28]Michaelis, op. cit.
[29]Vijayalakshmi Pandit, *Prison Days* (Signet Press, Calcutta, 1945), P. 60.
[30]Indira Gandhi, op. cit.
[31]V. Pandit, op. cit., P. 62.
[32]ibid., P. 63.
[33]Indira Gandhi, op. cit.
[34]V. Pandit, op. cit., P. 96.
[35]ibid., Ps. 97–99.
[36]ibid., P. 104.
[37]ibid., Ps. 107–108.
[38]Michaelis, op. cit.
[39]Hutheesing, *Nehru's Letters to his Sister*, P. 120, J. Nehru to K. Hutheesing, 14. 5. 43.
[40]Indira Gandhi, op. cit.
[41]ibid.
[42]Michaelis, op. cit.
[43]Indira Gandhi, op. cit.
[44]Indira Gandhi, *On Being A Mother*, article, P.M.S.
[45]Mohan, op. cit., P. 263.

CHAPTER V

[1]Socialist Congressman, Delhi, 25. 9. 63.
[2]Indira Gandhi interviewed by the author.
[3]Quoted in Mohan, op. cit., P. 184.
[4]Chalfont, op. cit..
[5]Indira Gandhi interviewed by Francis Watson of *The Guardian*, 1966, P.M.S.

[6]Chalfont, op. cit.

[7]Indira Gandhi, Speech at meeting of Council for Promotion of Communal Harmony, 23. 5. 65., P.M.S.

[8]Indira Gandhi, *Reminiscences of Bapu.*

[9]ibid.

[10]Manuben Gandhi, *Last Glimpses of Bapu* (S.L. Agarwala, India, 1962), P. 283.

[11]Indira Gandhi, op. cit.

[12]J. Nehru, *Independence and After* (Delhi, 1949), P. 17.

[13]Indira Gandhi, article for Gandhi Centenary Volume, 2. 10. 68., P.M.S.

[14]Indira Gandhi, *On Being a Hostess at Teen Murti House*, article in 'The International', Bombay, August 1957, P.M.S.

[15]ibid.

[16]ibid.

[17]ibid.

[18]Quoted in Time magazine, 28. 1. 66.

[19]Chalfont, op. cit.

[20]Indira Gandhi interviewed by Sita Crishna for *Junior Statesman*, P.M.S.

[21]Indira Gandhi, op. cit.

[22]Quoted in Seton, op. cit., P. 285.

[23]Indira Gandhi, op. cit.

[24]ibid.

[25]Mohan, op. cit., P. 257.

[26]Michaelis, op. cit.

[27]James Cameron, article in *Envoy*, London, June 1956, P.M.S.

[28]ibid.

[29]Quoted in K.P.S. Menon, *Russian Panorama*, P. 37.

[30]Ariel, *Success*, Times of India, 19. 6. 55.

[31]Indira Gandhi, op. cit.

[32]Indira Gandhi interviewed by Jeanne Gargi, *Femina*, Bombay, 22. 3. 68.

[33]Indira Gandhi, op. cit.

[34]Indira Gandhi interviewed by the author.

[35]Indira Gandhi, *On Being A Mother.*

[36]Indira Gandhi, *Design for Living*, Women on the March, January 1959, P.M.S.

[37]Indira Gandhi, *On Being A Mother.*

[38]ibid.

[39]ibid.

[40]ibid.

[41]*The Tribune*, Ambala, 5. 11. 57.

[42]Nayantara Sahgal interviewed by the author, 1971.

[43]Quoted in Seton, op. cit., P. 137.

[44]Indira Gandhi interviewed by the author.

[45]Hutheesing, *Dear to Behold*, P. 139.

[46]Nayantara Sahgal interviewed by the author, 1971.

CHAPTER VI

[1]Indira Gandhi, op. cit.

[2]Michael Brecher, *Succession in India* (Oxford University Press, London, 1966), P. 25.

[3]Hangen, op. cit., P. 177.

[4]M. Chalapathi Rau, article in *Indira Priyadarshini* (Popular Book Services, Delhi, 1966), P. 17.

[5]Indira Gandhi interviewed by Mme. Anne Cublier, 19. 12. 66., P.M.S.

[6]Michaelis, op. cit.

[7]Indira Gandhi interviewed by the author.

[8]ibid.

[9]Indira Gandhi, article in *Shankar's Weekly*, Silver Jubilee Number, 1973, P.M.S.

[10]National Herald, Lucknow, 12. 1. 59.

[11]Chalfont, op. cit.

[12]Kuldip Nayar, *Between The Lines* (Allied Publishers, India, 1969), P. 8.
[13]National Herald, 8. 2. 59.
[14]ibid., 10. 2. 59.
[15]ibid., 9. 2. 59.
[16]Times of India, Bombay, 15. 1. 59.
[17]Times of India, 10. 2. 59.
[18]Congress Bulletin.
[19]ibid.
[20]*The Organiser*, Delhi, 20. 4. 59.
[21]Congress Bulletin.
[22]Times of India, 11. 5. 59., P. 6.
[23]The Organiser, 12. 10. 59.
[24]The Hindu, Madras, 30. 4. 59., P. 5.
[25]ibid.
[26]*Link*, Delhi, 10. 5. 59., Ps. 7–8.
[27]*New Age*, 14. 1. 59., P. 17.
[28]National Herald, 26. 7. 59.
[29]Congress Bulletin.
[30]ibid.
[31]Hangen, op. cit., P. 176.
[32]Congress Bulletin, 4. 6. 60.
[33]ibid.
[34]Link, 17. 1. 60., P. 9.
[35]Times of India, 17. 12. 57.
[36]Congress Bulletin, 12. 5. 59.
[37]Chalfont, op. cit.
[38]Seton, op. cit., P. 288.
[39]Interviewed by the author.
[40]The Organiser, 13. 1. 64., P. 3.
[41]ibid., P. 15.
[42]Seton, op. cit., P. 373.
[43]Times of India, 2. 11. 62.
[44]Socialist Congressman, 1. 1. 63., Ps. 6–7.
[45]Michael Brecher, *India & World Politics: Krishna Menon's View of the World* (Oxford University Press, London, 1968), P. 7.

CHAPTER VII
[1]Hangen, op. cit., Ps. 183–184.
[2]Michaelis, op. cit.
[3]Kuldip Nayar, *India: The Critical Years* (Vikas, Delhi, 1971), P. 19.
[4]ibid.
[5]ibid., P. 20, footnote.
[6]Brecher, *Succession in India*, P. 76.
[7]Nayar, op. cit., P. 17.
[8]Nayar, *Between The Lines*, P. 8.
[9]Times of India, 19. 4. 64.
[10]ibid., 19. 5. 64.
[11]Seton, op. cit., P. 458.
[12]ibid.
[13]Chalapathi Rau, *Indira Priyadarshini*.
[14]Times of India, 1. 6. 64.
[15]Nayar, op. cit., P. 9.
[16]Brecher, op. cit., P. 51.
[17]ibid., P. 256, note 5.
[18]Chalfont, op. cit.
[19]Socialist Congressman, 15. 6. 64., P. 3.
[20]Link, 4. 10. 64.

[21]ibid., 13. 9. 64.
[22]ibid., 10. 1. 64, P. 9.
[23]Nayar, op. cit., P. 14.
[24]Socialist Congressman, 15. 8. 65., Ps. 17–18.
[25]Indira Gandhi interviewed by Marion Woolfson, P.M.S.
[26]Khushwant Singh, *Indira Gandhi*, Illustrated Weekly of India, 14. 3. 71.
[27]Brecher, op. cit., P. 193.
[28]ibid., P. 196.
[29]ibid., P. 202.
[30]ibid., P. 217.
[31]ibid., P. 218.
[32]Hindustan Times, Delhi, 16. 1. 66.
[33]ibid., 19. 1. 66.
[34]ibid., 17. 1. 66.
[35]ibid., 19. 1. 66.
[36]J. Anthony Lukas, *She Stands Remarkably Alone*, New York Times Magazine, 27. 3. 66., P.M.S.
[37]Abbas, op. cit., P. 15.
[38]Hindustan Times, 20. 1. 66.
[39]P.M.S.

CHAPTER VIII
[1]Hangen, op. cit., P. 22.
[2]Quoted in Khushwant Singh, op. cit.
[3]Economic & Political Weekly, Bombay, 20. 8. 66., Ps. 6–7.
[4]Khushwant Singh, op. cit.
[5]J. Anthony Lukas, op. cit.
[6]*Statesman*, Delhi, 20. 1. 66.
[7]*Dawn*, Karachi, 21. 1. 66.
[8]Hindustan Times, 21. 1. 66.
[9]Times of India, 20. 1. 66.
[10]Hindustan Times, 20. 1. 66.
[11]ibid.
[12]ibid., 25. 1. 66.
[13]ibid., 2. 3. 66.
[14]ibid.
[15]Times of India, 16. 3. 66.
[16]Hindustan Times, 17. 3. 66.
[17]Lukas, op. cit.
[18]Hindustan Times, 17. 1. 66.
[19]Link, 13. 2. 66.
[20]Lukas, op. cit.
[21]Hindustan Times, 13. 3. 66.
[22]ibid., 2. 3. 66.
[23]Link, 20. 3. 66.
[24]Hindustan Times, 29. 3. 66.
[25]Nayar, op. cit., P. 85.
[26]Hindustan Times, 1. 4. 66.
[27]Times of India, 1. 4. 66.
[28]Hindu, 26. 4. 66.
[29]Nandan Kagal, *The Limits of Dissent*, The Indian Express, Delhi, 12. 5. 66.
[30]Times of India, 27. 4. 66.
[31]ibid., 1. 5. 66.
[32]Indian Express, 24. 5. 66.
[33]Times of India, 13. 6. 66.
[34]Hutheesing, op. cit., P. 189.
[35]Link, 24. 7. 66.

[36]Seton, op. cit., P. 497.
[37]Interviewed by the author, 1. 7. 73.
[38]Times of India, 22. 7. 66.
[39]Hindustan Times, 13. 3. 66.
[40]Hindu, 21. 10. 66.
[41]Quoted in J. Anthony Lukas, New York Times, 30. 9. 66.
[42]Times of India, 1. 8. 66.
[43]Free Press Journal, Bombay, 27. 8. 66.
[44]Times of India, 13. 12. 66.
[45]Hindustan Times, 8. 11. 66.
[46]Times of India, 10. 11. 66.
[47]ibid., 6. 2. 67.
[48]ibid., 26. 12. 66.
[49]Socialist Congressman, 19. 1. 68.
[50]Quoted in *Some Thoughts of Indira Gandhi*, compiled in May 1968, P.M.S.
[51]Times of India, 20. 1. 67.
[52]Hutheesing, op. cit., P. 195.
[53]ibid., P. 196.
[54]*Some Thoughts of Indira Gandhi*, P.M.S.
[55]Hindustan Times, 16. 3. 67.
[56]Brecher, *Political Leadership in India* (Praeger, New York, 1969), P. 129.
[57]Hindu, 13. 3. 67.
[58]Lukas, New York Times Magazine, 27. 3. 66.
[59]ibid.
[60]Hindustan Times, 18. 3. 66.
[61]Lukas, New York Times, 30. 9. 66.
[62]Socialist Congressman, 19. 1. 68.
[63]Michaelis, op. cit.

CHAPTER IX
[1]Interviewed by the author, 1971.
[2]Times of India, 6. 1. 68.
[3]ibid., 10. 1. 68.
[4]*Selected Speeches of Indira Gandhi* (Government of India, 1971), Ps. 374–381.
[5]ibid.
[6]Quoted in Nayar, *India: The Critical Years*, p. 25.
[7]ibid., P. 26.
[8]ibid., Ps. 24–25.
[9]*Selected Speeches of Indira Gandhi*, P. 353.
[10]Quoted in Nayar, op. cit., P. 26.
[11]Statesman, 31. 12. 68.
[12]Quoted in Nayar, op. cit., P. 2.
[13]Congress Bulletin.
[14]ibid.
[15]Quoted in Nayar, op. cit., Ps. 35–36.
[16]Congress Bulletin.
[17]Nayar, op. cit., P. 37.
[18]Interviewed by the author, 18. 6. 73.
[19]Quoted in Nayar, op. cit., Ps. 41–42.
[20]Congress Bulletin.
[21]ibid.
[22]ibid.
[23]Indira Gandhi Correspondence, P.M.S.
[24]Nayar, op. cit., P. 59.
[25]Congress Bulletin.
[26]ibid.
[27]ibid.

28Quoted in Nayar, op. cit., P. 8.
29Congress Bulletin.
30ibid.
31ibid.
32ibid.
33ibid.
34New York Times, 22. 8. 69.
35M.C. Chalapathi Rau, *Indira Gandhi: Prime Minister of India* (Government of India, 1970).
36Hindustan Times, 5. 12. 68.
37Ariel, *The Sunday Standard*, 17. 11. 68.
38John Grigg, *Three Years of Indira Gandhi*, Times of India, 24. 1. 69.
39*Selected Speeches of Indira Gandhi*, P. 346.
40Quoted in *Socialist Congressman*, 19. 11. 68.
41Indira Gandhi's inaugural address to the All India Student's Convention, July 1961, quoted in *Socialist Congressman*, 19. 11. 68., Ps. 27–28.

CHAPTER X
1Nehru, *An Autobiography*, P. 365.
2Nehru, *A Bunch of Old Letters*, P. 309. J. Nehru to S.C. Bose, 4. 2. 39.
3Nayar, op. cit., P. 255.
4National Herald, 24. 1. 70.
5Statesman, 8. 1. 70.
6Nayar, op. cit., P. 252.
7Indira Gandhi's interview with an Indonesian woman M.P., 8. 5. 68., P.M.S.
8Times of India, 1. 2. 70.
9ibid., 11. 2. 70.
10Economic & Political Weekly, P. 470, 14. 3. 70.
11ibid.
1230. 7. 70., P.M.S.
13Indira Gandhi Correspondence, P.M.S.
14National Herald, 31. 1. 70.
155. 12. 70., P.M.S.
16Nayar, op. cit., P. 66.
17*Selected Speeches of Indira Gandhi*, P. 60.
18Nayar, op. cit., P. 107.
19*Socialist India*, All India Congress Committee, Delhi.
20P.M.S.
21ibid.
22Economic & Political Weekly, 12. 10. 70.
23P.M.S.
24Economic & Political Weekly, 2. 1. 71.
25Khushwant Singh, op. cit.
2611. 3. 71., P.M.S.
27Interviewed by the author.
28Indira Gandhi Correspondence, P.M.S.
29ibid.
30P.M.S.
31Debate in Lok Sabha, 27. 3. 71., *India & Bangladesh: Selected Speeches & Statements of Indira Gandhi* (Orient & Longman, Delhi, 1972), Ps. 9–10.
32Debate in Rajya Sabha, 27. 3. 71., ibid., P. 11.
3331. 3. 71., ibid., Ps. 13–14.
34Reply to Debate in Lok Sabha, 26. 5. 71., ibid., P. 20.
35ibid., P. 33.
36Interviewed by the author.
37Interviewed by the author, September 1971.
38Link, 15. 8. 71.

[39]*India Speaks* (Government of India), P. 3.
[40]Link, 3. 10. 71.
[41]*India Speaks*, P. 14.
[42]ibid., P. 49, 31. 10. 71.
[43]1. 11. 71., P.M.S.
[44]*India & Bangladesh*, P. 55, 1. 11. 71.
[45]1. 11. 71., P.M.S.
[46]*India Speaks*, P. 59, 4. 11. 71.
[47]ibid., P. 68, 5. 11. 71.
[48]Nayar, *Distant Neighbours*, P. 169.
[49]P.M.S.
[50]*India & Bangladesh*, P. 117, Debate in Rajya Sabha, 30. 11. 71.
[51]*India Weekly*, Vol. 7, No. 43, London, 4. 11. 71., P. 5.
[52]*India Speaks*, Ps. 123–124, 15.11.71.
[53]ibid., P. 117, Debate in Rajya Sabha, 30. 11. 71.
[54]ibid., P. 126.
[55]ibid., P. 130, 4. 12. 71.
[56]Amrita Bazar Patrika Supplement, 19. 11. 71., P. XXVI.
[57]K.A. Abbas, *That Woman* (India Book Co., Delhi, 1973), P. 159.
[58]Times of India, 17. 12. 71.
[59]P.M.S.
[60]Indira Gandhi Correspondence, P.M.S.
[61]Indira Gandhi interviewed by J. Datta of *The Hindustan Standard*, quoted in Times of India, 18. 3. 73.
[62]Quoted in Abbas, op. cit., P. 167.
[63]Amrita Bazar Patrika Supplement, 19. 11. 72., P. XXVI.
[64]Indira Gandhi interviewed by National Broadcasting Corporation of America, 22. 12. 71., *India & Bangladesh*, P. 159.
[65]The Statesman Weekly, 10. 6. 72., P. 13.
[66]Indira Gandhi interviewed by R.K. Karanjia, quoted in Abbas, op. cit., P. 214.
[67]28. 11. 71., P.M.S.
[68]Chicago Sunday Times, 13. 8. 72.
[69]Interviewed by the author.
[70]Indira Gandhi interviewed by the editor, Maharashtra Times, 11. 8. 72., P.M.S.
[71]J.D. Sethi, Hindustan Times, 7. 5. 72.

CHAPTER XI
[1]Mrs. Gandhi to Mrs. Darina Silone, 14. 3. 71., Indira Gandhi Correspondence, P.M.S.
[2]Interviewed by the author.
[3]Hangen, op. cit., P. 160.
[4]Mrs. Gandhi to Mrs. Mary Shelvankar, 3. 10. 71., Indira Gandhi Correspondence, P.M.S.
[5]Indira Gandhi interviewed by *Link*, 15. 8. 72.
[6]P. Kalhan, 'The Essential Indira', Hindustan Times, 30. 12. 74.
[7]Indira Gandhi interviewed by French National Radio, 12. 2. 71., P.M.S.
[8]Indira Gandhi, *Biographical Note for Lok Sabha Who's Who*, 1971, P.M.S.
[9]Indira Gandhi interviewed by *Eve's Weekly*, Bombay, 22. 11. 67.
[10]Oriana Fallaci, *A Talk with Indira Gandhi*, McCalls, U.S.A., June 1973.
[11]Interviewed by the author, 2. 8. 73.
[12]Times of India, 21. 12. 72.
[13]Indira Gandhi interviewed by Uma Vasudev, 25. 9. 73., quoted in U. Vasudev, *Indira Gandhi* (Vikas, Delhi, 1974), P. 542.
[14]Mrs. Gandhi to Mrs. Joseph, 26. 4. 71., Indira Gandhi Correspondence, P.M.S.
[15]Statesman Weekly, 2. 2. 74., P. 11.
[16]ibid.
[17]Kalhan, op. cit.
[18]Chalfont, op. cit.
[19]Inder Malhotra, *Nehru: Nine Years After*, Times of India, 27. 5. 73.

[20]John Grigg, *A Woman with the Heart of a King*, Sunday Times, London, 7. 3. 71.
[21]Fallaci, op. cit.
[22]Indira Gandhi Correspondence, P.M.S.
[23]Yashpal Kapur, 1 *Safdarjang Road*, article in *Saptahik-Hindustan*, 5. 3. 72., P.M.S.
[24]Interviewed by the author.
[25]ibid.
[26]Quoted in Vasudev, op. cit., P. 337.
[27]Interviewed by the author.
[28]Indira Gandhi interviewed by J. Datta of *Hindustan Standard*, Times of India, 18. 3. 73.
[29]Statesman Weekly, 24. 11. 73., P. 1.
[30]Times of India, 28. 6. 73.
[31]Kalhan, op. cit.
[32]ibid.
[33]Interviewed by U. Vasudev, 25. 9. 73., quoted in Vasudev, op. cit., P. 542.
[34]Interviewed by the author.
[35]Times of India, 30. 4. 73.
[36]Mrs. Gandhi to Chester Bowles, 6. 8. 72., Indira Gandhi Correspondence, P.M.S.
[37]Philip Norman, *The Most Powerful Woman in the World*, Sunday Times, London, P.M.S.
[38]Indian Express, 21. 6. 73.
[39]Dr. Karan Singh to Mrs. Gandhi, 24. 3. 73., Indira Gandhi Correspondence, P.M.S.
[40]Mrs. Gandhi to Karan Singh, 25. 3. 73., Indira Gandhi Correspondence, P.M.S.
[41]Indira Gandhi's replies to questions from Anne Cublier, 19. 12. 66., P.M.S.
[42]Indira Gandhi interviewed by Edith Nemy of the New York Times, 16. 11. 68., P.M.S.
[43]Yashpal Kapur, op. cit.
[44]Interviewed by the author.
[45]Chalfont, op. cit.
[46]Philip Norman, op. cit.
[47]Indira Gandhi, *Biographical Note for Lok Sabha Who's Who*, P.M.S.
[48]Mrs. Gandhi to Mrs. J.R. Davis, 24. 9. 72., Indira Gandhi Correspondence, P.M.S.
[49]Interviewed by the author.
[50]Replies to question from Dr. R.C. Nasso of Italian Television, June 1971, P.M.S.
[51]Fallaci, op. cit.
[52]*Selected Speeches of Indira Gandhi*, Ps. 254–255, address at S.N.D.T. University for Women, Bombay, 26. 6. 66.
[53]Indira Gandhi, Message to *Women on the March*, 30. 6. 71., P.M.S.
[54]Quoted in Amrita Bazar Patrika Supplement, 19. 11. 72., P. VI.
[55]*Selected Speeches of Indira Gandhi*, P. 260, speech to Maharashtra State Women's Council, Bombay, 9. 11. 68.
[56]Fallaci, op. cit.
[57]Mrs. Gandhi to E.G. Earley, 12. 5. 71., Indira Gandhi Correspondence, P.M.S.
[58]1971, P.M.S.
[59]Indira Gandhi, reply to question from *Mademoiselle* magazine, 2. 12. 69., P.M.S.
[60]Interviewed by ihe author.
[61]Kapur, op. cit.
[62]Quoted in Vasudev, op. cit., P. 39.
[63]Mrs. Gandhi to Pinto of the Aurobindo Ashram, 8. 8. 72., Indira Gandhi Correspondence, P.M.S.
[64]Chalfont, op. cit.
[65]Kalhan, op. cit.
[66]Quoted in Vasudev, op. cit., P. 310.
[67]Mrs. Gandhi to Devaraj Urs, 30. 9. 72., Indira Gandhi Correspondence, P.M.S.
[68]Times of India, 6. 4. 73.
[69]Interviewed by the author.
[70]ibid.
[71]ibid.
[72]ibid.

[73]Times of India, 8. 12. 72.

[74]Interviewed by Vasudev, 25. 9. 73., quoted in Vasudev, op. cit., P. 533.

[75]Quoted in Times of India, 12. 4. 73.

[76]Interviewed by Iqbal Singh of *Socialist India*, 29. 5. 71., P.M.S.

[77]Interviewed by K.A. Abbas, April 1972, P.M.S.

[78]Dilip Mukerjee, *A Bagful of Bogeys*, Times of India, 30. 12. 72.

[79]20. 5. 71., P.M.S.

[80]Statesman Weekly, 29. 12. 73., P. 13.

[81]Interviewed by Khushwant Singh, Illustrated Weekly of India, 13. 8. 72.

[82]Mrs. Gandhi to U.S. Joshi, 8. 8. 71., Indira Gandhi Correspondence, P.M.S.

[83]Quoted in Times of India, 12. 4. 73.

[84]Quoted in Ela Sen, *Indira Gandhi* (Peter Owen, London, 1973), P. 189.

[85]Indira Gandhi's replies to questions from Dr. R.C. Nasso of Italian Television, 15–16 June 1971, P.M.S.

[86]Times of India, 6. 4. 73.

[87]ibid.

[88]Times of India, 6. 1. 73.

[89]Hiren Mukerjee, *The Prime Minister & Parliament*, Amrita Bazar Patrika Supplement, 19. 11. 72., Ps. XII-XIII.

[90]*Selected Speeches of Indira Gandhi*, P. 189, 24. 6. 66.

[91]Article by Dom Moraes for New York Times, P.M.S.

[92]Interviewed by the author.

[93]Interviewed by the author, 1971.

[94]Moraes, op. cit.

[95]Kalhan, op. cit.

[96]Seton, op. cit., P. 498.

[97]S. Viswam, *The 'Unanimity' of One Opinion*, Statesman Weekly, 17. 6. 72., P. 9.

[98]Kalhan, op. cit.

[99]Khushwant Singh, op. cit.

[100]Interviewed by the author.

[101]Times of India, 15. 7. 73.

[102]Interviewed by the author, 18. 6. 73.

[103]Times of India, 3. 11. 72.

[104]ibid., 8. 7. 73.

[105]Interviewed by the author.

[106]Times of India, 23. 12. 72.

[107]ibid., 28. 12. 72.

[108]Interviewed by the author.

[109]Statesman Weekly, 27. 5. 72., P. 4.

[110]Economic & Political Weekly, 20. 5. 72., P. 1001.

[111]Quoted in ibid., 19. 5. 73., P. 894.

[112]Mrs. Gandhi to V.P. Naik, 11. 6. 71., Indira Gandhi Correspondence, P.M.S.

[113]Statesman Weekly, 10. 6. 72., P. 5.

[114]Times of India, 28. 12. 72.

[115]ibid., 12. 6. 73., Sham Lal, *The National Scene*.

[116]Khushwant Singh, op. cit.

[117]Interviewed by *Link*, 15. 8. 72., P. 19.

[118]Interviewed by the author.

[119]Times of India, 11. 7. 73.

[120]*India Speaks*, P. 65, 4. 11. 71.

[121]Times of India, 17. 11. 72.

[122]H. Mukerjee to Mrs. Gandhi, 24. 3. 72., Indira Gandhi Correspondence, P.M.S.

[123]Mrs. Gandhi to H. Mukerjee, 3. 4. 72., Indira Gandhi Correspondence, P.M.S.

[124]Interviewed by G.S. Talwalkar, Maharashtra Times, Bombay, 11. 8. 72., P.M.S.

[125]Interviewed by Abbas, *Blitz*, 22 & 29 April 1972, P.M.S.

[126]Interviewed by Datta of *Hindustan Standard*, Times of India, 18. 3. 73.

[127]Interviewed by Kaushik, 25. 12. 69., P.M.S.
[128]Interviewed by Talwalkar, op. cit.

CHAPTER XII

[1]Times of India, 7. 7. 73.
[2]B.M. Bhatia, *The Economic Crisis*, The Statesman, 31. 10. 72.
[3]B.G. Verghese, *The Hour of Decision*, Sunday World, 24. 3. 74.

# SELECT BIBLIOGRAPHY

(This bibliography only lists those primary sources to which extensive reference has been made and published works which have been cited in the notes).

Unpublished Sources:
1) Indira Gandhi Correspondence, Prime Minister's Secretariat.
2) Mrs. Gandhi's speeches, articles and press interviews, Prime Minister's Secretariat.
3) The Nehru Papers, Nehru Memorial Museum & Library, Delhi.

Newspapers:
1) The Times of India, Delhi.
2) The Hindustan Times, Delhi.
3) The National Herald, Lucknow and Delhi.
4) The Hindu, Madras.

Periodicals:
1) Congress Bulletin, All India Congress Committee, Delhi.
2) The Socialist Congressman, Delhi.
3) Socialist India, All India Congress Committee, Delhi.
4) Link, Delhi.
5) The Organiser, Delhi.
6) The Economic & Political Weekly, Bombay.
7) The Statesman Weekly, Delhi.

Published Works:
1) *Selected Speeches of Indira Gandhi* (Government of India, 1971).
2) *India Speaks* (Government of India).
3) *India & Bangladesh: Selected Speeches & Statements of Indira Gandhi* (Orient & Longman, Delhi, 1972).
4) K.A. Abbas, *Indira Gandhi* (Hind Pocket Books, India, 1966).
5) K.A. Abbas, *That Woman* (India Book Company, Delhi, 1973).
6) Michael Brecher, *Nehru: A Political Biography* (Oxford University Press, London, 1959).
7) M. Brecher, *Succession in India* (O.U.P., London, 1966).
8) M. Brecher, *India & World Politics: Krishna Menon's View of the World* (O.U.P., London, 1968).
9) M. Brecher, *Political Leadership in India* (Praeger, New York, 1969).
10) Eve Curie, *Journey Among Warriors* (Heinemann, London, 1943).
11) M.C. Chalapathi Rau, etc., *Indira Priyadarshini* (Popular Book Services, Delhi, 1966).
12) Manuben Gandhi, *Last Glimpses of Bapu* (S.L. Agarwala, India, 1962).
13) Emmeline Garnett, *Madame Prime Minister* (Farrar, Straus & Gironx, New York 1967).
14) Welles Hangen, *After Nehru Who?* (Hart-Davis, London, 1963).
15) Krishna Hutheesing, *With No Regrets* (Padma Publications, India, 1946).
16) K. Hutheesing, *We Nehrus* (Pearl Publications, Bombay, 1967).
17) K. Hutheesing, *Dear to Behold* (Macmillan, 1969).
18) K. Hutheesing, *Nehru's Letters to his Sister* (Faber & Faber, London, 1963).
19) Promilla Kalhan, *Kamala Nehru—An Intimate Biography* (Vikas, Delhi, 1973).
20) K.P.S. Menon, *Russian Panorama* (O.U.P., India, 1962).
21) Anand Mohan, *Indira Gandhi—A Personal & Political Biography* (Meredith Press, New York, 1967).
22) B.R. Nanda, *The Nehrus: Motilal & Jawaharlal* (Allen & Unwin, London, 1962).
23) Kuldip Nayar, *Between The Lines* (Allied Publishers, India, 1969).
24) K. Nayar, *India: The Critical Years* (Vikas, Delhi, 1971).

25) K. Nayar, *Distant Neighbours* (India, 1972).
26) Jawaharlal Nehru, *An Autobiography* (Bodley Head, London, 1936).
27) J. Nehru, *Letters from a Father to his Daughter* (O.U.P., 1929).
28) J. Nehru, *Glimpses of World History* (John Day, New York).
29) J. Nehru, *The Unity of India* (Lindsay Drummond, London, 1941).
30) J. Nehru, *Independence & After* (Delhi, 1949).
31) J. Nehru, *Discovery of India* (Signet Press, Calcutta, 1946).
32) J. Nehru, *A Bunch of Old Letters* (Asia Publishing House, India, 1958).
33) Vijayalakshmi Pandit, *Prison Days* (Signet Press, Calcutta, 1945).
34) Ela Sen, *Indira Gandhi* (Peter Owen, London, 1973).
35) Marie Seton, *Panditji* (Rupa, India, 1967).
36) Uma Vasudev, *Indira Gandhi* (Vikas, Delhi, 1974).

# INDEX